Chaucer's Knight

Terry Jones

Chaucer's Knight

The portrait of a medieval mercenary

EYRE METHUEN LONDON

First published in 1980 by Weidenfeld & Nicolson

First published in paperback 1982 by
Eyre Methuen Ltd
11 New Fetter Lane, London EC4P 4EE

Copyright © Terry Jones 1980, 1981

ISBN 0 413 49640 6

Printed by Butler & Tanner Ltd
Frome and London

Contents

Acknowledgements

I would like to express my thanks to Lyn Owen for all her assistance and many original ideas, and to Malcolm Andrew for his encouragement and valuable suggestions. I would also like to thank Claire Jakens and Graham Ley for their work on translating the Latin and Italian texts, and Brian Jeffery for his help on the Old French passages. My thanks also to Sue Waterston for editing my appalling manuscript and to Gregory Bainbridge for putting me right where I went wrong.

Preface

When I first read Chaucer at school, I remember having mixed feelings towards him and towards his work. I liked the witty yet compassionate man whom we all glimpse behind the portraits of the Prioress and the Monk and the Friar, but I could not understand why such a man would have written such apparently dull and interminable pieces as *The Knight's Tale*, *The Monk's Tale* and *The Tale of Melibeus*. At university I was able to spend a little more time on the subject and came to the conclusion that it was not Chaucer who had failed but my understanding of what he wrote. A key to the whole puzzle seemed to lie in the character of the Knight, as it is presented to us in the *General Prologue* – and, in particular, in the long list of battles with which he is associated. What does this list mean? If, as we are usually told, these battles were all glorious Christian victories over the infidel, and if they all, therefore, demonstrated the same thing – namely the Knight's remorseless enthusiasm for fighting the heathen – why should Chaucer have gone on at quite such length about it? Why take up thirty-six lines to make a point that is made in the first eight? Isn't such prolixity uncharacteristic of the pith and wit of the writing in the *General Prologue*?

Turning away from the books of literary criticism, I read Steven Runciman's account of the siege of Alexandria in 1366 – the first campaign with which the Knight is linked.[1] There I found a very different story from the glorious Christian victory I had learned about from the literary scholars. According to Runciman, the siege of Alexandria was a most appalling massacre and a complete waste of time with regard to advancing the Christian religion. What then, did the victory mean to Chaucer's own contemporaries? Furthermore, what did they think about the other campaigns and battles in which the Knight was supposed to have been involved?

I came down from university in 1964 and was unable to take up the problem again until about 1972. In the meantime an American scholar, Charles Mitchell, had written a brief article raising some of the same doubts that I had entertained.[2] Spurred on by this, I started reapplying myself to the Knight's battles, in my spare time. It has been a curious way of learning history. Starting from my hunches about these thirty-six lines of the Prologue, I began to learn about the changing military world of the late-fourteenth century, and, in trying to explain these six-hundred-year-old jokes, I found myself plunging ever deeper into the everyday detail of Chaucer's times. It has been an exciting chase, and confirmation of suspected ironies has turned up in the most unlikely places. For example, early on in the investigation, I had come to the conclusion that the Knight must have been a mercenary fighting in various corners of the globe for whoever would pay him – an interpretation of Chaucer's Knight which is apparently anathema to literary scholars but which is fairly self-evident to historians – particularly those familiar with the relationship between Europe and Islam in the fourteenth century.[3] My problem was then to find out what Chaucer's contemporaries thought about these mercenaries. In 1974 I was in Scotland, filming *Monty Python and the Holy Grail*, when I picked up the guide-book for the castle in which we were filming, and there I found that not only was Doune Castle built at the very time that Chaucer was writing the *Canterbury Tales* but it was specially constructed so as to minimize the kind of treachery which had come to be expected from the new breed of globe-trotting mercenary.[4] So there, expressed in the very fabric of the building we were using for our film, was the answer to my question about Chaucer's Knight – evidently the people of Chaucer's day were deeply suspicious of these mercenary knights.

Half the fun for me has been these sudden moments of discovery – the moment I first realized that Chaucer had carried out secret negotiations with the English mercenary captain John Hawkwood – the moment when, having already begun to suspect that the Knight interrupts *The Monk's Tale* because it is somehow getting too personal, I read the Host's remarks to the Monk in which he asks him to 'quit' the Knight's story.[5] The sequence in which discoveries are made gives them their excitement. When they are written down, however, they tend with hindsight to become yet another known, and therefore dull, fact with which

the poor student has to familiarize himself. However, I hope that
those who read this book will not think that it is all cut-and-
dried. I have only begun to scratch the surface; there are many
layers of eighteenth-century gilt, Victorian enamel and twentieth-
century brown paint to be scraped off before we can see the pure
metal of Chaucer's meaning, shining as bright as the day he wrote
the lines or read them to his first audience. Indeed, I suppose we
shall never be able to discover all the nuances that his words held
for his immediate contemporaries. After all, it is hard enough
now to explain why 'ITMA' made us laugh a mere twenty-five
years ago. I hope this book, with all its shortcomings, will at least
encourage people to turn to Chaucer's writing with fresh eyes
and with fresh confidence that there is always more to be discovered and enjoyed in this great poet and humorist.

Addition to Preface, July 1981

Since this book first appeared at the beginning of last year, I have
had many valuable discussions and a lot of interesting correspondence. I am particularly grateful to Derek Brewer for all the interest and kindness he has shown to me, and to Jill Mann especially
for pointing out an error concerning the translation of the word
'flauter' (pp. 211–12 and note on p. 286 in the first edition) which
I have taken the opportunity of correcting in the last two print-
ings. I am also indebted to A.A. Dent for some additional information on the branding of horses which I have included on
p. 29, and to Dr R.E. Alton, my old tutor, Norman Daniel and
Angela Dzelzainis for their assistance and encouragement.

I would also like to thank Dr P.W. Edbury for communicating
his two important articles on Peter of Cyprus, which considerably
amplify the picture of Peter I which I present here, and the nature
of Chaucer's Knight's service under him. Unfortunately I received
this information too late to be able to incorporate it in the text,
but my publishers have kindly allowed me to give a very brief
account of it here.

In 'The Crusading Policy of King Peter I of Cyprus', Peter
Edbury argues that Peter I's 1365 campaign to Alexandria was
motivated by commercial rather than crusading considerations.[6]
Dr Edbury also provides fascinating additional information
about the taking of Satalye in 1361, in which the Knight was
also involved. He points out that at Satalye the King of Cyprus
was simply pursuing his country's traditional military and

commercial policies, pre-empting further Turkish raids on Cyprus and protecting the all-important shipping lanes. More significantly, while the Alexandrian campaign at least carried the colours of a crusade, there was never any suggestion that the Satalye expedition was anything other than a military/commercial exploit.

Dr Edbury has also pointed out to me the possibility that Chaucer's reference to Satalye could even be to the mutiny of 1367 rather than to the 1361 expedition – a suggestion which I am sure is worth further investigation.

Dr Edbury's other article, 'The Murder of King Peter 1 of Cyprus',[7] considerably modifies my interpretation of the Knight's interruption of the Monk's Tale (see pp. 72 and 221 below). The significance of the Monk's reference to King Peter's murder by his *owene liges* is not, as I claim, that the Knight himself was one of those lieges, because he was not. The Knight was a foreigner in the service of the Cypriot King. In fact, the old Cypriot aristocracy murdered the king precisely because of his excessive reliance on such foreign adventurers, and because the expense of his military exploits with them were bankrupting the whole country. Indeed, in his attempts to remain solvent, Peter 1 was even alienating parts of the royal domain to these foreign mercenaries, thereby causing intense resentment amongst his *owene lieges*.[8] The Monk is thus referring to an incident which epitomised the antagonism between the old aristocratic knights and the new race of adventurers, such as Chaucer's Knight.

I might add that, in the context of this explanation, the Monk's use of the word *chivalrie* reinforces my interpretation of the Knight's own love of *chivalrie*. The Monk is employing the word in its strictly technical sense of mounted military exploits, and is demonstrating that in this sense it was even possible for *chivalrie* to be disapproved of by the old aristocratic knights.

The lines from the Monk's Tale (quoted on p. 72 below) might therefore be translated something like this:

> Full many a heathen you brought to grief,
> For which your own liegemen suffered great harm[9]
> And – purely because of your military adventures –
> They have slain you in your bed one morning.

Translated thus, it is even easier to see why Chaucer's Knight so rudely interrupts the Monk.

A Knyght ther was, and that a worthy man,
That fro the tyme that he first bigan
To riden out, he loved chivalrie,
Trouthe and honour, fredom and curteisie.
Ful worthy was he in his lordes werre,
And therto hadde he riden, no man ferre,
As wel in cristendom as in hethenesse,
And evere honoured for his worthynesse.
At Alisaundre he was whan it was wonne.
Ful ofte tyme he hadde the bord bigonne
Aboven alle nacions in Pruce;
In Lettow hadde he reysed and in Ruce,
No Cristen man so ofte of his degree.
In Gernade at the seege eek hadde he be
Of Algezir, and riden in Belmarye.
At Lyeys was he and at Satalye,
Whan they were wonne; and in the Grete See
At many a noble armee hadde he be.
At mortal batailles hadde he been fiftene,
And foughten for oure feith at Tramyssene
In lystes thries, and ay slayn his foo.
This ilke worthy knyght hadde been also
Somtyme with the lord of Palatye
Agayn another hethen in Turkye.
And everemoore he hadde a sovereyn prys;
And though that he were worthy, he was wys,
And of his port as meeke as is a mayde.
He nevere yet no vileynye ne sayde
In al his lyf unto no maner wight.
He was a verray, parfit gentil knyght.
But, for to tellen yow of his array,
His hors were goode, but he was nat gay.
Of fustian he wered a gypon
Al bismotered with his habergeon,
For he was late ycome from his viage,
And wente for to doon his pilgrymage.

General Prologue, 43–78

1 The traditional interpretation of Chaucer's Knight

Chaucer's Knight stands out as a key figure in one of the great landmarks of the English language: *The Canterbury Tales*. He is usually presented to the modern reader as the perfect Christian warrior. In 1907, J.M. Manly called Chaucer's Knight 'a figure at once realistic and typical of the noble and adventurous idealists of his day'.[1] This opinion has become generally accepted among academics. The most eminent of present-day editors, F.N. Robinson, commented in 1957: 'It is worthy of note that Chaucer presents in the Knight a completely ideal figure. Although chivalry in the fourteenth century was in its decline and had a very sordid side, Chaucer has wholly refrained from satirizing the institution.'[2] In 1969, Muriel Bowden – perhaps the best-known commentator on the *General Prologue* – still saw the Knight as the personification of the ideals of knighthood: 'The champion of the Church, the righteous and implacable enemy of the infidel, the compassionate protector of the weak and oppressed, the defender of all Right and Justice.'[3]

And if we are surprised that Chaucer, the humanist, should choose a man who has dedicated his life to bloodshed and warfare as 'a pattern of perfection against which all the other pilgrims should be measured',[4] we can rest assured that all the wars in which the Knight took part were holy wars. Thus E.T. Donaldson, in 1958, stated: 'Chaucer is careful to mention only his [the Knight's] participation in such wars as were in a sense holy wars, fought in defence of Christendom against the pagan incursions into Europe ....'[5] Similarly in 1973, Jill Mann was telling us: 'It seems clear that Chaucer wishes us to accept the Knight's motivation as religious. Not only do the historians tell us that all the campaigns named were against the heathen, but the vocabulary of the portrait stresses the opposition between "cristendom" and "hethenesse", that the Knight is a "Cristen man", who has "foughten for oure feith" and campaigned against the "hethen".'[6]

This interpretation of Chaucer's Knight as 'the quintessence of chivalry'[7] has achieved almost universal acceptance among literary scholars of the twentieth century.[8]

And yet, as 'the quintessence of chivalry' the Knight leaves much to be desired: he is not endowed with any physical beauty or grace; there is no mention of any family background, no coat-of-arms, no shield, no belt (crucial to the truly 'gentil' or noble knight), no manorial estates. He shows no interest in the courtly pastimes of hunting, hawking or courtly love. His dress is shabby, his retinue small, and his life-long career on the battlefield has been exclusively abroad and has apparently missed out on all the great English victories of the period – such as Crécy, Poitiers and Nájera – on which the reputation of English chivalry in the four-teenth century rested. On the contrary, throughout a period when England was constantly at war with her neighbours and repeat-edly threatened with invasion from the French, Scots, Spaniards and even Danes, the Knight has not once fought for his own king and country.

Moreover, the assertion that all the Knight's campaigns were idealistic crusades against the infidel is inaccurate and ignores the fact that there was, in Chaucer's day, a lively debate as to whether such 'crusades' were justifiable at all. In any case, is it credible that Chaucer – the humanist who chooses a polemical pacifist tract as his own tale – could really have believed that kil-ling heathens was the best way of converting them to the religion of love and peace?

I hope to show that the Knight's career, instead of conforming to a pattern of Christian chivalry, has more in common with the mercenaries who swarmed across Europe in the so-called Free Companies and who brought the concept of chivalry into dis-repute and eventual disuse. The campaigns in which the Knight has taken part – far from being 'a great rollcall of crusades against the infidels'[9] – were more often appalling massacres, scenes of sadism and pillage and, on one occasion (the siege of Alexandria) notorious for the disgrace which the English knights, in particu-lar, brought upon themselves.

This historical rather than purely literary approach to the Knight's character necessitates a new reading of *The Knight's Tale*, which emerges, in my view, as a sparkling and witty parody rather than as the philosophical but wooden romance it is usually regarded to be.

Our traditional image of Chaucer as the cool, courtly writer, detached from the turbulent politics of his own day, is also called into question. Re-evaluated in this historical context, he emerges as a writer more consistent, concise, humorous and politically aware than he is normally given credit for being.

2 The military background

What was a 'knight' in the fourteenth century?

From the moment I first read Chaucer's description of the Knight in the *General Prologue* to *The Canterbury Tales*, I felt I was missing something. I could never quite see the Knight as a real person. Eventually I realized that the main problem was that I didn't know what a 'knight' was. Were there really knights in shining armour riding around on white chargers in Chaucer's day? Or was knighthood simply an honour, as it is now, which could be bestowed for services to the catering industry as easily as to a man of war?

It seemed to me that I could not hope to understand Chaucer's portrait of the Knight in *The Canterbury Tales* until I had some idea of what a knight was at the time Chaucer was writing.

Unfortunately, I soon discovered that there is no cut-and-dried answer. Throughout the Middle Ages the meaning of the word 'knight' had been elastic, and by Chaucer's day it was full of ambiguities. For some people, knighthood was an ideal of military prowess. For some it was the embodiment of courtesy and noble deeds. For others it was nothing more than a hidden form of taxation. Some men refused to become knights when officially they should have done, while others styled themselves knights when, perhaps, they should not have. Some knights ranked with barons and earls. Some knights were despised as *parvenus*.

Originally, the word 'knight' did not necessarily indicate high social status. The Anglo-Saxon '*cniht*' primarily meant 'a youth'. It also meant 'a servant, man, follower', and in German the word '*Knecht*' still means 'servant', as does '*knegt*' in Danish, while '*knekt*' in Norwegian means 'rogue, rascal'. It was probably not until the tenth or eleventh century that '*cniht*' in England began to take on connotations of high rank.[1]

When William I invaded England, the native writers unhesit-
atingly applied the Old English word 'cniht' to his military followers. These were the followers whom William rewarded with
grants of the land they had helped him conquer, and so
William's cnihts became the landed gentry of the future.

These cnihts of the eleventh century were by no means
aristocrats. A recent study, by Sally Harvey, has shown that
many of them were 'often of lowly or even unfree origin and
in possession of minuscule fiefs and rents', and the same
author's analysis of Domesday Book shows that the majority
of knights at that time held only about 150 acres – which puts
them on a social level 'only just above the most well-to-do
peasants'.[2]

By the thirteenth century, however, a transformation had
taken place, and the knightly type had become an aristocratic
figure.[3] The main reasons were probably economic.

It may be difficult to imagine, but inflation was as topical in
the Middle Ages as it is today. Between 1180 and 1201, for instance, rents and prices more than doubled.[4] The daily wage rate
of a knight jumped from 4d a day to 2s.[5]

At the same time, it also became increasingly expensive to be
a knight. The responsibility of equipping and arming had
always rested with the knight himself. As increasingly sophisticated methods of killing were evolved – such as the long-bow
and the cross-bow and gunpowder – the knight found that he
needed more and more elaborate and therefore expensive
equipment for his own defence. In particular the introduction of
plate-armour started a chain reaction of escalating costs. It
meant, for example, that a knight-in-armour weighed far more
than his predecessors and therefore required a heavier and more
expensive horse.[6] In Chaucer's day a knight's horse could cost
up to two hundred times the price of an ordinary plough-horse,
or the equivalent of twenty years' rent on Chaucer's home in
Westminster.[7]

By the early-thirteenth century, only the wealthy could afford
to fit themselves up as knights. Those at the bottom end of the
income scale, living off perhaps 120 acres of land, could no longer
afford either the trappings of military service or to take time off
from the management of their estates. For them, knighthood was
not an honour so much as an intolerable burden, and not surprisingly they began trying to avoid their feudal obligations. By 1278

it has been estimated that only half of those eligible were taking up the order of knighthood.[8]

So there arose the rather odd custom whereby the king would *compel* men to become knights, if they possessed a certain amount of land. (From 1292 onwards this meant land worth £40 a year.)[9] Those who did not want to had to pay a fine, unless they could prove they had less land or had already been knighted by someone else.[10]

Exchequer returns are full of examples of men trying to avoid the honour – a notable instance being the first John Paston, who paid his fine to avoid knighthood in 1457 and eventually managed to get his son knighted in his stead.[11]

For those who could neither avoid nor afford it, a distraint of knighthood could spell financial ruin, and such ruined knights appear in the popular literature of the day as tragi-comic figures.[12] For example, in *The Geste of Robyn Hode*, Little John and Will Scarlet waylay a rather shabby knight and discover he has only ten shillings in his pocket. Robin Hood is immediately curious and wonders whether the knight isn't a victim of compulsory knighthood – 'a knyght of force':

> 'Tell me one thing,' said Robin,
>   'And secret it shall be;
> I'm sure you were made a knight by force
>   Or else out of yeoman stock.'[13]

The well-to-do, on the other hand, found it socially prestigious to be seen to be able to afford the time and money to go soldiering. Thus military service became, curiously enough, a status symbol.[14] By the mid-thirteenth century knighthood had taken upon itself the full colours of an aristocracy, laying emphasis on nobility of birth and passing its honours on from father to son.[15] The knight referred to above indignantly replies to Robin Hood that he is 'none of those' and that there have been knights in his family for a hundred years:

> 'I am not one of those,' said the knight,
>   'I swear by God that made me;
> A hundred winters here before
>   My ancestors have been knights.'[16]

During the fourteenth century the costs of knighthood continued to escalate, and the advent of the Hundred Years' War made knighthood even more unpopular among the lesser gentry, involving as it did the additional expenses and uncertainties of service abroad.[17] No one who was drafted into one of Edward III's armies in France could be sure if or when he might return home. It is scarcely surprising that in 1327 there were protests in Parliament, and the very legality of compulsory service on foreign soil was called into question.[18]

In order to offset this growing unpopularity, the kings of England tried to make knighthood more attractive by elevating its social status yet further. This they did with a sort of window-dressing technique, instituting fancy and elaborate rituals and coats-of-arms and by the founding of the Orders, for example, of the Garter, Bath and Round Table.[19] In 1363 there was even an attempt to increase the prestige of knighthood (and at the same time relieve the lesser gentry of the onus of military service) by restricting it to those with an income of £200 in lands or £1,000 in trade, and in 1379 there was an unsuccessful petition in Parliament to restrict the wearing of furs, jewellery, gold and silk to the knightly class.[20] The gulf between the 'gentil' knight and the ordinary man-at-arms thus widened visibly during the fourteenth century, so that, by the time Chaucer was writing, 'gentil' knighthood had become a jealously-guarded privilege.[21]

At the same time, however, there were other factors working in the opposite direction, which undermined this mounting prestige and which – to the horror of the gentry – began to make it possible for a mere grocer to become a knight.

The fact was that it had become virtually impossible to raise an army simply by compulsion.[22] A professional army, however, was distasteful to many men of Chaucer's day to a degree which it is probably difficult for us now to imagine.

Men had always been paid, of course, even within the feudal 'host', but the concept of a man offering his services in battle *merely* for monetary gain was repugnant to those who had been brought up in an older tradition. As a result the contractual system which eventually evolved under Edward III avoided being a full-blooded commercial system of recruitment such as had developed in Italy.[23] This arrangement is now generally referred to as 'the Indenture System'.

The Indenture System did not all at once replace compulsory service, but they co-existed for many years. At the same time increasing reliance was placed on a purely mercenary soldiery in the lower ranks.

An indenture was a mutually-agreed contract. To discourage forgery it was cut in two pieces: the irregularities (indentures) in the bottom of the one had to match those on the top of the counterpart. In these contracts, a great lord would agree to supply the king with a certain number of knights, men-at-arms and archers, all of whom would, in turn, contract with the lord to serve for a certain period at a fixed daily wage.[24]

Although the relationship between a knight and his lord was thus no longer truly 'feudal',[25] the men who drew up the indentures sought to retain some of the moral values that had been implicit in the older systems. Above all they sought to retain the tradition of loyalty to one lord and the sense of duty that lasted a man his whole life, in peace as well as in war.[26] And although all ranks and classes of soldier now received pay, there was a jealously-guarded distinction between the indentured retainer, who was fed and clothed by his lord, and merely paid 'for his trouble', and the out-and-out mercenary, who must needs live off his pay. A contemporary of Chaucer, the military theorist Honoré Bonet, explained it like this:

> Sometimes wages are given to a man for his labour and for his subsistence, as, for instance, to a man-at-arms, or a sergeant, or a crossbowman, who must live and clothe and equip himself with what he takes from his wages.... There are others who take wages rather for their trouble than for their subsistence, for they eat and drink of the subsistence of their lord, and take robes from his livery.[27]

An idea of how the Indenture System sought to preserve the values of the old feudal relationship is conveyed by the indentures drawn up between various knights and John of Gaunt between the years 1367 and 1399. Here, as an example, is the indenture made on 2 December 1386 between John of Gaunt and one Sir Thomas Beek. Note the insistence on service 'in times of peace as well as in times of war' and the life-long nature of the commitment – 'term of his life':

> This indenture, made between John, King of Castile and Leon, Duke of Lancaster, on the one part, and Sir Thomas Beek, on the other part, bears witness that the said Sir Thomas is retained and kept by the said King and Duke to serve him in times of peace as in times of war for the term of his life, and to work with him in whatever place should please the said King and Duke, well and suitably equipped for war.

And the said Sir Thomas in times of peace will have wages and food and fuel [*bouge et gages du court*] wherever he may be sent by the letters of the said King and Duke at his command.

And the said Sir Thomas will take for his fee, as well in times of peace as in times of war, twenty pounds a year, for the term of his life.

In time of war, the said Sir Thomas will take wages and board at court, as other bachelors of his condition will receive, from the hands of the treasurer of the said King and Duke for the war for the stated time.

With regard to prisoners and other profits of war taken or won by the said Sir Thomas or any of his men, from the commencement of his year of war and the equipping of himself, his men, horses and equipment, the said King and Duke will treat him as he treats other bachelors of his state and condition. . . .[28]

We even know that Chaucer himself was familiar with such indentures and – presumably – approved of them, since his son Thomas entered into an almost identical one with John of Gaunt three years later.[29]

This, then, was the style of knighthood encouraged by Chaucer's patron, and into which Chaucer himself saw his own son enter. It attempted to avoid being a mercenary institution by still regarding the knight in the style of the old feudal retainer – a blend of soldier and peacetime courtier, upholding the moral values of an older tradition. It applied, however, only to the upper ranks, and the fact that the bulk of the army was now recruited on a frankly mercenary basis was ultimately to prove the undoing of the whole system.

But, if many of Chaucer's contemporaries would have liked to confine the use of the word 'knight' to this sort of courtier-cum-man-at-arms, they were doomed to disappointment. In the first place, the use of the word in the fourteenth century was very fluid.[30] Primarily, of course, it indicated a military man, but there also were various ways in which the word had shed these exclusively military connotations. For example: knights of the shire were simply members of Parliament, representing their shires, and knights of the chamber were retainers concerned with the king's private quarters. In both cases the title had more to do with civil administration than with military affairs,[31] and it is worth remembering that the Knight of the *Prologue* was not the only knight on the pilgrimage: the Franklyn had on many occasions been a knight of the shire and so, of course, in reality, had Chaucer himself.[32]

In fact the words 'knights' and 'knighthood' were terms widely used to designate the upper class of laymen, the 'Second Estate' as it was then called. Medieval society saw itself divided into three clear groups or Estates: the priests, the knights and the labourers. Each group had its role to play in relation to the others, as a contemporary vernacular preacher, Master Thomas Wimbledon, explained in a sermon to the crowds at St Paul's Cross:

... These three offices are necessary: priesthood, knighthood and labourers. To the priesthood it falls to cut away the dead branches of sin with the sword of their tongues. To the knighthood it falls to prevent wrongs and thefts being done, and to maintain God's law and those that are teachers of it, and also to save the land from the enemies from other lands. And to the labourers it falls to work with their bodies and by their sore sweat to get out of the earth the bodily sustenance for themselves and the others.[33]

These ambiguities in the use of the word 'knight' were compounded by ambiguities in appearance. The flamboyant fashions of the fourteenth century caused much consternation not simply because they were considered outrageous but also because they blurred the boundaries of social distinction and status. Writers were constantly complaining that it was becoming more and more difficult to recognize a knight by the way he dressed. Shortly after Chaucer's death, Thomas Hoccleve wrote:

> Once there was a time when men could tell lords
> From other folk by their dress; but now
> A man must study and muse a long time
> To tell which is which.[34]

The preachers of the day, such as Thomas Wimbledon, complained that priests were aping knights in the way they dressed, while John Myrc even remarked that you could not tell one from the other any more since they both insisted on being called 'sir'.[35]

A further confusion resulted from the fact that the king was not the only person who could create knights. Edward I had tried to control this and establish a royal monopoly in knighting, but he failed, and knighthoods were still being bestowed by the lesser gentry on their followers even in Chaucer's day.[36] What is more, the less scrupulous would have no compunction about assuming the title themselves. There is, for example, no record of anyone officially knighting Sir John Hawkwood – that most famous English mercenary, who led the White Company in Italy for over a quarter of a century – yet he styled himself 'Sir John' and knighted his own followers.[37]

It can be imagined that all these anomalies were exploited to the full by the lower ranks of professional soldiers – especially by that phenomenon of the age: the itinerant mercenary. Travelling all over the known world, seeking their fortunes in battle, these ambitious soldiers of fortune would have had no hesitation in seizing on the dignity of the title 'knight'.

In this recent study, Richard Barber writes that, by the fifteenth century, 'the majority of so-called knights had no claim to the title. ... And the world of the lawless brigands who went under the once proud title was nearer to reality than that of the genuine knights, with their nostalgia for imagined glories of the past.'[38]

Such self-styled knights differed from the 'gentil' knight or in-dentured retainer in two very important respects. In the first place they served their masters *only* in times of war – peace was none of their business. And, in the second place, they served not just one master but any master who was willing to pay their wages. They had no feudal ties and no obligations of honour. They could transfer their allegiance as easily as their wage bills.

The 'gentil' knight, on the other hand, was seen as a man of culture as well as a soldier – a man of peace as well as a man of war. This was the sort of knight with whom Chaucer himself seems to have associated – men like Sir John Montagu, Sir John Clanvowe, Sir Lewis Clifford and Sir Richard Sturry. Some of them may have had distinguished military careers, but they were also men of letters – poets and thinkers who moved in the Court circles and who were often to be found in attendance at the king's council.[39]

The fact that common soldiers and itinerant mercenaries, who were going about in armed bands terrorizing the countryside and lording it over the peasantry, were also styling themselves knights, was a grim reminder of a changing world. It is hard to believe that Chaucer could have omitted from his great satire so important a figure as the soldier of fortune.

In the change-over from feudal host to mercenary army, Chaucer's contemporaries saw the breakdown not only of military honour as they conceived it but of the old order of society.

In familial, patriarchal or feudal relationships – whatever the very obvious short comings – men and women are nonetheless called upon to make such responses as loyalty, admiration and love – responses that are neither expected nor particularly encouraged where the relationship is a purely economic one.[40] The feudal relationship, as it had developed in the thirteenth and fourteenth centuries, involved values beyond the mere fulfilment of a military contract, as can be seen from the indenture of John of Gaunt quoted above. It was a real relationship, which made demands upon the loyalties and even the emotions of those involved.[41]

In the fourteenth century the hired mercenary became the mainstay of the army, and this reduction of a social relationship to a callous money relationship seemed particularly significant to many of Chaucer's contemporaries, because they saw the same happening throughout society.

In the same way that lawyers were condemned for defending accused men solely for gain and regardless of right or wrong, doctors were criticized for being prepared to use their skill to alleviate suffering only in return for payment.[42] Johannes de Mirfield, of St Bartholomew's, Smithfield, put the complaint thus: 'But the physician, if he should happen to be a good Christian (which rarely chances, for by their works they show themselves to be disciples not of Christ but of Avicenna and of Galen), ought to cure a Christian patient without making even the slightest charge if the man is poor; for the life of such a man ought to be of more value to the physician than his money.'[43] The selling of a particular skill or knowledge was seen as a corruption of a social relationship.

To us, living in an age when commerce is the heart-beat of our society, it is hard to see this as men of the Middle Ages saw it. Usury, for example, was universally despised as an anti-social activity throughout the period, and yet today 'banking' is considered to be a most respectable business – a curious reversal of ethics which is illustrated at some length by Corrado Pallenberg in his stimulating book *Vatican Finances*.[44]

The fact that modern society considers the professions – medicine, law, banking, the army etc – as the most acceptable of social roles, is an indication of the degree to which the mercenary ethic has become institutionalized.[45] Perhaps it is for this reason that scholars of the nineteenth and twentieth centuries have found it

so hard to believe that Chaucer could have had anything but unbounded admiration for this prototype of the professional
soldier. But back in the fourteenth century, although the professionalization of medicine and law had long been a target for
satire, the professionalization of the man of war was something
new and infinitely more horrifying.

To Chaucer's contemporaries, the growth of the mercenary
soldier represented, in the most dramatic terms possible, the
general erosion of social values.

It would not be surprising therefore if Chaucer had chosen the
portrait of such a knight as the centre-pin for his satire on the
society of his day.

The rise and rise of the mercenaries

Mercenaries had existed in England before the fourteenth century. The earliest written financial contract for military service
is dated 1270, but verbal contracts must have existed long before.[1]
The first *cnihts* who came across with William the Conqueror
were themselves indistinguishable from mercenaries.[2] In 1159
Henry II had used 'paid knights' (*solidarios milites*) to relieve his
'country knights' (*agrarios milites*) from the burden of military
service in Toulouse.[3] And in the early days mercenaries formed
the nucleus of many an abbot's household.[4]

Often these mercenaries performed well and faithfully, but as
soon as there was any lull in activities, the hired soldier only too
often became more trouble than he was worth. This is why, for
instance, Magna Carta in 1215 provided for the expulsion from
the realm of 'all alien knights, crossbowmen, serjeants and mercenaries'.[5]

In the fourteenth century, however, mercenaries came to be
used on a scale that was totally without precedent. The results
had a profound effect on the whole military scene. In the first
place, the character of national armies altered radically, as mercenaries were no longer used as mere auxiliaries but as the back-
bone of the army.[6] This meant that an English army fighting in
Scotland or Ireland or France in the late fourteenth century might
include in its ranks Scots, Irish and even French soldiers alongside
the Welsh, German and English. As a result, the commander in
the field could no longer rely on the unquestioning loyalty of his

troops, nor could he expect harmony to reign for long within the ranks of such a multi-racial hotch-potch, and brawling between the various factions became one of the major problems of the late fourteenth-century armies.

The second radical change was even more sinister and affected civilians as well as military personnel. The huge numbers in which these hired troops were now used meant that, when peace put them out of work, they were numerous enough to form themselves into autonomous, multi-national fighting units. These became infamous as the 'Free Companies' and were destined to be the scourge of Europe throughout Chaucer's lifetime.

The spawning-ground for the Free Companies was Italy, where, ever since the beginning of the century, the internal dissensions of the city-republics had led to the employment of organized gangs of paid desperadoes, in preference to the traditional levy of citizens.[7]

The conditions in which the Free Companies ultimately proliferated, however, were provided by the Hundred Years' War. By the time Chaucer was writing, the word 'Englishman' had become synonymous with the marauding freebooters of the Free Companies.[8]

In 1360, the Treaty of Brétigny brought a temporary cessation of hostilities between England and France. Welcome as this no doubt was to both sides, there were some for whom it spelled disaster. The soldiers who had grown up with the war over the past twenty years suddenly found themselves unemployed. Others – the *tard venus*, 'late-comers', as they were called – who arrived on the scene too late but who were still excited by rumours of the vast pickings to be had – were not to be put off by a mere peace treaty. It was all very well for Edward III to order his knights home, but many of the lesser fighting men had no homes to go to.[9] The only trade they knew was war. As the English chronicler Henry Knighton put it: 'At the same time sprang up a certain band of armed men called *Societas fortunae*, which some called the Great Company. It was recruited from men of diverse regions, who had no livelihood unless they actually worked, now that there was peace between the realms. They were strong men and war-like, accustomed to fine things and enterprising, who lived by what they gained in war, having nothing in time of peace.'[10] The French chronicler Jean de Venette, whose home town was devastated by the English, naturally records the formation of the Great Company with more passion: 'That same year arose those sons of Belial and men of iniquity, warriors from various lands who assailed other men with no right and no reason other than their own passions, iniquity, malice and hope of gain, and yet were called the Great Company.'[11]

As the fame of the Great Company spread, disbanded soldiers from both sides – French and English – began drifting towards it in increasing numbers. Before long the Company reached outrageous proportions – Froissart claims that it was over sixteen thousand strong, which would have made it larger than any legitimate army fielded by the English in France. But while Froissart's figure is hard to believe, it does give some idea of the scale on which the Company was operating and the impression it made on the people of the time. It was a disaster second only to the Plague itself.

As this autonomous force gathered momentum, the Courts of Europe grew alarmed and realized that they would eventually have to act. The French, whose peasants were now the chief victims, organized an army to destroy the Company once and for all. At least that was the intention, but by now the Great Company was stronger than almost any national force in existence. Its captains were old dogs of war, and its men experienced and disciplined. When an official French army, under Sir James de Bourbon, engaged the Company at Brignais on 6 April 1362, the French force was decimated.[12] In horror, Europe watched helplessly as the horde swept down towards Avignon. Accountable to no one and motivated by neither ideals nor patriotism, the Company was nothing but a bandit-gang blown-up to the nightmare proportions of a full-scale army. No village or town was safe, and even the Pope himself cringed in fear before its might. Jean de Venette takes up the story:

These miscreants, united in a large band and under arms, drew near to Avignon, desiring to subdue our lord the supreme pontiff, the cardinals and the Holy Church of God. They came to Pont-Saint-Esprit, a city near Avignon, and took it by force of arms. There they passed some time wasting the adjacent countryside horribly. They planned in some fashion or other to subjugate ultimately the whole city of Avignon, the residence of Pope Innocent VI and the cardinals, and the other towns and fortresses of that region as well, Montpellier and Toulouse, Narbonne and Carcassonne. Finally, however, after receiving large sums of money from the Pope and with his absolution, it is said, they left the country round Avignon and scattered in various directions through the world, doing harm wherever they went.[13]

After having been bought off by the Pope in this way (for sixty thousand florins, according to Froissart),[14] the Great Company seems to have split up. Many of these men, however, made their way down through Provence and into Lombardy, where they soon became equally notorious as the 'White Company'.[15] Their eventual leader typified the new style of self-made knight. He was an Englishman, whose name was to dominate Italian politics for the next thirty years: Sir John Hawkwood.

Hawkwood seems to have been impressed into the French wars as an archer in Edward III's army. In 1360 he was one of those poor soldiers who decided to make war their business, as Froissart describes:

When peace was made between the two kings at Brétigny, near Chartres ... he was but a poor knight and at that time he thought of returning again to England into his own country, but he realized he could win nothing there. And when he saw that all men-of-war must leave France by the ordinance and treaty of peace, he made himself captain of a certain number of companions, called the Late-Comers, and so went into Burgundy, and there he assembled a great numbers of such *routiers*, English, Gascon, Breton, German and companions of diverse nations. And this Hawkwood was one of the chief.[16]

Once he had assumed command of the White Company, in Lombardy, he never looked back.

Unlike previous *condottieri*, Hawkwood seems always to have made a point of honouring his contracts and thus earned for himself a reputation for honesty and fidelity which has lasted to this day.[17] But his was not the fidelity of vassal to lord; it was the fidelity of a businessman who cared for his reputation. Sometimes fighting for the Pope against the Visconti of Milan, but more often fighting for the Visconti against the Pope, or the Pisans against the Florentines, or eventually the Florentines against everyone else, Hawkwood became the symbol of efficient – even respectable – commercial soldiering. Bernabò Visconti gave him the hand in marriage of one of his daughters, and he became a man of substance and property, owning estates in Italy as well as the Leadenhall in London.[18] When he died in 1394, the city of Florence gave him a magnificent funeral and erected a huge fresco above his tomb, which still dominates the Duomo.

But no matter how respectable or honoured Hawkwood may have become in his own lifetime and after, the fact remains that, in return for payment, he dealt in the mercenary trade of death. For over a quarter of a century he and the 'Englishmen' under him slaughtered, pillaged, raped and burned their way throughout northern Italy. Pillars of strength they may have been to the 'tirauntz of Lumbardye' (*Legend of Good Women*, I, 374); to the ordinary Italian they were 'devils incarnate'. Throughout the land 'there was nothing more terrible than to hear even the name of the English.'[19] One contemporary Italian chronicler records how 'some men imprisoned themselves in their own dungeons and locked themselves in at night when they [the English] rode forth, and by day kept themselves locked-up and guarded, longing to evacuate this land...'[20] Another Italian chronicler of the period has left a very convincing picture of the men such as must have followed Hawkwood : 'These people, all young, and for the most part born and raised during the long wars between the French and English, hot and wilful, used to slaughter and rapine, were skilled in the use of cold steel, and had no thought for their own safety.'[21]

Hawkwood seems to have had no political ambitions and no illusions about chivalry.[22] To him war was just a job, which he performed to the best of his ability, whether it was offering information to the Florentines or massacring the defenceless inhabitants of Cesena.[23]

But though Hawkwood himself may have had no political ambitions, he did have a profound effect on the politics of his day. The Free Companies represented a military force which made itself felt at all levels. In the Italy of the 1350s, Fra Moriale's Company had numbered seven thousand men-at-arms and some two thousand archers.[24] And while Froissart's figure of sixteen thousand may have been an exaggeration, the Great Company of the 1360s was certainly more than a match for any national army of the day.[25] There is no doubt that these lawless, autonomous amalgams, without responsibility or loyalty and with no rule but self-profit, were able to dictate terms to the legitimate governments of Europe. In the 1360s, the Great Company became, militarily, more than a match for the French army, in the same way that in the twentieth century the modern global corporations are becoming, economically, more than a match for many nation-states.[26] In the same way that the Ford Motor

Company can now dictate terms to the British government, and ITT to the Chilean, so the Free Companies of the fourteenth century were able to dictate terms to popes and emperors and become a law unto themselves. Under the guise of commercial enterprises, the Free Companies became political forces which had to be reckoned with in their own right.

This was not the aspect of them, however, that most worried the writers and thinkers of the late-fourteenth century. For them, the main concern was the even more basic and more radical one of the whole commercial ethic itself. The disgust of the fourteenth century turned upon the very principle of the mercenary soldier.

Fourteenth-century attitudes to mercenaries

By the time Chaucer was writing, the mercenary soldier had become the main source of military power throughout Europe. Chaucer's fellow-writers had a great deal to say about these common fighters who dared to style themselves 'knights', and it would be extraordinary if Chaucer himself were to have totally ignored so momentous a change in society.

The dominance of the mercenaries represented a threat to the established order in more ways than one. In particular, the opportunities for self-advancement offered by the new commercial military ethic challenged the stability of the old hierarchical, feudal society, where social roles were normally established at birth. Now any man could become rich and famous through war. The theme of the poor squire made good was not just a fiction of the romances. Had not Roger di Flor – the humble falconer's son – been the last man on earth to have the title of Caesar conferred upon him?[1] Was not the mighty Sir John Hawkwood no more than a tailor's boy when he started out?[2] As C.T. Allmand puts it: 'War gave men opportunities for self-advantage which only the more foolish would not, or could not, seize upon.'[3] Even Froissart, for all his romanticism, was aware of this, and notes that Prussia (where Chaucer's Knight had sat at the head of the table so often) is typical of the places to which knights and squires 'go to advance themselves'.[4] In fact there is reason to suppose that the Prussian Court of the Teutonic Knights was a world centre of military self-advancement, the finishing school as it were for the self-made military man. (See commentary on lines 52–4 below, pages 49 ff.)

All this was deeply disturbing to many of Chaucer's contemporaries. Writer after writer complains that the order of knighthood was being demeaned, now that just anyone could become a man-at-arms or a captain. The French writer and diplomat Alain Chartier (c. 1385–1433) complained:

There are so many so-called captains and masters nowadays that a man can scarcely find a servant or a workman. But once it was otherwise, for then no man was called a 'squire' unless he was known to be of sovereign prowess. On the other hand, there was no man called to take wages as a man-of-arms unless he had taken a prisoner with his own hands. But nowadays every man that can gird himself with a sword and wear a habergeon dares boldly to take it upon himself to be a captain.[5]

Langland has his Dreamer complain that the social order is turned topsy-turvy in every walk of life:

... bondmen's children have been made bishops,
And those children's bastards have become archdeacons,
And soap-makers and their sons for silver have been
    made into knights,
And the sons of lords have become their labourers
    and had to pledge their incomes....[6]

Gower – perhaps referring to Hawkwood or Sir Robert Knolles – remarked that the pursuit of arms had been turned into a mere business like any other, now that any tailor's boy could wear a helmet or a gilded spur.[7]

It is, however, important to bear in mind that this indignation at the rise of the mercenaries and the consequent vulgarization of the Order of Knighthood was not simply the voice of pure snobbery. In part, the protest reflected genuine practical objections to the use of mercenaries.

In the first place, it was often pointed out that the prince who employed such professional fighters invariably put his own people at risk. After all, being a knight was an expensive business, and, in an age when pay was notoriously uncertain, loot was often the only means of subsistence for the low-born man-at-arms. If there were no war, or if the spoils of war were insufficient, they would all too readily turn to robbing, and plundering the local peasantry, whom they were supposed to be protecting. As Gower put it: 'Since the poor but proud man does not have the wherewithal to conduct himself with pride, he lives everywhere by plundering'.[8] This is precisely what happened when Andronicus II, Emperor of Byzantium, had employed the very first of the Free Companies – the Catalan Grand Company of Roger di Flor – in 1302. It was also a constant problem for the Italian city-states who employed Sir John Hawkwood's company between 1360 and the 1380s.[9]

It was because of this ever-present danger that people felt nobility of birth was important for a knight: it at least meant that he had his own inheritance to support him in his costly calling. As Ramon Lull said, it was not that a man of humble birth could never join the ranks of chivalry but just that it was easier for a man of means to stick to the ideals of knighthood:

Chivalry may not be maintained without the equipment which is necessary to a knight, nor without the honourable costs and expenses which are necessary to chivalry. Because a squire has no equipment, and no wealth of his own with which to defray his expenses, if he is made into a knight, he will perhaps have to become a robber or a thief, traitor, liar or beggar, or have some other vices which are contrary to chivalry.[10]

In Sicily and Germany, the knighting of men of low birth was made illegal for these very reasons.[11]

For the commander in the field, however, who was perhaps less squeamish about the sufferings of the peasants, there was an even more important practical objection to the use of mercenaries. When they were employed *en masse*, as became the custom in the fourteenth century, they could no longer be trusted in the same way as old-fashioned feudal or indentured retainers.[12] Machiavelli, looking back on the events of Chaucer's time a century later, drew the lessons to be learned with all the clarity of hindsight:

If any one holds his State founded upon mercenary armes, hee shall never be quiet, nor secure: because they are never well-united, ambitious, and without discipline, treacherous, among their friends stout, among their enemies cowardly, they have no feare of God, nor keep any faith with men, and so long only deferre they the doing of mischiefe, till the enemy comes to assayle thee, and in time of peace thou art dispoyld by them, in warre by thy enemies.[13]

This distrust of mercenaries was no less strong in Chaucer's own day. The French chronicler, Jean le Bel, records, for example, how Edward III rejected the assistance of foreign knights in 1359.[14] And Froissart describes how, in 1366, when the Black Prince was organizing his expedition to Castile, he turned down the help of many foreign mercenaries, preferring to have only his own men, who were tried and trusted, about him: 'The Prince might have had foreign men-at-arms, such as Flemings, Germans, and Brabanters, if he had chosen it; but he sent away numbers, choosing to depend more on his own subjects and vassals than on strangers.'[15]

But not all modern princes thought the same way. Peter of Cyprus, for instance, deliberately went out of his way to attract foreign mercenaries into his service, when he sacked Alexandria in 1365.[16] He discovered his mistake too late when, having burned, raped and looted to their hearts' content, his gold-hungry adventurers took to their heels. The city fell back into the hands of the infidel, and Peter was heard to cry: 'Honour, you are dead!'[17]

For many of Chaucer's contemporaries, the siege of Alexandria was the classic demonstration of the danger in relying on mercenaries. (See commentary to line 51 on page 42 below.) It is significant that the siege of Alexandria stands so proudly at the head of the Knight's battle honours.

With examples like this in mind, the military theorists of the day urged their leaders to rely not on foreign auxiliaries but on a well-trained, indigenous knighthood: 'It is more profitable for a king or prince to see his own men practised and well taught in the said art and deeds of arms, no matter how few or small a number of people he has, than to take and retain under him a great quantity of strange soldiers that he does not know.'[18] But by the time Christine de Pisan was writing this, the tide had turned. The mercenaries had become a hard fact of military life. If they were untrustworthy, then military life had to come to terms with their infidelity.

Before the century was out, even the design of castles had begun to change to allow for the notorious fickleness of the new breed of soldier. W. Douglas Simpson writes:

For the first time, such castles had to be devised so as to provide quarters, at need, for standing garrisons of professional soldiers. Now hirelings of this sort did not owe the natural allegiance of vassals to

their overlords. They were at all times liable to treachery, to be bought
over by a rival who could bid them higher wages. Moreover, at best
they were rough customers, turbulent and awkward neighbours in
one's household. So we find the designers of our later castles taking
two precautions. They built a separate hall, or mess-room, with its
own independent access, for their armed retainers. And for their own
households they provided quarters in the gatehouse, so that the en-
trance into the castle was always under the control of those whom
they could trust. Moreover, in these later gatehouses we often find
an inner system of defences – oaken doors, portcullis, iron gates, and
the rest – closing against the courtyard, so that the lord could still
hold out even in case of treachery within.[19]

An example of this is Doune Castle, in Scotland, which was built
in the decade that Chaucer started work on the *Canterbury Tales*.
It is clear from the plan that there was no connection between
the Retainers' Hall, where the mercenaries were quartered, and
the Lord's Hall, where the lord and his immediate household
lived. Here, then, expressed in stone and mortar for all to see,
is the new distrustful relationship between lord and vassal that
had replaced the old feudal ties. Nor was Doune an isolated
example. The same caution is displayed in other castles built during this period, such as Tantallon in East Lothian, Caerlaverock
on the Solway and Bodiam in Sussex.[20]
    But the greatest objections to the full-time professional soldier
were philosophical and moral. Rewards from warfare had always
been an important part of chivalry and were justified by the military theorists of the day,[21] but it was always stressed that payment
should never be the sole motive for going to war. The motivation
of the knight was all important, as Gower put it:

> According to the intention that you have
> You will receive good and bad,
> For God looks into your heart.
> Even in a just cause you may
> Do wrong, for if you set off
> More for gain from your pillage
> Than for the love of right, then your service
> Through your evil intent, will be its own
> Undoing and deserve no honour.
> But if you make your voyage for Right,
> Then Reward, Honour and Advancement
> – All three can be yours together.[22]

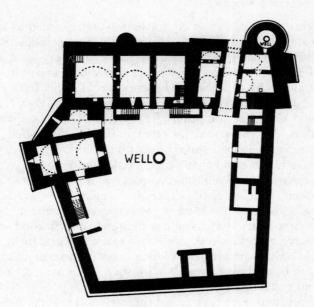

WELL○

GROUND FLOOR

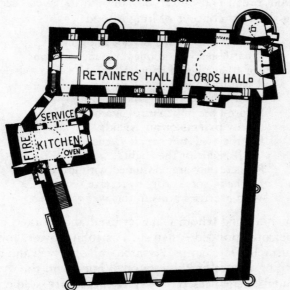

RETAINERS' HALL LORD'S HALL○

SERVICE

FIRE KITCHEN
OVEN

FIRST FLOOR

Plan of Doune Castle c. 1380

Men who went to war solely for gain were regarded as unable to pursue the true objectives of chivalry. For instance, Ramon Lull claimed that the ultimate objective of every true knight should always be peace,[23] but peace was anathema to a soldier who made his living by war. The story is told of Sir John Hawkwood that when two mendicant friars greeted him with the conventional 'God give you peace', he retorted: 'God take from you your alms.' When pressed for an explanation, he replied: 'Why do you pray God that I should die of hunger? Do you not know that I live by war and that peace would undo me?'[24]

Mercenaries, as Wyclif pointed out, had no real interest in and were often ignorant of the causes for which they were actually fighting.[25] Their only motive was self-advancement, which, according to Machiavelli, was not enough to ensure good service: 'They have no other love, nor other cause to keep them in the field, but only a small stipend, which is not of force to make them willing to hazard their lives'.[26] With such soldiers there could be no room for knightly ideals.

In short, wherever they called themselves 'knights', men who made their bread-and-butter out of fighting were seen to be debasing the very concept of knighthood:

> But certainly now I do not know
> What I shall say about these men-at-arms
> For I have heard them talking like this:
> 'I will make war my work.
> I will become rich or die,
> Before I see my country again
> Or my parents or my friends.'
> But they will not say, it seems to me:
> 'I will fight for the Right.'
> Rather, they are consumed with greed.
> But he is not worthy to receive reward
> Who practises arms in this way.[27]

The men among whom Chaucer lived and worked and with whom he corresponded – men such as John Gower, John Clanvowe, Eustache Deschamps, Petrarch – all observed and recorded the changing nature of knighthood.[28] For them, the drift away from feudal allegiances to a purely mercenary soldiery represented one of the greatest upheavals of contemporary social values. Is it conceivable that Chaucer himself could have written his portrait of a knight – the centrepiece of what is generally

regarded as the most penetrating satire of his day – without any
reference whatsoever to this revolution in social roles?

The poor knight

When we turn to the portrait of the Knight in the *Prologue*, it
is essential to see him, as Chaucer painted him, against this
backdrop of the declining status of the ordinary man-at-arms.[1]
With his stained tunic and meagre retinue, the Knight would have
been instantly recognizable to Chaucer's contemporary readers
as that familiar character: the poor knight.[2]

The poor knight was an all too common figure of the age.[3]
He might be a small landholder, ruined by trying to fulfil his military obligations, or perhaps the younger son out to make his fortune, or even an old 'gentil' man, like the poor knight in the *Geste
of Robyn Hode* who had been impoverished by his son's esca-
pades in the tournament.[4]

But by far the commonest kind of poor knights were the foot-
loose mercenaries of the Free Companies. Thrown up by the in-
cessant wars with France, with no other way of making a living
(or no other inclination) but to rob and plunder, these men were
big spenders. Some might have made vast profits in the course
of their marauding, but they lost them again as quickly, as Jean
de Venette wrote:

> But what availed them gains thus extorted? Truly, little or nothing.
> They all seemed to vanish from their hands like snow before the sun.
> Yea verily, coming into cities and expensive places, they were soon
> forced to sell their horses and to contract debts if they could find
> anyone to trust them, and in the end they became paupers and miser-
> able wretches in the sight of all, thus providing the truth of the popular
> saying, 'Gains ill got will be ill spent.'[5]

Confronted by all the attractions of dice, whores and taverns,
these adventurers were quite prepared to pawn their armour and
equipment as well as their horses – a situation their employers
tried vainly to prevent, as we read in one of the Italian military
rule-books of the period:

Concerning horses and arms not to be sold or pawned
Item, that no mercenary of the said company can or ought to sell or
barter any horse, war horse or hack registered for the said pay, or
pawn his arms to any person or place, without the permission of the

said Anziani, against a fine of one hundred denarii and more of his pay, according to the judgement of the commander of the said company, and no one can or ought to receive in pawn from these mercenaries their horses or arms. And if anyone contravenes this let him lose the pledge and restore the horses and arms that he shall have taken in pawn to their owners. And moreover, let him, at the discretion of the commanders, be condemned.[6]

In Florence, things were so bad by 1362 that the city actually opened a special bank specifically to provide loans to the mercenaries in order to prevent their arms and equipment falling into the hands of the usurers.[7] It was little wonder that when Pope Urban v tried to persuade the English mercenaries to leave Italy and join Peter of Cyprus's 'crusade' to Alexandria in 1364–5, one of his offers was 'the remission of usury due to Jews'![8] For many members of the White Company it must have been an offer they could not refuse – although what the Jews thought about this magnanimous gesture is not, to my knowledge, recorded.

Sometimes, however, would-be knights were ruined not by self-indulgence but simply by the sheer expense of providing themselves with equipment. Another French chronicler, Jean le Bel, describes how Edward III was confronted by a large Free Company at Calais in 1359. The knights put up a splendid show for him, but then 'most humbly explained to the king their poverty: how in attending him they had spent everything, on horses and equipment'. Edward, however, replied that, though he welcomed their assistance, he could not afford to pay them:

This reply did not please these foreign knights, who had thus struggled hard and suffered great hunger and poverty, as you have heard. Nevertheless, a certain sum of money was paid out to each as a loan so that he could return to his own country, but it was very small. So they went their ways, some poorly mounted, others on foot. Some sold their equipment or their bedding and others left their leggings in pawn to their hosts. It was total ruin for them.[9]

Without his armour and horse, a mercenary would naturally have great difficulty in finding further employment, and many a former adventurer found himself forced out on the streets to beg. These down-at-heel ex-soldiers, with their claims to be men-at-arms and even 'gentils', found their way back to England in such numbers in Chaucer's day that they became an urgent social problem, and in 1376 Parliament passed legislation to deal with them: 'And as for the others who claim to be 'gentils', and men-at-arms or archers who have fallen on hard times because of the wars or for some other reason, if they cannot prove their claim, and it can be proved that they are craftsmen and not in any service, they shall be made to serve or to return to their crafts which they practised hitherto.'[10] Such legislation could not be totally successful, however, and we find Wyclif complaining about these ex-soldiers some eight years later.[11]

This, then, is the immediate context in which Chaucer drew his famous portrait of a 'parfit gentil knyght'. It cannot be over-emphasized that the poor appearance of the Knight would immediately have alerted the suspicions of contemporary readers. Far from regarding his dingy tunic and lack of armorial bearings as signs of modesty (as modern commentators suppose), they would automatically have classed him either as one of the impoverished mercenaries described by Jean de Venette or else as one of the vagabonds detailed in the *Rolls of Parliament*. At best they might have classed him as a 'gentil knyght that is fal in pouerte' like the poor knight in the *Geste of Robyn Hode*. At all events, they would certainly have expected more explanation than Chaucer in fact provides.[12] This absence of explanation is, in itself, a sure sign that satire is in the air.

The Ellesmere illustration of the Knight

The picture of Chaucer's Knight on page 28 is from the famous Ellesmere Manuscript. The Manuscript was completed within a decade of Chaucer's death and may even have been commissioned by his son, Thomas Chaucer.[1] This picture, therefore, is a reasonable guide as to how Chaucer's own contemporaries interpreted the character of the Knight.

To the twentieth-century observer, the illustrations of the pilgrims which adorn this manuscript might appear at first sight to be somewhat crude, but they are, in fact, extremely accurate visualizations of Chaucer's descriptions. They depart from what Chaucer wrote only to add details which, though not in the poem itself, express something essential about the individual characters. Thus the Prioress is portrayed riding side-saddle – a detail which is not mentioned by Chaucer but which was the height of fashion in the 1380s, and just the sort of thing one would expect from that modish lady.[2]

When we look at the drawing of the pilgrims' horses, we find especially great attention to detail – as perhaps one would expect in an age when the horse was of tremendous social significance. It would be rather as if a modern artist were to draw a series of travellers and their cars – he would not represent them all driving the same car but would be careful to distinguish the driver of the Rolls-Royce from the driver of the old beat-up Morris Minor. So, with the Ellesmere Manuscript, the drawing of the

Chaucer's Knight as he appears in the earliest manuscript. Note the brand-mark on the horse's flank.

horses provides us with an accurate representation of the specific types of horse mentioned in the poem or else a reflection of the characters riding them. The Wife of Bath, for example, is described as sitting upon an *amblere* – and there, sure enough, in the Ellesmere illustration is an *amblere*, executing the particular gait known as 'ambling', in which the horse was trained to move both its right legs and then its left legs in unison, in order to provide an easy, relaxing ride.[3] The illustration of the Merchant's horse shows a thoroughbred of possibly oriental blood, executing a 'high school air' known as the *capriole* – thus indicating the sort of expensive, highly-trained mount one would expect the Merchant to ride, even though Chaucer doesn't actually specify his mount. The Squire's horse, on the other hand, is larger than the others and is 'a typical *stede* or *dexter*, recognizable by the thick crested neck, luxuriant mane, the feather above the heels and the small, wide-set inward-pointing ears, that one would expect to see in the male ancestors of the Shire breed'.[4]

When we come to the illustration of the Knight, we find that the artist has once again depicted a war-horse, larger than the others, but he has also made another very remarkable addition which shows us clearly what he at least thought of the Knight's character. On the horse's flank can be seen a brand-mark in the form of a letter 'M'. There is also another mark – a minuscule 'y', which is also conceivably some sort of brand – on the horse's neck.

Now why should the illustrator of the Ellesmere Manuscript have included such a detail? It is surely not an arbitrary addition – it must mean *something*.

One explanation of the brand-mark has been made by A.A. Dent, in his excellent article 'Chaucer And The Horse' (*PLPLS*, IX, 1959–62, p.9). He characterizes the Knight as: 'A recently retired cavalry officer; frankly mercenary' who had 'served in what was virtually a foreign legion ... under the command of the Teutonic Knights', and goes on to suggest that the 'M' might stand for Munster or Mecklenburg, since it is 'a characteristic habit of German horse-breeding establishments, especially those which formerly specialized in war-horses like the Hanoverian stud, the Trakehnen (ex-East Prussian) stud, and the Lipizza stud now domiciled at Piber in Styria, to brand stock bred by them in a certain position rather low down on the near hind quarter towards the front of the thigh'. To this I might add that the 'M' could also stand for 'Marienburg' which was, of course, the headquarters of the Teutonic Knights when the Knight of the *Prologue* was 'beginning the borde'. If this suggestion is correct, the brand-mark simply signifies a war-horse of German origin. There is another possible inference, however.

Such branding was customary in the Italian city-states which employed foreign mercenaries in the fourteenth century. In the *Rules for the Foreign Mercenaries in the Employment of the*

Republic of Florence in 1337, for example, we read: 'ITEM That each and every individual horse, palfrey, nag and mule must be branded over according to its skin colour and mark, and with a hot iron be branded with a clear sign; and that the said horses must be counted by those marshals chosen by the officials of the army who will be there at the time.'[5] The reason for this branding was that the mercenary was paid according to his equipment and according to the quality of his horse. Branding was one way of making sure that the mount of a soldier presented at muster was indeed the same animal he used at other times, and that he did not trade-in an expensive animal for a cheaper one – a practice which was evidently all too common, judging from the rule-books of the period. (See, for example, the *Military Code for the Troop hired by Pisa* in 1327–31, already quoted on page 25.)

Of all the Italian city-states employing English mercenaries in Chaucer's day, perhaps the best-known to Englishmen would have been Milan. Milan was one of the chief employers of the most famous of all English *condottieri*, John Hawkwood, and it was to Milan, of course, that Chaucer himself went on two occasions – in 1372 and 1378 (the latter time specifically to negotiate with Hawkwood). Indeed, *The Knight's Tale* itself contains allusions to the Visconti, who were then masters of Milan. It is, therefore, not an unreasonable guess that the unknown artist of the Ellesmere Manuscript intended this 'M' branded on the Knight's horse to stand for 'Milano', and for the reader to identify the Knight as a one-time member of that most infamous organization of Englishmen abroad – the White Company – the English tool of Italian tyrants and the scourge of Lombardy.

3 Commentary on the description of the Knight in the *General Prologue*

The Knight's ideals

> **A Knyght ther was, and that a worthy man,**
> **That fro the tyme that he first bigan**
> **To riden out, he loved chivalrie,**
> **Trouthe and honour, fredom and curteisie.**
>
> *General Prologue*, 43–6

In the preceding chapters I have outlined the changing nature of military service and the growing dominance of the mercenary over all other forms of soldiery. This was, for Chaucer's generation, a sociological change of such significance that Chaucer could surely not have ignored it. In the transformation, the ideals of an older order were thought to have been degraded, and a situation was created in which huge bands of bloodthirsty marauders roamed Europe, killing, raping, burning and pillaging without let or hindrance. At such a time, the poor knight – whether the self-made military man or the knight without independent means – was automatically an object of suspicion. The Knight of the *Prologue*, however, is introduced to us in glowing terms. He is a 'worthy man' who loves 'chivalrie' and 'trouthe and honour, fredom and curteisie'.

The apparently unequivocal praise of these opening lines, however, contrasts sharply with the picture of the Knight that would have unfolded to the contemporary reader throughout the rest of the description. This technique is typical of Chaucer's satiric portraits. He very often introduces a character with apparent praise before proceeding to reveal his true nature.

I say 'apparent' praise because even these opening lines would not have been as unequivocal to Chaucer's contemporaries as they appear to us. Many of the words have changed their meaning through the intervening centuries, and, when Chaucer wrote the lines, some of the words contained ambiguities which they no longer possess. A 'worthy man' for example, did not primarily mean a man 'deserving honour' or 'of great merit' as it does now; an analysis of Chaucer's own use of the word shows that he almost invariably used it to mean 'well-to-do' or 'of high social status' and that he applied it most frequently to characters whom he was satirizing.[1] Similarly, although 'chivalrie' could be used to denote the whole system of knightly ethics, in Chaucer's day it was even more commonly used in a purely technical sense to denote the cavalry officers or cavalry warfare in general.[2] Thus the second half of line 44 could mean '... he loved the ideals of chivalry' or it could just as easily have meant no more than '... he loved cavalry warfare' or '... he loved being a cavalry officer'.

In fact, when the line is considered in context, these latter interpretations make, perhaps, better sense, for Chaucer also tells us that the Knight loved 'chivalrie' 'fro the tyme that he first bigan/ To riden out ...'. This does not mean that the Knight had loved 'chivalrie' since he could first ride a horse.[3] 'To riden out' was another technical military term: it meant 'to go on raids'.[4] These were pillaging raids, undertaken away from the main body of the 'host' or army. As such, they were understandably popular with the knights, since – away from the watchful eye of superior officers – there were no controls on what the knights did or how much booty they picked up or – more importantly – how much booty they kept for themselves. 'Riding out' was such a temptation for knights, so detrimental to discipline and so bad for the reputation of any army, that it had to be strictly controlled. Every army of the day included in its regulations a clause to this effect. Here, for example, is one taken from Richard II's 'Statutes & Ordinances To Be Keped In Time of Werre':

No man to make roode withoute licence.
Also that no man make no riding by day nor by night, except by licence and with the knowledge of the chieftain of the battle ... upon pain of surrendering their bodies and goods to the king.
Also that no ward captain allow any roode without licence of the king.
No man is to be absent from any array nor to go out of the host without licence.[5]

Chaucer then goes on to list another four qualities which the Knight admires: 'Trouthe and honour, fredom and curteisie'. This line is, in many ways, the most difficult in the whole portrait for the modern reader. The nuances of these four words are extremely elusive and, moreover, debatable, so that it is very difficult to know for certain just what they would have conveyed to the fourteenth-century reader. A discussion of these words will be found in the Appendix to this book, but for now I will summarize their likely meanings.

'Trouthe' could mean either 'fidelity' or simply 'trustworthiness, honesty'; 'honour' meant primarily 'worldly glory' (not honourable conduct); 'fredom' is usually translated as 'generosity', but, in my opinion, it is far more likely to have meant 'freedom of action' to Chaucer's contemporaries; and 'curteisie' meant 'fine manners'.[6] Now these are all ideals which one might expect any knight to admire – the aristocrat as well as the mercenary – but they are not the ideals of the pious ascetic the Knight is generally represented as being.

'Trouthe' in the sense of 'fidelity', for example, is a fine quality for the nobleman warrior to admire, but in the sense of 'trustworthiness' or 'honouring pledges' it was also something which many a *condottiere* would have professed – indeed John Hawkwood built his very reputation on his love of such 'trouthe' and his zeal in honouring contracts.[7] Similarly, 'fredom' may have carried connotations of generosity, but Chaucer normally used the word to indicate the quality known in French as *franchise*.[8] By this was meant a certain freedom of action – an independence – and in this sense it was an important quality of knighthood – but it had an ironic slant when applied to the itinerant freebooters of the mercenary companies who, of course, prized their freedom of action only too highly. The Knight's love of 'honour' or 'worldly glory' was something else that most noble knights and mercenaries shared in common, but it was also something for which they were constantly criticized by their contemporaries. It was certainly not an ideal by which Chaucer himself laid any store, and the Poor Parson condemns this love of 'honour' as something which damns a man to the eternal fires of hell.[9] Likewise, although a love of 'curteisie' was only natural for any noble knight or would-be knight, it is by no means a spiritual quality. In fact for Chaucer, unless fine manners were tempered by the all-important quality of pity, they were all too likely to be nothing more than a cloak for evil:

> Eke what availeth Maner and Gentilesse
> Without yow, benygne creature?
> Shal Cruelte be your governesse?
> Chaucer, *Complaint Unto Pity*, 78–80

[Also, what avail are fine manners and noble birth without you (Pity), benign creature? Shall Cruelty be your guiding influence?]

And this brings us to what is perhaps the most important point about these lines from the *Prologue* – what they *don't* say. Chaucer's contemporaries would probably have understood as much from the words which are omitted from this list as from those which are included. The absence of such crucial words as 'largess', 'loyalty' and 'pity' would probably have spoken volumes in an age when the ideals and qualities of knighthood were under constant discussion and debate.[10]

However, for the moment, Chaucer merely leaves these hints in the air. It is only as the portrait moves on remorselessly through the catalogue of battles and military campaigns in which the Knight is supposed to have fought, that the satire begins to bite.

Crusading into Christendom

> **Ful worthy was he in his lordes werre,**
> **And therto hadde he riden, no man ferre,**
> **As wel in cristendom as in hethenesse,**
> **And evere honoured for his worthynesse.**
> *General Prologue*, 47–50

These lines introduce the list of battles and campaigns which occupy lines 51 to 66. Many commentators have remarked on the length of this list, and some have been driven to the conclusion that Chaucer is guilty here of uncharacteristic prolixity. The passage is certainly long-winded, if one accepts the usual interpretation that each of these campaigns merely demonstrates, over and over again, the Knight's dedication to championing Christianity by force of arms.

I have always been convinced, however, that Chaucer avoided verbosity and that the essence of his style is, as Caxton put it, 'short, lively and dignified expressions, avoiding prolixity, casting away the chaff of superfluity and showing the choice grain of meaning'.[1] It seemed to me necessary, therefore, to take a closer look at this list of battles and campaigns.

Chaucer prefaces his review of the Knight's military career with what many modern commentators take to be a eulogy to the Knight's martial defence of Christianity. They see the 'lorde' in whose 'werre' the Knight had fought as none other than God.[2] There are, to be sure, other interpretations of the phrase 'his lordes werre' (which are discussed in 'Where had the Knight not fought?' below, p. 94), but here I wish to concentrate on the religious interpretation of these lines because it is so fundamental to the traditional image of the Knight. Invariably scholars have seen him as 'the champion of the Church' and 'the implacable enemy of the infidel'.[3] They tell us that his campaigns 'have one obvious characteristic in common: they are all struggles between Christians and pagans'[4] and that the Knight has not fought in the Hundred Years' War because he is more concerned with the broader, spiritual task of expanding the borders of Christendom.[5]

It is a mistake, however, to assume that all Chaucer's contemporaries shared the unbounded enthusiasm of modern commentators for knights who went off to kill Arabs, Turks and Lithuanians in the name of Christ. They did not.

Even in the previous century, St Thomas Aquinas had held that crusades should only be defensive, while Roger Bacon condemned them outright as a 'cruel and useless waste of time', maintaining that 'the infidel should be converted not attacked.'[6]

By the time the *Prologue* came to be written, the golden age of crusading had long since lost its lustre, and more and more men were questioning whether killing the infidel really was the best way of converting him to the religion of Love and Peace. As Gower put it:

> And for to slay the heathen all,
> I know not what good there might fall,
> No matter how much blood be shed.
> This find I written: how Christ bid
> That no man should another slay ...
>
> If I should slay a Saracen,
> I also slay his soul withal,
> And that was never Christ's law.[7]

Even some of those who conceded the Church's right to win back the Holy Land, felt that the Pope had no right to encourage Christian aggression in other places, such as Prussia and Lithuania.[8] Honoré Bonet, for example, wrote in 1386: 'Further, I say that the Pope cannot reasonably declare war against the unbelievers for the conquest of other lands or kingdoms that they hold, unless those lands were lawfully subject to the Church or the Roman Empire.'[9]

In 1395, while Chaucer was still working on *The Canterbury Tales*, there was uproar in London when a document was nailed on the doors of St Paul's and of Westminster Abbey, which included the following attack on the whole crusading ethic and the papal use of indulgences and pardons to propagate wars in distant lands:

It is a holy robbing of the poor people, when lords purchase indulgences *a poena et a culpa* for those who ally themselves with his host and gather to slay the Christian men in far lands for temporal goods, as we have seen. And knights, who run to 'hethnesse' to get themselves a name for slaying men, are greatly blamed by the King of Peace; for by humility and tolerance our faith was multiplied, and Jesus Christ hates fighters and manslayers and threatens them: *Qui gladio percutit, gladio peribit.* [Who strikes with the sword, shall die by the sword.][10]

The reasons for this disillusionment with the crusades among thinkers and writers are not hard to find. In the first place there was the growing realization that heathens were human beings the same as Christians. As Honoré Bonet pointed out, 'God does not make the sun to shine hotter or stronger for the one or for the other.'[11]

Thinking men of Chaucer's day must also have been acutely aware that the Saracen was not a mere barbarian, fit for nothing better than to be run through by the shining sword of Christian bigotry. Contact with the Arab world was surprisingly close. The Saracen maintained an easy-going attitude to Christian pilgrims: the pilgrimage to Jerusalem was a comparatively common experience (the Wife of Bath, for example, has been there no less than three times), and one could hardly travel to such a place without being impressed by Muslim architecture and craftsmanship.[12] Even more impressive was the debt of the Western world to Arab culture and learning. It was, after all, through Islamic scholarship that many of the great works of Classical Greece were preserved and transmitted to Medieval Europe.[13] Chaucer himself demonstrates his own familiarity with the names of several Arab scientists.[14] His *Treatise on the Astrolabe* is based ultimately on the work of Mashallah, a Jewish astronomer of the eighth century, and in his introduction he holds up Arab scholars as an example to the English – a proposition which must have shocked many of his more conservative readers.[15]

A more pragmatic reason for the diminishing enthusiasm for the crusade into 'hethenesse' was the realization of its futility – the appalling knowledge that all this bloodshed achieved so little – especially in the areas in which the Knight has been engaged. Alexandria had been won and lost again within days, and the net result was merely the disruption of Christian trade and an escalation in the price of some foodstuffs – precisely the same outcome as resulted from the Duke of Bourbon's futile expedition to Tunis in 1390.[16] In the previous century Roger Bacon had attacked the Teutonic Order for the futility of its 'crusade' in Germany and Poland,[17] while in Lithuania – where the Knight has 'reysed' more often than any other Christian of his rank – the cost (according to Walsingham) was something like four thousand slain or captured for eight Lithuanians converted.[18] Not much of a success rate for even the most ruthless evangelist!

Above all, the fact that the crusaders into 'hethenesse' received the blessing and active encouragement of the Pope did little to enamour them to Englishmen. At a time when the Pope in Avignon was generally accounted an enemy of England and a supporter of the French cause, it was all too easy to suspect that he was using the crusades to divert English arms away from the war with France.[19]

All these attitudes found their way into the literature of the day. Monarchs and romantics paid lip service to the virtues of fighting the heathen, but many writers of the age recognized the real motives that impelled knights to venture into 'hethenesse'. Gower said that the only reason men-of-arms travelled 'over the grete Se' or to Prussia, Rhodes or Tartary, was to gain 'worschipe' (i.e. fame and honour) whereby to impress their ladyloves:

There as these men-of-arms are
Sometimes over the Great Sea   [Mediterranean]
So that by land and also ship

He had to strive to gain worship,
And make many hasty raids
Sometimes into Prussia, sometimes into Rhodes
And sometimes into Tartary   [the land of the Tartars]
So that these heralds would shout in front of him:
'His worthiness! His worthiness! Lo! Here he comes!'
And then he gives them gold and cloth
So that his fame might grow
And to his lady's ears might bring
Some tidings of his worthiness;
So that because of his prowess,
Which she heard others talk about,
She might the better to his love accord.[20]

The French poet Guillaume de Machaut consistently treated fighting in heathen lands as merely a way of impressing the ladies.[21]
Even Froissart – that great apologist of chivalry – noted Prussia
as a place of profit and self-advancement.[22]
   Chaucer himself identified the places where the Knight had
fought (Prussia, Alexandria, Turkey and Wallachia) as the sort
of place to which ladies sent their lovers to prove themselves
rather than as the resort of dedicated soldiers of Christ. In *The
Book of The Duchess*, the Black Knight praises his lady, Blanche,
because she does not follow the fashion:

Nor send men to Wallachia,
To Prussia and into Tartary,
To Alexandria, nor into Turkey,
And bid him at once that he
Go hoodless to the Dry Sea   [Gobi Desert]
And come home via Qara Na'ur;   ['Black Lake' on the
And say: 'Sir, you must now realize   eastern side of
That I must hear fine things said   the Gobi, Outer
Of you, before you come again!'   Mongolia]
She used no such little tricks.[23]

In fact, it was a commonplace of contemporary satire that the
crusade into 'hethenesse' was no longer an evangelical mission
but an exercise in greed and worldly vanity.[24]
   If there was this much opposition to the crusade into 'hethenesse', it can be imagined how much greater was the outcry
against the crusade into Christendom itself. And this is, after all,
what Chaucer emphasizes in these lines – that the Knight had
ridden as far '*in cristendom* as in hethenesse'.

We should not have any illusions about what this would have meant to Chaucer's contemporaries. The crusade into Christendom was not against heathens but against Christians. In the fourteenth century there were comparatively few battles between Christians and heathens on Christian soil. On the other hand, the increasing readiness of the popes to preach crusades against their fellow-Christians was one of the scandals of the age.[25]

Already in the previous century there had been mounting resentment at the papal use of the holy war to enlarge the temporal power of the papal see, as witnessed in the substantial body of protest literature in Old French and Provençal.[26] At the beginning of the century Chaucer's own hero, Dante, angrily indicted Pope Boniface VIII for using the crusades in Europe against his own opponents within the Church:

> The Prince of the new Pharisees
> Waging war close to the Lateran
> Instead of against the Saracens or the Jews,
> For every one of his enemies was Christian.[27]

By the time Chaucer came to write *The Canterbury Tales*, the crusade in Christendom had become even more notorious. In 1377, it brought about one of the most horrifying massacres of the century, at the little Italian town of Cesena, which had dared to oppose the might of one of the most powerful cardinals in the Roman Church. According to even the most conservative estimates, 'about 2,500 Christians' (men, women and children) were slaughtered in one day on the orders of the papal legate Cardinal Count Robert of Geneva.[28]

The next year, this supposed man of God, who had craved 'blood and more blood', to quote his own words, was elected Pope in opposition to the French pope in Avignon. The Great Schism tore the Church apart, and Europe recoiled before the spectacle of the two popes locked in bloody conflict with each other. From now on, any war that suited their own ends became dignified with the title of 'crusade'.[29] By 1397, the meaning of the word had altered so radically, that Pope Boniface IX could even talk about 'a crusade to Italy'![30]

To many observers, it seemed as if the Christian Church were tearing itself apart. Gower complained:

> Alas! it is by the Christians
> That Holy Church is destroyed,

> And Justice in her freedom
> Now no longer protects the people.[31]

Honoré Bonet, in his *L'Apparicion Maistre Jehan de Meun*, pictured the Saracen gloating over the conflict, while Wyclif expressed his own horror with characteristically passionate clarity:

> Bodily torment is great nowadays, when one pope sends bishops and many men to slay men, women and children, and on behalf of the other pope come more against them. And the cause of this fighting is a fiend's cause, for no man on earth knows which of these popes is a fiend to be damned in hell, or indeed whether they both are. ...
> For if one of these popes is to be damned – and God alone knows whether they both shall be – then men are fighting for a falsehood in the cause of a fiend, and such a cause was never heard so plainly against the truth.[32]

And perhaps one should bear in mind here that in Chaucer's day Wyclif's views were not confined to some lunatic minority but were widely held, as Henry Knighton records: 'They gained to their sect half or more than half the population ... the sect was growing so much in repute and number that you could hardly see two people on the street but one was a Wycliffite.'[33]

What made the crusade in Christendom particularly obnoxious to many of Chaucer's contemporaries was the fact that the Church had become a main employer of the notorious Free Companies. John Hawkwood's White Company, for example, was employed by the Pope between 1372 and 1374 and again between 1375 and 1377. Langland blasted away at the Pope for paying mercenaries to make war upon their fellow-Christians:

> For were the priesthood more perfect than it is,
>   especially the pope;
> Who with money maintains men to war upon Christians,
> Against the law of our Lord as St Luke witnesses:
>   *Mihi vindictam, et ego retribuam, dicit dominus etc.,*
> His prayers with his patience would bring peace
> And love to all lands, and that in a little time;
> The Pope with all priests *pax-vobis* should make![34]

And of course since so many of these mercenaries were Englishmen, like their leader, Hawkwood, the whole subject had a particular relevance for Chaucer's fellow-countrymen.

There was also another peculiarly English reason for resenting the crusade within Christendom: the conviction that it was being financed by taxes levied from within the English clergy – in other words that money collected in England was being used to finance the enemies of England. An entry in the *Rolls of Parliament* for 1376 reads:

... as soon as the pope needs Money to maintain his Wars in Lombardy, or elsewhere, for distributing favours or for ransoming any of his French friends captured by the English, he demands a subsidy of the Clergy in England. And immediately it is granted to him by the Prelates, because the Bishops do not dare to contradict him, and it is levied from the Clergy against their wishes. And the Secular Lords take no notice of this, and are not dismayed that the Clergy is destroyed and the Money of the Realm is wickedly taken away.[35]

The continuator of Adam Murimath's *Chronicle* records the general feeling that at this time the English were being taken for a ride by the papal see: 'Among the courtiers of the papal see it has become a proverb that the English are good asses, bearing all the intolerable burdens imposed upon them.'[36] Clearly the sight of Christian fighting Christian hurt not only the Englishman's sense of propriety, it also hurt his pocket.

If these wars within Christendom were of great interest to Englishmen in general, they were especially so to Chaucer, for he had been there, right in the thick of it. He had twice travelled through Italy at times when the activities of the Free Companies were at their height. In 1378 he was sent to carry out top-secret negotiations with John Hawkwood, the chief of the English *condottieri* and the very man who was employed by Cardinal Robert of Geneva to carry out the massacre at Cesena![37] So we know for a fact that Chaucer had met face-to-face with these men whom the Pope 'with money maintains to war upon Christians'. Chaucer must have known as well as any Englishman living exactly what it cost in terms of human misery and suffering, when men waged the crusade 'As wel in cristendom as in hethenesse'.

It is against this backdrop that Chaucer's contemporaries would have interpreted this line. At a time when many thinking men (including men in Chaucer's own circle) were questioning the right of the Church to wage wars even 'in hethenesse', the extension of the holy war within the borders of Christendom itself was a scandal, and the readiness of some Englishmen to sell their services to either side in the Pope's wars a source of shame and anger.

The fact that, in the course of this, the Knight has been 'evere honoured for his worthynesse' merely compounds the irony – as if to say: not only has he slaughtered his fellow-Christians, as well as heathens, but he has done very well for himself out of it.[38]

Chaucer now goes on to enumerate a number of specific campaigns in which the Knight has been involved. All of them refer to actual historical events. The first is the Siege of Alexandria in 1365 by King Peter of Cyprus.

The Knight and Peter of Cyprus at Alexandria

At Alisaundre he was whan it was wonne.

General Prologue, 51

The Knight's involvement in the siege of Alexandria is usually represented as the jewel in his crown of Christian knighthood.[1] And yet contemporary accounts of the siege read more like the recent massacre at Mai Lai than some glamorous exploit of chivalry.

Alexandria had a large Christian population and a flourishing trade with all Western Europe – being, among other things, the centre of the important spice trade. It was not really expecting to be attacked.[2] When Peter of Cyprus's armada turned up in the Old Harbour in 1365, the unsuspecting citizens of Alexandria assumed it to be an unusually large merchant fleet. On the morning of 10 October they thronged onto the beaches to witness such an unusual sight 'with no idea of the misery and desolation which lay in store for them. ... Some were spectators and some were vendors. There was much buying and selling and bargaining in full Oriental fashion, notwithstanding the impending calamity.'[3]

By the time they realized their mistake, it was too late. The result was an appalling massacre. One citizen, who was lucky enough to escape but who later returned to collect eye-witness accounts, reported: 'An old man found in al-Khalasiya School was thrown to his death from an upper floor. ... Women and children were slaughtered, and it is even said that infants were torn in two in a kind of tug-of-war, and that boys were dashed

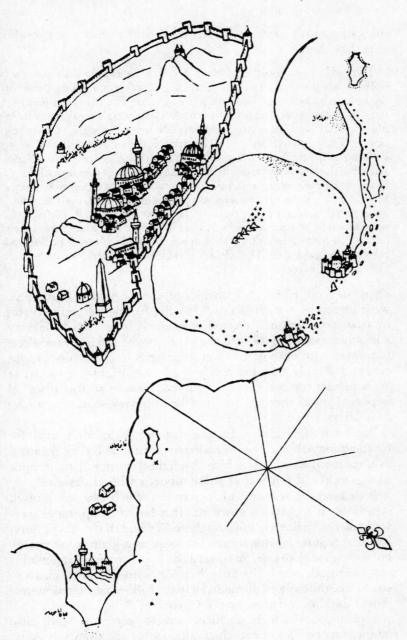

A sixteenth-century plan of Alexandria

to death against stone walls.'⁴ A modern historian sums up the siege like this:

> Two and a half centuries of Holy Warfare had taught the Crusaders nothing of humanity. The massacres were only equalled by those of Jerusalem in 1099 and Constantinople in 1204. The Moslems had not been so ferocious at Antioch or at Acre. Alexandria's wealth had been phenomenal; and the victors were maddened at the sight of so much booty. They spared no one. The native Christians and the Jews suffered as much as the Moslems; and even the European merchants settled in the city saw their factories and storehouses ruthlessly looted. Houses were entered, and householders who did not immediately hand over all their possessions were slaughtered with their families. Some five thousand prisoners, Christians and Jews as well as Moslems, were taken to be sold as slaves. A long line of horses, asses and camels carried the loot to the ships in the harbour and there, having performed their task, were killed. The whole city stank with the odour of human and animal corpses.⁵

Even the Coptic churches of their fellow-Christians in the East were looted by the crusaders.⁶ Finally, having perpetrated this holocaust, the knights deserted *en masse* with their booty, leaving Alexandria to fall back into the hands of the infidel – and Peter of Cyprus with nothing but a pointless piece of vandalism to his credit. The only tangible result of the whole sorry episode, as Walsingham rather sourly observed, was that the price of imported spices shot up, and they became very scarce for a long time afterwards.⁶

But what significance did the siege of Alexandria hold for Chaucer himself and for his contemporaries? Did they regard it as a spectacular success which 'brought great rejoicing in most of the courts of Europe' as some modern scholars assert?⁸

If we read the accounts of Alexandria which Chaucer himself is most likely to have seen, we find that his contemporaries were well aware of what had gone on there. We find that poets of international repute did not regard the siege as a glamorous victory but as a cause of shame. So too did the Pope's own representative on the crusade. Even the Pope himself, who had done much to encourage the exploit, dismissed it in the following year as merely 'a few days' occupation by the Christians'.⁹

The account which Chaucer almost certainly read, also happens to be one of the chief sources for the events at Alexandria. It is the long poem called 'The Capture of Alexandria'

('*La Prise d'Alexandrie*') written between 1369 and 1373 by the French poet Guillaume de Machaut.[10]

In his poem, Machaut constantly contrasts the nobility of Peter of Cyprus with the treachery of the knights who served under him. In particular, he puts the blame for the desertion firmly on the shoulders of the foreign knights – the *estranges chevaliers*.[11] Machaut describes how King Peter holds a council of war on the beach. The king tells the knights that it is their duty to hold the city against the infidel,[12] but the knights reply *sans conseil*[13] that they cannot and that they are not going to stay any longer.[14] When Peter reminds them that they have promised to serve him for an entire year, the foreign knights merely reply that they are not prepared to talk any more.[15] Peter then delivers an impassioned but futile plea to their sense of honour, ending:

> I will never again rejoice
> For your honour or for mine,
> Which I consider as lost
> If your valour does not urge you on.
> So I beg you, each one, to stay
> Otherwise it is dishonour.[16]

To all of which, the foreign knights reply in a most un-ceremonious manner:

> When he had finished these words,
> The foreigners, of whom I speak,
> Replied that they were off
> And that they could not help him.[17]

The Papal Legate, Pierre de Thomas, joins in the king's exhortations, saying:

> 'You came here
> Saying that you were pledged
> To perform his service with devotion,
> From which to depart would be too great a vice,
> And would lose and undo
> All the good you have done.
> For Good and Dishonour
> Cannot go together, it seems to me.
> And so they say that he who serves
> If he does not complete his service – loses his reward.'
> He showed them the Holy Scripture,
> But he wasted his breath,

>For their reply was brief and curt:
>'We're off. Life is running away.
>We don't want to die.'[18]

King Peter even tries to set them an example by riding back into the city, but it is no good. As he sees the Saracens re-enter the city and all his work undone, he cries out:

>'Honour, you are dead!
>Without a shadow of doubt we have lost you
>Beyond recovery, and well we know it!'[19]

So Guillaume de Machaut, whose work Chaucer apparently admired, and whose account of the siege of Alexandria Chaucer in all probability read, did not regard the siege as an occasion of great honour but as an infamous display of treachery and a disgrace to the knights who served there. It is a strange beginning to the career of the 'parfit, gentil knyght'. It is certainly a peculiar sort of 'victory' for Chaucer to spotlight rather than the genuine English triumphs of the age, such as Crécy and Poitiers.[20]

There is another account – this time from an eye-witness – which puts the Knight's presence at the siege of Alexandria in an even more suspicious light. This is contained in a report sent back to the Pope by his chief representative on the crusade – Pierre de Thomas, formerly Archbishop of Crete. According to Thomas, those responsible for the treacherous defection were none other than the English knights:

>Alas! An intolerable grief! Its like has never been heard of. Those whom God had brought together, in order to conquer the city, were split apart by wickedness. ... And the English retreated, who previously had seemed the bravest acting in league with their chief, whose name I had better keep quiet in view of his parentage and the treachery that follows. ... For when their leader, the King, like a good soldier, wanted to resume the fight, these men refused to resist, but with his English troops, who refused to spend the night in the conquered city ... [the chief] ostentatiously marched away and completely withdrew from the King's company.[21]

Although we do not know whether this actual letter reached Chaucer's eyes, its contents must have been widely circulated in the Courts of Europe, and Chaucer and his readers must have been aware of the implied stain against English knighthood.[22]

Another significant account of the siege of Alexandria is contained in a letter which Petrarch wrote to Boccaccio. It is by no means as unlikely as one might at first think that Chaucer should have seen such a piece of correspondence, since Petrarch's letters appear to have been a good deal more public than Petrarch himself would have liked and were constantly being copied or stolen as they crossed the border between France and Italy.[23] We certainly know that Chaucer had read at least one other letter which Petrarch wrote to Boccaccio, since he based his *Clerk's Tale* on it.[24] In any case, Chaucer, with his keen interest in Italian literature and affairs, would have been extremely sensitive to Italian reactions to contemporary events – especially the reactions of a poet such as Petrarch, whom he admired and, quite possibly, even met.[25] With regard to the siege of Alexandria, Petrarch was quite certain that those who fought under Peter of Cyprus were not true 'knights' but freebooters or, as he puts it, 'men recruited from beyond the Alps':

Peter of Cyprus seized Alexandria in Egypt – a great and memorable feat and of immense value in widening the empire of our religion, if only there were as much worth in taking the city as holding on to it. Not that Peter himself, according to what reports tell us, tarnished his own glory in any way, but his troops, who all consisted of men recruited from beyond the Alps (the kind of men always keener to undertake such exploits than to finish them) left him in the thick of the battle and showed that they had followed him in the first place not out of piety but out of greed. Once they'd got their booty, they took to their heels, little caring that the King's solemn vow remained unfulfilled, once their own covetous desires had been satisfied.[26]

And this brings us to what appears to have been the crucial significance of the siege of Alexandria for Chaucer's contemporaries: it epitomized all that was worst about the new breed of mercenary soldier. Although Peter of Cyprus had set off with the intention of leading an army of kings, princes, dukes, barons and earls, what he in fact ended up with was little more than a gang of adventurers and paid desperadoes. When he toured Europe in 1364 to whip up support for a crusade, he was feasted royally but obtained little real support from the nobility of France, England or Germany.[27] Edward III for example, was very lukewarm and merely promised not to oppose any English knights who might want to go. 'And the King of Cyprus', says Froissart, 'never could obtain any more of him.'[28]

On the Continent, Peter's crusade was openly regarded as an opportunity for getting rid of the Free Companies who were currently burning, pillaging and blackmailing their way across Europe. The Pope seized on it as a chance to get the English Free Companies out of Pisa, expressing the hope that with a little encouragement 'other companies in those parts' (Hungarians, Germans and French were also active) 'may be induced to do the like, or may be so weakened as to be resisted, and thereby both Italy be freed and the crusade greatly helped....'[29] He made no bones about his motive, which was nothing less than 'the total extinction of the vicious Companies now devastating many parts of Ecclesiastical and Imperial Rome'.[30]

In France, so Froissart tells us, the king promised his support to Peter for two reasons: 'One was, that King Philip, his father, had formerly made a vow to do the same; the other was, to draw out of his kingdom all those men-at-arms called free companions, who pillaged and robbed his subjects without any shadow of right.'[31]

King Charles of Bohemia made a compact with the Pope in which they

planned to summon all the robbers who had long been in France and were now devastating Lorraine and other companies like them as well and, if they would agree to go, to grant them the remission and absolution of their sins, provided they were penitent, to give them generous pay, and immediately to assign them the task of aiding and defending the faithful in the name of Christ against the infidels and the enemies of the cross of Christ.[32]

Even the Cypriot chronicler Makhairas, whose chief intent is to eulogize Peter, makes it quite clear that the king was actively recruiting mercenaries from the Free Companies in Lombardy on the basis of a mere monthly wage.[33]

So whatever had been Peter of Cyprus's original intentions, the army which he finally took to Alexandria consisted in the main of lawless adventurers and desperadoes from the Free Companies. His crusade was openly used by the Pope and many of the crowned heads of Europe as an opportunity to draw off the military detritus left behind by the cessation of hostilities between England and France.

This was all common knowledge to Chaucer's contemporaries, and the débâcle at Alexandria was seen as a textbook example of the danger in relying on such mercenary riff-raff, and the need for troops with some commitment or loyalties beyond the acquisition of hard cash.

Although Alexandria may have been reckoned as a credit to Peter of Cyprus himself, it was long regarded as a stain on the honour of the knights who served under him – particularly the English. When Chaucer blithely informed his audience that this 'verray, parfit gentil knyght' was one of those very English knights who took part in the siege of Alexandria and so shamefully betrayed the King of Cyprus, his eye must have been sparkling with irony.

The Knight and the Teutonic Order

Ful ofte tyme he hadde the bord bigonne
Aboven alle nacions in Pruce;
In Lettow hadde he reysed....

General Prologue, 52–4

Chaucer now proceeds to paint a picture of the Knight presiding like a figure from Arthurian legend at a table of honour in Prussia (*Pruce*). At first sight, this once again seems to confirm his reputation as a pious, militant Christian, since Prussia and Lithuania (*Lettow*) were the stamping ground of a crusading order, known as the Teutonic Knights.[1] But there is another side to the coin.

Although the Order of Teutonic Knights had, indeed, started out as a crusading order, dedicated to winning the Holy Land from the Saracen, this was no longer the case by Chaucer's day. At the beginning of the thirteenth century the Order turned its attentions away from the Holy Land, where the Saracen was becoming increasingly effective as a military power, and towards the Baltic, where the enemy was less potent.[2] By 1283 they had more or less exterminated the Prussians and were able to move their headquarters to Prussia in 1309. They now turned their eyes towards neighbouring Lithuania.

The Lithuanians were pagans, and so the new campaign could still carry the official colours of a crusade. But already, in the previous century, the aggressive expansionist policies of the Teutonic Order had provoked much hostile criticism. Roger Bacon pointed out that the heathens of Germany and Poland were not resisting the arguments of a superior religion but fighting against oppression.[3]

By the time Chaucer was writing, the Teutonic Order was first

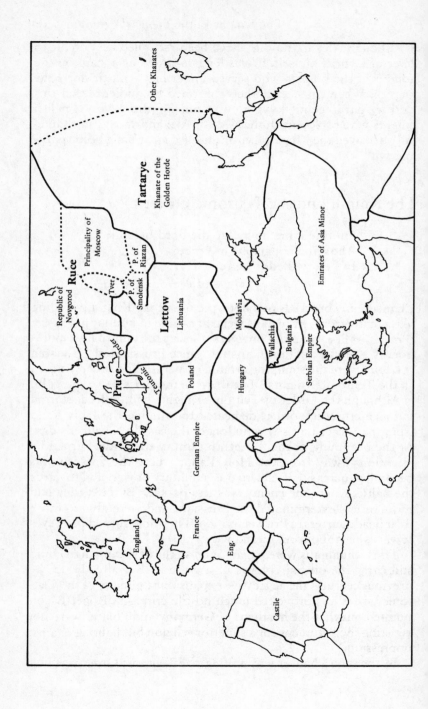

and foremost a political and economic institution: 'Their aim
was no longer in the first place the practice of chivalry; that element, as well as their spiritual aspirations, had been more or less
effaced by their political and financial importance.'[4]

On 12 November 1308 they had demonstrated just how far
they had abandoned both their Christian and their chivalric
ideals. Having been admitted into Danzig as allies of Wladislaw
Lokietek, the Grand Prince of Poland, the Knights turned on their
hosts, seized the city and massacred its inhabitants.[5]

From then on it must have been increasingly clear to all Europe
that the '... original spiritual ideals of the order were subordi-
nated to political ambitions. The Teutonic Knights indiscriminately attacked Christians and heathens in eastern Europe. They
were fundamentally a state in the guise of a religious order.'[6]

The Teutonic Order was not only a fully-fledged secular power
but one renowned for its savagery.[7] And the Lithuanian campaign, with which Chaucer associates his Knight, was infamous
even in an age of brutal and savage campaigns. The contemporary chronicler John of Posilge records an example of their
ruthlessness, in an incident in 1390 which involved many English
knights, including the Earl of Derby (later Henry IV):

On September 4 they arrived at Vilna and set up their bombards,
catapults and mangonels, and stormed the upper house vigorously,
so that they gained possession of it. From this house over two thousand persons were captured and slain, and the fire was so great that
they perished there all together, for inside were many goods, and the
people from all about had fled thither, and piteous it was how they
all burned.[8]

Another chronicle records that in 1378 the Livonian Master
(the chief of the Teutonic Order in Livonia) 'killed, burned, laid
waste and destroyed everything for nine days and nights' ('*per
ix dies et noctes occidit, cremavit, vastavit et destruxit omnia*').
Indeed 'seldom has a war been waged so stubbornly and with
such ferocity'.[9]

Why, then, did English, French, Hungarian and Italian knights
travel so far – often at their own expense – merely to assist this
ruthless German expansionism?[10]

In the opinion of Chaucer's literary colleagues there were two
obvious attractions: glory and loot.

Froissart categorically identifies Prussia as one of those places where, in 1366, a soldier could 'take his profit' and where 'all knights and squires go to advance themselves'.[11] So too, Gower complained that knights went off to Prussia and Tartary to win fame and glory, or else to win their ladies, and all too seldom to serve God:

> Oh knights, I will speak to you,
> You who seek to prove yourselves
> In Prussia and in Tartary.
> I don't know the reason why you go.
> Three causes I can describe to you:
> Two of them aren't worth a sorb-apple:
> The first is, if I may say so,
> 'Because of my prowess and pride,
> I will journey afar to win praise'
> Or else: 'It is for my lady-love
> Therby to gain her affection
> That I labour' ...
> The third cause for which the 'prudhomme'
> Strives is not like this,
> But it is for the sake of Him
> Through whom all good is rewarded. . . .
> But, on the other hand, without fear of contradiction
> The present generation has a large following
> Of those who serve themselves.
> In the present day, as it is said,
> Chivalry is maintained
> For pride and foolish delight.[12]

As I have already pointed out, Gower makes the same association in his *Confessio Amantis*, where he described 'Prus' as the sort of place to which a knight will 'travaile for worschipe' to impress his lady.[13] Chaucer himself, in *The Book of the Duchess*,[14] specified Prussia as one of the places to which it was then the fashion for ladies to send their lovers. It was, in fact, a commonplace of literary satire.

It is no wonder that Prussia became associated with knightly vainglory, for the Teutonic Order deliberately set out to attract foreign knights to its service with glittering promises of prestige and public displays of pomp and circumstance. One of the devices used was the table of honour: 'In order to attract to themselves more powerfully the foreigners who poured in to show their prowess, they caused proclamations to be made at fixed times that they would, at a certain date, such as seemed to them most convenient for undertaking such an inroad, set up a so-called table of honour, known in German as *eretysche*, for those who should come to them.'[15] These tables of honour have clearly been the high point of the Knight's career in Prussia:

> Ful ofte tyme he hadde the bord bigonne
> Aboven alle nacions in Pruce ...

And nobody ever got to sit at the head of a table of honour by being modest and retiring. Among all the other adventurers, jostling for a place, the Knight would have had to make sure that he impressed the heralds who appointed the places at table. This is how the custom was described by one contemporary:

> Now the custom was and is, with respect to this so-called table of honour devised by the vanity of the said friars, that, the said friars having prepared a solemn banquet for a certain number of such persons and guests, say for ten or twelve, or some other small number, only those persons who were selected from the knights by the heralds there present were assigned to places at the aforesaid table, those persons being such as, by the testimony of the heralds, had traversed various parts of the world as errant knights and had been seen by the heralds in various other regions; and, according as one individual from the number of these knights and persons seemed to surpass another in this respect, the places about the table were assigned.[16]

This process, as we have already seen Gower pointing out, usually meant that knights had to bribe the heralds with 'gold and cloth':

> So that these heralds would shout in front of him:
> 'His worthiness! His worthiness! Lo! Here he comes!'
> And then he gives them gold and cloth
> So that his fame might grow
> And to his lady's ears might bring
> Some tidings of his worthiness.[17]

The whole concept of the table of honour was, in fact, so far removed from the religious ideal of knighthood that it was one of the grounds on which the Teutonic Order was accused of heresy.[18]

The other great attraction which the Teutonic Order offered the knightly adventurer was the prospect of prodigious amounts of loot – especially against an enemy 'less powerful and less well-

organized than the Turks in the Holy Land or in the Balkans'.[19]
An account by a contemporary wandering minstrel makes it clear
that there were often easy pickings to be made by the Christians:

> God gave the Christians the good fortune to come unannounced,
> to the sorrow of many a heathen. The knights hunted them down and
> brought them to a standstill with thrust and stroke. Woe was it for
> them, but well for us. The land was full of people and goods, so that
> we held revel with them, for what was loss to the heathen was gain
> to the Christians, as the scales of battle inclined; merry in truth was
> the day.[20]

The lure of glory and easy booty brought soldiers of all sorts
to Prussia and Lithuania – not just great lords such as the Earls
of Derby and Gloucester but also soldiers of fortune and mercenaries. In fact the popes did everything they could to encourage
this flow of mercenaries into Prussia, since, like Alexandria, it
offered an alternative theatre of war for the mercenaries who
were currently terrorizing Italy.[21] The Teutonic Knights themselves seem to have been happy to welcome these adventurers
and desperadoes into their midst – indeed they even started to
adopt their fighting tactics.[22]

The Teutonic Court was in some ways the natural haunt of
the itinerant mercenary. It was the one Court where martial
values had eclipsed all others and where the successful man of
war or the simple adventurer was likely to find advancement
more easily than in the established Courts of Europe. To repeat
Froissart: it was a place where all knights and squires 'went to
advance themselves'. There was opportunity for a would-be
knight of dubious origins to win status unimaginable at home,
where low birth would inevitably hold him back. 'The soldiery
of various Christian regions of the world *of all ranks*', says a Pol-
ish contemporary, 'came in great numbers to gain this special
honour. . . .'[23] As the late Professor Coopland observed: 'We need
not credit Bolingbroke and others [who undertook the journey
to Lithuania] with any burning zeal for the conversion of the
heathen Lithuanians to Christianity.'[24] The same may be said of
Chaucer's Knight.

It is to this polyglot nature of the Teutonic Court that Chaucer
gently draws his readers' attention when he mentions that the
Knight had begun the board 'aboven alle nacions in Pruce'. The
Knight would have found himself rubbing shoulders with penni-

less adventurers as well as some of the wealthiest nobles in Europe. In such an atmosphere, having to keep up appearances while receiving no pay, it is no wonder that many knights over-reached themselves and, like so many military adventurers of the time, were ruined in the process.[25]

The Teutonic Order itself did what it could to assist the process of parting these men from their money. As they kicked their heels in the Court, waiting for action sometimes for months together, many Christian knights 'lost the great sums which they expended among the brethren. And thus the said brethren, by this their craft and cunning, drew gold and silver from them, for the most part under the pretext of fair dealing, that is, through the agency of persons who furnished them food in return for money. This was and is a truth public and notorious.'[26] Could this be one reason why the Knight of the *Prologue* cuts such a poor figure on the road to Canterbury? To have sat at the head of the tables of honour so many times 'aboven alle nacions in Pruce' must have cost him a lot of Gower's 'gold and cloth'. How else is it that such a highly-honoured man looks so like a 'poor knight' return-ing from abroad down-at-heel and broke.[27]

By having his Knight serve in Prussia, Chaucer was not, as modern critics suppose, associating him with the highest aims of old-style chivalry. The Prussian Court was one of the main centres of military opportunism and one of the few Courts of Europe that made little distinction between the old feudal knight and the new-style military entrepreneur.

Any doubt as to what kind of a soldier the Knight is, disappears in the very same line, when Chaucer reveals that the Knight had 'reysed' not only in Lithuania but also in Russia (Ruce) ...

What was the Knight doing in 'Ruce'?

> ... and in Ruce,
> **No Cristen man so ofte of his degree.**
> *General Prologue*, 54–5

Unlike Prussia and Lithuania, 'Ruce' (Russia) is not a place which is usually associated with knightly adventures in the literature of the day.[1] Neither Gower, Froissart nor Chaucer himself – aside from this occasion – ever mentions it as a focus for Christian military expeditions against the heathens.[2] This is scarcely surprising, since Russia was already a Christian country and had been for over four centuries.[3] It was a land abounding in fine churches and monasteries – 'a refuge for Christians, a joy to Angels and ruin to the Devil',[4] where men sang the *Te Deum* and kissed the holy Bible just as they did in England or in Rome.[5] For all the hostility between the Greek Church, to which Russia belonged, and the Latin Church, it was still a part of Christendom.[6] There was certainly no question of any 'crusade' into Russia during the fourteenth century.

Chaucer seems to imply that the Knight had 'reysed' (or 'raided') in Russia during his time with the Teutonic Order. And yet the last important conflicts between the Teutonic Knights and the Russians had been in 1242 and 1268.[7] By the mid-fourteenth century the only German attacks on Russia were lawless pillaging raids on the border towns of Novgorod. Presumably it was in such a raid as the following (described in a contemporary Russian chronicle for 1367) that the Knight is supposed to have taken part:

The same year, for our sins, there was no understanding between Pleskov and Novgorod; and a force of *Nemtsy* [Germans or 'unintelligible ones'] and men of Velney [Vilna in North Pruce] came and ravaged about Izborsk, all the Pleskov district as far as the Great river [the Velikaya] and having forded the Great river they came to the town of Pleskov and burned the town around the fort and did much damage, and then retired, suffering no harm, because neither Knyaz Alexander nor the Posadnik Lenti [Leontius] nor any other good men were in town at that time; many were away in travel.... And at that time Novgorod merchants had been detained in Yurev [Dorpat in North Pruce] and in other towns of the *Nemtsy*, and *Nemetski* merchants were detained in Novgorod.[8]

The only other kind of 'reysing' the Knight could have done in Ruce would have been plain and simple banditry. The Prusso-Russian border was, in fact, notorious as the haunt of robbers who waylaid merchants on the way to and from Novgorod. And the official government of the Teutonic Knights, far from being totally hostile to the Russians, actually relied on their co-operation for the suppression of this banditry.[9]

When Chaucer's Knight 'reysed' in Ruce, there is no way he could have been a 'soldier of Christ'. He was either a marauder, burning and looting undefended border towns in a Christian country, or else a bandit ambushing Christian and heathen merchants alike.

Chaucer's irony grows even darker in the next line, when he tells us that not only had this 'verray, parfit gentil knyght' ravaged in Russia but he had done so 'No Cristen man so ofte of his degree'. The nuances in this are not hard to pick up.

The troubles which the Russians experienced on their Prussian border at the hands of Christian pillagers were almost nothing compared with what they were suffering elsewhere at the hands of the pagans. In the west, Russia was under constant pressure from the Lithuanians, who pushed as far east as Smolensk, under Olgierd (1339–77). In the south and east, the threat came from the fearsome Mongol Tartars – the Golden Horde who sacked Moscow itself in 1382.[10]

It is to this pagan onslaught that the Knight's own son, the Squire, refers in his Tale, when he describes the Tartar Khan as 'a kyng that werreyed Russye' (*Squire's Tale*, 5, 10). In fact the Squire is full of praise for the Khan and apparently quite un-perturbed by the suffering which the Tartars were inflicting on the Christians of Russia. One contemporary Russian chronicle for 1327, however, describes what it meant when the Tartars 'werreyed Russye': 'The lawless Shevkal, the destroyer of Chris-tianity, went to Rus with many Tartars. He came to Tver, drove the Grand Prince from his Court and entrenched himself there with great haughtiness and violence. He inaugurated great perse-cution of the Christians [using] force, pillage, torture and abuse.'[11]

In 1380, the Russians enjoyed their first success against the Tartars, but it was short-lived, and in 1382 they were over-whelmed again. Another chronicler has left a description of the devastation which the Golden Horde left in their wake and which was still visible on a journey from Moscow to Constantinople in 1389:

We resumed our journey on Sunday [21 May]... The journey was mournful and dismal. Everywhere prevailed a desert-type [environ-ment]. We did not see anything – neither cities nor villages. Yet, in the years gone by, beautiful and well-populated towns had been located there. Now everything was deserted. No people could be seen anywhere – just one empty space. There were many animals, however, such as goats, elks, wolves, foxes, martens, bears [and] beavers, [and such] birds as eagles, swans, cranes and others. But emptiness reigned everywhere.[12]

By the time Chaucer was writing *The Canterbury Tales*, the Russians were so hard-pressed that Philippe de Mézières announced that it was the Church's duty to bring 'effective aid to the Eastern Christians'.[13]

So when Chaucer says that the Knight had raided in 'Ruce' 'No Cristen man so ofte of his degree', the emphasis is not – as at first appears – on the Knight's 'degree' (his rank or status) but on the fact that he had done so more often than any other Christian. In other words, the Knight had been the keenest Christian to go pillaging another Christian country at a time when it was already reeling from the devastating incursions of the pagans!

Indeed, there may be further irony in the mention of 'degree', since it is conceivable (though not proven) that only Christian knights of 'low degree' – such as the ruthless mercenaries – would have stooped to this sort of unethical banditry.

It might be argued, however, that the Knight could have been fighting in Russia *for* the Russians *against* the Tartars. But the sense of the line is against this. To have 'reysed' in Ruce meant to have gone on military expeditions or raids into Russia – it hardly implies fighting on behalf of the Russians. Besides, there is no evidence of Teutonic Knights or even mercenaries giving such support. It is more likely, in fact, that the Knight had been actually fighting *for* the Tartars.

In the conflict of 1380 against the Christians of Moscow, the Tartars were assisted, according to one chronicler, by Turkish and Genoese mercenaries:

That year [1380] Prince Mamai of the [Golden] Horde, accompanied by other princes and all the Tartar and Polovtsi forces, and joined by such mercenaries as: the Turks, Armenians, Genoese, Cherkessians, Burtasians, and supported by [Grand Prince] of Lithuania Iagello and [Prince] Oleg of Riazan, advanced against Grand Prince Dmitri, and on September 1 made a camp on the bank of the Oka River.[14]

And since Chaucer also tells us that the Knight had fought as a Turkish mercenary in Palatye (cf. commentary on line 65, below) it is equally possible to suppose that he might have travelled north, with other Turkish mercenaries, to offer his services at the Court of the Golden Horde – especially since his own son displays such familiarity with the Tartar Court and even frank admiration for the great Khan himself.[15]

To sum up: when Chaucer tells us that his Knight had fought in Prussia and in Lithuania, he leaves it wide open as to what kind of a knight he is talking about – he could be a nobleman or a mercenary. When, however, Chaucer adds that the Knight had also 'reysed' in Russia, he is branding him as a brigand and a mercenary, prepared to pillage and destroy Christian cities as soon as heathen.

Chaucer's final observation that the Knight had ravaged in Russia 'No Cristen man so ofte of his degree' is one of the most bitter comments that he makes on any of the pilgrims.

What was the Knight doing at Algezir?

> **In Gernade at the seege eek hadde he be**
> **Of Algezir ....**
>
> *General Prologue*, 56–7

Chaucer now traces the Knight's career down into another major theatre of war – southern Spain. 'Gernade' was the independent Moorish kingdom of Granada, which had been ruled by a Muslim dynasty, the Nasrid, since 1235. It survived as an independent state for something like two and a half centuries.[1]

'Algezir' (Algeciras) was a strategically important seaport.[2] The siege of Algezir was a long-drawn-out affair in which Alfonso XI of Castile attempted to drive out the King of Granada. It lasted from 1342 to 1344.

Because the siege of Algezir was fought against the Moors, most modern commentators assume that Chaucer is once again simply reinforcing the image of the Knight as a crusading Christian, dedicated to fighting the infidel – no matter where.[3] But there is more to it than this.

In the first place, there is no reason to suppose that Englishmen would have attached any specifically religious significance to the siege of Algezir any more than they did to any other victory against the infidel – or against anyone else for that matter.[4] The Castilian campaign against the Moors in Granada was not a holy war in any true sense of the word – it was simply 'a political war on the part of the ruling classes in Spain'.[5] This must have become quite obvious to Chaucer's contemporaries as the century wore on, from the ease with which the Spanish royal Houses allied themselves as it suited their convenience either with the Moors of Granada or with the Marinids of Morocco.[6]

As a religious enterprise, the siege of Algezir was certainly overshadowed by other military adventures of the day. If Chaucer

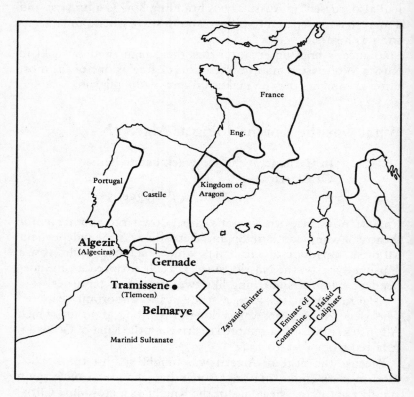

had really intended to associate the Knight with a great religious victory of this particular period, he could have sent him off on the crusade which succeeded in capturing Smyrna in October 1344, which has been described as 'the first expedition to come within the category of holy warfare at this time'.[7] Or else he could have had him take part in Alfonso's far more famous victory over the King of Belmarye four years earlier, on the River Salado. The victory on the Salado was indeed seen by contemporaries as a religious triumph – perhaps because Alfonso deliberately went out of his way to give it the colours of a 'crusade' and even advanced behind the papal banner.[8] The Spanish, *Crónica de Alfonso XI* (written c. 1370) regarded it as 'the greatest Christian victory ever won over Islam in Spain'.[9] And the French chronicler Jean le Bel spends six whole pages enthusing over the Salado victory (as against one paragraph on Algezir): 'I do not wish to forget the great deeds and the very happy fortune which fell to the King of Spain, at Castelet ... against the Saracens, for which all Christianity must forever give thanks to Our Lord for the great strength he showed them.'[10]

It is also interesting to compare the letters of congratulation which Edward III sent to Alfonso on each occasion. The letter of 1340 refers to 'the glorious triumph granted to you by Heaven over the enemies of the faith', whereas the letter of 1344 for all its fulsome phrases merely refers to 'the subject of the surrender of the town of Algezir and your prosperous successes in that area'.[11]

In fact, the conclusion to the two-year siege of Algezir was, in comparison with the victory on the Salado, scarcely a victory at all. The end came not with a crushing defeat for the infidel but merely a ten-year truce with the Moors in return for twice the normal tribute.[12] Even the Moors themselves regarded it as 'an honourable capitulation', according to the Arab chronicler Ibn-Khaldun.[13]

Another main feature of the siege of Algezir for contemporary chroniclers seems to have been the great sufferings of the Christian knights.[14] Jean le Bel attributes the cause of this to the fact that Alfonso had in attendance at his Court some of the grandest nobility of Europe – the Earls of both Salisbury and Derby were there, for example. Such a glittering Court inevitably attracted vast numbers of poorer knights all eager to impress the great lords – so eager in fact that, according to Jean le Bel, they became quite reckless: 'The Christians perished more often than the Saracens, by sword and other arms, for they abandoned themselves too much to folly in order to advance their honour amongst the great lords and barons who had come there from all countries as pilgrims. ...'[15]

The *Crónica de Alfonso XI* provides the details of such an incident, which makes it clear that these foreign knights were none other than the itinerant mercenaries of the Free Companies

('companies of foot-soldiers from outside the kingdom') who were acting without authorization from the official besiegers:

> And one day, at the beginning of the month of August, foreign companies of foot-soldiers entered the barricade which the Christians had built and commenced to fight the Moors of the city in between the villas. And when he saw this, the King realized that if these men were not given help, they would be in danger of death, since the Moors were numerous and more were coming out of the city. For this reason he commanded several of his own men to arm themselves and go in to get these men out. And those whom the King commanded, went in but were not able to extricate them immediately, as the Moors began straight away to fight with them as hard as with the others. And the Earls of Derby and of Salisbury were present, as well as other English and German knights, and they armed themselves and entered eagerly into the battle. And all the Moors of the city came out, both on horseback and on foot, and awaited them in the field, and the battle was very fierce between them. But the Christians who were involved in the battle, did not stand firm with the Earls but abandoned them as men who had entered rashly into the battle. And the King, seeing this, straight away ordered all those who were lodged round about the barricade to arm themselves and go in to help the Christians. And this they did.[16]

In other words, the siege of Algezir, like the siege of Alexandria, witnessed the betrayal of the old feudal knightly class by the modern itinerant mercenary.

The preceding extract from the *Crónica de Alfonso XI* clearly demonstrates Chaucer's ambivalence in associating the Knight with the siege of Algezir rather than more important victories of the period such as the victory at the Salado. The Knight might well have been legitimately in attendance on one of the great English nobles, such as Salisbury or Derby, but he might equally well have been one of the poor mercenaries attracted thither by the presence of these great lords. Chaucer doesn't say which he was – he leaves the reader to draw his own conclusions.

It is worth pointing out, however, that if the Knight *had* been one of these wandering freebooters, there is even some doubt as to whether, legally speaking, he should have been at the siege of Algezir at all, for in the years which it occupied, Edward III issued several proclamations forbidding English knights to fight abroad in foreign service. Four years earlier, at the battle of the Salado, Edward had felt himself able to give Alfonso support because of the truce of 1340 between England and France.[17] But when the siege of Algezir took place, things were very different. In 1341 the English alliance had received a severe blow by the transference of the Emperor Louis IV of Bavaria to the French cause; the Scots had renewed their raids on England's northern borders, and the French were gaining ground in Gascony.[18] In 1342 the French again burned Portsmouth, and the south coast of England was on constant alert against a French invasion that was expected at any moment.[19] Edward, however, took the initiative by overrunning Brittany, and it is probable that he now planned a final decisive strike against the French.[20] He required every available knight and man-at-arms to be at his disposal, and in 1343, when the siege of Algezir was at its height, he decreed that no ordinary knight ('simple Chivaler') or sergeant should henceforth undertake any commissions abroad without special licence.[21] In 1344 it was asserted in Parliament that the French intended 'to destroy the English language and occupy the territory of England, which God forbid unless a remedy of force is found against their malice'.[22] The uneasy truce was again broken, and the very month before Algezir fell, Edward issued yet another proclamation specifically forbidding 'any earl, baron, knight, squire or other man-at-arms' from undertaking any foreign adventure without his express permission.[23]

It was also during the siege of Algezir that Alfonso started to receive support from England's arch-enemy – Philip VI of France. This may account for the speedy recall of the Earls of Derby and Salisbury.[24] Certainly fighting in a foreign war for a foreign king in a campaign financially supported by the King of France himself could not have been a very popular activity among Englishmen, even when it was not actually illegal.

Such suspicions about the legitimacy of the Knight's presence at Algezir are dramatically confirmed when Chaucer goes on to reveal that the Knight had also 'riden in Belmarye'. For his contemporary readers, this would have left no question as to what kind of a knight this was ...

What was the Knight doing in Belmarye?

... and riden in Belmarye.
General Prologue, 57

'Belmarye' refers to the area of North Africa occupied by the Banū-Marīn or Marinids (from whom the 'merino' sheep derives its name)[1] and roughly corresponds with present-day Morocco and part of Algeria (see map, p. 60). Once again the Knight's service there is usually seen as a part and parcel of his crusading activities against the Moors.

Chaucerian scholars are mistaken, however, when they claim that there were many Christian expeditions into Belmarye during the fourteenth century.[2] There were not. J.N. Hillgarth, the historian, writes that there was 'no attempt to penetrate politically into North Africa west of Tunis' during the whole of this period.[3] There were, indeed, occasional plans for such expeditions (such as Henry of Trastamara's in 1366)[4] but they all came to nothing. There was not even a raid on any Marinid port until 1399. The Duke of Bourbon's expedition to Barbary in 1390 was to Tunis – some eight hundred miles away – and although the threat of a Christian invasion of Belmarye itself had been present ever since 1260, when the Christians occupied Sala, it did not become a reality until the Portuguese occupied Tetuan in 1415, long after Chaucer's death.[5]

So whatever the Knight had been doing in Belmarye, Chaucer's contemporaries would have known that he had not been on a crusade there.

There were, however, a considerable number of Christian soldiers in Belmarye throughout the fourteenth century; they were not crusaders – they were mercenaries *in the pay* of the Moors. Belmarye was, in fact, a happy hunting-ground for soldiers of fortune from all over Europe. Norman Daniel, in his recent book *The Arabs and Medieval Europe*, notes that 'the picture of the loyal Christian knight in Arab service ... seems to have been a pattern of employment, especially in North Africa, over a very long time'.[6] In fact, ever since the middle of the thirteenth century the Berber tribe of Zayanids had employed Catalonian and Castilian mercenaries, and their rivals, the Marinids of 'Belmarye', continued the practice throughout the fourteenth century.[7] J.N. Hillgarth wrote recently:

> There were Christian mercenaries, merchants and slaves in North Africa, and Muslim mercenaries, merchants and slaves in Castile and Aragon. In the twelfth century Christian mercenaries had fought for the Almoravids against the Almohads in Morocco. In the thirteenth century the declining Almohads depended largely on Castilian and Portuguese mercenaries. When the Almohads fell, Castilian and, at times, Catalan mercenary captains recruited bands to serve the new masters of Morocco, the Banū-Marīn. There were Catalan militias in Tunis and Tlemcen from the 1250s onwards for at least two centuries.[8]

The reason that the rulers of the Maghrib saw fit to employ Christian mercenaries was mainly tactical, as the famous fourteenth-century Arab historian, Ibn-Khaldun, explains:

> We have mentioned the strength that a line formation behind the army gives to the fighters who use the technique of attack and withdrawal. Because of [this fact], the Maghribî rulers have come to employ groups of European Christians in their army.... The Maghribî rulers do that despite the fact that it means utilizing the aid of unbelievers. They do think much of it, because the necessity [of using such men] exists, as we have shown. They fear that their own line formation might run away, and [they know that] the European Christians know only how to hold firm, because it is their custom to fight in closed formation. They are, therefore, more suitable for the purpose than others. However, the Maghribî rulers employ [such European Christians] only in wars against Arab and Berber nations, in order to force them into submission. They do not use them for the holy war, because they are afraid that they might take sides against the Muslims. Such is the Maghrib at this time.[9]

Another reason for the Christian mercenary presence in 'Belmarye' at this time was that the Maghrib, like northern Italy, represented the archetypal situation which fostered the employment of mercenaries. As the nineteenth-century French historian le Comte de Mas Latrie put it: 'Exposed without ceasing to betrayal or massacre, in the midst of the rivalry of local tribes and in the heart of a social organization where every successful revolt was legitimate, many sultans found more security in entrusting the safety of their palaces to foreign troops.'[10]

There is also no doubt that Chaucer and his audience would have been familiar with the activities of these soldiers of fortune in Arab service. They provided, after all, one of the main points of contact between Christendom and the Muslim world: 'Official diplomatic envoys were the exception rather than the rule. The main contacts between Christian and Islamic countries were provided by the mercenaries, merchants, missionaries and slaves who shuttled between Castile and Catalonia-Aragon and Granada, North Africa and the East.'[11] And it was on Arab culture, transferred in this way, that Western writers and thinkers had to rely for their knowledge of the learning of Classical Greece. Besides, these were famous men: their commanders were well paid – often earning more than the officers of state of Christian kingdoms. At the beginning of the century the kings of Aragon had been drawing a substantial income from their salaries.[12] At times they even exerted a considerable political influence in Islam,[13] although we should always bear in mind that, like Hawkwood and the *condottieri* of northern Italy, the men who served in 'Belmarye' and 'Tramyssene' were motivated purely by self-advancement: 'The Christian mercenaries had, at times, great political influence in the Islamic states of North Africa. They exercised it almost entirely for their own profit. One can trace little systematic attempt to use mercenaries to undermine Islamic rule politically in North Africa. The mercenaries had no effect on Islamic religion.'[14]

Nor would Chaucer's readers have confused activities in 'Belmarye' and 'Tramyssene' with more creditable adventures such as the 1390 attack on Tunis. Medieval Europeans were perfectly aware of the distinct principalities which made up the North African coastline.[15] Some of them were, moreover, surprisingly well informed about the affairs of the Muslim world. The full text of the *Crónica de Alfonso XI*, for example, contains over fifty chapters devoted to the history of the Banū-Marīn of Morocco.[16] So when Chaucer says that his Knight had 'riden in Belmarye', his readers would have known where he meant, and, what is more, they would have been well aware that the only Christian soldiers in Belmarye were mercenaries in the service of the infidel.

In the late-thirteenth-century book of miniatures known as the *Cantigas of Alfonso X*, we actually have a picture of a Christian knight pledging friendship with a Muslim, just as Chaucer's Knight must have done, and another showing Christians fighting alongside Saracens against other Christians (see illustration).

Any doubts as to what Chaucer's Knight was doing in 'Belmarye' have been purely in the minds of literary scholars. To historians who have studied the relationship between Christian Europe and the Arab world in the fourteenth century, it is perfectly obvious what Chaucer intended. As long ago as 1886, the French historian de Mas Latrie noted that Chaucer's Knight was typical of the freebooting men-at-arms, Castilian, Italian, German and English, who drifted in and out of the service of the kings of Morocco and Tlemcen during this period.[17] More recently, Norman Daniel put it more brutally: 'There were always experienced and unscrupulous mercenary soldiers', he writes, 'ready to take expeditions in Africa or Asia; it is of these that Chaucer's knight is the type.'[18]

13th-century illustrations of a Christian mercenary pledging friendship to a Muslim, and fighting alongside Muslims

In short, lines 56–7 execute one of Chaucer's favourite joke patterns. He first of all presents us with a piece of equivocal information as if it were certainly praise and then knocks it flat with a deft and unexpected *coup de grâce*:

> In Gernade at the seege eek hadde he be
> Of Algezir, and riden in Belmarye.

The fact that the Knight had been in Granada, at the siege of Algezir, could possibly be interpreted as praise, for he may have been in the retinue of those great lords who joined Alfonso's host at the beginning of the campaign, but as soon as Chaucer adds: 'and riden in Belmarye', his audience would have recognized him as a mercenary, prepared to serve Christian and heathen alike.

Further adventures with Peter of Cyprus

**At Lyeys was he and at Satalye
Whan they were wonne ...**
General Prologue, 58–9

Chaucer now returns to the Knight's service with Peter of Cyprus, under whom he would have been fighting at both 'Lyeys' and 'Satalye'.

'Lyeys' and 'Satalye' represent the beginning and end of Peter of Cyprus's career as a crusading king. But while Satalye (1361) was a fast, if bloody, victory, Lyeys (which came towards the end of Peter's reign, in 1367) was a dismal failure. The fact that Chaucer mentions them both in the same breath as being 'wonne' may be nothing less than a cheerful irony.

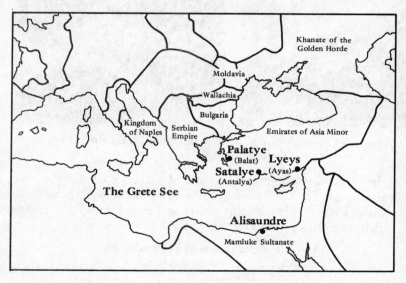

Satalye is the modern town of Antalya in southern Turkey[1] (see map). In Chaucer's day, it was such a fabulously wealthy city that even apologists for Peter of Cyprus suspect that he may have had 'his crusading spirit mixed with a touch of human greed' when he set out to regain the city.[2]

There is some difference of opinion as to whether this conquest was characterized by the usual pitiless savagery of Peter of Cyprus's crusades.[3] However, Guillaume de Machaut describes it as the familiar blood-bath in which Turks and Saracens, and fellow-Christians as well as women and children, were slaughtered indiscriminately by the Christians:

> He [Peter of Cyprus] set off, with his men.
> They sailed on the high seas
> Until they came to Satalye,
> A city that is in Turkey,
> Great and powerful, fortified and strong.
> But there was neither wall nor door,
> Nor anyone that could defend it,
> When the good king went to take it,
> And destroyed it and put it to the sword.
> And so he set fire to all and burned it,
> One saw there many fine robes of silk
> And of fine gold burnt up
> In flames. And many a beautiful lady,
> Many a Saracen, many a young girl,
> Many a Turk, and many a child died
> By fire or by the sword.[4]

Bloody outrage or not, the winning of Satalye was undoubtedly a conquest, and one which earned Peter of Cyprus quite a reputation. But what happened at Lyeys was a very different story.

In Machaut's description, which follows, it is important to note the distinction between the citadel (*chastiaus*) and the undefended town which lies beside it (the *ville*):

> Lyeys is a castle stronghold
> Strong and powerful and beautiful.
> There is a town there, and it sits by the sea....
> When he [Peter of Cyprus] came there, he attacked
> The castle, but he failed to take it
> Because his men were exhausted,
> Wounded and tormented and crushed
> By the great heat and the battle,
> And they had so little food.
> And the Saracens who were
> In the castle defended it well.
> But the town was burned and destroyed,
> So that it wasn't worth a trout.[5]

It appears, then, that the only thing that Peter could be said to have 'wonne' at Lyeys was the undefended *ville*, by then 'not worth a trout'.

So when Chaucer announced that the Knight had been at Lyeys 'whan it was wonne', as well as at Satalye, his audience may well have known he was pulling their legs by lumping together a bloody victory with a worthless fiasco. Perhaps the implication is that this is exactly what the Knight himself was doing – passing off failures as victories to impress his less well-informed companions.

Nor could the attack on Lyeys be said to have been a religious undertaking. Philippe de Mézières may have recommended Peter of Cyprus as a model for Christian chivalry and listed Alexandria, Satalye and Lyeys among his victories,[6] but then Philippe de Mézières, like the Knight, was not only a former follower of Peter, but also his chief aider and abettor in those very campaigns – he would be bound to see them in the best light possible.[7] The political reality was different. In the case of Lyeys, for example, Machaut, with whom Chaucer had more acquaintance and more affinity than with Mézières, emphasized that Peter of Cyprus was attacking as part of an agreement with the Armenians – a fact which seems to have left a rather sour taste in his mouth (see the following extract). He also notes that Lyeys was the Sultan's legitimate heritage but that, as it lay on the borders of Armenia, it was a constant source of trouble for the Armenians. Moreover, the Armenians coveted Lyeys because it would give them access to the Mediterranean. Having thus pointed out the political implications of Peter's 'crusade', Machaut goes on to detail the atrocities committed by the 'good king' on the way to Lyeys, with such bland indifference that I find it impossible not to believe that he is being ironic:

> Lyeys is a castle stronghold
> Strong and powerful and beautiful.
> There is a town there and it sits by the sea,
> And, I can tell you truly
> It has been a great nuisance to the Armenians.
> It is the inheritance of the sultan
> And it sits on the border of Armenia
> And cuts Armenia off.
>
> The noble king, with stout heart,
> Set out once more across the sea,

And came to the country of the Saracens.
Thus he wished to help the Armenians.
The king set out from Tripoli
And went on his way, his heart divided
Between joy and melancholy,
For he was often melancholy
At hurting his enemies
And at helping the King of Armenia,
And at the same time he had joy in his success
At taking the city of Tripoli.
On the sea from Tripoli he rode
But there was not a house of *bauge* [clay and straw]
Nor of mud nor of any other wood
Which he didn't burn. He spared nothing.
Often his sword was stained with blood,
He killed everyone he came across.
Thus he went about, fighting all
And killed the Saracens,
Straight to Alayas,
Spreading fires. What more can I say?

Three beautiful towns he took,
And destroyed – this famous king.
These are their names, without doubt:
There was Tourtouze, Liche and Valence.
And men old and young there were
Who lost their skins.
For they were all killed and burnt to cinders,
Without sparing anyone or taking prisoners.
And when he saw the night coming,
He retreated to the boats,
And commanded his men to retreat.
But by day they set about doing ill
To the Saracens, and destroyed
And killed whomsoever they found.

The illustrious King, so frank and free,
Was so intent upon his deeds
That he could think of nothing else,
Nor thought of going elsewhere.[8]

So, once again, the Knight is being associated with a bloody
and callous campaign, which, under the pretext of a religious
war, was in reality a sordid political exercise.

In view of this close association of the Knight with Peter of
Cyprus, it is obviously worth paying some attention when Peter

reappears in *The Canterbury Tales*. This occurs in *The Monk's Tale* where the Monk says:

> O worthy Petro, kyng of Cipre, also,
> That Alisandre wan by heigh maistrie,
> Ful many an hethen wroghtestow ful wo,
> Of which thyne owene liges hadde envie,
> And for no thyng but for thy chivalrie
> They in thy bed han slayn thee by the morwe.
> Thus kan Fortune hir wheel governe and gye,
> And out of joye brynge men to sorwe.
>
> *The Monk's Tale*, 2391–8

> [O worthy Peter, King of Cyprus, also,
> That won Alexandria by great leadership,
> Full many a heathen you brought to grief,
> For which your own liegemen became envious
> And – for nothing but your 'chivalry' –
> They have slain you in your bed one morning.
> Thus Fortune governs and guides her wheel,
> And out of Joy brings men into sorrow.]

The fact that *The Monk's Tale* is actually 'quitting' *The Knight's Tale* often seems to be forgotten, but it is the case, nevertheless (see *Miller's Prologue*, l. 3119). So when the Monk narrates the downfall of the Knight's own former war-lord and even manages to bring in the siege of Alexandria, which the Knight proudly boasts he attended, he is obviously taking the offensive right into the Knight's home territory. In particular, his remark that Peter of Cyprus was murdered by his 'owene liges' would have struck very near home, since the Knight has already reckoned himself as one of those 'liges'. In addition, the Monk's suggestion that Peter was murdered 'for no thing but [his] chivalrie' is plainly ironic, since anyone familiar with Machaut's account of Peter, as Chaucer was, would have known that Peter was murdered because he had become a notorious tyrant,[9] accusing his own mother of treason, putting his son in irons, forcing the Viscount of Nicosia's daughter to marry a serf and putting her in the pillory, and treacherously killing his hostage, Sir John Visconti.[10] Even Makhairas, the Cypriot chronicler and apologist for Peter of Cyprus, acknowledges that he ends up as a tyrant.[11] He describes how the King went against his promise to free Sir John Visconti and treacherously allowed him to die, and then, not content with this, 'he began to insult all the high-born ladies, from the least to the greatest'. Furthermore he tried to marry Marie de Giblet to a tailor and, when she ran away to a convent, he sought her out and had her tortured: 'And the lords seeing this said: "Such things did we ever expect to see now and hence-forward done to our daughters and to our sons and to our widowed ladies!"' [12]

Peter's end was suitably grisly. Makhairas describes how, after his assassination, James de Nores came into his chamber and 'he found him rolling in his blood, without his breeches and with his head cut off – he drew his sword and cut off his member, and said to him: "It was this which cost you your life."' [13]

Chaucer's association of the Knight with Peter of Cyprus appears to have been typically double-edged. On the one hand, the King of Cyprus and his apologists claimed a reputation for keeping the tattered banner of chivalry flying in an age of general disillusionment, but at the same time he was equally renowned for the bloody savagery of his campaigns, for the treachery of those who served under him and finally for the fact that he ended up as the most unspeakable of tyrants. It is, as we shall see later, obviously a very sore point with the Knight. [14]

Why does Chaucer use the word 'armee'?

> ... and in the Grete See
> **At many a noble armee hadde he be.**
>
> *General Prologue*, 59–60

Chaucer now proceeds to add one more detail about the Knight's service in the Mediterranean. For the modern reader, the unfamiliar phrase in this passage is the 'Grete See', which means the Mediterranean – for Chaucer's contemporaries, however, the unfamiliar word was *armee*. [1]

First of all it should be stated that there is some doubt as to what word Chaucer did write here – whether he wrote *armee* or *arive* or *aryve*. Skeat for example came down in favour of *aryve*, but most modern editors favour *armee*. For this discussion I will follow the authority of J.M. Manly, Edith Rickert, the Middle English Dictionary and others, and assume that *armee* is correct. [2]

'Army' is now such an everyday word that it is difficult to realize that to the Englishmen of Chaucer's day it was totally foreign. In fact, before Chaucer used it here, it had never been used in a work of written English (to the best of our knowledge) and was not to be used again until almost a century later.[3] It was, for example, too new a word to be included in the first ever English–Latin dictionary of c. 1440.[4] In fact its very unfamiliarity may explain the appearance of *aryve* in some fifteenth-century manuscripts. Perhaps some scribe, confronted with the word *armee* which he had never seen before, made a guess and wrote *aryve* instead – a word which had never been used in that way before and was never to be used again.

It would be a mistake, however, to suppose that Chaucer was trying to introduce the word into the English language. He himself never used it again. He was quite simply employing a foreign word to achieve a specific effect – as a modern English writer might use '*gendarme*' or '*Polizei*' instead of 'police'.

The question is: what associations *did* this foreign word carry for Chaucer's contemporary English readers?

The word *armee* was first used in Italy c. 1320, where it indicated 'a troop of armed men' or *soldatesca* (undisciplined soldiery).[5]

Some time between 1360 and 1370 the word was imported into France, and during the following century it gradually replaced the Old French word '*ost*'.[6]

It has been suggested that the importation of *armee* from Italian into French 'was occasioned by a radical reorganization of the French army'.[7] And certainly the substitution of the one word for the other parallels the change-over in military organization from the old feudal levy to the modern paid army. *Ost* seems to die out with the feudal levy itself, while *armee* becomes more and more common as increasing reliance is placed on the use of mercenaries.

In England, where the transition from feudal to mercenary army took place later than on the Continent and where it was buffered by the intermediate Indenture System, the word 'host' remained in general use much longer, and did not even begin to be supplanted by 'army' until the second half of the fifteenth century.[8]

To us, this distinction between feudal levy and hired troops may seem a mere technicality, but to the men of the fourteenth century it was an urgent social problem as we have already seen. It affected the way they built their castles; it affected the way they went to war; it affected the whole fabric of society even in peacetime (see above, pp. 21–5). In war it was vital for a leader to distinguish between his own men and those whom he had hired, for, as Machiavelli put it: 'An army of strangers [i.e. mercenaries] will sooner harm the public good than a Prince's own men, because it is more easily corrupted.'[9]

So when Froissart speaks of *l'ost et l'armee de Monseigneur Charlon de Blois*, he is not simply throwing in superfluous words for the sake of it.[10] He is being technically precise, informing the reader that Blois was employing both his own men and hired troops. A century later Rabelais still distinguished between *ost* and *armee*, using *ost* to refer to the armies of antiquity and *armee* to designate a contemporary armed troop.[11] A similar distinction is also observed in the English *Brut*, c. 1500.[12]

This identification of the word *armee* with the growing use of mercenaries is supported by the fact that the Knight had served in many such *armees*. For it was in the very nature of the freebooter to travel around from country to country and from company to company, wherever the pickings were fattest, whereas the old-style feudal retainer or indentured knight (as he had become) undertook to serve only one lord and to serve that lord for the duration of his own life. (This was, as we have already noted, the form of agreement that Chaucer saw his own son enter into with John of Gaunt in 1389.[13])

The word *armee* was also used in French, however, to mean a 'military raid' or 'expedition', and this makes, perhaps, even better sense here. [14] The lines could thus be translated:

> ... and in the Mediterranean
> He had also been on many a noble raid.

The irony of this would scarcely have needed underlining for Chaucer's contemporaries, since the Mediterranean was, throughout this period, notorious for piracy on the high seas. In any case, whether the Knight has served on 'many a noble raid' or 'in many a noble army', the important point remains the choice of the word *armee*. The application of this Italian–French word to an English knight would have further identified him as one of the many thousands of English mercenaries who formed, at this time, our chief export to the continent of Europe. In France 'the English' was a synonym for ravaging freebooters (whether in the Free Companies or in the pay of the French themselves),[15] while in Italy the savagery of the English soldiers of fortune became enshrined in Italian proverbs such as: '*Inglese italianato è un diavolo incarnato*' ('An Italianized Englishman is a devil incarnate').[16]

One thing is certain – with all Chaucer's military and diplomatic experience of the English in France and Italy, his choice of this Franco-Italian word *armee* was no mere slip of the pen.

The Knight as an efficient killer (1)

At mortal batailles hadde he been fiftene,
General Prologue, 61

Chaucer now adds a general observation which tells us yet more about the Knight's character. At first sight, this line is simply helping to build up the picture of a brave and fearless warrior, but let us, for a moment, consider its implications.

A 'bataille' could be either 'a hostile encounter between two armies' (as in the modern sense) or 'a single combat, especially as a customary or legal device for settling an issue'.[1] Whichever it means in this context, the significant feature about these particular 'batailles' is that they have been '*mortal* batailles' – exactly the kind of battle that the Knight's own hero Theseus abjures at the last moment:

> The lord hath of his heigh discrecioun
> Considered that it were destruccioun
> To gentil blood to fighten in the gyse
> Of mortal bataille now in this emprise.
> Wherfore, to shapen that they shall nat dye,
> He wol his firste purpos modifye.
>
> *The Knight's Tale*, 2537–42

[Our lord, in his noble wisdom,
Has considered that it would be a destruction
Of noble blood to fight in the manner
Of 'mortal battle' now in this enterprise;
For which reason, in order that no one shall die
He will modify his first intention.]

The whole point about a 'mortal bataille' (whether a single combat, mêlée or actual battle) was that it was a battle *to the death*. The implication of this, of course, is that on the fifteen occasions when the Knight has fought in 'mortal batailles' he must have killed everyone he fought with, since otherwise he would not have survived himself.

We thus know that he has killed at least fifteen men. The significance of this will become apparent a couple of lines further on, when we find out that he has also always killed his foe in the lists. The Knight, it appears, is a very efficient and merciless killer. (For the further argument see commentary on line 63, below, p. 81.)

The Knight's tournaments in Tramyssene

And foughten for oure feith at Tramyssene
In lystes thries ...
General Prologue, 62–3

For the moment, Chaucer returns to the Knight's exploits in North Africa. He tells us that he had fought at 'Tramyssene', now the modern city of Tlemcen in Algeria[1] (see map p. 60).

It is usually assumed, quite naturally, that the Knight would have been in Tramyssene fighting the Moors – defending the Faith against the infidel.[2] But, as I have already observed (see Commentary on l. 57), North Africa was a favourite resort of the itinerant mercenary throughout the thirteenth and fourteenth centuries. Tramyssene was the focal point.

In 1248, when the Almohad Caliph Sa'id invaded Tlemcen, he used a militia of Spanish mercenaries, and after his death these soldiers of fortune divided themselves between the two factions: the Zayanids and the Marinids. In 1286 there was a treaty between the Catalonians and the Zayanids (who then held Tlemcen), and we read that the salary of the chaplain of the Christian militia was actually paid by the Sultan himself. Throughout the fourteenth century whenever the Marinids occupied Tramyssene, they inherited the practice of using these Christian mercenaries as the Sultan's bodyguard.[3]

So although there certainly was a lot of fighting in and around Tramyssene (the city changed hands something like seven times between 1337 and 1388), it was nothing to do with the crusade against the infidel.[4] It was simply the result of the inter-tribal rivalry between the Marinids and the Zayanids, and the only Christian involvement was that of the mercenaries habitually employed by either side.

There can be no doubt that Chaucer would have been familiar with the existence of these Christian mercenaries in Arab service.[5] The situation was even tolerated, to some extent, by the Church. In 1290, Pope Nicholas IV wrote to the 'noblemen, barons, notables, knights and all mercenary Christians serving in Morocco, Tunis and Tlemcen: they are to watch their manner of life, and ensure that the Christian religion is honoured both by Christians and by Muslims, and must obey the bishop the Pope has sent'.[6]

When Chaucer says that his Knight has been at Tlemcen, his readers would have known that he had not been there as a crusader.

In the very next line, Chaucer confirms that the Knight had not been fighting in a crusade at Tramyssene, for he tells us he was fighting *in the lists*.

There was nothing especially odd about fighting in the lists on enemy soil – even among the heathens – though it may seem bizarre to us. It was in fact, quite a common practice.[7] But the idea that the Knight has been fighting in the lists 'for oure feith' is not without its irony. For, contrary to the impression one gets from literary commentators, fighting in the lists was not universally regarded as a sign of religious devotion.

To many people in Chaucer's day, tournaments were, on the contrary, the summit of worldly vanity. After all, the whole point of fighting in the lists was for a knight to gain glory *as an individual*.

According to Honoré Bonet, such single combat was the resort of men who were 'so full of pride and with so little love for God that they have no trust except in their worldly strength'.[8] In a fifteenth-century French novel, *Le Jouvencel*, two knights seek permission to fight in the lists against two of the enemy, but they are rebuked by the hero (le Jouvencel) who tells them that such exploits are

... forbidden things, which should not be done at all. Firstly, those who do it wish to take away the good of others, that is to say their honour, in order to gain for themselves a vainglory which is of little value, and in so doing he does a service to nobody, he spends his money, he endangers his body to take the life or the honour of his opponent, which is of little value; as long as he is occupied in doing this, he fails to advance the war, the service of his King and the public good; and no one should endanger his body except in deeds of merit.[9]

One of the most famous of these tournaments was the Combat of the Thirty which took place in 1351 at Ploërmel, in Brittany, between the French under the command of Robert de Beaumanoir and a mixed company of English, Germans and Bretons under the leadership of 'a man who called himself Brandebourch'. Even Froissart cannot help noting that, 'Some regarded it as a courageous exploit, but others as an outrage and an overweening conceit.'[10] The Dutch historian Johan Huizinga remarks that, 'The uselessness of these chivalrous spectacles was so evident that those in authority resented them. It was impossible to expose the honour of the kingdom to the hazards of a single combat.'[11] Thus when an English knight, Sir Peter Courtenay, came to Paris in 1386 and challenged Guy de la Trémoille to single combat for the honour of their countries, the King of France and the Duke of Burgundy prohibited the contest at the last moment. And when, eventually, the Lord of Clary fought Sir Peter in secret, dangerously injuring him, 'the King and the Duke of Burgundy and especially Sir Guy de la Trémoille were incensed with the knight and said he had done enough to lose his lands and be banished from the realm of France for ever'.[12]

If fighting in the lists was sometimes disapproved of on purely military or political grounds, it can be imagined that it met even stronger disapproval from religious quarters. It was certainly not the act of an austere Christian idealist.

One ecclesiastical contemporary of Chaucer's, the Dominican friar John Bromyard, for example, roundly condemned the vanity of knights, which prompted them to seek praise 'in prohibited deeds of arms, as in tournaments and the like' and made them neglect their real duties (such as defending the country).[13]

Fighting in tournaments, in fact, is incompatible with the image of the Knight as the devout and dedicated crusader. The chief propagandist of the crusades in Chaucer's time, Philippe de Mézières, regarded tournaments as the very antithesis of crusading and thought that all knights who took part in them should be fined, and the proceeds devoted to the cost of the Holy War.[14]

Moreover, fighting in the lists was so far contrary to 'oure feith' that it was actually prohibited by the Church.

Throughout the previous centuries, tournaments had been repeatedly banned under pain of excommunication – by Pope Alexander II in 1179, by the Lateran Synod in 1215, by Pope Gregory IX in 1228, by Innocent IV in 1245 and by Clement V in 1313.[15] In Chaucer's own day there seems to have been some softening of the Church's attitude, but it still maintained an official stance of disapproval.[16] And during the Knight's period of active service, Pope Urban V once again condemned them outright. In 1368 we find him writing:

> To Master Robert de Stratton, DCL, canon of Lincoln, papal chaplain and auditor. Mandate to go to Lionel, Duke of Clarence, and warn him, under pain of excommunication, not to hold the tournament (in itself reprobated by the sacred canons) which he and many other nobles are said to have agreed and sworn to carry on as a hostile and deadly combat. Faculty is granted for the relaxation of any oaths and obligations that have been made and taken.[17]

Of course, the fact that the Pope disapproved of tournaments does not mean that Chaucer himself disapproved of them (on the contrary, as Clerk of the King's Works, he helped organize one in 1390),[18] but it does mean that there is a cheerful incongruity between the suggestion that the Knight has 'foughten for oure feith' and the revelation the next line that it has been 'in lystes thries'.

In any case, is it not manifestly an absurd idea to seek to prove religious truth by a contest of arms? It certainly seemed so to some of Chaucer's contemporaries, Christine de Pisan regarded it as blasphemous:

> ... to ask a thing against nature or above nature is a presumption and is displeasing to God, and to believe that the feeble shall overcome the strong, or the old the young, or the sick the healthy because of the justness of their cause ... is but tempting God. And I say, for certain, if it happens that they should win it is but chance and not because they are in the right.[19]

On that often quoted occasion in 1390, when the Saracens challenged the Christians to a tournament during the siege of Mahdia, there was, in fact, a considerable difference of opinion among the Christians as to whether or not they should accept it. The

Lord of Coucy said that where the Christian faith was called into question, it was too serious a matter to be answered by one knight and that, 'such defyaunce in armes for suche a quarell ought nat to passe without great deliberation of good counsayle'.[20]

In *Monty Python's Flying Circus*, the TV show in which I have been involved over the last ten years, we once did a sketch in which, instead of debating the existence or non-existence of God, a bishop and a humanist philosopher fought each other for it.[21] It seems to me that Chaucer made this same joke almost six hundred years ago.

In his day, however, it had even more relevance, since he was in effect commenting on the Church's double-think on the subject of war. For the same Church that condemned tournaments, condoned and encouraged crusades in which, instead of two men, two nations fought each other to the death to prove the superiority of one religion over another. We shall hear a further echo of this in *The Knight's Tale* itself, when Theseus stops the two young princes fighting each other for the fair Emily and, in his wisdom, declares, instead, a battle to the death between two hundred knights! (It is only on the day of the tournament itself that he modifies the event to non-mortal combat.)[22]

Once again this whole passage has followed the classic Chaucerian joke form. He first raised a balloon of expectation by telling us that the Knight had 'foughten for oure feith'. He then showed us the pin, when he told us that it was 'at Tramyssene'. He then applied the pin to the balloon by telling us it was 'In lystes thries' and the whole thing will burst in our faces in the next half line, when he cheerfully adds: 'and ay slayn his foo.'

The Knight as an efficient killer (2)

... and ay slayn his foo.
General Prologue, 63

Chaucer now adds one small detail which tells us more about the Knight's character than almost anything else. He tells us that every time the Knight has fought in the lists, he has killed his foe. Of course, from the way it is tossed in, it sounds like the final accolade. But is it?

The whole spirit of the tournament lay in displaying skill,

courage and generosity – not in killing your opponent. To be sure, the more skilful the jousters, the more liable they were to do each other serious damage, but this was not at all the object of the exercise, and it was always a cause for rejoicing when they did not. Here, for example, is Froissart's description of a particularly dangerous bout during the jousting at Calais, in 1390, between one John Savage and Sir Reginald de Roye, which conveys the ideal spirit in which these events took place:

An English squire, a good tilter, called John Savage, squire of honour and of the body to the Earl of Huntingdon, sent to touch the shield of Sir Reginald de Roye. The knight answered, he was ready and willing to satisfy him. When he had mounted his horse, and had his helmet buckled and lance given to him, they set off at full gallop, and gave such blows on the targets, that had the spears not broken, one or both must have fallen to the ground. This course was handsome and dangerous; but the knights received no hurt, though the points of the lances passed through the targets, and slipped off their side-armour. The spears were broken about a foot from the shaft, the points remaining in the shields; and they gallantly bore the shafts before them, as they finished their career. The spectators thought they must have been seriously wounded; and the French and English hastened each to their companion, whom, to their joy, they found unhurt. They were told they had done enough for that day; but John Savage was not satisfied and said he had not crossed the sea for only one tilt with a lance. This was reported to Sir Reginald, who replied, 'He is in the right; and it is but just that he should be gratified, either by me or by one of my companions.' When they had rested themselves a while, and received new lances, they began their second course, each aiming well at the other; but they failed, from the swerving of their horses, to their great vexation, and returned to their posts. Their lances, which had been accidentally dropped, were given to them, and they set off on their third course. This time they hit on the vizors of their helmets; and, by the force and crossing of their lances, both were unhelmed as they passed. The tilt was much applauded for its correctness and vigour. When they were returned to their posts, the English told John Savage that he had very honourably performed and that it was now time for him to make way for others to tilt as well as himself. He complied with this and, laying aside his lance and target, dismounted and rode on a hackney to witness the performances of others.[1]

The essence of the chivalry lies in the willingness of the two contestants to face a mutual danger. It has nothing to do with their obvious ability to hurt each other. On the contrary, Froissart often seems to go to great lengths to emphasize how little damage has actually been done in a joust. Usually the combatants do no more than unhelm each other, break their lances or unhorse themselves – as in the jousting at Smithfield in 1390 (which Chaucer himself helped to organize) in which the worst that befell any of the knights was that 'some were stryken down fro their horses.'[2]

The fact is, by the late-fourteenth century death in the lists had become an increasingly rare occurrence.[3] Where it did occur, it was usually the result of the participants having lost their self-control or disregarded the prescribed laws, and the survivor – far from being a hero – very often had to take to his heels.[4] This happened, for example, in 1389, when the seventeen-year-old Earl of Pembroke was accidentally killed during a tournament. The continuation of Higden's *Polychronicon* tells us: 'The knight who had wounded him took to flight; if he had remained, he would undoubtedly have lost his own life.'[5] Even as far back as 1318 we read of a knight having to be pardoned for having killed his opponent in a tournament at Luton.[6] And in the *Geste of Robyn Hode*, Sir Richard Atte Lea explains that he is a ruined man because his son killed 'a knight of Lancaster' in a joust:

'In what manner', then said Robin,
   'Have you lost your riches?'
'Because of my great folly,' he said,
   'And my natural affection.

'I had a son, in truth, Robin,
   Who should have been my heir.
When he was twenty winters old
   In the field he'd joust full fair.

'He slew a knight of Lancaster,
   And a squire bold.
In order to save him in his suit
   My goods were put up for sale and sold.

'My lands as well were pledged, Robin,
   Until a certain day,
To a rich Abbot who lives near here
   Of St Mary's Abbey.'

'What is the sum?' asked Robin;
   'Tell the truth to me.'
'Sir', he said, 'four hundred pounds
   The Abbot reckoned it to me.'[7]

Even in judicial duels in the list it was not expected that the two contestants should kill each other – only that one of them should be 'convicte and discomfite'.[8]

So whoever the Knight of the *Prologue* had been fighting in the lists at Tramyssene (whether Saracens or fellow-Christians), his proficiency at killing his opponent is not an attribute of knightly perfection, as Chaucer pretends. It is more the mark of the seasoned, cold-blooded professional soldier. This is especially so since the tournaments held in the Arab world, in places like Tramyssene, were not considered to be as dangerous as those held in Europe. An Irish traveller of 1323 tells us that the military exercises in the *maidan* (the courtyard or parade ground outside a town) were 'playful and effeminate in comparison with European tournaments'.[9] It looks as if the Knight was able to achieve this slaughter in the lists because he was playing by different rules from his opponents'!

And this takes us back to that earlier line: 'At mortal batailles hadde he been fiftene.' From this we know that the Knight must have killed at least fifteen men (see above, p. 76); now Chaucer tells us he has killed another three in the lists – giving a grand total of, at the very minimum, eighteen killings.

I believe that this bloody record of killings should be read alongside Wyclif's blistering attack on the knights of the day as worse than butchers and hangmen:

Lord! What honour is it to a knight that he kills many men? Well I know that the hangman kills many more, and with more justice, and therefore more right, and so they should be praised more than such knights. And the butcher of beasts does his office many times with right and charity, and therefore does it well; but there is not as much evidence that the butcher of his brother slays men in charity, and therefore not so justly. Why should not this butcher, since he does better, be praised more than this knight that the world glorifies? Since the more virtuous deed is the more to be praised. And therefore it were better to be a butcher of beasts than to be a butcher of one's brother, for the latter is more unnatural. The suffering of Christ is much to be praised, but the slaying of his tormentors is odious to God.[10]

The Knight's record of killings should also be read alongside Gower's description of mercenaries as vultures and wolves: 'It is the vulture's ghastly nature to want [to eat] men, and to follow the camps of war in order to seize upon its food.... This bird is terrifying since it plunders like the swift hawk, and every flock of them is like a cruel wolf.'[11] And it should be read alongside Pope Urban v's account of the mercenaries in Italy, with whom Chaucer came into contact in 1378:

That multitude of villains of divers nations, associated in arms by avidity ... unbridled in every kind of cruelty, extorting money; methodically devastating the country and the open towns, burning houses and barns, destroying trees and vines, obliging poor peasants to fly ... torturing and maiming those from whom they expected to obtain ransom, without regard to ecclesiastical dignity or sex or age; violating wives, virgins and nuns, and constraining even gentlewomen to follow their camp, to do their pleasure and carry arms and baggage.[12]

The Knight's homicidal character should be read in the context of the massacre at Alexandria in which the Knight himself participated, the rape and pillage of the peasantry that he would have performed in Lithuania, and the suffering he would have brought to the countryside every time he had 'riden out'.[13]

To the Gawain poet, the most important quality for the true knight to possess was 'pitie'.[14] Yet what pity has this Knight

The Knight as the angel of death, pictured by Bruegel

shown in his career of active service, or when he has so mercilessly and so unnecessarily killed his foes in the lists? Pity is a quality that is entirely missing from his portrait. It is also missing from the tale he tells. Whether he is describing the bloody slaughter of the tournament, the bitter enmity of the two heroes or the death of Arcite, the Knight consistently removes all the elements of 'pitie' that are certainly present in Boccaccio's original story.[15]

But then pity was not a quality which carried much weight among the new-style 'knights' of the fourteenth century. Where was the profit in pity for men such as Hawkwood and the other commanders of the Free Companies?

The Knight of the *Prologue* may behave with dignity; he may cultivate a manner 'as meeke as is a mayde', but for all that, he has been the angel of death for all too many of his fellow-men.

The sight of the proud knight, clad in his armour, seated up on his high horse, with his rod of authority in his hand, calmly ordering the death and destruction of the peasants and their countryside, must have been as familiar to Chaucer's Europe as it was two hundred years later to contemporaries of Bruegel.

The Knight in the service of a heathen

> **This ilke worthy knyght hadde been also**
> **Somtyme with the lord of Palatye**
> **Agayn another hethen in Turkye.**
>
> *General Prologue*, 64–6

And now, lest any of his readers have missed the true nature of this 'parfit gentil knyght', Chaucer spells it out in black and white.

Palatye (Palatia) was one of the many Turkish emirates which maintained independence from the expanding Ottoman Empire throughout the fourteenth century.[1] During this period, there was constant conflict between Palatye and the neighbouring emirate of Menteshe, so it was presumably in this struggle that the Knight was involved, when he fought with the Lord of Palatye 'agayn another hethen in Turkye'.

The Emir of Palatye was a Seljuk Turk who appears to have maintained a fairly easy-going attitude towards the Christians – by no means an uncommon phenomenon at the time.[2]

The capital, Palatia – modern Balat or Milet (on the site of or near the ancient Miletus) – was an important trading centre for such commodities as saffron, sesame, wax, alum and slaves from the archipelago.[3] From 1345 to 1405 the Venetians had interests in Palatia and maintained there a consul and a church.[4] But the Lord of Palatye was nonetheless a heathen – moreover a heathen under whom the slave trade and piracy flourished.[5]

Modern critics, who wish to present the Knight as a crusading idealist whose only motive for fighting was religious fervour,

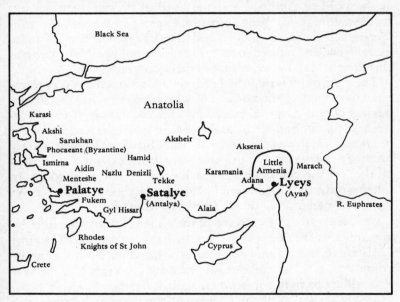

explain this rather startling revelation that he has fought for one heathen against another by the fact that in 1365 the Emir of Pala-tye entered into a treaty with Peter of Cyprus.[6] But this treaty was in no way a religious pact.

At this time Peter of Cyprus was ravaging, pillaging, looting and burning towns all along the coastline of Asia Minor. The Lord of Palatye, as emir of a rich port with valuable international commercial interests, had even more to lose than most. But fortu-nately for him he was wealthy enough to be able to buy off the Cypriot king. It was simply a case of paying what we should now call 'protection money'. Perhaps the Venetians also put pressure on him, in order to safeguard their own interests in Palatia, as they had in 1361.[7] Another possibility is that the Lord of Palatye could not risk reducing his military strength on the inland border with the Menteshe in order to meet the Christians on the coast. But whatever the reasons there is no doubt that the treaty was the result of fear rather than any sudden enthusiasm for Christianity.

Philippe de Mézières has left an eye-witness account of the Lord of Palatye's motives: 'God filled the hearts of the Turks with such fear and terror, that the main Turkish Princes, such as the Lord of Altologo and the Lord of Palatye, sent solemn ambassadors to the King [Peter of Cyprus] in Rhodes and presented their castles, men, food and friendship to the King by these messengers, and offered to serve him under tribute.'[8] The Cypriot chronicler, Makhairas, confirms this account.[9]

The main point is that the Lord of Palatye was in no way interested in extending the borders of Christendom – he was simply buying off the Cypriot crusaders and conserving his military strength for fighting off the Menteshe. So when the Knight fought in his service, it was not as a militant Christian. He was simply offering his services to an extremely wealthy heathen who needed all the help he could get against his belligerent neighbours. In other words, the Knight would fight for anybody: Moor, Turk, Cypriot, Spaniard, German, Christian or heathen.

Chaucer started this résumé of the Knight's military career by informing us that he was willing to fight for Christian against Christian (General Prologue, l. 49) so what could be more appropriate than to close the section with the corollary that he was also willing to fight for heathen against heathen?

Significantly it is in the context of this ultimately pragmatic attitude of the Knight that Chaucer remarks, with that wonderful insouciance of his, that the Knight had always come away with a good bit of booty – or, as he puts it, a 'sovereyn prys'.

Was the Knight too successful?

And everemoore he hadde a sovereyn prys
General Prologue, 67

Chaucer concludes his review of the Knight's career with a remark that seems to beg no question: And evermore he had a sovereign 'prys'. This is usually translated as: 'He was of supreme value' or 'He was always outstandingly successful'.[1] The word 'prys' in Middle English was widely used in this sense of 'personal or social worth, excellency, honourableness' (OED), but there were other meanings to the word 'prys', and there is a multiple pun in the line which, I think, would have been obvious to Chaucer's contemporaries.

As well as meaning 'honour, value, praise', 'prys' was also used in the more mundane sense of 'a price'. Chaucer uses it in this way on several occasions, as when Harry Bailey says that he will order a supper 'at a certeyn prys'.[2] 'Prys' could also take on the even more tangible meaning of 'a reward, trophy or symbol of victory' (OED) – in other words, a prize. Thus Chaucer tells us of the Friar's ability to make up little songs: 'Of yeddynges he baar outrely the pris.'[3]

In all these senses, the word 'prys' is ultimately derived from the Latin *pretium*, meaning 'price, value, wages, reward'. There was, however, another meaning to the word in Middle English which derived from the Latin *praehendere* – 'to seize'.[4] This other sense was particularly applied to things seized or captured in war – 'prizes of war, loot, booty'. Chaucer's readers would have been perfectly familiar with this sense; Gower uses it and so does Chaucer himself, when in *The Parson's Tale*, the Devil claims: 'I wol departe my prise or my praye by deliberacioun.'[5]

How readily Chaucer's audience would have recognized all the meanings present in this line about the Knight is, of course, a matter of conjecture, but the syntax is sufficiently curious to suggest that Chaucer intended his readers to see them. 'Prys' was frequently applied to knighthood in the sense of 'value, esteem, worth', but usually in the phrase 'of prys': 'With fourscore knihtes al of prys', 'Knightes to hauen and holden of pris'.[6] If Chaucer had wished to say merely that the Knight had always been 'of supreme repute' he could have easily written: 'And everemoore he *was of* sovereyn prys'. However, in his parody, *Sir Thopas*, Chaucer makes fun of this expression as a typical cliché of the popular romances: 'Men speken of romances of prys' (*Sir Thopas*, 7, 897), so it seems reasonable to conclude that he is here playing on the same expression.

In the first place Chaucer allows the suggestion that the Knight had always obtained 'a good price' – in other words that he had always been well paid for his services. The syntax certainly supports this interpretation, since Chaucer never used the indefinite article with the word 'prys' anywhere else where it meant 'honour, praise, esteem'.[7] In general, people could be 'wurthy of prys' or 'holden in prys' – they could even be said to *have* 'prys', but they never had *a* 'prys'.[8] The only other time that Chaucer speaks of 'a prys' is when he refers to Harry Bailey's supper. The suggestion that the Knight had always obtained 'a good price' for his services would certainly have made a lot of sense to Chaucer's contemporary readers, and nobody familiar with the military affairs of the period could doubt that payment was a major preoccupation of all mercenaries. According to the Pope, it was particularly the preoccupation of English mercenaries.[9] Moreover one of the most outstanding features of a successful *condottieri* such as Sir John Hawkwood was the high price they could command for their services – sometimes even in advance![10] The irony of this interpretation would have needed no elaboration for the fourteenth-century audience.

The third punning sense of the word 'prys' – that the Knight had always obtained a good 'prize of war' – needs, however, more attention. On the surface it seems yet another point in favour of the Knight – what could be more admirable than to fight in battle and win 'a sovereign prize'? But a closer consideration of the spoils of war in the fourteenth century – both booty and ransoms – reveals yet more layers of irony behind the line.

No soldier of the fourteenth century ever made his fortune out of the wages he was paid. His real chance for profit and, perhaps, undreamed-of wealth, lay in the acquisition of loot. It was the nearest chance he had to winning the pools or a TV game show. In fact, all too frequently, these spoils of war became a substitute for pay.[11] Throughout this period, the winnings of war were of overriding importance to the participants. As Denys Hay puts it: 'Spoils mattered equally to the rank and file soldier, to the magnate and to the crown.'[12]

But there were strict rules governing the division of the spoils of war. A knight could not simply keep whatever he won for himself. As Christine de Pisan explains, it was up to the king who paid for the war to distribute the prizes to his knights: 'For that which they do is done as by the king's own workmen whom he has set to work for him and in his name; therefore the prize [*proye*] should not be theirs as well as their wages, but only what the prince gives them of his special grace.'[13] More importantly, certain prizes belonged only to the King.

In Chaucer's day, all the most valuable prizes won in battle – the most important castles and lands and all ransoms above £500 – had to be handed over *in toto* to the King. For example, Denis de Morbec, who captured King John of France at Poitiers, had to hand him over to the Black Prince and later had to yield all rights and claims on him to Edward III.[14] Such prizes were known as 'the King's prize'.

So Chaucer has obviously chosen his words with ironic circumspection, and if the Knight had indeed always come away with a 'sovereyn' prize of war, he probably should not have done. Any prize worthy of a sovereign ought to have gone to the sovereign.

Chaucer is, in fact, putting his finger unerringly on one of the most sensitive areas in the military affairs of the day. The division of the spoils of war was often a sore point – particularly in the English army. Any knight who served a great English lord, such as the Black Prince or John of Gaunt, might find he had to give up as much as half of his winnings – whereas if he fought for a foreign master, such as the Spanish Crown, he would only have to give up one fifth.[15] If he had served in Prussia with the Knights of the Teutonic Order, he might even secure the right to take 'the king's share of the spoils, if the king shall not be in person in the host'.[16]

It is perhaps significant that Chaucer's Knight has served in both these foreign armies, in preference to the English host.

The unpopularity of the forfeits which were claimed by the English nobility may be gathered from the fact that, after 1360, as the war with France became less and less attractive, most barons and nobles were forced to reduce their claim to one third.[17]

In 1385 Richard II decided to put this obligation down in writing: 'Also, that each man pay the third to his lord or master, of all manner of winnings of war, and this applies as well to those who are not retained but merely lodging under the banner or pennant of any captain.'[18]

This ordinance gives us the flavour of Chaucer's line, for the way in which it emphasizes that this ordinance applies not only to the retained knights but also the non-retained men and mercenaries who were 'merely lodging under the banner or pennant of any captain', makes it clear that among these freebooters there was a considerable amount of evasion going on.

For the itinerant soldier there was obviously a better chance of avoiding these forfeits. If he happened to win any particularly valuable bit of spoil – 'a sovereyn prys' – all he had to do was move on to the next assignment. His former master stood little chance of catching up with him to exact his due.

That this sort of thing was rife is clear from Richard's ordinance, from references in Honoré Bonet's *Tree of Battles* and from both Philippe de Mézières's and Guillaume de Machaut's accounts of the siege of Alexandria – at which of course, the Knight himself was present.[19]

In fact the Knight's career, spread over many lands and under many different masters, represented the perfect situation for avoiding the customary obligations of dividing spoil. It is not surprising that he was always able to get away with 'a sovereyn prys'.

But in any case, although Chaucer cheerfully pretends that it is greatly to the Knight's credit that he has always claimed great amounts of spoil or huge ransoms, this was not actually regarded as true knightly conduct.

Honoré Bonet said that a knight should 'ask a reasonable and knightly ransom, such as is possible for the prisoner to pay'. If he does not, he concludes, he is 'not a gentleman but a tyrant and no knight'.[20] Froissart praises Sir John Chandos at the battle of Poitiers for staying by the side of the Black Prince, instead of looking for prisoners.[21]

But it was a common cause of complaint that modern knights did not observe this decorum. On the contrary, they extorted huge amounts from their captives and plundered the countryside without restraint, as Bonet says:

> But God well knows that the soldiery of today do the opposite, for they take from their prisoners, or cause them to pay, great and excessive payments and ransoms without pity or mercy, and this especially from the poor labourers who cultivate lands and vineyards, and, under God, give sustenance to all by their toil.[22]

The general complaint was that those knights who looked for great prizes of war, as Chaucer's Knight has done, very often neglected their real duties:

> ... and when they have captured [*pris*] them and other goods, they have greater will and desire to keep their prisoners and their gains, than to rally round and help bring the day to a successful conclusion. And it can well happen that in this way, the day can be lost altogether.

And one might well ask what profit it is, that makes one lose honour, life and fortune.[23]

For we should be under no illusions – a knight could not win 'a sovereyn prys' by mere good luck, he would have to be ever on the look-out for the main chance and prepared to plunder and pillage where he could; it is no wonder that Gower saw such knights as vultures and wolves.

In short, the fact that Chaucer's Knight has always won 'a sovereyn prys' has nothing to do with knightly honour. The true spirit of chivalry lay in what you did with your spoil – how much of it you gave away – not in how much of it you acquired.[24] This spirit of largess was valued as one of the most important qualities which a knight could possess, because it implied a disregard for wealth and, hopefully, a freedom from corruption.

An early-fourteenth-century handbook on good government tells us that of the 'twelve requisites for a good ruler' the sixth is 'that he be not covetous of money, or led by his other inclinations. For these are two things that cast the sovereign from his throne.'[25]

Yet Chaucer's 'parfit gentil knyght' displays a total lack of interest in this crucial quality. It does not come into his portrait and he himself never mentions the word – not once in the three thousand lines of his *Tale*.[26]

On the contrary, the Knight displays a quite unbecoming competitiveness, making no bones about the fact that he is in the story-telling competition to win the free supper that the Host has suggested:

> I wol nat letten eek noon of this route;
> Lat every felawe telle his tale aboute,
> And lat se now who shal the soper wynne
>
> *The Knight's Tale*, 889–91

[I will not hinder any of this crew;
Let every fellow tell his tale in turn,
And let's see now who will win the supper.]

Even on the pilgrimage to Canterbury, it seems, the Knight still had his eye on the 'sovereyn prys' – no matter how trivial it might be.

Where had the Knight not fought?

Line 67 concludes Chaucer's summary of the Knight's career. It certainly has been a remarkably long and varied one. From 1344 to 1387 (approximately) he has fought in Egypt, Prussia, Lithuania, Russia, Spain, Morocco, Turkey and all round the Mediterranean. He has fought under Spanish, German, Cypriot, Turkish and even Moorish masters – in fact it has been *such* a cosmopolitan career that one is almost bound to ask: whom has he not fought for? The answer, of course, is painfully obvious: he has never once fought for his own country – and that in an age when England stood in almost continuous peril and when the defence of the realm was an active concern not just of governments but of ordinary men and women.[1]

It is easy to forget the apprehension with which Englishmen of the fourteenth century must have looked across the English Channel. Invasion scares were rife throughout the period, and the citizens of coastal towns and of London itself practised their home-guard drill with no less a sense of urgency than they did in 1939–45.

In 1338–40 there had been French raids all along the Channel coast. Southampton had been burned to the ground, and there had been attacks on Hastings, Sandwich and Rye.[2] Even during the 1350s and 1360s, when England's military stock was at its height, there were Scots, Spanish and even Danish raids.[3] The England of Edward III was not the self-assured nation that it was to become under Elizabeth and Victoria. It was a land that lived in almost constant fear of its neighbours, where Parliament itself believed that the French intended 'to destroy the English language and occupy the territory of England, which God forbid, unless a remedy of force is found against their malice'[4] and where, for many years, churches on the coast were permitted to ring only one bell, reserving the full peal as a warning should the French land.[5]

In the years before Chaucer started to write his portrait of the Knight, this national insecurity reached its peak, as the tide of the war in France started to go against the English with the fall of Poitiers, La Rochelle and Angoulême. In 1370 a daily watch of forty armed men and sixty archers was set up along the Thames between the Tower and Billingsgate, when the enemy's fleet was reported in the area. A couple of years later, 'all manner of men-at-arms and archers' were despatched to Sandwich 'as the enemy threatened to attack the navy assembled in that port'.[6] Meanwhile the Bishop of Winchester opened Parliament with an appeal for advice as to how the realm might be protected from French aggression.[7] The war that had devastated so much of Normandy was being brought home to the Englishmen's doorstep.

The Abbot of Battle Abbey, Hastings, for one, decided to take matters into his own hands and marched his men to the defence of nearby Winchelsea when it was attacked by the French in 1377. While he was gone, however, the French diverted some of their ships to Hastings and burned it. In the same year, the French marched into Rottingdean and there actually captured the Prior of Lewes in hand-to-hand fighting. Three years later they were back, burning, robbing and killing in Winchelsea, Rye and Hastings. One French fleet even sailed up the Thames and burned Gravesend.[8] Even towns far from the coast no longer felt safe, and in 1378 orders went out for the fortification of Oxford 'in case our enemies the French should land in our kingdom of England ...'.[9]. The *Rolls of Parliament* at this time make pathetic reading with petition after petition from small towns and villages appealing for charity for their sufferings at the hands of both the Scots and the French.[10]

But if fear of a French invasion was acute throughout the late 1370s, it was nothing compared with the panic which swept the country in the very year before Chaucer began work on *The Canterbury Tales*. In 1386, when England had hardly recovered from the cataclysm of the Peasants' Revolt in 1381, the country was shaken by the news that the French had assembled a huge armada at the port of Sluys. 'I believe,' wrote Froissart, 'since God created the world, there was never so many great ships together as was that year at Sluys ... their masts seemed in the sea like a great wood.'[11]

If the French intention was to put the fear of God into the English, they succeeded only too well. Rumour and panic spread through the land like wildfire.[12] Every town and every city held processions through the streets three times a week praying for deliverance. There was a run on the pound as people tried to get rid of their money, reckoning it would be worthless once the French landed, and those who were already in debt refused to settle, hoping that the invasion would cancel all debts. The current joke was that the creditors would be paid by 'the new florin they forge in France'.[13] There was a mobilization of a hundred thousand archers and ten thousand men-at-arms – a truly massive call-up out of a total population of under a million and a half.[14] And there were even extensive plans worked out for a resistance movement, which would retreat to the hills and carry on guerrilla warfare, should the French invade.[15] In London, where Chaucer was attending Parliament as a knight of the shire, mass hysteria gripped the city, according to the chronicler Walsingham, sending its citizens running here and there looking for hiding-holes and ripping down the houses adjacent to the town wall in their panic.[16]

This, then, was the atmosphere in England when Chaucer began work on *The Canterbury Tales* – a far cry from the idyllic eternal April that most of us have in our minds when we read those opening lines of the Prologue. To be sure, foreign travel held a tremendous fascination for people – as the success of *Mandeville's Travels* bears witness – but knights who abandoned their own country for foreign adventures were an almost universal focus for criticism. Some time between 1376 and 1379, Chaucer's colleague John Gower put it like this:

> Oh knight, who goeth far-off
> Into strange lands and seeketh only
> Praise in arms, know this:
> If your country and your neighbour
> Are at war themselves, all the honour
> Is in vain, when you flee from
> Your country and estrange yourself.
> For he who abandons his duties
> And does not wish to fulfil his obligations
> But rather fulfils his own desires
> Has no right to be honoured
> No matter how mighty he may be.[17]

England had been drained of man-power during the Black Death, and knights were in desperately short supply.[18] The true knight's place was seen to be at home, fulfilling his role in the Three Estates, defending the realm against foreign invasion or – as in 1381 – against internal revolt.

Walsingham even dares to criticize the Duke of Gloucester for setting out for Prussia in 1391, despite fears that in his absence 'some new evil would follow'.[19] And the same misgivings were felt in France, when the French King tried to limit the Duke of Bourbon's expedition to Barbary in 1390 because he 'wolde nat that so many shulde have gone, to leave the realme destitute of knyghtes and squyers'.[20]

What, then, would Chaucer's fellow-countrymen have made of this 'parfit gentil knyght' who has travelled 'no man ferre' in the service of foreigners – Spaniards, Germans, Cypriots and even Turks – without once offering his sword in the defence of his own country? The satire could scarcely be more biting – especially at a time when it was the firm conviction of most people that English knighthood was not doing all it should to defend the realm.

At least one private citizen became so exasperated by the failure of the knightly class to do its duty that he took matters into his own hands: a wealthy London grocer, by the name of John Philpot, equipped a fleet at his own expense and captured a Scottish pirate in 1378. Turning on the knightly establishment, he claimed that he had acted out of pity for

the afflictions of the common people and of our native land which now, through your indolence, has fallen from being the most noble kingdom and mistress of nations into such wretchedness that it lies open to plundering by whom it please of the most ruthless people; so long as none of you applies his hand to its defence, I have exposed me and mine for the salvation of my own countrymen and the liberation of my native land.[21]

Froissart records the prevailing mood of gloom that hung over the country in the very year that Chaucer began the *Canterbury Tales*:

In England there began different murmurings in various places ... And those that loved evil rule rather than good said, 'Where are now these great enterprises and these valiant men of England that were in the days of King Edward III and the Prince his son? Oh! What a deed was that, when the noble King Edward landed in Normandy ... and passed through the realm of France, and what goodly deeds he achieved on the way. After Crécy he beat King Philip and all the power of France, and before he returned, won the town of Calais. But nowadays the knights and men-of-war do no such feats. Also the Prince of Wales, son of this noble king, did he not take the French King John and defeat his power at Poitiers with a small number of people against all the men that King John had? In those days, England was feared and respected, and we were spoken of through all the world as the flower of chivalry, but nowadays no man speaks of us, for now there is no war made, but at men's purses.[22]

And here Froissart brings us to the crucial factor in the extraordinary career of Chaucer's 'verray, parfit gentil knyght' – his conspicuous absence from all the great English victories of the century: Crécy (1346), Calais (1347), Poitiers (1356) and Nájera (1367). It was on these glorious victories that the whole reputation of English knighthood rested, and Englishmen looked back to them with nostalgia, even as they reproached modern knights for failing to live up to such an illustrious past. If Chaucer really were painting a portrait of a true and noble representative of English chivalry, he simply could not have omitted all mention of these triumphs. Yet he not only omits them – he omits any mention of the Hundred Years' War itself – a war which 'directly or indirectly ... influenced the lives of all Englishmen from its inception in 1337 to the end of the century'.[23] It would be like describing a twentieth-century American hero who has fought in Spain, in China, in Biafra, the Congo, Angola and Chile without any mention of the Second World War, Korea or Vietnam.

It's all very well for modern scholars to praise the Knight's dedication to fighting in 'holy wars' in distant lands, but the average Englishman of Chaucer's day, who lived under the constantly recurring threat of invasion from France or Scotland, must have viewed such single-minded dedication to other people's wars with a healthy scepticism.

It may be objected, however, that all this could – at a pinch – be covered by lines 47–8, in which Chaucer tells us:

> Ful worthy was he in his lordes werre,
> And therto hadde he riden, no man ferre ...

This is, in fact, very often interpreted as 'He has fought worthily in the service of the King.'[24] And yet if this is correct, there is a very obvious irony in the ensuing revelation that the Knight has ridden in this service *further than any other man*. How could the Knight possibly have been serving the King of England in such remote places as Turkey, Africa, Lithuania and Russia, when the King of England's preoccupations were on his own doorstep and in France and in Scotland?

In fact, the kings of England were, understandably, unenthusiastic at the prospect of their knights taking off on remote cam-

paigns and crusades.[25] In 1349, for example, when the Pope declared a general absolution and many men set out to travel to
Rome, Edward 'prohibited their passage on account of the war
with France', and, moreover, ordered all those Englishmen
already abroad to return to England at once 'under pain of for-
feiting their body and all goods'.[26] Indeed, as we have already
seen, Edward was constantly making proclamations forbidding
men-of-arms and knights 'leaving the kingdom for foreign parts'
or 'seeking adventures'.[27]

And, significantly, in 1363, when Peter of Cyprus came to England to enlist Edward III's support for his forthcoming crusade
to Alexandria (which, again, the Knight was involved in),
Edward was very non-committal and would never give Peter any
concrete assistance[28] (see commentary on line 51).

So if 'his lordes werre' refers to the King of England's war (as
many modern editors believe it does),[29] then the fact that the
Knight has travelled thereto 'no man ferre' could hardly be more
ironic.

Nevertheless, it is often claimed by modern scholars that the
Knight's career is not merely unremarkable but is actually typical
of many real-life knights of the period – men such as Henry of
Grosmont, first Duke of Lancaster, and certain members of the
Scrope family.[30]

It is true that these men, between them, fought in most – but
not all – of the remote regions in which the Knight of the *Prologue*
has fought, but there is one very obvious difference: not one of
them has served *exclusively* in such places and *exclusively* under
foreign masters. Henry of Grosmont, for example, was present
– like the Knight – at the siege of Algezir. He also went on expeditions to Prussia and Poland, but – unlike the Knight of the *Prologue* – the rest of his career was dedicated to fighting the French
or the Scots (see page 102). Similarly, Sir William Scrope (1325–
67) was certainly at Satalye in 1362, but, unlike the Knight, he
had defended the English coast at Winchelsea in 1344 and had
fought alongside the Black Prince at Nájera in 1367.[31]

This pattern is repeated in the careers of the knights whom
Chaucer himself knew personally.[32] Sir John Montagu may have
been to Prussia once, but he had also served his own country
before and after, both in France and in Ireland. Sir John Clanvowe
and Sir William Neville may have obtained permission to join
the Duke of Bourbon's expedition to Barbary in 1390, but

throughout the 1370s they had been fighting in France; Sir Richard Sturry and Sir Lewis Clifford (after whom Chaucer may have named his own son) never served under any foreign masters.

A glance at the tables on pp. 102–6 shows that far from being typical, Chaucer's Knight is quite exceptional for his total lack of patriotism in having ridden 'no man ferre'. At a period of crisis for the English nation, he has failed to serve his own country with spectacular single-mindedness and has ranged all over the known world in search of fat pickings. In short, the Knight's career has not been that of a responsible member of the knightly class, nor even of a dedicated militant Christian but of a self-serving itinerant mercenary, and this would have been quite obvious to Chaucer's contemporary readers.

The wisdom of being meek

> **And though that he were worthy, he was wys,**
> **And of his port as meeke as is a mayde.**
>
> *General Prologue, 68–9*

Chaucer now moves on to describe the Knight's principal virtues – and an odd lot they turn out to be. The first thing that Chaucer tells us, however, echoes the very first line of the portrait: '... and that a worthy man'. But, Chaucer says, although he was 'worthy', he was 'wys'. Now this statement has always posed a problem for those who wish to see the Knight as the Christian epitome of knighthood. If worthiness and wisdom are *both* desirable moral qualities, why does Chaucer put in that little word *though*? Why could not the Knight be both worthy and wise?

Some critics solve the problem by translating *worthy* as 'brave' – 'Though he was brave, he was wise.'[1] This would certainly make good sense of the line, since the conflict between great courage (which, though praiseworthy in itself, may demand actions which might be foolhardy) and wise caution is a commonplace in medieval literature about conflict.[2] There is, however, no evidence to suggest that the word 'worthy' was ever used to mean 'brave'. It is certainly not a meaning given by the *Oxford English Dictionary*, and there is no etymological evidence to support such an interpretation. The claim by Muriel Bowden that

Chaucer uses 'worthy' to mean 'brave' in his translation of Boethius' *De Consolatione* is based on a misunderstanding of the Latin *valentia*.[3]

According to the OED, 'worthy' was applied to people either 'distinguished by good qualities; entitled to honour or respect ...' or 'holding a prominent place in the community; of rank or standing'. It could also be applied to things in the sense of 'strong, powerful'. Clearly, in the present context, an obvious sense of 'worthy' would have been 'distinguished by good qualities etc'. But then – as so often with Chaucer – the construction of the rest of the line begs the question: 'And *though* that he was worthy, he was wys.' Why should not a 'distinguished' or 'honoured' knight also be wise? After all, knights were regularly described as 'worthy and wise' in medieval romances, and, more significantly, that is the way in which Chaucer combines the words on every other occasion.[4] Why – this *one* time – does he say, '*Though* he were worthy, he was wys'?

The reader is sent back to reconsider that word 'worthy'. Perhaps it is not being used in its immediate, positive sense after all. Perhaps it is being used in its other sense of 'holding a prominent place – of rank or standing'.

This was certainly a widely understood sense of the word – in fact the phrase a 'worthy man' often appeared as one word to denote 'a man of note or standing'.[5] Chaucer himself frequently used the word specifically to indicate social rank as opposed to any admirable quality of character. In *The Tale of Melibeus*, for example, Dame Prudence tells her husband, Melibeus, that 'worthiness' is simply one of those things that money can buy. Because Chaucer was translating, very closely, a French text, we can ascertain with accuracy what he meant by the word by referring back to the original. The French text reads: '*Et encores dit Pamphiles que richesses font nobles ceulz qui sont villains de lignages*' ('And moreover, Pamphilles says that riches make noble those who are base-born').[6] When Chaucer translated this, he deliberately added the word 'worthy' to the word 'noble' with the apparent purpose of making it clear that he is talking about nobility of social rank and not nobility of character:

> They that been thralle and bonde of lynage
> shullen be maad worthy and noble by the richesses
>> *Tale of Melibeus*, 1560

The career of Chaucer's Knight
compared with those of other knights of the period, and English military involvement with France and Scotland

It is often claimed that the career of Chaucer's Knight was typical of those of many knights of this period, and that parallels can be found with certain knights fighting in Alexandria, Lithuania and Prussia. This view, however, ignores the point that these knights with whom Chaucer's Knight has been compared (particularly Henry of Lancaster, Sir John Chandos and the Scropes) only went off crusading during lulls in the Hundred Years' War, and all at some time served in France or defended their home country. The career of Chaucer's Knight is exceptional in that it is devoted solely to the service of foreign masters at a time when England was pre-occupied with wars against France and Scotland.

Key

In service of the English crown ☐   In service with foreign masters ▨

English military engagements	Chaucer's Knight	Henry of Lancaster (1299-1361)	Sir John Chandos	Sir William Scrope of Masham	Sir Stephen Scrope (1345-1405)	Sir Geoffrey Scrope (1340-62)
1337 Edward III claims French crown. French invasion rumoured		With Edward III in Flanders	Cambrai			
1338 French burn Portsmouth, Southampton. Warning beacons on south coast		With Edward III in Flanders				
1339 Edward III invades France. French burn Hastings; attack Sandwich and Rye		Hostage in Flanders, against Edward III's return				
1340 English defeat French at Sluys	Sluys	Sluys				Sluys

Year		...the Scots			
1342 Edward III to Brittany. English victory at Morlaix. French burn Portsmouth again		Arranges Scottish truce. With Edward III in Brittany. Embassies to Pope & Alfonso of Castile			
1343 Edward III forbids knights to travel abroad	Siege of Algezir (fighting for Alfonso of Spain)	Algezir. / Negotiates with Scots			
1344 Edward III recalls knights from Spain. Fears of French invasion expressed in parliament		Steward of England. / Negotiates with Castile; Portugal; Aragon			
1345 Edward III to Flanders. English defeat French at Auberoche	Fighting in North Africa and Turkey for a Turk (the Lord of Palatye) and for the Moors, in Belmarye and at Tramissene	Takes Bergerac and many Upper Gascony towns			
1346 Edward III defeats French at Crécy. Derby takes Poitiers. English defeat Scots at Neville's Cross		More gains in Gascony; Poitiers		Crécy	Crécy; Neville's Cross; Calais
1347 English defeat French at La Roche. Surrender of Calais		Calais with Edward III			

	English military engagements	Chaucer's Knight	Henry of Lancaster (1299-1361)	Sir John Chandos	Sir William Scrope of Masham	Sir Stephen Scrope (1345-1405)	Sir Geoffrey Scrope (1340-62)
1348		Fighting in North Africa and Turkey for a Turk (the Lord of Palatye) and for the Moors, in Belmarye and at Tramissene	Negotiating with French				
1349	Edward III to Calais; beats off French attack						
1350	English defeat Spanish at Winchelsea		Winchelsea		Winchelsea		
1351	'Battle of the Thirty'. English against Bretons		Boulogne and Flanders				
1352	English in Brittany defeat Montfort faction at Mavron. English capture Guisnes		Prussia and Poland. France				
1353	Edward III proclamation forbids tournaments and 'adventures'		Negotiating with French				
1354	Scottish alliance with France		Peace conference at Avignon. Raids in Artois, Picardy with Edward III				
1355	Scots defeat English at Nesbit. Proclamation forbids armourers to leave the country						
1356	English raid Scottish border. Edward III recaptures Berwick. Black Prince defeats French at Maupertius		Campaigns in Normany & Brittany. Siege of Rennes etc.	Poitiers (saves Black Prince's life)			

Year	Historical events	Chaucer's Knight (under Peter of Cyprus)	Campaign / biographical notes
1357	Treaty of Bordeaux. Treaty of Berwick		Seige of Rennes
1358	Edward III proclamation forbids men-at-arms to leave the realm		
1359	Treaty of London. Edward III invades Northern France, Champagne & Burgundy		Raids in Normandy with Edward III · With Edward III in France
1360	Treaties of Guillon, Brétigny and Calais. Special councils in England to consider possibility of French invasion		Takes command in France · With Edward III in France
1361		Satalye (under Peter of Cyprus)	Dies · Satalye · With Edward III in France
1362		Presumably fighting with Peter of Cyprus	In France · With Edward III in France
1363			
1364			Brittany
1365		Alexandria (under Peter of Cyprus)	Alexandria · With Edward III in France
1366	Sir Owen ap Thomas allies with France. Attempted Danish invasion		Slain in Lithuania
1367	John of Gaunt in Brittany. Black Prince's expedition to Spain. Victory at Nájera	Lyeys (under Peter of Cyprus)	Nájera (dies there) · With John of Gaunt in Brittany, Nájera

English military engagements	Chaucer's Knight	Henry of Lancaster (1299-1361)	Sir John Chandos	Sir William Scrope of Masham	Sir Stephen Scrope (1345-1405)	Sir Geoffrey Scrope (1340-62)
1368			Guisnes in command of English army			
1369 Rebellion against Edward III in Gascony. France redeclares war on England			Dies in France			
1370 French victories near Paris, in Gascony and Maine. Black Prince sacks Limoges. Daily watch in London for French invasion	With Teutonic Knights in Pruce and Lettow and raiding into Ruce					
1371 English defeat Flemish off Bourgneuf. Bishop of Winchester asks for help against French aggression						
1372 John of Gaunt claims Castile. Owen of Wales takes Guernsey and aids French. French recapture Angoulême						
1373 John of Gaunt invades France from Calais to Bordeaux						
1374 English and French truce for Picardy						
1375 Truce of Bruges						

(Those that are bound and unfree by birth shall be made worthy and noble by wealth.) The connection between this sort of 'worthinesse' and wealth was a close one. Thus, when the Friar pays his attentions to the 'worthy wommen of the toun', he is after the well-to-do ones, not the virtuous ones.[7] Similarly, the Wife of Bath is mightily concerned about the 'worthiness' of her deceased husbands, and the context makes it clear that she is primarily thinking of them as men of substance.[8]

In view of this materialistic meaning of 'worthy', it is scarcely surprising that when Chaucer applies the word to the Knight's fellow-pilgrims, he is usually being ironic. In fact, he almost invariably applies it to the rogues and rascals. That unscrupulous trickster of a Canon, the hedonistic Franklin, the pompous, hard-nosed Merchant, the status-seeking Wife of Bath and even the lecherous, despicable Friar are all 'worthy' people – not a very strong recommendation for 'worthiness' one would have thought. The Knight, however, is the 'worthiest' of them all.[9]

Being 'worthy' begins to appear slightly less than complimentary in Chaucer's book. The statement: 'though the Knight was worthy, he was wise', *could* be interpreted as: 'though he was distinguished he was wise', but it makes far better sense as: 'though he was of high social rank [or else wealthy or even powerful] he was *wise*'.

This is exactly the sense in which Chaucer uses 'worthy and wys' elsewhere in his work. In his translation of Guillaume de Lorris' *Roman de la Rose*, Chaucer describes the allegorical figure of Largess (reward, bounty, generosity) as 'worthy and wise'.[10] Now quite clearly Largess is not *brave* and wise. Chaucer is, in fact, using 'worthy' to translate the French word *vaillant*, and, contrary to what one might perhaps expect, *vaillant* does not mean 'valiant' but 'valuable' – 'being of worth', 'rich'. In other words, Largess is well-off, but she is also wise enough to give some of her wealth away. And this brings us to a consideration of how the Knight was 'wise'.

Knightly wisdom was frequently associated with largess in Middle English literature. A knight was said to be 'wise' if he was generous in his gift-giving. In the romance of *Havelock the Dane* (c. 1300), for example, when Havelock gives Ubbe a gold ring worth a hundred pounds, the poet remarks that he is being 'wise' in the same way that the first man who ever gave *mede* (reward, largess) was 'wise':

> A gold ring drow he forth anon
> An hundred pund was worth the ston
> And yaf it Ubbe for to spede.
> He was ful wis that first yaf mede;
> And so was Hauelok ful wis here.[11]

Similarly, in his *Chronicle* (c. 1425) Andrew of Wyntoun says that Henry of Grosmont, the first Duke of Lancaster, was 'ay worthi wycht/And wysse, and mast ranownyt of bownte' ('ever a worthy man/And wise, and most famous for his generosity').[12]

Bounty or largess was seen as a political necessity – it was the way you kept your followers happy, and the 'wise' ruler gave generously. In the previous century, Guillaume de Lorris outlined the theory:

> A lord can have no kind of vice
> That will hurt him more than avarice;
> For a miserly man cannot conquer
> Either lordship or great territory,
> Since he does not have plenty of friends
> With whom to accomplish his will.
> And he who would have friends
> Must not love his own wealth too dearly.[13]

So when Chaucer says, 'And though that he were worthy, he was wys', his contemporary readers, familiar with the chivalric values of the day, might well have expected the next line to be a description of the Knight's generosity. Instead all Chaucer offers is: 'And of his port as meeke as is a mayde.' Of course, you could say that a leader who adopts a meek manner towards his inferiors is also being 'wise', but pleasant manners are no substitute for hard cash. Unless a knight were generous with his giftgiving, he could be as polite as he liked, but he would not have many followers.[14] Perhaps we should take a closer look at this meekness of the Knight's.

Meekness, or *humblesce*, was another important quality for a knight to possess. According to Henry of Lancaster, it was the quality from which all other virtues sprang.[15] *The Middle English Dictionary* gives the following meanings for 'meeke': gentle, humble, unassuming, submissive, patient, merciful. Yet how can the Knight be said to be truly meek in any of these senses? He cannot be *humble* or *unassuming*, for he has sought out the most ostentatious displays of worldly honour that he could – sitting at the head of the board in Prussia and fighting in the lists at

Tramyssene.[16] Nor is he *submissive*. When the Monk 'quits' *The Knight's Tale*, the Knight is unable to remain 'in adversitee ful pacient' – as is the Poor Parson – and cuts the Monk off most unceremoniously: ' "Hoo!" quod the Knyght, "good sire, namoore of this!" ' (Prologue to *Nun's Priest's Tale*, 7, 2763). Nor is the Knight *merciful*. With uncanny sure-footedness, he seems to have steered himself around Europe from one bloody massacre to another. Moreover, when he has fought in the lists, he has never shown any mercy and, contrary to the general practice of the day, he has always killed his opponent. Altogether, he has slain at least eighteen of his fellow-men (see The Knight as an efficient killer, above, p. 81).

But then, Chaucer only says that he is meek 'of his port' – i.e. in his manner.[17] Meekness, as defined by the MED and as spoken of by Henry of Lancaster, is an interior quality – a matter of character. Chaucer is always careful to distinguish between those who are genuinely meek and those who are only meek in appearance – like 'hende Nicholas' in the *Miller's Tale*:

> This clerk was cleped hende Nicholas.
> Of deerne love he koude and of solas;
> And therto he was sleigh and ful privee,
> And lyk a mayden meke for to see.
> *The Miller's Tale*, 3199–202

[This scholar was called courteous Nicholas./He knew about secret love and pleasure;/And at it he was sly and very discreet,/And as meek as a maid to look at.]

The Knight is meek 'of his port'; Nicholas is meek 'for to see'. Similarly, in the *Merchant's Tale*, the beautiful, young May appears meek – 'so meke a look hath she', but, continues Chaucer, 'God woot what that May thoughte in hir herte', and she soon plays old January false.[18] So too, in *The House of Fame*, Chaucer describes the nine Muses: 'That in her face semen meke' ('That in their faces seem meek') and yet are the attendants of Fame – that least meek of all allegorical figures.[19] 'Hende Nicholas' is 'sleigh and ful privee' and cultivates a meek exterior because it speeds him in his love affairs; the Knight is 'meke' because he is 'wys' enough not to go throwing his weight around. In fact, his own career of blood and slaughter is such a startling contrast to any concept of 'meekness' that the irony must surely be intentional. It recalls one of the Knight's own former warlords – Pedro the Cruel, King of Castile – about whom it was said that, although given to wanton slaughter and murder on the slightest pretext, he was himself 'the mildest mannered man ...' who would 'see no murder done by others'.[20] It recalls once again Bruegel's figure of a knight on horseback in his *Massacre of the Innocents* with baton of office in one hand, mildly ordering his thugs to break open doors and windows, and to kill the children and babes still in their mothers' arms. The traditional 'meek' behaviour of knights beside the horror and bloodshed they created must have been a grim joke to the peasants who suffered at their hands.

In the next line, Chaucer goes on to describe exactly *how* the Knight's manner was 'meek', and it is a very parody of the true '*humblesce*' of chivalry.

The Knight's lack of bad language

> He nevere yet no vileynye ne sayde
> In al his lyf unto no maner wight.
>
> *General Prologue*, 70–1

The word 'vileynye' originally meant action or conduct befitting those of 'villein' status – that is, the unfree peasants, bound to their feudal lords.[1] So it is rather thin evidence from which to conclude, as Chaucer does in the next line, that the Knight was therefore 'a verray, parfit gentil knyght' ('gentil' means nobly born).

Why does Chaucer even mention 'vileynye-saying' at all? Did it have any special significance in the fourteenth century? Did it imply anything more than mere bad language?

In fact, 'vilony saying' was a serious military offence. So far from aspiring to the pinnacle of 'gentil' behaviour by not saying any 'vileynye', the Knight was merely observing the regulations and avoiding an offence which Henry V considered so serious that he made it punishable by death, as we read in his Ordinances of War for 1419:

For those that insult others.
Also that no manner of man shall insult another because of the country he comes from, whether he is French, English, Welsh or Irish or from any other country, and that no man shall say any *vilony* to any other, through which *vilony saying* hasty manslaughter or general disturbance might arise; all such trouble-makers shall stand at the King's pleasure for what death they shall have for their noise-making.[2]

Henry V's ordinance is clearly aimed at the hired men-at-arms and mercenaries of mixed nationalities who increasingly made up the bulk of the contemporary army.

But in the world of true knighthood it went without saying that people did not insult one another. Such matters belonged among the peascods and the ploughshares of the village not in the refined circles of gentlefolk.

In the *Durham Halmote Rolls* for 1375, for example, we find frequent prohibitions on bad language. Sandwiched between orders preventing peasants selling their home-brewed beer at more than 1½d a gallon, and receipts such as: 'From Thomas Rois – 18d because his dog ate a pea-hen', we find:

West Merrington. It was ordered that no tenants of the vill should insult one another by word or deed.
Hedworth ... It was ordered that no tenant of the vill should permit his wife to vilify or insult any persons of the neighbourhood. ... It was ordered that all women of the vill should hold ther tongues and should not scold or curse any one.[3]

Even in military circles, bad language was associated with the taverns and brothels and with dice-playing. When a herald was

sworn in, in Chaucer's day, he had to agree to the following oath:
'Item: you shall promise, as far as it lies in your power, to forsake
all vices and dedicate yourself to all virtues, and not to be a
common frequenter of taverns, which might give rise to unvirtuousness and unclean language, and that you shall not be a
dice-player nor any other kind of gambler, and that you avoid
trouble-spots and unhonest places and the company of unhonest
women. . . .'[4] But then military service had been, traditionally, the
concern of the nobility and landed gentry. The new-style mercenary army of the fourteenth century was no longer such a classy
affair. It attracted whoever it could with the promise of wages
and the possibility of prodigious amounts of loot. It was the gold-
rush of the fourteenth century, and, like the Klondike, it brought
together the roughnecks and desperadoes. It has been estimated
that 'from two to twelve per cent of most armies of the period
consisted of outlaws'.[5] Not surprisingly, military manners
declined with the class of recruits, and even at the beginning of
the century men were complaining that 'vileynye-saying' was rife
among the new order of so-called knights:

Thus the order of knighthood is now turned so upside-down
That a knight knows how to swear as well as any common scold.
They should be as well-mannered as any lady in the land,
But now no knight refrains for shame to speak all manner of *vilanie*
And thus is knighthood crippled and grown all foot-lame.[6]

And for Jean de Meung 'Wicked-Tongue' was epitomized by the
soldiers of Normandy'.[7]

The new-style army not only mixed men from different classes,
it also mixed together men of different nationalities. Englishmen,
Frenchmen, Welshmen, Irishmen, Germans, Italians, Hungarians
often rubbed shoulders under a common paymaster. National
jealousies and rivalries, mutual distrust, bragging and insults,
must have been the order of the day. Some of the men may even
have been fighting on opposite sides a few months before, only
to be joined together by their common interest in loot. It is little
wonder that trouble-making in the ranks was one of the major
preoccupations in the military organization of the day.

For example, in the conditions of employment for the English
Company (the White Company) under Albert Stertz laid down
by the Republic of Florence, 28 July 1364, almost a quarter of
the document deals with the problem of trouble making.[8]

Similarly in Richard II's army there were fierce penalties for quarrelling:

Also that no man, for any argument over arms, prisoners or lodgings, or any other thing, shall make a disturbance, dispute or argument in the host ... on pain of losing his horse and harness, and his body placed under arrest at the King's pleasure. Or, if he is a groom or page, he shall lose his left ear.... Also that no one be so bold as to make a dispute or argument in the host, for any hatred of time past or time to come; from which dispute or argument if someone is killed, the person or persons who were the cause of it shall be hanged.[9]

It is a measure of just how serious a problem these disputes were that Henry V felt obliged to increase the penalty for 'vilony-saying' to death.[10] And it is in the context of this crisis in military discipline, precipitated by the change-over from the feudal host to the paid armies of the fourteenth century, that Chaucer's remark about the Knight's restraint in not saying any 'vileynye', should be seen – especially since the sort of armies in which the Knight is supposed to have served were among the most notorious for their lack of discipline.

In 1360, for example, when Peter of Cyprus was recruiting men for the crusade which was eventually to take the Knight to Alexandria, he sent envoys to recruit mercenaries from the ranks of the Free Companies in Lombardy. When he introduced these English, German and Hungarian soldiers of fortune into his feudal host, trouble at once broke out. The Cypriot chronicler Makhairas has left us a record of the incident:

And when they were returning to Cyprus, they fell in with John of Verona, whom the King had sent to recruit men-at-arms at a monthly wage. And at once they landed in Lombardy and recruited many men-at-arms and came back together to Cyprus in company with the said John of Verona.

And on Sunday the twenty-second of April 1360 after Christ, when King Peter was at Famagusta, there arose a great stir and strife amongst the men-at-arms, the new recruits [who had been brought from abroad] against the older ones [of the country], Cypriots and Syrians, and two of the strangers were killed. Then there arose a great tumult between them. When the King saw that many were likely to be killed, a proclamation was made by his command that no one should dare to carry arms or to make any quarrel, on pain of losing his head. And the sheriff went out with a strong force and found those who had made the quarrel, and hanged them upon the gallows. And with this the people and the tumult were stilled.[11]

'Vilony-saying' was a typical problem of the new-style mercenary armies with their mixture of men-at-arms from different classes and different nations. It may have been to the Knight's credit that he didn't enter into this, but the fact that Chaucer mentions it at all is scarcely kind. Instead of elevating the Knight into the ranks of chivalry, by the very fact of bringing up the subject Chaucer wryly keeps the Knight among the ranks of the hired troops.

It is often pointed out, however, that these words of Chaucer's correspond fairly closely to those of an earlier French poet, Watriquet de Couvin.[12] And Watriquet is *not* being ironic when he describes his patron, Gauchier de Chatillon, in similar terms:

> He was never so full of wrath or anger
> That there ever issued from his mouth
> A villainous word; he had a softer manner
> Than a lady or a maiden.[13]

But let us look again at what Watriquet wrote. He does not just say that his patron never used bad language – he says that Gauchier de Chatillon was *never so full of wrath or anger* that a 'villainous word' ever came to his lips. The truly *gentil* thing was not simply to refrain from using bad language but to avoid the sin of Anger.[14]

Anger, according to the Poor Parson, is defined as: 'the passionate blood of a man, quickened in his heart, so that he wishes harm to him whom he hates',[15] and war and killing were the inevitable expression of this sin.[16] To the Knight, war and killing are a way of life. His career is a catalogue of bloodthirsty massacres and of his success in killing. Quite obviously he has *done* many a 'vileynye' to his fellow-men. The fact that Chaucer merely emphasizes that he has never *said* a 'vileynye' is an essential irony, for Chaucer is being quite specific when he uses the word 'said'. Out of the seventy-one or so occasions when he uses the word 'vileynye', on only five is it a question of *saying* a 'vileynye' rather than *doing* one.[17] Once again, Chaucer is only praising the Knight's outward appearance and telling us nothing of the man himself. In the same way that he is meek 'of port' only (in his appearance), the restraint which he shows to his fellow-men is a matter of words not deeds.

In any case, isn't Chaucer rather damning the Knight with faint praise? Of course 'vylaynous and foule wordes ben ageynst thordre of chyualrye', as Caxton put it,[18] but 'chyualrye' was not *just* a case of avoiding bad language, it was also a question of speaking nobly and courteously – it all went together with having splendid equipment, being well dressed and keeping a good household: 'It behoves a knight to speak nobly and courteously and to have fine equipment and to be well dressed and to keep a good household and an honest house, for all these things are necessary to the honour of chivalry.'[19] As we shall see, in the next line or two, the Knight does not live up to any of these requirements. He is poorly dressed and under-equipped and has only the most basic retinue. Similarly he fails in his language. When he speaks, in the headlinks and in his own Tale, his imagery is never courtly, it is drawn from the plough and the common soldier's view of battle.

Simply to say that the Knight never used bad language to anyone is a long way from saying that he used the 'teccheles termes of talkyng noble' which were the mark of the truly gentil knight like Sir Gawain.[20]

Placed in the context of his bloody career, the emphasis given to this mere observation of military regulations is bitterly ironic.

It is even more ironic when he goes on to conclude that this lack of bad language was the thing that made the Knight beyond any doubt: 'a verray, parfit gentil knyght'...

Is the Knight 'gentil'?

He was a verray, parfit gentil knyght.
General Prologue, 72

The word *gentil* started out in life as the Latin *gentilis*, meaning 'of the same stock' or 'belonging to a good family'.[1] Thus in medieval times it came to mean: 'of noble rank or birth, belonging to the gentry'. By extension, it also came to be applied to those qualities which the 'gentry' liked to consider themselves as possessing. In Chaucer's day, which of these two characteristics most deserved the name 'gentil' – nobility of birth or nobility of character – was the subject of much debate. And it is essential to follow this debate in order to understand Chaucer's use of the word and why he should call the Knight 'gentil'.

In the fourteenth century nobility of birth was certainly considered by many people to be an important factor in being 'gentil'. In 1354, for example, Henry of Grosmont (whose daughter Blanche Chaucer celebrated in *The Book of The Duchess*) wrote:

> It seems to me that he who wishes to judge the 'gentilesce' of a person, must know three things, before the man is established by him as truly 'gentil'. First he must know if his father is gentil. Second: if his mother is also a gentle woman. The third is to know whether he behaves himself in words and deeds as a gentil, and loves the company of other gentils – and a great shame it is to his mother, if he does not take after his father in goodness. And if he is thus 'gentil' through his father and mother and also through himself, then, as I have said before, it is right for men to call him and hold him 'gentil'.[2]

In particular, nobility of birth and knighthood had long been considered inseparable, as Ramon Lull wrote (*c.* 1265): 'Noble birth and chivalry belong together for ... if you make a knight out of someone who is not nobly born, you make chivalry to be contrary to noble birth, and by the same reasoning, he whom you made a knight is also contrary to noble birth and therefore to chivalry....'[3]

In Chaucer's own day, when the traditional feudal retainer was being ousted by the mercenary, nobility of birth naturally had an added importance for the knighthood. It was an essential way in which the retained knight, serving his lord in peace and war for the duration of his life, could distinguish himself from the hired man, engaged for a specific occasion (see 'What was a Knight in the Fourteenth Century?' above, p. 4).

What, therefore, could be more natural than for Chaucer to dub his Knight of the *Prologue* – that flower of chivalry – 'a verray, parfit gentil knight'?

On the other hand, the writers who most influenced Chaucer's thought all reckoned that the gentility of one's parents meant nothing at all.[4] Thus, some eighty years before Chaucer, Jean de Meung wrote:

> If anyone should dare to contradict
> What I have said, and vaunt his gentle birth
> And name of gentleman, declaring he
> Is better by nobility of race
> Than those who cultivate the fields, and live

By their own labor, I should answer thus:
That no man's gentle who is not intent
On virtue, and that none ungentle are
Except by foolish outrage or by vice.
  Nobility comes from an upright heart;
Gentility of birth is nothing worth
If he who has it lacks goodheartedness.
In him the prowess should be shown of those
Who were his forebears, and their name achieved
By the good works to which they set themselves.
When from the world they went, they with them took
Their virtues, leaving only to their heirs –
Who nothing more could claim – their property.
These have their fathers' wealth, but nothing more –
No nobleness or worth – unless they do,
By reason of their virtue or good sense,
That which discloses true nobility.[5]

And eight centuries earlier, Boethius (another seminal influence on Chaucer's thought) said:

But now who does not see how empty and vain a thing is a reputation for nobility? If it is related to fame, it belongs to another: for nobility seems to be a kind of praise deriving from the deserts of one's parents. Now if being talked about produces fame, then those must be famous who are talked about; wherefore the fame of others, if you have none of your own, does not make you renowned.[6]

Perhaps equally important for Chaucer was Dante's discussion of *gentilezza* in the Fourth Treatise of the *Convivio*, and in the canzone prefixed to it,[7] in which he put forward the rather convincing argument that if virtue or baseness were inherited, then all men would have to be like Adam since he was their common ancestor. If Adam was base, all men must be base; if Adam was noble, all men must be noble; but since this similarity does not exist in men, virtue and baseness cannot be inherited.[8]

It is very easy for us nowadays to think of this debate about the word 'gentil' as a sterile argument confined to polite literary circles. But in the reality of Chaucer's day, it was political dynamite.

In Italy it presented a direct challenge to the right to rule of the 'tyraunts of Lumbardy'[9] such as the Visconti of Milan – as Dante wrote: 'Let not him of the Uberti of Florence, nor him of the Visconti of Milan, say: "Because I am of such a race I

am noble"; for the divine seed falls not upon the race, that is
the stock, but falls upon the several persons; and, as will be
shown below, the stock does not ennoble the several persons,
but the several persons ennoble the stock.'[10] Chaucer, of course,
knew Bernabò Visconti from personal experience, and on his
journeys of 1372 and 1378 he would have found the Italian cities
which he visited buzzing with this very debate.[11]

In England, the argument took on even more radical colours.
From the argument that 'gentillesse' lies in the individual and
not in his birth, John Ball, for example, concluded that there
should be 'equality of liberty and nobility as well as of dignity
and power'.[12] The peasants of 1381 chanted:

> When Adam delved and Eve span
> Who was *then* a gentleman?

The debate on 'gentillesse' – far from being a mere philosophical
or literary conceit – was a desperately important political issue
which was shaking Europe to its very foundations.

In *The Canterbury Tales* the 'noble is as noble does' school
of thought is vigorously represented by the Wife of Bath, who,
despite the fact that she is herself a social climber (or perhaps
because of it), does not give a fig for nobility of birth. For her,
as for John Ball, 'gentillesse cometh fro God allone':

> But, for ye speken of swich gentillesse
> As is descended out of old richesse,
> That therfore sholden ye be gentil men,
> Swich arrogance is nat worth an hen.
> Looke who that is moost vertuous alway,
> Pryvee and apert, and moost entendeth ay
> To do the gentil dedes that he kan;
> Taak hym for the grettest gentil man.
> Crist wole we clayme of hym oure gentillesse,
> Nat of oure eldres for hire old richesse.
> For thogh they yeve us al hir heritage,
> For which we clayme to been of heigh parage,
> Yet may they nat biquethe, for no thyng,
> To noon of us hir vertuous lyvyng,
> That made hem gentil men ycalled be,
> And bad us folwen hem in swich degree.
> *The Wife of Bath's Tale*, 1109–24

[But if you speak of the sort of 'nobility' that is handed down by virtue of ancient wealth, claiming that because of it you are therefore noblemen, such arrogance is not worth a hen. Discover who is always the most virtuous, both privately and publicly, and who always tries to do the noblest deeds that he knows how: Take *him* as the greatest nobleman. Christ wishes us to claim our nobility through him, not through our forebears because of their ancient wealth. For even though they give us all of their heritage on account of which we claim to be noble of birth, yet they cannot bequeath, by any means whatsoever, to any of us their virtuous way of life which caused them to be called noble in the first place, and it is in this manner he [Christ] bade us follow them.]

Further on the Wife of Bath returns to this theme for yet more clarification (see *The Wife of Bath's Tale*, 1150-65).

It seems reasonable to assume, as Nevill Coghill does, that this is also Chaucer's own point of view,[13] for when he writes a ballad on the subject of 'Gentilesse', he writes:

> This firste stok was ful of rightwisnesse ...
> And, but his heir love vertu, as dide he,
> He is noght gentil, though he riche seme,
> Al were he mytre, croune, or diademe.
>
> Vyce may wel be heir to old richesse;
> But ther may be no man, as men may wel see,
> Bequethe his heir his vertuous noblesse....
>
> *Gentilesse*, 8–21

[The first ancestor was full of righteousness ... and, unless his heir loves virtue as he did, he is not noble, though he seem rich, even though he wears a mitre, crown or diadem. Vice may well be heir to old riches but, as men may see plainly, no man can bequeath his nobility of character to his heir....]

But although this may represent Chaucer's own view of what is 'gentilesse', to most people of his day 'gentil' still meant 'noble by birth'. Consequently, unless he is actually *defining* it, Chaucer's use of the word 'gentil' is almost always ironic.

This is how the Manciple and the Pardoner both come to be dignified as 'gentil', while the Parson and the Ploughman (who so clearly fit Chaucer's own definition) are not. Similarly the Host uses the word ironically of the Cook, and Chaucer himself when he calls the Tabard Inn 'this gentil hostelrye'.[14]

By which definition of the word, then, can the Knight of the Prologue be said to be 'gentil' – by Chaucer's own definition (nobility of character) or by the popular definition (nobility of birth)? Indeed, can he be said to be truly 'gentil' by either?

The qualities which Chaucer assigns to 'gentillesse' in his own ballads on the subject are: truth to promises, sobriety, pity, generosity, a clear spirit and honest industry.[15] In *The Parson's Tale*, the Poor Parson distinguishes three 'generale signes of gentillesse': 'eschewynge of vice', 'to be liberal' and 'pitee'.

If one compares these qualities with those ascribed to 'virtue' by both Aristotle and Dante,[16] one notices that Chaucer has made one very significant addition: pity.

Pity is crucial to Chaucer's concept of 'gentillesse'. Without it, he says, all the good attributes of men of power, such as strength, intelligence, drive, etc, become potential evils:

Wherfore seith Senek, 'Ther is no thing moore convenable to a man of heigh estaat than debonairetee and pitee. And therfore thise flyes that men clepen bees, whan they maken hir kyng, they chesen oon that hath no prikke wherwith he may stynge' (*The Parson's Tale*, 466–7).

[Wherefore, says Seneca, 'There is nothing more fitting to a man of high social position than kindness and pity. And for this reason these insects that men call bees, when they choose their king, they choose one that has no barb with which he may sting.]

This association of 'gentillesse' and pity recurs again and again throughout Chaucer's writing.[17] The Squire, looking at the world through rose-tinted spectacles, claims:

> That pitee renneth soone in gentil herte,
> Feelynge his similitude in peynes smerte,
> Is preved alday, as men may it see,
> As wel by werk as by auctoritee;
> For gentil herte kitheth gentillesse.
> *The Squire's Tale*, 479–83

[That pity runs soon in a noble heart which feels the sharp pains of others like his own is proved all day, as men may see, both by experience and by learned books; for the noble heart proclaims its own nobility.]

In truth, of course, the experience of the fourteenth century was quite the opposite, and the supposedly 'gentil' folk were all too often without pity. Chaucer himself would have witnessed some of the outstanding examples of this, such as at Cesena in 1377 when Cardinal Lord Robert of Geneva wreaked his vengeance on the innocent citizens of that town, or, in England, the fearful suppression after 1381.[18] Without pity, manners and gentillesse are nothing:

> Eke what availeth Maner and Gentilesse
> Without yow, benygne creature
> Shal Cruelte be your governesse?
> Allas! what herte may hyt longe endure?
> *Complaint Unto Pity*, 78–80

[Also, what do Fine Manners and Gentility avail without you, benign creature, shall Cruelty be your governess? Alas! what heart could long endure it?]

And yet, when we turn to the portrait of the Knight in the *Prologue*, it is precisely this quality of pity which is most obviously missing. Moreover, when we examine the *Knight's Tale*, we shall find that pity plays little, if any, part in his concept of chivalry.[19]

By the same token, that other important ingredient of Chaucer's 'gentillesse' – generosity or largess – is also markedly absent from both the portrait of the Knight and his *Tale* (see Commentary on lines 68–9 above).

Against this implied lack of pity and generosity, the only positive proof of the Knight's 'gentillesse' we are offered is that his manner was as meek as a maid's and that he never used bad langauge, which are exactly the sort of superficial qualities which Chaucer rejects as meaningless without pity.

If the Knight cannot be said to be 'gentil' by Chaucer's own definition of the word, neither can he be said to be 'gentil' in the popular sense of 'gentil' by birth.

There is nothing in the Knight's appearance to suggest 'high parage'. He has no livery, no coat-of-arms, no shield, no belt and only a minuscule retinue. He has no name, no family seat, no manor house and no lands that Chaucer thinks worth mentioning. Furthermore, his obsession with foreign service indicates a lack of feudal ties and bears all the marks of the career of a landless knight without family or possessions in England.[20]

To us these omissions may seem very much by-the-way, but to the men of the fourteenth century they would have been highly relevant. It was essential for a knight to display his rank. To have appeared as the Knight does would have been improper, imprudent and even illegal for the truly 'gentil' knight (see commentary on lines 75–6 below).

And yet the Knight himself appears to share this popular concept of 'gentillesse'. For him, 'estaat and heigh kynrede' are equally as important as 'trouthe, honour, knyghthede' (see *The Knight's Tale* 2788–91).

It appears, then, that the Knight is not 'gentil' by Chaucer's definition of the word, nor by the popular definition of the word, nor even by his own definition of the word. He is no more truly 'gentil' than the Manciple, The Pardoner, the Monk, the Cook or even the Tabard Inn itself.

A gay horse?

> **But, for to tellen yow of his array,**
> **His hors were goode, but he was nat gay.**
>
> *General Prologue*, 73–4

Having dealt with the Knight's supposed virtues, in lines 68–72, Chaucer now proceeds to give us a description of the Knight's physical appearance – and a very surprising description it turns out to be. He starts with his horses.

The grammar of these lines appears to be as follows: 'His hors were goode' is plural, while 'he was nat gay' is singular.[1] The line therefore reads: 'His horses were good, but he [the Knight himself] was not gay.'

The quality of his horses was of paramount importance for any knight – for the hired mercenary no less than for the aristocrat – since it was according to the quality of his mount that the mercenary was, to a large degree, paid. Indeed, if his horses were not 'goode', a knight would have found it very difficult to obtain any employment at all. The Military Code governing the employment of mercenaries by the town of Pisa, for example, laid down: 'that the superintendents ... are required on oath not to accept any horse, courser or hack which is broken-winded, obstinate, affected by rheum or otherwise sick'.[2] Moreover the same regulations laid down that any horse that was taken into service had to be worth at least twenty-five gold florins.

But while it should thus be no surprise that the Knight of the *Prologue* had good horses, we are still faced with the very odd syntax of these lines. Why does Chaucer place the Knight's own lack of gaiety in antithesis to the quality of his horses? Why should not the Knight be 'gay'?

It is usually assumed that 'gay' here means 'gaudily dressed',[3] and Muriel Bowden sums up the traditional interpretation of the line:

> It is very much to the credit of the Knight that he is not overdressed, not too 'gay', for, according to the sermon literature of the fourteenth century, the upper classes are continually censured for their 'synful costlewe array of clothynge'. The homilists often coupled 'the synne of adornement or of apparaille' with the possession of 'to manye delicat horses that been hoolden for delit', so that Chaucer's *but* in line 74 has added force. The Knight's horses are good, but since their owner is soberly clad, we realize at once that he has not an excessive number and that they are maintained solely because a knight must be fittingly mounted.[4]

'Gay' could indeed mean 'finely or showily dressed' (OED), but it did not necessarily mean this in a bad sense. An angel, for instance, could appear in 'gay gear':

> He come in als gay gere
> Ryte as he an angelle were.[5]

And the Wife of Bath tells us that she always loved to be gay: 'For evere yet I loved to be gay' (*The Wife of Bath's Prologue*, 545, see also 337–56). In the first sense it means: 'shining, glittering, bright', and in the second: 'joyous, merry, light-hearted, carefree'. 'Gay' could also mean: 'excellent, noble, beautiful' and even 'strong and gallant' (MED).

In all these senses, being 'gay' was an important part of knighthood. The Knight's own son associates being 'gentil born' with being 'gai': 'Though he were gentil born, and fressh and gay' (*The Squire's Tale*, 622). Indeed, 'gay' was often used as a substantive for 'a noble lady' or 'a gallant knight'.[6]

So gaiety is a very odd quality for Chaucer's 'verray, parfit gentil knight' to lack. The readers of the fourteenth century, far from feeling it was to the Knight's credit, would have felt there was something decidedly peculiar about it.

What is more, Chaucer himself seems to have approved wholeheartedly of being 'gay'. Indeed, it is sometimes the very object of his writing:

> Nowe this dreme wal I ryme aright,
> To make your hertes gaye and lyght.
> *The Romaunt of the Rose*, 31–2

[Now this dream will I rhyme aright, to make your hearts gay and light.]

And for his contemporaries, 'gaity' was the very essence of his style:

> Chaucer is deed ...
> We may assay for to countrefete
> His gay style but it wyl not be.[7]

The official church may well have disapproved of 'gaiety', but this was often seen as a prime example of ecclesiastical hypocrisy.[8] Chaucer himself never once uses the word 'gay' in a pejorative sense – even though he uses it on no less than forty-four occasions.

It seems very strange that here – and only here – he should commend the Knight for *not* being 'gay'.

But why the antithesis between the good horses and the Knight's lack of 'gaiety'? It seems as if Chaucer is making a play on some connection between 'gay' and 'horses' which his contemporary readers would have understood though it is obscure to us.

In Medieval French '*gai*' was often applied to animals in the sense of 'lively and spirited'[9] (this is probably the sense in which Chaucer's style was also considered to be 'gai'). In Middle English too we find 'a gay falcon and swifte'[10] and in Modern French '*un cheval gai*' still means 'a lively horse'.[11] So by putting the Knight's lack of 'gaiety' in antithesis to his horses, Chaucer might be implying that the Knight was not 'gay' like a horse – i.e. lively and spirited. The line would thus signify that 'his horses were good [and therefore 'gay' – lively and spirited] but the Knight himself wasn't.'

But there is also another connotation to the line – more ludicrous and at the same time more sinister.

'A Gay Horse' was also a popular term for a certain kind of carnival figure. An English–Latin Dictionary of 1530 renders 'a gaye horse' as: '*ioculator, ore turpiter manducans, vel ore hians*' ('a jester with an ugly chewing mouth, or his mouth gaping open').[12] An earlier dictionary, of 1483, gives 'a gay horse' as the Latin *manducus* – 'a glutton' or an image 'carried in pageants with great cheekes, wyde mouthes & makyng a great noys with their iawes'.[13] So perhaps the antithesis in the line is suggesting that the Knight was not 'a gay horse' – i.e. a carnival figure: 'His hors were goode, but *he* was nat gay' ('His horses were good and therefore gay, but he was not a gay horse'). What would this have meant?

Perhaps the most relevant feature of 'a gay horse' or *manducus* was its frightening appearance. It was a carnival figure that was made as terrible-looking as possible, with great jaws and crashing teeth, and was used to make people fall back and give way.[14] In other words 'a gay horse' was a frightening figure, which at the same time made people laugh because they knew it was harmless – a paper dragon. With the Knight it is just the other way round. On the surface he appears harmless enough and cultivates a manner as meek as is a maid. But, like Pedro the Cruel, beneath that modest exterior he is a deadly killer. He is anything but a paper dragon or, in the terms of Chaucer's day, 'a gay horse'.

Once again I am reminded of the figure of the Knight in Bruegel's *Massacre of the Innocents* – that venerable figure of authority, calmly supervising the atrocious slaughter of children and babes-in-arms (see above, p. 86).

The shabby Knight

> **Of fustian he wered a gypon**
> **Al bismotered with his habergeon.**
>
> *General Prologue*, 75–6

When Chaucer gets round to describing what the Knight wears, he is even more perfunctory. From the way the Knight has been built up as:

> ... a worthy man,
> That fro the tyme that he first bigan
> To riden out, he loved chivalrie.
>
> *General Prologue*, 43–5

one might have expected a glorious figure in shining armour, with banners flying, a dragon on his shield and a crested helm glinting in the sun. But, instead, Chaucer merely says that he wore a 'gypon' of 'fustian' and that it was actually marked in some way – 'bismotered' – by his 'habergeon'. There is no mention of any of the usual knightly trappings – no helmet, no belt, no spurs, no shield, not even any heraldic device.

What a contrast to the hero of almost any medieval romance you care to mention.[1] And what a contrast to the Knight's own descriptions of how a noble knight should appear: Lycurgus, for example, standing in his chariot of gold, pulled by four white bulls, or Emetreus, mounted on a bay, trapped out in steel and covered with a cloth of gold, or Theseus himself 'arrayed as he were a god in trone'.[2] It is obvious that the Knight of the *Prologue* admires splendid accoutrements and rich attire. Why, then, is he so shabby himself?

Let us look at the details of his dress. Once again, all Chaucer says is:

> Of fustian he wered a gypon
> Al bismotered with his habergeon.

The 'habergeon' was a coat of mail. It was, in fact, the shortened and therefore lighter version of the 'hauberk' – the word is the diminutive of 'hauberk'.[3] The 'gypon' or 'jupon' was a tunic worn over it.

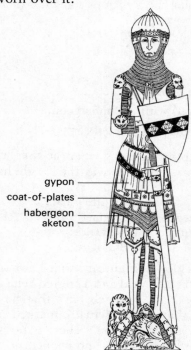

gypon
coat-of-plates
habergeon
aketon

Brass of Sir John de Creke

The 'gypon' was a sleeveless, tight-fitting outer garment, worn over the rest of the armour. A more general name was 'coat-armour'. All the gypons of which we have any record were splendid affairs. Edward III had gypons of blue taffeta, velvet and satin.[4] The Black Prince's was of blue and red velvet, and Charles VI of France, as a boy, wore a gypon of white linen faced with silk brocade.[5]

The 'fustian' from which the Knight's gypon was made, on the other hand, was a strong, thickish material made of cotton, flax or wool, which was often also used for blankets and bed-covers.[6] It was the sort of material you would normally expect to find worn *under* the armour rather than over it. It would certainly not have borne any armorial bearings.[7] In the fifteenth century the fustian tunic became known as the 'doublet of defence' or 'arming-doublet', and it was worn under the full plate-armour in place of the old chain-mail habergeon.[8] A manuscript of the period describes how to arm a man for fighting on foot: 'He shall have no shirt upon him but a doublet of fustian lined with satin cut full of holes....'[9] The same manuscript includes a rare illustration of the fustian doublet.

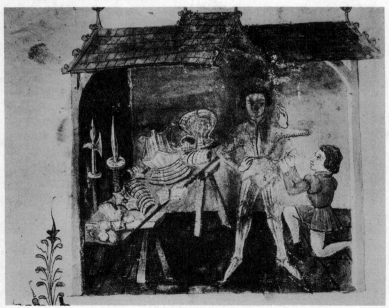

A rare illustration of the fustian doublet

So the Knight's fustian 'gypon' would have been a practical fighting garment worn for protection rather than display, and in marked contrast to the elaborately-decorated gypons worn by the true gentry at the end of the fourteenth century.[10]

The 'gypon' as worn by the nobility of Chaucer's day

However, the most remarkable feature of the Knight's gypon is that it has been marked or stained in some way by his chainmail habergeon.[11] Presumably this means either that the chainmail itself has made indentations on the gypon or that rust or oil from the mail has rubbed through and stained it.

Now *why* should Chaucer make this – his only – observation about the Knight's dress unless it tells us something about the character of the Knight? After all, a dirty tunic is not really the sort of thing one would expect from a man who 'loved chivalry'. A knight was supposed to:

> ... teach chevaliers under his care,
> Right as himself to turn out in their gear,
> The brigandine, helmet and all to procure
> To often wipe clean – and to know for sure
> With harnessing and mighty port afraid
> Is often a foe, and for to fight dismayed.[12]

More importantly, why does Chaucer say that the jupon was marked by the Knight's *own* habergeon? Why is he so specific that the marking is merely from another piece of the Knight's own equipment?

If you look again at the illustration of Sir John de Creke (p. 126), you notice that in between his gypon and his habergeon is another garment – the 'coat-of-plates', or 'hauberk of plates', which consisted of a series of metal plates sewn or riveted onto a cloth facing.

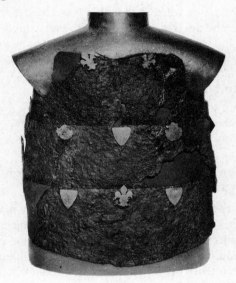

The important point about the coat-of-plates is that it was worn *in between* the chain-mail habergeon and the gypon or coat-armour, as can be seen in the illustration.[13] Chaucer himself records that this was usual practice when he decribes how Sir Thopas was armed. Like Sir John de Creke, Sir Thopas first puts on an 'aketoun', then a habergeon, then a 'hawberk ... of plate' and then his 'cote-armour':

> And next his sherte an aketoun,
> And over that an haubergeoun
> For percynge of his herte;
> And over that a fyn hawberk
> Was al ywroght of Jewes werk,
> Ful strong it was of plate;

And over that his cote-armour
As whit as is a lilye flour,
In which he wol debate.
Sir Thopas, 860–8

[And next to his shirt: an *aketon* and over that: a *habergeoun* to prevent his heart being pierced. And over that: a fine *hauberk*, which was all made by Jewish craftsmen very strong and made of steel plates; and over that: his coat-armour, as white as a lily flower, in which he will fight.]

The Knight also confirms that this was the order for wearing armour, when he describes the hundred 'wel armed' knights who accompany Palamon to the tournament: they wear a habergeon, then a breastplate and then a gypon. (Incidentally, it is noticeable that the knights of his imagination wear a *light* gypon, in contrast to his own heavy fustian one.)

With hym ther wenten knyghtes many on;
Som wol ben armed in an haubergeoun,
And in a brestplate and a light gypoun.
The Knight's Tale, 2118–20

[With him there went many a knight: some were armed in a *habergeoun*, and in a breastplate and in a light gypon.]

Yet, since the Knight's own gypon has been marked by his habergeon, he has obviously not been wearing any form of plate-armour in between. This is surprising, since plate-armour was very much an essential part of the nobleman-knight's equipment. No truly *gentil* knight would have left it off deliberately.

The question is: what would Chaucer's contemporaries – as familiar with armour as the modern reader might be with makes of cars – have understood from this surprising omission?

The development of plate-armour was one of the great revolutions in the warfare of the late-thirteenth and early fourteenth centuries. Claude Blair writes: 'From the last decade of the thirteenth century, references to it [the coat-of-plates] become increasingly common, until after *c*. 1320 there is hardly an inventory, account or will in which armour is mentioned that does not include one or more examples.'[14] Towards the end of the century it began to be replaced by the independent breastplate, but this was still very often worn over the habergeon and under the gypon – as the Knight himself bears witness, referring to it as

the 'newe gyse' (*Knight's Tale*, 2125). By 1384, breastplates had
become so common that the wearing of them had to be banned
throughout the City of London, and by the end of the century
you might find any rich merchant keeping a couple lying around
his counting-house.[15] A memorandum of 1387 records that one
merchant of Bohemia had no less than six hundred 'white plates',
fifty 'long plates' and thirty-three plates for the breast in his
house.[16] Even the ludicrous Sir Thopas wore a coat-of-plates.
Every noble knight and every would-be noble knight, it seems,
wore some form of plate-armour under his gypon – everyone,
that is, except for our perfect, nobly-born knight of the *Prologue*.
Why?

The question becomes even more puzzling when we consider
that what a knight wore was not simply a matter of personal
taste – like choosing the right tie or wearing odd socks. Ever
since 1181 the exact arms and armour that were required of every
Englishman between the ages of fifteen and sixty had been laid
down by statute.[17] In 1285 the Statute of Winchester once again
painstakingly spelled out what was required of each man according to his wealth. A man with land worth £15 a year and forty
marks' worth of goods was supposed to provide himself with a
hauberk (a long coat of mail), an iron helmet, a sword, a knife
and a horse. A man with land worth £10 a year and twenty marks'
worth of goods had to provide himself with a habergeon (short
coat of mail), helmet, sword and knife; and a man with only a
hundred shillings' worth of land: a doublet, helmet, sword and
knife, and so on.[18]

In the fourteenth century the requirements for defensive
armour grew even more stringent as the techniques of warfare
developed. In 1318, for example, we find ordinary infantrymen
being required to wear habergeons and helmets, which previ-
ously had been demanded only of the relatively wealthy £10-a-
year class.[19] In 1324, there was even an attempt to make some
of the foot soldiers who went across to Gascony wear habergeouns *and* plate-armour, but the expense provoked such a storm
of protest that the demand had to be dropped.[20] Nevertheless,
by 1335 we find that the coat-of-plates has become a standard
requirement even for simple spearmen or 'hobelars'.[21]

In short, our Knight of the *Prologue* has not been wearing the
legal minimum required of a knight by English law.

Of course, as the Knight of the *Prologue* has not been in England

very often, he may not have considered it worth his while to con-
form to the laws of England. But wherever he *had* fought, he
would have found similar requirements demanded of him. In
Italy, for example, the military codes drawn up by the various
city-states, Florence, Pisa, Milan and so on, laid down elaborate
systems of fines for any soldier reporting for duty without the
required equipment.[22]

These same Italian military codes also make it quite clear, however, that the style of armour adopted by the English freebooters
was considerably lighter than that of other nations or of soldiers
of noble birth.

In the first place, the English Company did without horse
armour entirely. They also went without cuirass or coat-of-plates
(*corazza*), throat-guard, chin-guard, sleeves of mail and gorget.[23]
Instead they wore what is referred to in contemporary documents
as a *pancerone*. Now what this is, is open to some debate. In
Italian, *panciera* (of which *pancerone* is the diminutive) seems
to have referred to a plate designed to protect the belly. In the
French of Chaucer's time, however, it was also used to refer to
the coat-of-mail or habergeon.[24] But whatever the exact details,
it is quite clear that, like Chaucer's Knight, the English mercenaries in Italy wore no plate-armour or coat-of-plates between
their habergeon and gypon. When they did wear a small plate
or heart-piece, it was always worn on top of their other dress.
Thus, according to the contemporary Italian chronicler Matteo
Villani, their arms shone like mirrors:

The armour of almost all of them was: pancerones, and in front
of the breast heart-pieces of iron, thigh-pieces, and leg-pieces, daggers
and sharpened swords, all with lances ... each of them had one or
two pages, some more, depending on how powerful they were. When
they removed their armour, these pages kept it so polished that when
they appeared at a skirmish, their arms resembled mirrors, making
them all the more frightening.[25]

Another Italian chronicler of the period gives the impression that
armour was in short supply among these English mercenaries and
so had to be shared out among them: if someone wore a helmet,
he did not wear a heart-piece, and if he wore a heart-piece, he
did not wear a helmet: 'For the most part they are armed only
in a thick doublet [*diploide*] and either have their heads un-
covered and a single iron plate upon their chests, or else they

wear only a cap and chin-guard ...'[26] One might also note that the 'thick doublet' is reminiscent of the Knight's fustian jupon.

But if one reason for the light armour of the English Company was economic, a more important reason was tactical. The English took great pride in their speed and ability to appear when and where they were least expected – often by forced night marches. Moreover their method of fighting made lighter armour a necessity. They rode in a basic unit of three called a 'lance', which consisted of a mounted soldier, a page and an archer. When it came to a pitched battle, they would all dismount and form a tight-knit pack, with two to each lance, and with lances lowered they would advance on the enemy with slow steps and blood-curdling shouts.

These tactics were so successful that other nationalities were soon following suit, and the *Codex for Mercenaries in the Service of Florence for 1369* had to make special provisions for other nationalities who wanted to follow the English style of arms.[27]

But, successful or not, the fact remains that the English mercenaries in the White Company in Lombardy were nothing more nor less than brigands, and by Chaucer's day light armour, such as the Knight of the *Prologue* has evidently been wearing, had become synonymous with brigandry. Indeed, the very word '*brigand*' originally simply meant: 'a lightly-armed foot soldier' (from the Italian '*brigante*' c. 1350).[28] By 1387 '*brigantes*' was already being used in English to mean bandits, just as, in French, the word '*coterel*' (meaning 'a short coat') was being used to mean 'a mercenary'.[29]

The shabby appearance of Chaucer's Knight was, by the mid-fourteenth century, the very trademark of the new breed of professional soldier. More than one writer complained that, as the mercenary had become the predominant element in the army, so the glamour of the battlefield had almost entirely disappeared.

The French chronicler Jean le Bel, writing between 1352 and 1356, contrasted the glitter of the knights of twenty years before with the drab figures of the present day:

In those days, the great lords reckoned nothing of men-of-arms, unless they possessed a helm with a crest on it, whereas nowadays they recognize anyone with a sword, *panchiere*, habergeoun and iron helmet. Thus it seems to me that times are very changed from what I remember, for the armoured horses, the crested helms which used to be worn, the plate-armour, the surcoats bearing the coat-of-arms, have all disappeared into oblivion, and habergeouns – which are now called *panchieres* – thick padded gypons and iron helmets are all you see. A poor groom is now armed as well and as nobly as is a noble knight.[30]

Exactly the same phenomenon is recorded by an obscure clerk of the court in Liège, named Jacques de Hemricourt. Lamenting the vanished glories of the chivalry of his youth, when knights went into battle on chargers draped with embroidery, riding high tournament saddles and looking 'so beautiful that they seemed like winged angels', he contrasts the drabness of the modern knight.[31] In doing so, he gives an almost word-for-word description of the Knight of the *Prologue*: 'But nowadays, each one is armed in a coat of mail called a *panchire*, rides a small horse and is dressed in a jupon of fustian, regardless of the fact that one cannot distinguish one man from his companion ... thus is all honour and nobleness perished.'[32]

Here at last, we can clearly see the significance of Chaucer's Knight's fustian gypon. It is not simply that it was a drab garment – it was directly contrary to the true spirit of chivalry. The whole point of the gypon or coat-armour was to display a knight's coat-of-arms. The plain fustian gypon, as Hemricourt points out, made one knight 'indistinguishable from his companion'.

Now the ability to distinguish one knight from another was absolutely essential to the pursuit of chivalry, since a knight displaying his family coat-of-arms on his back was fighting for more than his life – he was fighting for his honour: '... it was the greatest joy one could have, to see the noble men-at-arms in such array. For then no one dared to be a coward, since the good and the bad were recognizable by their coats-of-arms. And one battle in those days would last as long as three do now.'[33]

There was too a very practical reason for any nobleman who possessed a coat-of-arms to display it. At a time when the common soldier was usually slaughtered indiscriminately after the battle or else was simply left to die, the coat-of-arms acted as a sort of life insurance. The wealthy knight, who might be worth a handsome ransom, would be picked out by his coat-armour and would be rescued and given every necessary first aid, so that the ransom could be claimed. The Knight himself illustrates this practical function of the coat-armour in action, when he

describes how Palamon and Arcite are rescued from the pile of
dead and wounded at the opening of his *Tale*:

> ... by hir cote-armures and by hir gere
> The heraudes knewe hem best in special....
> Out of the taas the pilours han hem torn,
> And han hem caried softe unto the tente
> Of Theseus....
>
> *The Knight's Tale*, 1016–22

[... by their coat-armours and by their gear, the heralds knew them
to be especially high-ranking.... Out of the heap, the pillagers have
them torn, and have them carried softly to the tent of Theseus....]

For the mercenary, fighting for neither honour nor loyalty but
for hard cash, such recognition was the last thing he wanted –
especially when he might wish to extract himself from a battle
that became too dangerous, or perhaps even change sides altogether! Besides, the desperadoes of the Free Companies would
have had no coats-of-arms to display – they were for the most
part mere soldiers of fortune – veterans of the Hundred Years'
War, thrown out of work by the treaty of 1361.[34] Theirs was a
very different world from the world of chivalry that many of
Chaucer's contemporaries recalled.

Jacques de Hemricourt may have been just an obscure clerk
in a magistrate's court, but he was a dedicated admirer of
chivalry,[35] and to him, as to Jean le Bel, the Knight of the *Prologue's* plain habergeon and fustian gypon epitomized the decay
of chivalry. In other words, Chaucer has dressed his only representative of chivalry – a man who claims to love chivalry before
all else – in the style that symbolized to his age the decline of
that very institution.

Is the Knight's shabbiness a sign of piety?

> **For he was late ycome from his viage,**
> **And wente for to doon his pilgrymage.**
>
> *General Prologue*, 77–8

Chaucer now tries to tell us that the Knight's shabby turn-out
is merely the result of his pious enthusiasm: he has no sooner

landed from his latest crusade or 'voyage' than he sets off at once on his pilgrimage without even bothering to change his clothes. Chaucer's explanations of this sort are usually tongue-in-cheek[1], but this one is taken at face value by most modern critics.[2] It is assumed that the same Christian idealism which sent the Knight off on crusades against the heathens in distant lands prompts him to avoid ostentation in his dress. Muriel Bowden writes: 'The appearance of Chaucer's Knight is entirely in keeping with his virtues. . . . It is very much to the credit of the Knight that he is not over-dressed, not too "gay", for according to the sermon litera-ture of the fourteenth century, the upper classes are continually censured for their "synful costlewe array of clothynge".'[3] This reasoning, however, represents a considerable over-simplifica-tion.

Muriel Bowden is quoting Chaucer's *Parson's Tale*, and the Par-son is certainly no member of the religious establishment – Harry Bailey even smells 'a loller in the wind'.[4] Consequently, his attack on fine clothes has a totally different basis from the criticisms levelled by the orthodox clergy.

The Poor Parson condemns the 'superfluitee of clothinge' among the rich because it deprives the poor: '. . . the superfluity in length of the aforesaid gowns, trailing in the dung and in the mire, on horses as well as on foot, and of men as well as of women, all that trails is truly in effect wasted, consumed, thread-bare and made rotten with dung, instead of being given to the poor, to the great damage of the aforesaid poor folk.'[5] He is, in fact, making an attack on the inequality of society and, therefore, on the established order of the day.

The orthodox, on the other hand, complained not that fine clothes were inegalitarian but that they were *too* egalitarian and that they threatened the *status quo*. Consequently the orthodox attacked not only the rich for dressing too finely but also the poor:

. . . Now a wretched knave that goes to the plough and the cart, and has no more means than to serve from year to year for his livelihood, whereas once a white tunic and a russet gown would have served such a one perfectly well, now he must have a new doublet worth five shil-lings or more, and besides that a costly gown with bag-sleeves hanging down to his knee, and pleated under his belt like a newly worked sur-plice, and a hood on his head, with a thousand rags on his tippet, in gay stocking and shod as though he were a country squire.[6]

And there lies the crux of the matter: a knave dressed 'as though it were a squyer of cuntre' – in other words: a knave dressing above his station.

Another orthodox sermon of the day makes it quite clear that fine clothes were seen as the symptom of a more general social discontent and upheaval:[7] 'The garments, I say, of the proud and those who once were noble are now divided as spoil along with their bed-quilt, amongst grooms and maid-servants.... Hardly anyone now is satisfied with his status but pants after a higher one and inanely affects to be reputed better than he is by other people.'[8] In short, the orthodox religious establishment attacked those who dressed too finely not simply for their vanity but because they posed a threat to the established order of society. It was a political as well as a moral criticism.

Dress in the fourteenth century was all-important as a badge of social rank. Perhaps one reason for this was the greater physical contact between social levels which existed then.[9] In an age in which the only means of travel was to walk or ride a horse,[10] when a rich man's home was populated by servants and menials, and when the beggar sat outside the rich man's gate, waiting for the alms-dish that always stood on the great lord's table,[11] rich and poor rubbed shoulders together daily in a way which modern society constantly invents new means of preventing.[12] There is, for example, no social obligation to fill any alms-dish on the table of a modern restaurant, and the private car and the aeroplane safely insulate the well-to-do from the beggar on the street. But there was no first-class compartment on the pilgrimage to Canterbury, and the Knight rides cheek-by-jowl with the Miller and the Ploughman.

Dress was one way in which the structure of society was preserved, and the exuberant fashions of the late-fourteenth century were regarded as not merely the extravagance of *haute-couture* but a direct political threat.

At the beginning of this book I quoted Thomas Hoccleve's observation:

> Once there was a time when men could tell lords
> From other folk by their dress; but now
> A man must study and muse a long time
> To tell which is which[13]

but I did not then go into the conclusion which Hoccleve drew from it. According to Chaucer's self-confessed disciple, such homogeneity heralded a breakdown in the order of society:

> O lordes ...
> If twixt you and youre men no difference
> Be in array, lesse is your reverence.[14]

Alain Chartier, the French writer and diplomatist (c. 1385–1433), echoed the same thing – perhaps at the same time making a passing reference to that most infamous of all ex-tailor's men: John Hawkwood:[15] '... show me a tailor's man and a woman of poor

The ever-present beggar at the gate, waiting for the alm's dish from the rich man's table

degree and see if they are not bold enough to wear such array as does a worshipful knight or a noble lady ... in this way every man has learned this conceit so that it is a hard thing to know the status of people by their appearance, or to know a worshipful man from a craftsman.'[16]

Another way in which the fashions of the fourteenth century were regarded as socially disruptive was as a primary cause of inflation. In 1363, a petition in Parliament spelled out to the Commons:

> how various Foodstuffs in the Realm have been made much more expensive because various people of various Conditions use various Apparel that is not appropriate to their Status. That is to say: Menials use the Apparel of Attendants, and Attendants use the Apparel of Squires, and Squires the Apparel of Knights; anyone uses Fur which by reason ought to be worn only by Lords and Knights: poor Women and others dress like Ladies, poor Clerks dress in Fur like the King and other Lords. Thus are the said Goods made more expensive than they should be, and the Treasure of the land is destroyed to the great damage of the Lords and Commons. . . .[17]

In Chaucer's day, then, dress was not just a status symbol – it was a vital prop to the social order, and if it was important not to dress above your rank, it was equally important not to dress below it.

This was especially true of the knightly class, since the poor knight was an object of suspicion and might as easily be a robber as a soldier (see The Poor Knight, above, p. 25). It was therefore in the Knight's own interests to dress according to his rank. In the same way that the knight was under a legal obligation to equip himself correctly, he was under a social obligation to dress correctly – as an anonymous poet of Edward III's time put it:

> Knights should wear their clothes in their manner
> As their order demands just as much as should a friar.[18]

Chaucer's Knight fails on both counts: legally and socially (see commentary on ll. 75–6 above).

It was the religious anti-establishment who called for total simplicity in dress and the renunciation of all finery, and their aim was to change society. The religious establishment, on the other hand, attacked extravagant dress only when it was disruptive of the existing social order. The Knight, by his shabby turn-out and lack of plate-armour, was being as disruptive of that social order as if he had been over-dressed.

Chaucer is executing the final irony in his portrait of the Knight. He describes him in the gear of a typical freebooter, epitomizing the breakdown of the old order of society, and yet attributes this appearance to the Knight's dedication to the religious establishment, with its holy wars and pilgrimages.[19]

Thus by the end of Chaucer's description of the Knight no contemporary reader would have been left in any doubt as to what sort of a fellow this was. They would not have seen a militant Christian idealist but a shabby mercenary without morals or scruples – the typical product of an age which saw war turned into a business.

In the next chapter I shall consider how this view of the Knight's character affects our reading of the Tale which he tells, and turns it from a rather wooden philosophical romance into a highly entertaining satire on the pretensions of this new breed of military adventurers.

4 *The Knight's Tale*

The Tale which the Knight tells is given pride of place in Chaucer's masterwork. It is clear that Chaucer had no doubts about its merits, and since he most probably read his work aloud, he must have had plenty of opportunity to test its success with a live audience. Nevertheless twentieth-century commentators seem to be happier pointing out deficiencies in the *Tale* than in praising it. In 1933 no less a person than A.E. Housman wrote: '*The Knight's Tale* of Palamon and Arcite is not one of Chaucer's most characteristic and successful poems: he is not perfectly at home, as in the *Prologue*, and his movement is a trifle languid.'[1] More recently, Ian Robinson came out with perhaps the real truth of the matter when he claimed that many people 'find the tale tedious or uninterestingly obscure'. With admirable honesty he remarks: 'I will confess that it took me several years of admiration for Chaucer before I could see the tale as more than the lengthy gesture towards literary decorum which he felt he had to make ...'[2] – an observation which will, I am sure, strike home in many hearts.

The critics and *The Knight's Tale*

Perhaps the key to the problem lies in the fact that most new readers are encouraged to approach the poem as a courtly, philosophical romance,[3] despite the fact that almost all modern commentators have noted that one or more of these elements is missing. As far back as 1915, Stuart Robertson pointed out that much of the poem is far from romantic.[4] He drew attention to many instances where Chaucer has deliberately introduced a harsh realism into Boccaccio's original narrative – the *Teseida* – on which Chaucer based his poem. In 1939 H.R. Patch wondered 'why Chaucer failed to write an actual romance', and came to the conclusion that 'his humour was far too mischievous when he told his story'.[5]

More recent commentators have drawn attention to the un-courtly nature of much of the language, the introduction of comic, low-life observations at moments of otherwise high trag-edy, and the strange mixture of styles. All of which Paull F. Baum, in 1958, branded as more or less serious blemishes.[6] Critics have also pointed to the apparent excesses of much of the writing – for example the lengthy descriptions of the temples of Mars and Venus, and the apparently absurd account of Arcite's funeral, where Chaucer spends fifty lines telling us in great detail exactly what he is *not* going to tell us. In 1950 Charles Muscatine noted the length and apparent irrelevance of many of the descriptive passages (for example the sixty-one lines devoted to Emetreus and Lycurgus – two characters who do prac-tically nothing in the *Tale*), the non-dynamic quality of the speeches and the whole style of the poem, the wooden con-ventionality of much of 'the stage business' – (what he calls 'the swoons and cries, fallings on knees and sudden palenesses') and the general lack of characterization and failure of the plot to fasci-nate.[7] To explain how such a disaster of a poem ever came to figure in one of the greatest masterpieces of the English language, Muscatine supposes that the medieval reader must have looked at things differently from the modern reader: 'It seems reasonable to conclude', he writes, 'that the *Knight's Tale* is of a kind having a much closer affinity to the medieval tradition of conventional-ism than to realism.' He concludes that the real meaning must lie in the symmetrical structure of the poem, which he takes to be symbolic, and that 'order which characterizes the framework of the poem, is also the heart of its meaning'.[8] Within this structure, however, he also discerns a 'subsurface insistence on disorder'. This, according to Muscatine, is 'the poem's crowning complexity, its most compelling claim to maturity.' True nobility as expressed in the poem, Muscatine claims, lies in 'a per-ception of the order beyond chaos. When the earthly designs sud-denly crumble, true nobility is faith in the ultimate order of all things.' This view, supported by two other eminent commenta-tors, W.H. French and William Frost, became established in the early 1950s as a critical orthodoxy regarding the interpretation of the poem.[9]

However, to reach this view of the poem as a sort of hymn to law and order, these commentators have been forced to suspend all normal critical judgements. 'We can neither examine nor evaluate it', claims Muscatine, 'according to canons by which it patently was not written and could never satisfy.'[10] Nevertheless, only in this way can Theseus, the central figure, be regarded as 'an embodiment of earthly authority and an interpreter of the ways of Divine Providence'[11] and the poem itself be seen as a triumphant expression of Christian philosophy, told by a devout and deeply serious narrator: 'The lessons of the Tale,' writes Frost, 'if such they may be called, imply a pious and logical mind in the instructor, a deep acceptance of Christian faith and chivalric standards, and a heroic disposition to face the vicissitudes and disasters of a dangerous calling.'[12]

More recently still, however, even this claim to philosophical greatness has been called into question – particularly as embodied in the figure of Theseus. In 1959 Dale Underwood pointed out the problematic nature of many of Theseus's actions and the inadequacies of his philosophical outlook.[13] In 1962 R. Neuse noted that Theseus is made to appear in a very ambiguous light and that in his final oration he not only 'fails to see the crux of the human situation'[14] but also appears 'as spokesman and representative for a world-view which the entire narrative places in an ambiguous light'.[15] That same year, Elizabeth Salter also remarked on the philosophical shortcomings of Theseus's final speech and observed that, when examined closely, it is 'a withdrawal from rather than a solution of the problem'.[16] Even she, however, never doubts that Theseus's intention in his final speech is also Chaucer's intention and that the poet's ultimate aim in the poem is to achieve 'final and total reconciliation' – it is just that Chaucer allows darker, more realistic elements to intrude on the original narrative, and this has 'made his task of final and total reconciliation much more complex'. In fact, she concludes that Chaucer fails to achieve his objective in the poem because: 'the prescribed story is an inadequate vehicle for the emotions so powerfully expressed by the poetry.... Chaucer allows the poem to raise imaginative issues which are not resolved by the final philosophical summing-up.'[17]

It is this basic assumption, that *The Knight's Tale* must be an expression of Chaucer's own personal philosophy, that forces even the most perceptive of critics onto unsafe ground. Ian

Robinson, for example, notes the irony by which all Theseus's acts of 'pity' end in bloodshed and concludes that the *Tale* is 'Chaucer's criticism of the nature of the noble life'.[18] But he never for one moment doubts that the Knight who tells the *Tale* is an idealized character and that therefore he must ultimately represent Chaucer's own point of view. He is therefore forced to the conclusion that 'Chaucer, the most intelligent and sceptical man of his century, works in *The Knight's Tale* to a position of trust in the military aristocracy. . . . Chaucer knows all about the shortcomings of Theseus, but he *doesn't* want the philosophers to be kings.'[19] And yet such an interpretation is scarcely supported by the rest of Chaucer's writing. He was outspoken against wars in which the innocent suffered and looked back to the former age when:

> No trompes for the werres folk ne knewe,
> Ne toures heye and walles rounde or square.
> *The Former Age*, 23–4

[No trumpets for the wars were known, no towers high, nor ramparts round or square.]

Most significantly, as his own *Tale*, he chose to translate an uncompromising pacifist tract. Critics have, in the past, tended to minimize Chaucer's anti-war statements, dismissing them as either 'wholly conventional' or unoriginal.[20] But they overlook the political climate in which Chaucer was writing, which would have given tremendous impact to any statement on the subject that he made. The peace with France was, of course, one of the major political controversies of the day. The 'hawks' versus 'doves' confrontation in Richard II's Court was no less dramatic than it was in this century in President Johnson's or President Nixon's Senate during the Vietnam War. In the *Chronique de la Traison et Mort de Richard II*, for example, there is a vivid account of the Duke of Gloucester, in 1397, goading Richard and the Court party for their pacifist aspirations.[21] There was even a tradition on the Continent that Richard II was murdered precisely because of his peace policy towards France,[22] and it was certainly a direct cause of the Cheshire rebellion in 1393.[23] And yet in such an atmosphere Chaucer was bold enough to present *as his own personal statement* a pacifist tract – and a French one at that – opposing all wars:

Ther is ful many a man that cryeth 'werre! werre!' that woot ful litel what werre amounteth.... For sothly, whan that werre is ones bigonne, ther is ful many a child unborn of his moder, that shal sterve yong bycause of that ilke werre, or elles live in sorwe and dye in wrec-chednesse.... And for ther is gret peril in werre, therfore sholde a man flee and eschewe werre, in as muchel as a man may goodly. (*The Tale of Melibeus*, 2226–31, 2860.[24])

[... There is many a man that cries 'War! War!' who knows very little about what war involves.... For truly, when war is once begun, there is very many a child yet unborn of its mother who shall die young because of that war, or else live in sorrow and die in wretchedness.... And because there is great peril in war, therefore a man should fly from and avoid war as much as he possibly can.]

Melibeus is, however, more than just a pacifist tract – it is also a manual of philosophy and practical guidance for the medieval ruler. It is clear that Chaucer did *not* trust the militarists of his day and wished that kings *were* philosophers.

It seems to me that the main problem which *The Knight's Tale* poses for its critics lies in the character of the Knight who is telling it. As soon as one avoids the assumption that the Knight is an idealized Christian warrior who represents Chaucer's own personal philosophy, the whole poem begins to fit into place. Areas which formerly seemed illogical, banal or simply boring are suddenly invested with meaning and wit.

The Knight's Tale is, indeed, a courtly, philosophical romance, but it is told by an uncourtly, unphilosophical and totally un-romantic professional soldier who nevertheless pretends to the dignity of knighthood. Such pretensions were, indeed, character-istic of the mercenaries of Chaucer's day, as M. H. Keen has re-cently made clear: men such as John Hawkwood, he writes, 'were a scourge to the lands over which they campaigned' and yet 'still the tinsel glint of chivalry clung about their calling'.[25] Chaucer's Knight is a man who is obsessed by pomp and display but who has grown up in the vicious, brutal reality of the mercenary armies of the fourteenth century. He is a man who yearns after the courtly trappings of knighthood but who has, himself, no courtly background, no education and little understanding of the ethical basis of courtly behaviour or the values that underpin the chivalric code.

The clearest evidence for such a reading lies in a close compari-son of Chaucer's poem with the *Teseida* of Boccaccio from which he took the story. It is an extraordinary failing on the part of

English and American scholarship that there was no English translation of the *Teseida* until 1974.[26] With the publication of Bernadette Marie McCoy's translation, it is at last possible for all English-speaking readers to discover exactly what Chaucer did to Boccaccio's story. The result confirms, in the most startling way, the characterization of the Knight as a rough-shod mercenary and makes it quite plain that the *Tale* is a dramatic reflection of the narrator.

Boccaccio's *Teseida* is written in vernacular Italian, but it is undoubtedly an elegant courtly romance. Chaucer himself was perfectly able to write in the courtly love style – one has only to read the graceful courtly love debate between the three eagles in *The Parliament of Fowls* to find all 'the teccheles termes of talkyng noble'[27] one could want. Among his contemporaries Chaucer was renowned as a courtly love poet; they called him: 'God of Love in Albion' (Eustache Deschamps c. 1386) and 'Venus's disciple' (Gower c. 1390).[28] Yet in *The Knight's Tale* he has taken Boccaccio's story and systematically stripped it of all the underlying values of courtly love: generosity, sympathy, respect, humility and even love itself.

I am not suggesting that Chaucer intended *The Knight's Tale* as a mere parody of the *Teseida*, meaningful only to those who had read the original, but a comparison of the two poems makes Chaucer's intention clear by setting it in its immediate literary context. It is sometimes difficult for the modern reader to know what the medieval audience would have been expecting and thus to realize how Chaucer meets or fails to meet those expectations. Perhaps the greatest surprise for Chaucer's own contemporaries would have lain in his treatment of love in the poem.

Courtly love in *The Knight's Tale*

A most peculiar thing happens when the Knight enters (in his imagination) the Temple of Venus (*Knight's Tale*, 1918–66). In the *Teseida*, Boccaccio found a garden of delights, where Comeliness, Elegance, Affability and Courtesy wandered arm in arm; where gentle beasts played and youth disported itself (*Teseida*, 7, 50–5). The Knight discovers a world 'ful pitous to biholde' (*KT*, 1919). He sees only the broken sleeps, the sighs, the tears, the lamenting and the 'fiery strokes' of desire that Love's servants endure in this life (*KT*, 1920–3). He sees debauchery, expenses, magic spells, lying, flattery and even 'force' (*KT*, 1926–8). Instead of birds of every kind, sparrows and doves (*T*, 7, 52, 57) he sees only the cuckoo sitting on the hand of Jealousy, in itself a parody of the courtly hawking image (*KT*, 1930). On the walls of the temple, where Boccaccio saw depicted such stories of real love as that of Pyramus and Thisbe (*T*, 7, 62), the Knight sees only the self-love of Narcissus and the polygamy of Solomon (*KT*, 1941–2). Instead of Hercules' great love for Iole (*T*, 7, 62), he sees only his 'grete strengthe' – which in the context of Venus's temple seems to be a ludicrous reference to Hercules' sexual powers (he is supposed to have made all fifty of the King Thespius's daughters pregnant in one night!)[29] And instead of the true, though incestuous, love of Byblis and Caunus, he sees only the bought love of Medea, who secured Jason's attentions in return for allowing him the use of her *enchauntmentz* (*KT*, 1944), the treacherous voluptuousness of Circe and the proud vengeance of Turnus (*KT*, 1944–6). What a contrast all this is to Chaucer's own description of Venus's temple in *The Parliament of Fowls* (lines 183–294). There, in the true courtly love style, Venus's temple is seen as a beautiful garden abounding in birds and gentle animals, flowers and music, pleasure, youth and beauty, and where the walls are decorated with the histories of true lovers, such as Dido, Pyramus and Thisbe, Tristan and Isolde, Paris and Helen, Cleopatra, Troilus etc (*PF*, 288–92).

The Knight's account of Venus's temple is a travesty of the conventional courtly love imagery. It would not have been boring to a fourteenth-century audience – they would have found it outrageously amusing. Perhaps the thing which would have struck them most about this temple of Love is that Love itself is conspicuously absent. The *Teseida* and *The Parliament of Fowls* both offer a temple of Love presided over by Dame Peace (*T*, 7; *PF*, 240), but the Knight sees love in terms of conflict and bitter battle, and Venus herself as a tyrant:

> Thus may ye seen that wysdom ne richesse,
> Beautee ne sleighte, strengthe ne hardynesse,
> Ne may with Venus holde champartie,
> For as hir list the world than may she gye.
>> *The Knight's Tale*, 1947–50

[Thus may you see that neither wisdom nor riches, beauty nor cunning, strength nor bravery, may with Venus hold dispute, for as she will she guides the world.]

This is not the love-vision of a man who has grown up in the civilized elegance of the Court. It is the vision of a man for whom true affection between the sexes is unheard of and who is more familiar with scenes of rape and coercion (as he would have observed at the sacking of Alexandria and Satalye and so on) or whose chief contact with the other sex has been in the tavern and the dark alleys of the town.

For the Knight, Love is just another battle. His *Tale* is 'an essentially loveless love-story', as R. Neuse has pointed out.[30] Nowhere is this more clearly demonstrated than in his account of the relationship between the two protagonists, Palamon and Arcite.

In Boccaccio's story, the most important love is not that of Palamon for Emilia or of Arcite for Emilia, but the love which Palamon and Arcite have for each other. The whole story hinges on the fact that such is their love for each other and such is their true *courtesy* that they can become rivals for the same lady without falling out with each other. In fact, it is this tension between their mutual affection and their inescapable rivalry that provides the chief motor for the poem and the mainspring for its courtly chivalry.

In the *Teseida* it is Arcite who first sets eyes on the lovely Emilia. He calls Palamon over as an act of pure friendship: 'As he turned back in he said softly: "O Palaemon, come and see. Venus has truly come down here. Do you not hear her singing? O, if I mean anything to you, come here quickly. I believe for certain that it will please you to see the angelic beauty down there which has descended to us from the sovereign heights."'[31]

As they feel themselves falling in love, the two friends are careful not to make any claims or to offend each other. They express their feelings with elegance and lightness – sharing and adding to the same metaphor as they are the experience itself.

Meanwhile, they enjoyed themselves, breathless and attentive, keeping their eyes and ears fixed on her, and marveling much over her and over the time they had lost in their grieving, time which had passed before they saw her. Arcites said: 'O Palaemon, do you see what I behold in those beautiful immortal eyes?'

'What?' answered Palaemon. Arcites said: 'I see in them the one who wounded the father of Phaeton because of Daphne, if I am not mistaken. In his hands he holds two golden arrows, and now he is placing one on his bowstring as he looks at no one else but me. I do not know if it displeases him that I should look at what gives me so much pleasure.'

'Indeed,' answered Palaemon then, 'I do see him. But I do not know if he has shot one arrow, for he does not have more than one in his hand now.' Arcites said: 'Yes, he has wounded me in such a way that pain will pierce my heart if I am not helped by that goddess.' Then Palaemon, utterly astonished, cried out, 'Alas, the other has wounded me.'[32]

And from this moment on, the two friends never lose their concern for each other: 'So the two new lovers talked in this fashion and each spoke words of comfort to the other.'

In the Knight's version, by way of contrast, Palamon and Arcite are totally preoccupied each with himself. From the moment they set eyes on Emily they start fighting like two dogs over a bone (*KT*, 1177). Palamon drops to his knees and, oblivious of his friend, offers up a prayer to Venus. Arcite sets eyes on Emily, and he too declares his passion. Whereupon Palamon turns on him angrily ('dispitously') and demands: 'Weither seistow this in ernest or in pley?' (*KT*, 1125). Within a few lines they are calling each other 'traitor' and 'false' (*KT*, 1130, 1153) and embroiled in a ludicrously futile argument as to which of them loved her first. It is only seconds since Palamon first set eyes on the girl, and yet he is already accusing Arcite of betraying him by plotting to love the lady whom he 'loves and serves'. It is interesting to note that even the imagery is taken from military life:

> Thus artow of my counseil, out of doute,
> And now thow woldest falsly been aboute
> To love my lady, whom I love and serve,
> *The Knight's Tale*, 1141–3

[Thus you know my plans, without doubt, and now you're falsely setting out to love my lady whom I love and serve.]

With equal banality, Arcite replies:

> ... thou art fals, I telle thee outrely,
> For paramour I loved hire first er thow.
> *The Knight's Tale*, 1154–5

He goes on to claim that Palamon did not even know whether Emily was a real woman or a goddess; his was just a religious emotion while Arcite's was the love of man for woman:

> Thyn is affeccioun of hoolynesse,
> And myn is love, as to a creature;

Such abusive squabbling is not only ridiculous: it is a travesty of the true courtly love debate. Contrast, for example, the love debate between the three tercel eagles in *The Parliament of Fowls* (416–83). These noble creatures would never dream of abusing their rivals – on the contrary, the more noble the bird, the more humble his manner, and throughout the whole debate they are careful to defer to the wishes of the lady. In the Knight's world-view, Venus is the sower of discord not harmony.

The same bitter enmity is revived when Palamon and Arcite meet later, after Arcite has been released and after Palamon has escaped. Whereas Boccaccio has them meet in the wood and make merry together, calling each other 'sweet, dear friend' (*T*, 5, 39) the Knight plunges them immediately into a slanging match (*KT*, 1586). They insult each other gratuitously, calling each other 'fool', 'madman', traitor' etc (*KT*, 1585–6, 1600, 1606) and blackening each other's characters with the kind of 'vileynye-saying' that was so notorious in the ranks of the modern mercenary armies.[33] Even their language descends to the level of the tavern:

> ... 'Arcite, false traytour wikke,
> Now artow hent, that lovest my lady so, ...
> And hast byjaped heere duc Theseus,
> And falsly chaunged hast thy name thus!
>   *The Knight's Tale*, 1580–6 .

['Arcite, false, wicked traitor, now you are caught, you who love my lady so. ... And have tricked Duke Theseus like this, and have deceitfully changed your name thus!]

Compare the first words which Boccaccio gives to Palamon, when he arrives in the grove to find Arcite asleep: 'O beautiful and most praiseworthy friend, if you should awaken now ...' (*T*, 5, 36).

In the *Teseida*, Palamon has to *beg* Arcite to fight with him as a favour, and Arcite consents only with a heavy heart. And when they do fight, it is with 'nobility, courage and great skill' (*T*, 575). In *The Knight's Tale* they fight like wild beasts (*KT*, 1655–60) and end up to the ankle in their own blood. In the *Teseida* Palamon is unhorsed by the first blow, and Arcite, believing him to be dead, starts to grieve over his friend (*T*, 5, 70–1).

The Knight significantly omits this incident. Similarly he omits the fine words which the two knights deliver to each other before they fight (*T*, 5, 61–4). In *The Knight's Tale* they specifically dispense with the usual chivalrous preliminaries: 'Ther nas no good day, ne no saluying' (*KT*, 1649).

Never is their lack of chivalry towards each other more obvious, however, than when Theseus eventually interrupts them and demands to know why they are fighting. In Boccaccio's version Arcite refuses to betray his friend's identity unless Palamon wishes to reveal it himself, which he does. In the Knight's version they display no concept of loyalty to each other whatsoever. Palamon's main concern is to ensure that Arcite does not escape punishment. He points to Arcite and not only reveals his identity to Theseus but paints as black a picture as he can of his supposed friend's conduct. The total effect is ludicrous and the language uncourtly:

> This is thy mortal foo, this is Arcite,
> That fro thy lond is banysshed on his heed,
> For which he hath deserved to be deed.
> For this is he that cam unto thy gate
> And seyde that he highte Philostrate.
> Thus hath he japed thee ful many a yer,
> And thou hast maked hym thy chief squier;
> And this is he that loveth Emelye.
> *The Knight's Tale*, 1724–31

[This is thy mortal foe, this is Arcite, who was banished from your land, on pain of losing his head, for which he deserves to be dead. For this is he that came unto your gate and said that he was called Philostrate. Thus he's made a fool of you for many a year and you have gone and made him your chief squire! And this is he that loves Emily.]

It hardly needs to be said that such conduct breaks every rule in the book of chivalry.

The mutual animosity of Palamon and Arcite, however, finds its ultimate expression in the great tournament (*KT*, 2599–635). In the *Teseida*, Teseo explicitly states that the tournament must be fought in a spirit of love – not hate: '... love is the reason for this contest ... therefore this contest ought to be a matter of love, if I judge aright, not hate. Let hatred be the business of anyone who works to do evil, or of anyone who does not have good sense for other things.... Let it not exist among us who, although we take our origins from this place or that, are yet born of the same blood.'[34] Throughout the tournament, Boccaccio emphasizes the skill, courage and beauty of the contestants. The Knight reduces it to a blood-bath. He records the hewing through of helmets, the bursting out of blood, the breaking of the bones, the stumbling of the steeds and the trampling under foot of riders. The contestants are fierce as tigers, cruel as hunters or dangerous as lions mad with hunger (*KT*, 2599–635) but he makes no mention of their courage, skill or generosity to opponents. Yet these were, the qualities for which tournaments were fought (see the courtly descriptions of tournaments in Froissart, or romances such as *Sir Degaré* and *Sir Launfal*).[35]

The tournament ends in both the *Teseida* and *The Knight's Tale* with Arcite suffering a fatal fall from his horse as he is going to claim Emily's hand. But here, as usual, the similarity ends. In the *Teseida* Arcite's misfortune provides a final opportunity to demonstrate the depth of the love between Palamon and Arcite. Palamon is desolate at his friend's accident (*T*, 9, 21) and orders all his men to accompany Arcite in his triumphal procession in order to give Arcite as much pleasure as possible (*T*, 9, 34). Arcite, for his part, orders that the 'prisoners' should be excused from wearing chains (*T*, 9, 47). On his deathbed Arcite bequeaths all his possessions to his friend (*T*, 10, 21) and then, in a final gesture of self-sacrifice, implores Palamon to take his beloved Emily to wife, on the grounds that he, Arcite, will draw comfort from the knowledge that Palamon is worthy of her and will be able to look after her (*T*, 10, 38–47). Palamon's resistance to the idea is such that Arcite is forced to make him swear to marry her as a dying wish. The way in which the Knight's Arcite recommends Palamon to Emily is, by comparison, lukewarm. Far from *commanding* the two to get married, he leaves it entirely up to her, adding rather half-heartedly that if she ever *does* think of getting married not to forget Palamon (*KT*, 2796–7). Similarly, the Knight's Palamon pays no final tribute to his relationship with Arcite such as the elegy which Palamon delivers in the *Teseida*: 'And as the gods who know the hearts of men can testify without fail, there was never such fervent love between two men, whether for blood relationship or familiarity, than that which I bore, little enough, for Arcites, since the time that I was born in this sad life.'[36]

In Boccaccio's poem, the love between Palamon and Arcite is one of the pivots of the whole story. In *The Knight's Tale* it is non-existent, and instead of a courtly tale of chivalry between the two young knights, all we are left with is a barrack-room brawl dressed-up in the fine rags of pageantry.

Since we know that Chaucer was a past-master in the courtly love *genre*, it would be absurd to conclude that in *The Knight's Tale* he somehow failed to hit the right style – the gulf is too large. It is more reasonable to suppose that he is telling the tale in the *persona* of the Knight and that it is the Knight-narrator who misunderstands the nature of courtly chivalry. One of the ways in which this is most clearly manifested is in the attitudes to women in the *Tale*.

Courtesy to women or '*druerie*' was, of course, one of the cornerstones of Chivalry – as one of the many Courtesy Books of the period put it:

> Speak never unhonestly of womankind,
> Nor let it ever run in your mind;
> The book calls him a 'churl of cheer' [a peasant in manner]
> That speaks ill of women here,
> For we are all of women born.[37]

The practice of *druerie* was considered an art.[38] In *Sir Gawain and the Green Knight*, for example, much of the enjoyment of the story lies in Sir Gawain's mastery of *druerie* which enables him to refuse the pressing advances of the lady without once giving her offence.

Nor was this *amour courtois* an empty ideal of the story-books. It was a political reality that was publicly seen to be embodied in the Court marriages of the day, such as that of Edward III with Philippa of Hainault, the Black Prince with Joan of Kent, John of Gaunt with Blanche of Lancaster, and Richard II with Anne of Bohemia.[39] It was considered especially uncourtly to lump all women together as if they were all the same. As Christine de Pisan wrote and as Hoccleve translated:

> To slander women thus, what may it profit?
> Especially to gentlemen that should arm themselves
> And delight in the defence of women
> As the Order of Gentleness would have it....
> Albeit that men find one woman 'nice',
> Inconstant, ruleless or variable,
> Devious, or proud, filled with malice,
> Without faith or love or deceptive,

> Sly, crafty and false – in all wrongs culpable,
> Wicked or fierce or full of cruelty,
> It follows not that such all women be.[40]

Chaucer's Knight, however, frequently tosses off male chauvinist generalizations about women, which are often quite outrageously unchivalrous, as when he accuses all women of being born opportunists:

> (For wommen, as to speken in comune,
> Thei folwen alle the favour of Fortune)
> *The Knight's Tale*, 2681–2

[For women, to speak of them in general, all follow the favour of Fortune.]

For him, women 'all weep the same' (*KT*, 1770–1), and he clearly has no time for the sort of sentimental nonsense they indulge in:

> What helpeth it to tarien forth the day
> To tellen how she weep boothe eve and morwe?
> For in swich cas wommen have swich sorwe,
> Whan that hir housbondes ben from hem ago,
> That for the moore part they sorwen so....
> *The Knight's Tale*, 2820–4

[What good is it to waste away the day in telling how she wept both eve and morrow? For in these cases women have such sorrow, when their husbands are parted from them, that for the most part they sorrow so....]

This is not the elegant concern of the courtier. It is the dismissive pragmatism of the professional soldier, hardened to scenes of domestic tragedy, as when husbands are torn away from their families to be carried off to the wars.

It is scarcely surprising that this rough, practical fellow is at a loss when he comes to deal with more intimate feminine matters. When he describes Emily's rites in the Temple of Diana, his manner hovers between that of a Peeping Tom ('and yet it were a game to heeren al') and the male chauvinist ('But it is good a man been at his large', that is, a man has a right to be free):

> This Emelye, with herte debonaire,
> Hir body wessh with water of a welle.
> But hou she dide hir ryte I dar nat telle,
> But it be any thing in general;
> And yet it were a game to heeren al.

To hym that meneth wel it were no charge;
But it is good a man been at his large.
The Knight's Tale, 2282–8

[This Emily with a devoted heart, washed her body with water from the well. But how she did her rites I dare not tell, unless I talk of it in general; and yet it would be fun to hear it all. To him that means it well, it's no dishonesty; and it is good for a man to feel quite free.]

Perhaps no characters in the *Tale* are less courtly in their attitude to women than the two principal lovers, Palamon and Arcite. Arcite, for example, disguises himself as a humble servant in Theseus's Court, just so that he can see Emily, and then complains bitterly about his loss of social status (*KT*, 1550–62). In the world of courtly love, the noble lover gladly accepted hardships and humiliation in order to serve the lady he loved. In Boccaccio's poem, although Arcite bemoans his loss of station, as soon as he returns to Theseus's Court and can see Emily, he counts himself as the happiest man alive (*T*, 4, 52–4). At no time is either Boccaccio's Palamon or Boccaccio's Arcite so uncourtly as to suggest that it is Emily herself who is the cause of their misfortune. They rail against Fortune, Love and Cupid, but *never* against Emily herself (*T*, 4, 75–7).

In the *Teseida* the essence of the young men's love for Emily is that it is selfless (*T*, 4, 5). In *The Knight's Tale*, Palamon and Arcite's passion is totally self-centred. Not only does the one never consider the feelings of the other, they never even consider the feelings of Emily. When Palamon prays to Venus, he does not pray for Emily's love: 'But I wolde have fully possessioun of Emelye' (*KT*, 2242). Whereas Boccaccio's lovers yearn for her affection (*T*, 4, 7), Chaucer's treat her as little more than a prize of war.

The climax of this insensitivity towards the girl is reached with Arcite's death. In the *Teseida* this provides the opportunity for the ultimate display of gallantry and selfless devotion. Even at the moment of his own death, Boccaccio's Arcite tries to comfort Emily: 'Arcites said to her, "Beautiful friend, be comforted, and do not trouble your soul over my passing. Be pleased to take comfort for love of me, if ever you decide to do in the future what I am about to say. I have found a very fitting way to console you and with just cause."'[41] He then sets about persuading her to accept Palamon as a substitute for himself, because he believes

that it will make her happier. In doing this, he displays true
courtly *humblesce*, deprecating his own victory in the tournament and asserting that the gods had always meant Emily for
Palamon (*T*, 10, 61–2). He is noble, generous, humble and selfless
– all the things that Chaucer's Arcite is not. In fact Chaucer's
Arcite is ungallant enough to express regret for all that he has
suffered because of Emily:

> Allas, the wo! allas, the peynes stronge,
> That I for yow have suffred, and so longe!
> *The Knight's Tale*, 2771–2

[Alas, the woe! Alas the bitter pains that I have suffered for you, and
for so long!]

What is worse, he then proceeds to blame her – to her face
– for being the cause of his death:

> Allas, myn hertes queene! allas, my wyf!
> Myn hertes lady, endere of my lyf!
> *The Knight's Tale*, 2775–6

[Alas, my heart's queen! Alas, my wife! Lady of my heart, ender of
my life!]

He is so bound up in his own misery that he is totally blind to
the effect that his words must have on his lady – here she is, a
young girl, faced with a dying man, being told that she is the
cause of his death! Hardly words to bring her comfort.

The love of man and woman, in *The Knight's Tale*, is a self-
centred passion, light-years removed from the courtly ideal of
druerie. As a result it is not the bringer of peace and harmony
(as in the *Teseida*) but the herald of discord and strife. The Knight
sees love as a battlefield, and his description of Venus's temple
is an image of his own vision of love itself.

The absence of 'largess'

Though the Knight's ignorance of the true nature of courtly love
and his outrageously ungallant attitude to women are the most
obvious indications of his unchivalrous character, they are not
the only ones.

One of the prime chivalric ideals was what was called 'Largess'.[42] Gervase Mathew, in his study of chivalry in Chaucer's time, defines Largess as 'a prodigal generosity. It is primarily valued', he continues, 'because of the detachment from possession and the disregard for wealth that it implies....'[43] This 'detachment from possession and disregard for wealth' was considered vital to any man who held jurisdiction over his fellowmen, because those who sought wealth were considered incapable of forming correct judgements. Greed clouds a man's mind, since the greedy man can act only from his own desires. This is what Boethius taught[44] and what Chaucer himself translated in his *Tale of Melibeus*:[45]

And trust wel that a coveitous man ne kan noght deme ne thynke, but oonly to fulfille the ende of his coveitise; and certes, that ne may nevere been accompliced; for evere the moore habundaunce that he hath of richesse, the moore he desireth.

The Tale of Melibeus, 1130–1

[A covetous man can neither judge nor think but only to fulfil the end of his greed; and certainly that may never be accomplished, for ever the more abundance of wealth he has, the more he desires.]

The Knight, however, does not seem to possess this 'disregard for wealth' – on the contrary, he displays an almost obsessive fascination for material possessions. The predilection which he exhibits throughout his *Tale* for money, power, rich clothing and huge retinues, gives the lie to any suggestion that his own shabby personal appearance on the road to Canterbury is the result of his own disapproval of fine clothes.

The heroes of Boccaccio and Statius (whose *Thebaid* was another source of the story) are admired for their beauty, courage, skill in arms and generosity. The Knight admires his hero, Theseus, for his riches (*KT*, 864), his power (*KT*, 861–5), his huge retinue (*KT*, 874), his luxurious style of living (*KT*, 2523–9) and his extravagant entertaining (*KT*, 1881–2088). In the Knight's eyes, the great tournament is remarkable mainly for its extravagance and for the glitter and splendour of the contestants. This is why he spends those sixty-one lines describing Emetreus and Lycurgus in such detail, even though their roles are so limited. When he describes the temples of Venus, Mars and Diana, which Theseus has built, he seems to be preoccupied with how much it all cost:

> For in the lond ther was no crafty man
> That geometrie or ars-metrike kan,
> Ne portreyour, ne kervere of ymages,
> That Theseus ne yaf him mete and wages,
>   The theatre for to maken and devyse.
>   *The Knight's Tale*, 1897–1901

[For in the land there was no craftsman who knew about geometry and arithmetic, nor portraitist, nor carver of images, to whom Theseus did not give food and wages, to make and to devise the theatre.]

> Of Mars, he maked hath right swich another,
>   That coste largely of gold a fother.
>   *The Knight's Tale*, 1907–8

[To Mars he made another in that style that cost in gold a generous load.]

> Wel koulde he peynten lifly that it wroghte;
> With many a floryn he the hewes boghte.
> Now been thise lystes maad, and Theseus,
> That at his grete cost arrayed thus
> The temples and the theatre every deel,
> Whan it was doon, hym lyked wonder weel.
>   *The Knight's Tale*, 2087–92

[Well could the man who made it paint and lifelikely too; with many a florin he the colours bought. Now have these lists been made, and Theseus, who at his own great cost thus arranged the temples and the theatres, when it was done, liked it wondrous well.]

And when the women mourn Arcite's death, gold takes on, in the Knight's mind, an almost magical power over life and death:

> 'Why woldestow be deed', thise wommen crye,
> 'And haddest gold ynough, and Emelye?'
>   *The Knight's Tale*, 2835–6

['Why would you be dead,' the women cry, 'when you had gold enough, and Emily?']

– as if the Knight imagines that with gold enough you could buy off death itself.[46]

This preoccupation with worldly wealth and display reaches its climax in the Knight's description of Arcite's funeral. He describes the funeral pyre with a lavish love of detail: its height, exactly how it was constructed, the huge variety of trees that were cut down for it, the consequent dismay and flight of the woodland spirits from the decimated forests, the spices and costly scents that are put on the pyre, the elaborate coffin decked out with gold and furs, and the precious jewels and the spears and shields and vestments that are all thrown onto the fire that burned 'as if it were mad' (*KT*, 2919–50). Even Arcite's body is clad in cloth of gold, and white gloves are put on his hands (*KT*, 2874). The modern reader might be forgiven for thinking it is all a disgraceful waste and that it is not the fire that is mad but the people who throw all this finery upon it. Nor would the modern reader be alone in thinking this. There were a considerable number of people in Chaucer's own day who would have agreed. In fact the lavish expense and pomp of fashionable church funerals met with fierce opposition from a very influential body of opinion, including some of Chaucer's closest friends. Sir Lewis Clifford, for example, who brought Chaucer the ballad addressed to him by the French poet Eustache Deschamps in 1386 and who may have been godfather to one of Chaucer's sons, prescribed for himself in his Will a most austere form of burial, very different from that which the Knight so relishes:

...I pray and charge my Survivors and executors, as they shall answer before God, and as all my whole trust in this matter is in them; that on my stinking carrion be laid neither cloth of gold, nor of silk, but a black cloth, and a taper at my head and another at my feet; nor stone, nor any other thing, whereby any man may know where my stinking carrion lies. And to that Church [i.e. where he is buried] my executors should do all the things which ought by right to be done in such circumstances without any more cost – save to poor men [i.e. except for alms to poor men]....[47]

Two other members of Chaucer's circle, Sir John Cheyne and Sir Thomas Latimer (for whom Clifford acted as an executor), left almost identical Wills. Latimer requested, 'that there be no manner of cost incurred for my burial, neither in meat nor in drink, nor in any other thing unless it be given to anyone that needs it, according to the law of God, except for two tapers of wax, and as soon as I am dead "thud me in the erthe".'[48]

The whole spirit of these Wills, as K.B. McFarlane pointed out, is in key with the writing of yet another of Chaucer's intimate friends, Sir John Clanvowe,[49] and although we do not possess Clanvowe's own Will, we do have evidence that the same austere tradition remained in his family, since his daughter-in-law, Lady Peryne Clanbowe, in 1422 requested: 'poorly to be buried without great expense being spent thereon'.[50] Other Wills in English have survived containing the same strict injunctions against funeral pomp – referring to the body as 'stinking carrion' and requesting 'cheap russet cloth', only 'two tapers' and that the money which would have been lavished on the funeral should be given instead to the poor.[51] This last was no mere empty utterance of piety – it was in itself a bitter condemnation of the contemporary fashion for burying the wealthy in their finery. Such a practice was seen as robbing the poor, for instance by Thomas of Wimbledon in a sermon in 1388: 'Whoever tries to keep a difference between poor and rich, should wait until they have lain a little while in the grave, and then open it up and look amongst the dead bones: who was rich and who was poor? Unless it is that more clothes rot with the rich man than with the poor, and that harms those that are still alive and profits not the dead.'[52]

Since so many of Chaucer's closest associates joined in the opposition to extravagant Christian funerals, it would not be unreasonable to expect that Chaucer himself would have been sceptical in his treatment of the lavish pagan rites in *The Knight's Tale*. He was clearly dealing with a highly topical subject of controversy and of immediate public concern, and, when viewed in the context of the contemporary criticism of such lavish spectacles, the Knight's preoccupation with the elaborate details of Arcite's funeral begins to take on more than a tinge of irony.

The whole passage is given a ludicrous ring by the way in which the Knight constantly insists that he is not going to tell us about it and then proceeds to do exactly that – plunging into ever more elaborate detail:

But how the fire was made up high, nor also the names that the trees were called.... Nor how they were felled, shall not be told by me. Nor how gods ran up and down.... Nor how the beasts ... fled.... Nor how the ground was aghast of the light nor how the fire was first made-up with straw and then with dry sticks ... and then with green wood ... and then with cloth of gold ... and garlands.... Nor how Arcite lay ... nor what riches.... Nor how Emily.... Nor how she swooned.... Nor what she said.... Nor what jewels.... Nor how some threw their shields.... Nor how the Greeks.... Nor how ... Nor how ... Nor how ... Nor how the Greeks play the wake-plays, I shall not bother to say; Nor who bore himself the best... I also will not tell how they went home.

Finally he concludes:

> But shortly to the point than will I wend,
> And make of my long tale an end.[53]

Now of course some critics have seen this as a fine example of the stylistic device known as *occupatio*, used as 'a part of the general sense of *amplificatio*',[54] which no doubt it is, but the fact still remains that, as William Frost hinted, the whole passage adds up to a piece of high comedy.[55]

A comparison of this passage and the equivalent section in the *Teseida* makes it clear that Chaucer is making fun of the pomposity of the Knight-narrator. In the *Teseida* the list of trees that are cut down for the funeral pyre forms an elaborate conceit: each tree is recorded for its military use – as lances, ships, shields, symbols of victory (*T*, 11, 22–4).[56] In the Knight's description it becomes a mere catalogue 'with no more ceremony of adjective than it is customary now to give names in a telephone directory'.[57] Boccaccio himself hints at the absurdity of such extravagant pagan customs when he notes the sadness of the woodlands and the nymphs who know that the area will never be reforested (*T*, 11, 25) and when he compares the building of such a huge pyre to 'the foolish race' of giants in Thessaly who placed five mountains one on top of the other in order to seize the heavens (*T*, 11, 26). The Knight has no such doubts. For him the list of trees adds to the spectacle, and the distress of the woodland gods 'disinherited of their habitation' is merely another indication of Theseus's power (*KT*, 2925–32). The elaborate trappings placed on the pyre are seen merely as instances of magnificence and pomp (*KT*, 2935–40), and the casting of jewels and weapons onto the flames appears to him as a culmination of worldly honour (*KT*, 2947–50). The conspicuous waste of the whole charade which would have been condemned by Chaucer's own friends, entirely escapes him, so thoroughly material are his values. In content, style and relevance to a topical controversy of the day, this whole passage is a piece of biting social satire.

The Knight's preoccupation with wealth and money is, as I have already indicated, the antithesis of 'largess' – that special generosity which was so crucial to true knighthood.[58] Yet although Chaucer uses the words 'largess' and 'bounty' with comparative frequency,[59] he never once uses either in connection with the Knight. The Prioress, the Poor Parson, the Monk, the

Wife of Bath, the Doctor of Physic, the Clerk of Oxford, the
Merchant, the Shipman and Chaucer himself, all use these words
or have them used about them, but the Knight – this supposed
epitome of chivalry – never mentions either – not once in a tale
of nearly three thousand lines. Such an omission simply could
not be accidental.

In the *Teseida* largess is continually emphasized. Palamon and
Arcite, for instance, are prodigious in the largess which they distribute in the months leading up to the tournament (*T*, 6, 7–9).
In *The Knight's Tale* this is never mentioned. In the *Teseida*
Theseus (Teseo) is careful to distribute largess after his successful assault on Thebes: '. . . he had his men bring him whatever they
had won, and freely and generously divided their shares amongst
his knights. . . .'⁶⁰ The Knight makes no mention of this. He
stresses, instead, that Theseus refused to allow any ransom for
Palamon and Arcite – which was in itself an act contrary to the
spirit of largess – unless accompanied by some sort of compensation to those of his men who had caught them.⁶¹

Even on the two occasions when Theseus does distribute gifts,
we are never allowed to feel that it is an expression of largess.
In the first instance (*KT*, 2190–2208) the gift-giving is all part and
parcel of Theseus's ability to do things properly – it is all part
of the Knight's concern with 'degree' and form and with
Theseus's desire to display his wealth:

> He festeth hem, and dooth so greet labour
> To esen hem and doon hem al honour,
> That yet men wenen that no mannes wit
> Of noon estaat ne koude amenden it.
> *The Knight's Tale*, 2193–6

[He feasted them and did such great labour to put them at ease and
do them all honour that men still think that no man's wit of any rank
could have improved it.]

In the second instance (*KT*, 2731–40) the gift-giving is clearly a
political expedient to pacify fractious knights who felt cheated
by Theseus's extraordinary judgement at the tournament (see
below, p. 183). Despite the most flagrant breaches of all the rules
of tournament, Theseus awards the prize to Arcite, and then,
when the inevitable arguments develop, he declares a feast and
distributes gifts, 'To stynten alle rancour and envye' (*KT*, 2732).
When he has nothing to gain by bestowing gifts, he does not

bother to do so. Thus, when he releases Arcite from prison, he does not give him any gifts, as Boccaccio's Teseo does – an important act of generosity since, as Boccaccio points out, Arcite would otherwise be destitute (*T*, 3, 56). Even when Theseus takes Arcite into his service, disguised as Philostrate, he gives him only enough to 'mayntene his degree' – i.e. to dress and equip himself – and Arcite has to rely on secret remuneration from Athens for his 'rente' – i.e. his subsistence (*KT*, 1439–43).

Largess was the very foundation-stone of the old feudal system, and it always remained a political necessity, since it was the way in which a lord provided for his retainers and bound their loyalty to him.[62] In the days before fixed wages became *de rigueur*, the lord was honour-bound to reward his faithful followers freely and generously. Such arbitrary payment was, however, anathema to the fully-fledged professionals of the fourteenth century, who sought hard cash and, where they could, often demanded it in advance. The expansive, gentlemanly days of largess, when remuneration was a matter of discretion, had vanished, to be replaced by hard-headed cut-throat competition. Among the mercenaries of Chaucer's day it was every man for himself, as Arcite remarks to Palamon, with remarkably frank uncourtliness:

> . . . at the kynges court, my brother,
> Ech man for hymself, ther is noon oother.
> *The Knight's Tale*, 1181–2

[. . . at the king's court, my brother, each man for himself – there is none other.]

This is the world into which the Knight fits. He is a fiercely competitive animal in everything he does. He automatically sees the courtly pastimes of dancing, singing and talking of love in a spirit of competition (*KT*, 2201–3). And he makes no bones about the fact that he is in the business of telling tales to win the prize that Harry Bailey has proposed. Indeed he is the only one of the pilgrims to be so indelicate:

> I wol nat letten eek noon of this route;
> Lat every felawe telle his tale aboute,
> And lat se now who shal the soper wynne;
> *The Knight's Tale*, 889–91

[Besides I will not hinder any of this crew; let every fellow tell his tale in turn and let's see now who shall the supper win!]

Such a sense of competition may have been second nature to the self-made men of the Free Companies, but, outside the lists, it had no place among courtly ideals.

The Knight's false modesty

With this in mind, one should perhaps take the Knight's protestations of modesty with a pinch of salt. Indeed, one might ask: is he truly modest at all? Does he really display that chivalrous quality of *'humblesce'*? Close examination of his character as it is revealed in his *Tale* makes it quite clear that he is, as Chaucer himself told us in the *Prologue*, meek only 'of port' – i.e. in his manner – and that this overt meekness is often no more than a cloak for simple, straightforward bragging.

For instance, when he confesses with apparent self-effacement: 'wayke been the oxen in my plough' ('weak are the oxen in my plough', *KT*, 887), he is in fact doing no more than impressing on the other pilgrims (whom he clearly regards as rivals) that he is going to tell an extremely long and imposing story – perhaps one might even go so far as to say that he regards the story-telling as a battle and is indulging in the time-honoured custom of all warrior-knights of vaunting their own prowess before going into action.

This tendency towards self-advertisement is expressed chiefly in the Knight's extensive use of a stylistic device which we have already touched on: *occupatio* – 'describing something while apparently refusing to describe it'.[63] Critics generally assume that this device must have been regarded as 'having some elevation',[64] and this is no doubt true when the device was used in moderation, as in the *Teseida*, but in *The Knight's Tale* its use is so extensive and, at times, so *extended*, that it ceases to be merely a literary flourish and starts to become a significant expression of the Knight's character. In the description of Arcite's funeral it pointed up the Knight's absurd pomposity (see above, p. 160), but by and large he appears to use the device as a means to impress his audience with what a splendid story-teller he is. He is forever reminding us how concise he is being:

> But shortly for to speken of this thyng ...
> But shortly for to telle is myn entente ...
> As shortly as I kan, I wol me haste ...

> But shortly to the point thanne wol I wende,
> And maken of my longe tale an ende.[65]

[But to speak briefly about this matter ... But my intention is to speak briefly ... as briefly as I know, I will make haste ... but I will come quickly to the point, and make an end of my long tale....]

He is always pointing out how he is selecting only the most important things:

> Of al this make I now no mencioun,
> But al th'effect, that thynketh me the beste.
> *The Knight's Tale*, 2206–7

[I do not mention all this now, but only what matters, that seems to me the best]

or else warning us that he is coming to the important part: 'Now cometh the point, and herkeneth if yow leste' ('Now comes the point – if you will be pleased to listen').

All this is said without the slightest hint of modesty – on the contrary, the tone is sometimes almost peremptory: 'This is th'effect; ther is namoore to seye. (*KT*, 2366) ('This is the essence, there is no more to say') and authoritarian:

> Why sholde I noght as wel eek telle yow al ...
> Now demeth as yow liste, ye that kan,
> For I wol telle forth as I bigan.
> *The Knight's Tale*, 1967, 1353–4

[Why should I not also tell you all as well ... Now judge as you wish, you that know, for I will tell on in the same way as I began....]

Constantly he draws our attention to the fact that he is not omitting all this detail because he cannot remember it but merely because it does not suit him or he has not the time:

> Greet was the strif and long bitwix hem tweye,
> If that I hadde leyser for to seye....
> But of that storie list me nat to write....
> Suffiseth heere ensamples oon or two,
> And though I koude rekene a thousand mo....
> Ther saugh I many another wonder storie,
> The which me list nat drawen to memorie....
> *The Knight's Tale*, 1187–8, 1201, 1953–4, 2073–4

[Great was the strife and long between those two, as I could describe if only I had the leisure.... But I don't want to write about that story.... Let one or two examples here suffice, although I could add a thousand more.... There saw I many another wondrous history, which I do not feel like calling to mind....]

This last example captures the tone of the worldly-wise traveller teasing his home-spun audience with glimpses of the wonders he has seen. He even forgets for the moment that he is telling a tale of olden time and relapses into the first person singular: 'Ther saugh I...' (*KT*, 1995), '...yet saugh I ther' (*KT*, 2005), 'Yet saugh I ...' (*KT*, 2011) etc. Perhaps it is not too far-fetched to imagine the simpler pilgrims listening open-mouthed, and the Knight, encouraged, reiterating that he has seen all these things with his own eyes – but then suddenly he cuts short his description (*KT*, 2073-4) as if it were all really a bit of a bore to someone like himself who has seen it all.

When he reaches the finale of his story, he makes no bones about reminding us that this is the 'great climax':

> Now wol I stynten ...
> And telle yow as pleynly as I kan
> The grete effect, for which that I bygan.
> *The Knight's Tale*, 2479–82

[And tell you as fully as I can the great climax for the sake of which I began.]

This is not true courtly modesty, and would have jarred on the ear of the medieval listener used to the conventional self-deprecation of most story-tellers. Compare the Knight's tone, for example, with John Gower's stylized modesty in his *Confessio Amantis*:

> But since my wits are too small
> To tell a tale to suite everyone,
> I send this book unto my lord,
> With whom my heart is in accord,
> To be amended as he shall command it[66]

or the poet's subjection to correction at the start of *Mum and the Sothsegger*:

> And if you find untruths, or foolishness amongst it,
> Or any feigned fantasy in which there is no fruit,
> Let your advice correct it, all you clerks together,
> And amend what is amiss, and make it better.[67]

The Knight's story-telling manner is certainly a contrast to Chaucer's own habitual self-effacement:

> And though I nat the same wordes seye
> As ye han herd, yet to yow alle I preye
> Blameth me nat....
>
> *Sir Thopas*, 959–61

[And though I do not use the same words that you have heard before, yet I beg you all, do not blame me....]

> O moral Gower, this book I directe
> To the and to the, philosophical Strode,
> To vouchen sauf, ther nede is, to correcte....
>
> *Troilus and Criseyde*, v, 1856–8

[O moral Gower, I direct this book to you, and to you, philosophical Strode, to be good enough to correct it where there is need.]

Contrast especially the true courtly 'humblesce' that Chaucer displays in his Prologue to *The Legend of Good Women*:

> Allas, that I ne had Englyssh, ryme or prose,
> Suffisant this flour to preyse aryght!
> But helpeth, ye that han konnyng and myght,
> Ye lovers that kan make of sentement;
> In this cas oghte ye be diligent
> To forthren me somwhat in my labour,
> Whethir ye ben with the leef or with the flour.
> For wel I wot that ye han her-biforn
> Of makyng ropen, and lad awey the corn,
> And I come after, glenyng here and there,
> And am ful glad yf I may fynde an ere
> Of any goodly word that ye han left.
> And thogh it happen me rehercen eft
> That ye han in your fresshe songes sayd,
> Forbereth me, and beth nat evele apayd,
> Syn that ye see I do yt in the honour
> Of love, and eke in service of the flour
> Whom that I serve as I have wit or myght.
>
> *The Legend of Good Women*, 66–83

[Alas, that I have not English, rhyme nor prose, sufficient to praise this flower aright! But help me, you that have knowledge and power, you lovers, that know how to make poems of feeling; in this case you ought to be diligent in furthering me somewhat in my labour, whether you side with the 'leaf' or with the 'flower'.]

For well I know that you have been here before and reaped the field of poetry, and taken away the corn and I come after, gleaning here and there, and am full glad if I can find an ear of any goodly word that you have left. And though it falls to me often to repeat what you have already said in your fresh songs, bear with me and be not displeased, since you see that I do it in honour of Love ... and also in service of the flower whom I serve as long as I have wit or strength.]

Above all, the Knight's pseudo-modesty contrasts unfavourably with the true courtly humility of his own son. From the moment when the Host calls upon the Squire to tell a tale of love (because he looks as if he knows more about that subject than anyone), the young Squire is 'humblesce' personified:

> 'Nay, sire', quod he, 'but I wol seye as I kan
> With hertly wyl ... a tale wol I telle.
> Have me excused if I speke amys:
> My wyl is good, and lo, my tale is this'.
> *The Squire's Tale*, 4–8

['Nay, sir', said he, 'but I will say as best I can with a hearty will ... a tale will I tell, excuse me if I speak anything amiss: my will is good, and lo! my tale is this.']

And so on through his *Tale.*... He regrets that he is not clever enough to describe a lady's beauty:

> But for to telle yow al hir beautee,
> It lyth nat in my tonge, n'yn my konnyng;
> I dar nat undertake so heigh a thyng.
> *The Squire's Tale*, 34–6

[But to be able to describe to you all her beauty, it lies not in the power of my tongue, nor in my knowledge: I dare not undertake so high a matter.]

He makes apologies for his lack of style:

> Al be it that I kan nat sowne his stile,
> Ne kan nat clymben over so heigh a style...
> *The Squire's Tale*, 105–6

[Albeit that I cannot imitate his style nor cannot clamber over so high a stile.]

He pleads his ignorance about dancing and flirting (which we know from the *General Prologue* to be his forte):

> Who koude telle yow the forme of daunces
> So unkouthe, and swiche fresshe contenaunces,

Swich subtil lookyng and dissymulynges
For drede of jalouse mennes aperceyvynges?
No man but Launcelot, and he is deed.
Therfore I passe of al this lustiheed;
   The Squire's Tale, 5, 283–8

[Who could tell you the form of dances so unknown, and such fresh countenances, such subtle looks and dissembling for dread of jealous men's perceiving? No man but Lancelot, and he is dead, therefore I pass over all this pleasure....]

When measured up against such examples of true courtly 'humblesce', the Knight's meekness can be seen for what it really is: a wafer-thin veneer which has little to do with chivalry or courtliness. This lack is also reflected in the Knight's language.

The Knight's uncourtly language

In his *Tale* the Knight sets out to narrate a dignified courtly romance. His opening words set a tone of stately rhetoric, leisurely and ceremonious:

Whilom, as olde stories tellen us,
Ther was a duc that highte Theseus;
   The Knight's Tale, 859–60

[Once, as old stories tell us, there was a duke named Theseus....]

And yet, within thirty lines, he has dropped into a colloquial idiom quite at odds with this, referring to his fellow-pilgrims as 'felawes' – a word which, in Chaucer's day, carried strong connotations of low-life and the tavern.[68] Even his imagery is of the farmyard: 'And wayke been the oxen in my plough' ('And weak are the oxen in my plough'). You do not find the Squire using such metaphors, nor the tercel eagles in *The House of Fame*, nor Chaucer in *The Book of the Duchess*. It *is*, however, the imagery of the drunken Miller to the Reeve:

I have a wyf, pardee, as wel as thow;
Yet nolde I, for the oxen in my plogh,
Take upon me moore than ynogh...
   The Miller's Prologue, 3158–60

[I have a wife, by god! as well as you! Yet I would not – for all the oxen in my plough – take upon myself more than enough....]

And the Nun's Priest reserves 'oxen of the plogh' as an image epitomizing lowliness (*The Nun's Priest's Tale*, 7, 2997).

Time and again the Knight's bluff, uncourtly manner breaks out in his language: 'What sholde I al day of his wo endite?' ('What! Should I write about his woe all day?'), he exclaims, when he comes to describe Arcite's sufferings. Or again when he is faced with the task of detailing the feelings of lovers, instead of summoning up elegant, ennobling imagery, his images are a washerwoman's – comparing the changing moods of lovers with 'a bucket in a well' or 'just like a Friday' – he sounds more like the Goose in *The House of Fame* than the royal eagles:

> Into a studie he fil sodeynly,
> As doon thise loveres in hir queynte geres,
> Now in the crope, now doun in the breres,
> Now up, now doun, as boket in a welle.
> Right as the Friday, soothly for to telle,
> Now it shyneth, now it reyneth faste,
> Right so kan geery Venus overcaste
> The hertes of hir folk; right as hir day
> Is gereful, right so chaungeth she array.
> Selde is the Friday al the wowke ylike.
> *The Knight's Tale*, 1530–9

[Into a study he fell suddenly, as do these lovers in their curious changes, now in the top, now in the briars, now up, now down, as a bucket in a well. Just like the Friday, truthfully to tell, now it shines, and now it rains hard, just so changeable Venus can overcast the hearts of her own folk, just as her day is changeable, so she changes her array. Seldom is Friday all the week alike.]

The same lapses are observable when Theseus declares that only one of the two lovers can have Emily and as for the other: 'He moot go pipen in an yvy leef' (*KT*, 1838), ('He must go and pipe into an ivy leaf' – 'to be left out in the cold'); or, when he holds up the two lovers to ridicule in front of Emily herself and all the ladies of the court:

> But this is yet the beste game of alle,
> That she for whom they han this jolitee
> Kan hem therfore as muche thank as me.
> She woot namoore of al this hoote fare,
> By God, than woot a cokkow or an hare!
> *The Knight's Tale*, 1806–10

[But this is yet the best joke of all: that she for whom they're having all this sport knows how to thank them for it no more than me. She knows no more of all this hot affair, by God! than does a cuckoo or a hare!]

These lapses in the Knight's language have already been noted by many critics and have always been regarded as somewhat of a puzzle. 'Even the diction and figurative speech in *The Knight's Tale*', writes Charles Muscatine, 'for all its noble characters, classical setting and elevated theme, is sprinkled with rural familiarity....'[69] William Frost observed the 'ingenuousness of the Knight as a commentator on his own story' and drew attention to several passages where a high style suddenly descends to the colloquial, while Elizabeth Salter remarked that 'in passing so swiftly from powerful expression to comment which is trivial, almost flippant, he [Chaucer] seems to be using two voices....'[70] Both Muscatine and Salter regard these lapses in style as lapses in Chaucer's own style. Muscatine put them down to 'something deep in the grain of his [Chaucer's] own discourse, that, at times, seems to transgress literary decorum itself', while Elizabeth Salter saw them as the result of the conflict between the tragic implications of the story – reinforced in Chaucer's treatment of it – and the 'limiting features of the set narrative structure'. A much simpler explanation, it seems to me, is that the lapses in style are lapses in the style of the Knight as a story-teller. He is trying to tell a courtly romance, but he is a brusque man-of-action, more used to the black and white situations of the battlefield than the sophisticated circumlocutions of the Court. He simply cannot achieve the courtly style to which he aspires.

And yet it is clear that he does aspire to courtliness. In fact, not to put too fine a point on it, the Knight is a bit of a social climber.

The Knight and social status

There can be little doubt what Chaucer himself thought about social status and high birth. Right at the beginning of *The Canterbury Tales* he wryly excuses himself from setting every one in 'their degree':

> Also I prey you to foryeve it me,
> Al have I nat set folk in hir degree

> Heere in this tale, as that they sholde stonde.
> My wit is short, ye may wel understonde.
> *General Prologue*, 743–6

[Also I pray you to forgive me though I have not put folk according to their rank here in this tale, as they ought to stand. My talents are limited, you well may understand.]

The dismissiveness of that last line leaves no doubt as to how seriously Chaucer took such matters. And as for 'nobility of birth', I have already outlined Chaucer's own probable attitude (see above, pp. 118–19). At all events, he closely echoed his favourite authors, Jean de Meung and Boethius, when he wrote his ballad on the subject:

> Vyce may wel be heir to old richesse;
> But ther may no man, as men may wel see,
> Bequethe his heir his vertuous noblesse...
> *Gentilesse*, 15–17

[Vice may well be the heir to old riches, but there is no man, as men can well see, who can bequeath to his heir his own nobility of character.]

In fact Chaucer would probably have agreed with the Wife of Bath that claims of nobility based upon inherited wealth were 'not worth a hen!'[71]

> But, for ye speken of swich gentillesse
> As is descended out of old richesse,
> That therfore sholden ye be gentil men,
> Swich arrogance is nat worth an hen.
> *The Wife of Bath's Tale*, 1109–12

Yet the Knight takes both rank and high birth very seriously indeed. He does not try to disguise the fact that the only reason that Palamon and Arcite are rescued from the heap of dead bodies after the battle, and carried 'softe unto the tent of Theseus' (*KT*, 1021), is because the pillagers recognized their coat-armours as 'best in special' and of royal blood (*KT*, 1016–19).

In the Knight's mind, high birth is the only thing that makes Palamon and Arcite worthy of Emily (*KT*, 1829), whereas in Boccaccio it is because they have proved already how ardently they love her – their compatibility of birth is only a secondary consideration (*T*, 5, 95–6). When the Knight marvels at the equality of the two sides drawn up for the grand tournament, it is not their 'prowess' that makes them equal as Boccaccio insists (*T*, 7, 19) but their 'worthiness', 'estaat' and 'age' (*KT*, 2592) (see commentary on lines 68–9). And when Arcite recommends Palamon to Emily, 'estaat and heigh kynrede' play an important part in his definition of knighthood (*KT*, 2790). As for the Knight's hero, Theseus, in practically everything he does, whether organizing a tournament, providing entertainment, arranging a funeral or making a marriage, he is besotted with the question of rank and degree (see *KT*, 2196, 2200, 2855–6, 2887–91). Even his apparent pity for the mourning women is triggered off by their high rank. The eldest lady asserts that they are all qualified by social standing to deserve pity:

> Som drope of pitee, thurgh thy gentillesse,
> Upon us wrecched wommen lat thou falle.
> For, certes, lord, ther is noon of us alle,
> That she ne hath been a duchesse or a queene.
> *The Knight's Tale*, 920–3

[Some drop of pity, through your nobility, let fall upon us wretched women, for certainly, lord, there is not one of us that has not been a duchess or a queen.]

As Ian Robinson points out: 'Why should that have seemed less snobbish to Chaucer than to us?'[72] There is certainly no glimmer of doubt in the Knight's mind that it is their high rank that principally moves Theseus to 'pity':

> Hym thoughte that his herte wolde breke,
> Whan he saugh hem so pitous and so maat,
> That whilom weren of so greet estaat;
> *The Knight's Tale*, 954–6

[It seemed to him his heart would break, when he saw them so pitiable and brought low who formerly had been of such high rank.]

Throughout his *Tale* the Knight consistently displays the automatic respect for rank that one would expect of an old professional soldier – it is the same respect for established law and order that John Hawkwood showed throughout his long career, regardless of right or wrong.[73] But the Knight goes even further – he is a true snob. He even regards the joys of spring as the preserve of the aristocracy – for him, spring pricks only 'every gentil herte' (*KT*, 1043), whereas for Chaucer, of course it was the great leveller.[74] Just as the Knight himself has sat 'full many a time' at the head of the tables of honour in Prussia, so he notes how correctly Theseus arranged 'who sat first or last upon the dais' (*KT*, 2200). The Knight displays exactly that same vanity which Chaucer satirizes in the Wife of Bath and the five guildsmen and their wives, and from which he consciously dissociates himself at the end of the *Prologue*.[75]

Yet, although the Knight is so preoccupied with social status and nobility of birth, he himself bears distinct signs of low birth. Chaucer's description of the Knight in the *Prologue* has significantly omitted any mention of the outward signs of a pedigree – such things as family, a coat-of-arms, a manorial seat or lands. This impression is corroborated in his *Tale*.

The Knight's lack of education

One of the most important marks of an aristocratic upbringing was education. It was also a crucial quality for the whole concept of chivalry.[76] As one manual put it: 'Knights should be learned, so that by learning they are fit to be judges. No office is more suitable to make judges than that of chivalry.'[77] And even if knights were not always expected to write or read themselves, a knowledge of books seems to have been generally admired.[78] Yet Chaucer's Knight displays no such learning. The Wife of Bath and even the Miller display more familiarity with books than our 'parfit gentil knyght'. The Wife of Bath, for example, refers to Dante, Valerius, Tullius, Seneca and Boethius, whilst the Miller mentions Cato, Ptolemy's astronomical treatise *The Almageeste*, St Benedict and the Bible.[79] Even Mine Host of the Tabard is able to quote Seneca![80] Yet the only time that the Knight attempts a literary reference he gets it ludicrously wrong, when he refers his listeners to Statius or 'Stace of Thebes' (*KT*, 2294) for a description of Emily's religious rites. Emily does not figure in the *Thebaid*, and Statius himself did not come from Thebes but from Naples. Among the literary *cognoscenti* there must have been a few muffled guffaws at the Knight's expense.[81]

For the most part, the Knight relies on proverbial wisdom which he sometimes tries to pass off as learning (cf. *KT*, 1521–2, 2447–9). Indeed, his hero, Theseus, whom he presents as the 'flower of chivalry' (*KT*, 982), proudly spurns book-learning alto-

gether and claims no authority for his pronouncements beyond
his own:

> Ther nedeth noght noon auctoritee t'allegge,
> For it is preeved by experience...
> *The Knight's Tale*, 3000–1

[It is unneccesary to cite any authority for it is proved by experience.]

Such contempt for the wisdom of books puts Theseus on a
level with the shallow, worldly Friar, who turns to the Wife of
Bath, after her *Tale*, and rebukes her for being so serious:

> Ye han seyd muche thyng right wel, I seye;
> But, dame, heere as we ryde by the weye,
> Us nedeth nat to speken but of game,
> And lete auctoritees, on Goddes name,
> To prechyng and to scole eek of clergye.
> *The Friar's Prologue*, 1273–7

The scorn for authorities which both Theseus and the Friar display would have been more shocking to medieval audiences than
it is to us, perhaps, because they were all too familiar with the
extensive use of authorities such as we find in *The Tale of
Melibeus*, *The Parson's Tale* and even, to our amusement, in the
mouth of Chanticleer the cock, in *The Nun's Priest's Tale*.[82] The
Friar, however, rejects ancient wisdom because he is interested
only in the present – in eating, drinking and womanizing. Theseus, on the other hand, rejects any authority other than his own
because, as we shall see, the essence of his character is that of
a tyrant.

The absence of 'pity'

Perhaps the most important quality of 'gentillesse' in Chaucer's
own view was the quality of pity.[83] And yet in the same way that
this quality is missing from the Knight's portrait in the *Prologue*,
so it is missing from *The Knight's Tale*. We have already noted
how Theseus's 'pity' for the weeping women is adulterated by
ulterior motives; in action too Theseus displays no pity whatsoever: Chaucer has, for example, omitted elements of pity which
are found in Boccaccio. The Knight's Theseus puts the folk to
flight and then destroys the city of Thebes without mercy, tearing

it down 'bothe wall and sparre and rafter' in a holocaust
reminiscent of the one in which the Knight himself had taken
part at Alexandria.[84]

> He ... putte the folk to flyght;
> And by assaut he wan the citee after,
> And rente adoun bothe wall and sparre and rafter;
> *The Knight's Tale*, 988–90

[He ... put the folk to flight, and by assault he won the city after,
and tore it down both wall and spar and rafter.]

Boccaccio, in contrast, specifically notes that Teseo did not
pursue those who fled; he entered Thebes unchallenged and was
so impressed by the beauty of the city that he wandered around
lost in admiration, and then gave orders that the temples were
to be spared (*T*, 2, 72–3). Similarly, Boccaccio's Teseo gives
Creon an honourable funeral (*T*, 2, 74) and has the wounded
of either side cared for: 'Theseus had the plain searched, and
every wounded man who was found was given medical aid, and
every corpse was buried. ...'[85] The Knight's Theseus has no time
for such niceties – he has the battlefield searched but only to pillage the equipment and gear of the dead and wounded, and then
he does as he likes with the countryside – and there would have
been little doubt what that would have meant to Chaucer's contemporaries (*KT*, 1004–6).

Unromantic elements in the *Tale*

Another important quality of chivalry was physical beauty.
When Walsingham described Edward III as an ideal of knighthood, for example, he was careful to stress the King's physical
appearance: 'He was elegant of body, as his height neither
exceeded that which was seemly nor yielded overmuch to short-
ness. He had a countenance like an angel, the more venerable
for its human mortality, in which shone forth such extraordinary
beauty that if anyone had openly looked upon his countenance
or dreamed of it by night, he would without doubt hope for de-
lightful solaces to befall him that day.'[86]

The same importance is given to the physical appearance of
the hero of almost any romance of the period. Sir Gawain, for

instance, is a knight of 'good looks, gracious manner and great courtesy'.[87] Yet this is another quality which neither Chaucer applies to the Knight, nor the Knight to any of the characters in his *Tale*: not Theseus, nor Arcite, nor Palamon, nor any of the famous kings attending the great tournament, is ever described as handsome or straight-backed or broad-shouldered or even tall. He sees them only in terms of their power and rank and wealth. Whereas Boccaccio portrays both Palamon and Arcite as so handsome that Emily scarcely knows which to choose (*T*, 2, 97), the Knight tells us nothing of their looks, and Emily – perhaps not surprisingly – wants neither of them (*KT*, 2304–21).

This lack of interest in physical beauty goes hand-in-hand with that total lack of feeling for romance which we have already noted. As H.R. Patch observed: romance is a quality which 'hardly predominates in *The Knight's Tale*'.[88] Patch goes on: 'In revising Boccaccio's story, it does not appear that Chaucer made any changes in the general direction of what we have described as romantic.' Indeed, as we have seen, Chaucer seems to have gone out of his way deliberately to reduce the romance of the original to a mundane level.

To the examples which I have already offered, I would add just one more, which seems to me to encapsulate an essential ingredient of the Knight's character. When Arcite goes into exile, Boccaccio records how his love-longing changes his appearance. The Knight also notes it but adds that the change in Arcite's appearance was not just like 'lover's malady' but was more like some sort of manic depression:

> And in his geere for al the world he ferde,
> Nat oonly lik the loveris maladye
> Of Hereos, but rather lyk manye,
> Engendred of humour malencolik,
> Biforen, in his celle fantastik.
> *The Knight's Tale*, 1372–6

[In his behaviour he was for all the world not only like one afflicted with the lover's malady of Eros, but more like a man with mania caused by some melancholic humour in his frontal brain cells where fantasy is located.]

The pedestrian accuracy of the medical diagnosis cuts across the traditional description of *amor hereos* with a touch of bathos.

Chaucer had no need to make such an addition unless he were deliberately creating a *persona* for the narrator-Knight of a down-to-earth pragmatist – a man who has no time for the nonsense of romantic love, even if his story demands it.

The unromantic eye of the Knight is also evident in all his descriptions of conflict. Whether it is the attack on Thebes, Palamon and Arcite's duel in the forest, or the grand tournament of the two hundred knights, he consistently fails to include the elements which made feats of arms chivalrous. He wallows in the ferocity of the combatants, the destruction and the violence, but never records heroism, skill or magnanimity. The supreme example of all this is the tournament which the Knight succeeds in stripping of every vestige of chivalry or romance.

The great tournament

When Boccaccio describes the tournament, he depicts the skill, bravery, grace, noble gestures and chivalrous sentiments of the contestants (*T*, 8, 1–131). Chaucer's Knight dwells at length on the mutual hatred and jealousy of the two principal combatants. The imagery of wild beasts (a recurrent theme in *The Knight's Tale*)[89] comes to the surface again, as the Knight compares Arcite with a tigress whose whelp has been stolen, and Palamon to a lion, mad with hunger:

> Ther nas no tygre in the vale of Galgopheye,
> Whan that hir whelp is stole whan it is lite,
> So crueel on the hunte as is Arcite
> For jelous herte upon this Palamon.
> Ne in Belmarye ther nys so fel leon,
> That hunted is, or for his hunger wood,
> Ne of his praye desireth so the blood,
> As Palamon to sleen his foo Arcite.
> *The Knight's Tale*, 2626–33

[There was no tiger in the vale of Gargaphia, whose whelp is stolen from her when it's small, so cruel to the hunter as Arcite for his heart's jealousy of Palamon. Nor in Morocco any lion so savage, that is hunted or is with hunger mad, or so desires the life-blood of its prey as Palamon to slay his foe Arcite.]

Such personal animosity in the lists was, in itself, directly contrary to the true spirit of chivalry. At their inauguration, knights were supposed to take an oath that they would 'only frequent tournaments to learn the exercises of war' and not to use them as an opportunity for personal revenge.[90] In the *Teseida*, Teseo expressly states that hatred should have no part especially in this particular tournament:

There is no quarrel here over the acquisition of a kingdom, or the seizure of a lost inheritance. There is no mortal hatred between them, no search, here, for revenge of an outrage committed. But love is the reason for this contest, as I have already said. Therefore, this contest ought to be a matter of love, if I judge aright, not hate. Let hatred be the business of anyone who works to do evil, or of anyone who does not have good sense for other things, or of the crude Centaurs of Thessaly, who never know how to be at rest. Let it not exist among us who, although we take our origin from this place or that, are yet born of the same blood.[91]

The fact that personal animosity did sometimes enter into such tournaments, so that they turned sour, was inevitable, but it is important to realize that when this happened it was considered a disgrace to chivalry. (See for example Henry Knighton's account of the tourney at Chalon in 1274.[92]) In any case, by Chaucer's day tournaments tended to be grand ornamental affairs rather than mere blood-baths.[93] The mêlée in which all the participants took to the field at once, like a miniature battle, had long since been replaced by elaborate jousts which generally featured single combat.

The Knight presents as the apex of chivalry-in-action a degrading spectacle of violence, void of any redeeming features:

> Ther shyveren shaftes upon sheeldes thikke;
> He feeleth thurgh the herte-spoon the prikke.
> Up spryngen speres twenty foot on highte;
> Out goon the swerdes as the silver brighte;
> The helmes they tohewen and toshrede;
> Out brest the blood with stierne stremes rede;
> With myghty maces the bones they tobreste.
> He thurgh the thikkeste of the throng gan threste;
> Ther stomblen steedes stronge, and doun gooth al;
> He rolleth under foot as dooth a bal;
> He foyneth on his feet with his tronchoun,
> And he hym hurtleth with his hors adoun;
> He thurgh the body is hurt and sithen take,
> Maugree his heed, and broght unto the stake;
> As forward was, right there he moste abyde.
>
> *The Knight's Tale*, 2605–19

[There spear-shafts were shivered upon the thick shields; one feels the blow through his heart's bone (breastbone). Up spring the spears, twenty feet in height; out come the swords, like silver bright; the helmets they hack to pieces and shred; out bursts the blood in violent red streams; with mighty maces the bones they break. One man through the thickest of the throng starts to thrust. There strong steeds stumble and down go all! Another man rolls under foot like a ball; that one strives on foot with his spear-shaft, and another one hurtles down with his horse; he through his body is hurt and then taken despite his efforts, and brought to the stake: as was agreed, and there he must stay.]

All this is on the level of mere physical violence and should be contrasted with the true spirit of the tournament as caught in the pages of Froissart, where the violence serves only to highlight the bravery and skill of the participants.[94]

Malcolm Andrew has made the fascinating observation that the alliteration adopted for this description would have had a slightly ironic, mocking effect 'in the work of a southern cosmopolitan poet'[95] – he reminds us of the Parson's comment:

> ... I am a Southren man,
> I kan nat geeste 'rum, ram, ruf' by lettre.
> *The Parson's Prologue*, 42–3

[... I am a Southern man, I cannot recite alliteratively 'rum, ram, ruf'.]

But the ultimate demonstration of the Knight's failure to understand chivalry comes with the capture of Palamon, which also forms the climax of the tournament. In the *Teseida*, Palamon is attacked by Chromis's ferocious horse, which Boccaccio reminds us, used to eat men (*T*, 8, 120). The horse bites Palamon's arm and pulls him to the ground: 'And had Palamon not been helped by the enemy, the horse would have killed him' (*T*, 8, 122). Thus in Boccaccio's version even Palamon's capture is an opportunity for his captors to display gallantry. In *The Knight's Tale*, Palamon's capture is an outrageous violation of all the rules of fair play and of tournaments.

'Som tyme an ende ther is of every dede,' says the Knight (*KT*, 2636) with a nod in the direction of the language of romance, and then goes on to describe how King Emetreus wounds

Palamon (presumably from behind) while he is busy fighting Arcite:

> The stronge kyng Emetreus gan hente
> This Palamon, as he faught with Arcite,
> And made his swerd depe in his flessh to byte;
> > *The Knight's Tale*, 2638–40

[The strong king Emetreus began to take Palamon, as he fought with Arcite, and made his sword bite deep into his flesh.]

To attack someone thus, when his back was turned fighting someone else, would have meant automatic disqualification, according to the Ordinances of Tournament. The rules drawn up by Lord Tiptofte, Earl of Worcester, in 1464, for example, specifically state: 'Who so striketh a man, his back turned, or disgarnished of his speare, shall have no prize.'[96]

Over sixty years ago Stuart Robertson noted the unfairness of Palamon's capture, but he concluded: 'It did not, however, occur to any of the spectators or participants, even Palamon to protest; so that we cannot doubt that this was considered to be in quite good form....'[97] This conclusion, however, is not justified. A foul blow in a tournament that Froissart observed in 1381 certainly provoked indignation,[98] and when an incident similar to the present one occurs in the early-fourteenth-century romance *King Alexander*, a tremendous debate ensues. In the poem, a Persian, disguised as one of Alexander's own men, attacks the King from behind 'when he saw Alexander was busy'.[99] The Persian is eventually captured, and the next day Alexander turns on him:

> 'Thou traitor!' he said,
> 'Yesterday you came into battle
> Armed like one of my men,
> From behind my back
> You smote me with your spear;
> And if my hauberk had not been so strong,
> You would have vilely slain me.
> You shall be hung and drawn
> And burnt to nothing,
> For doing such treachery.'[100]

Chaucer's Knight, however, tries to pass off an attack from behind as if it were perfectly acceptable.

To make matters worse, once Palamon has been wounded, he is set upon by no less than twenty of Arcite's followers, who carry him off to the stake:

> And by the force of twenty is he take
> Unyolden, and ydrawe unto the stake.
> *The Knight's Tale*, 2641-2

[And by the force of twenty he is taken unyielding, and dragged unto the stake.]

Once again the Knight does not offer a word of surprise or condemnation, even though such 'combining' is clearly a breach of the rules of chivalry. In *Havelock the Dane* it is compared with bear-baiting, and the men who take such unfair advantage are equated with dogs.[101] Nor should we necessarily assume that the incident provoked no protest from either spectators or participants – on the contrary there are hints, later on, that the result of the tournament generated a great deal of ill-feeling. Fair play meant the same in the Middle Ages as it does today, and what must have struck Chaucer's audience was the Knight's calm acceptance of an obvious injustice. In fact, the more the Knight elaborates on how satisfactory a result to the tournament it was, the more he unconsciously reveals the full extent of the outrageousness of the whole episode.

After the tournament, the Knight explains, Theseus

> ... made revel al the longe nyght
> Unto the straunge lordes, as was right.
> *The Knight's Tale*, 2717-18

[... made revel all the night long for the foreign lords, as was right.]

And why not – asks the Knight. After all, Palamon had not done anything wrong or suffered any dishonour in the way he was captured since he was set upon by so many and had had his horse driven off. But of course the Knight is completely side-stepping the issue: it was not Palamon's behaviour that would have provoked protests but the behaviour of Arcite's followers. Palamon was not driven to the stake by force of arms or led off yielding victory but physically carried, still struggling, 'by arm and foot and toe'!

> Ne to be lad by force unto the stake
> Unyolden, and with twenty knyghtes take,
> O persone allone, withouten mo,
> And haryed forth by arme, foot and too.
> *The Knight's Tale*, 2723-6

[... to be led by force unto the stake unyielding, and captured by twenty knights, one person alone, without any more, and dragged away by arm and foot and toe.]

And even worse is to follow, for, it turns out, Palamon's horse was driven off by Arcite's menials:

> And eke his steede dryven forth with staves
> With footmen, bothe yemen and eek knaves....
> *The Knight's Tale*, 2727–8

[And also his horse driven off with sticks by footmen, both yeomen and even knaves....]

One of the first essentials of chivalry on the battlefield was that a knight should fight only his peers. J.F.C. Fuller writes: 'According to the code of chivalry it was beneath a knight's dignity to attack infantry because infantry had little or no ransom value.'[102] To be actually defeated by menials was a cause for scandal. Jean de Venette notes the mourning over knights cut down by a peasant force at Longueil: 'It was too much that so many of their good fighters had been killed by mere peasants.'[103] In any case, what sort of a tournament was this that allowed yeoman and even 'knaves' (boys employed as servants) to invade the lists with sticks and beat off a knight's horse? According to the Rules of Tournament drawn up by the Duke of Gloucester for Richard II, by which the tournament in which Chaucer assisted was probably organized, it was essential that everyone should be cleared from the lists: once the tournament started, no one was to go within four feet of the lists.[104] The circumstances of Palamon's capture may not be reckoned a 'vileynye' or a 'cowardye' on Palamon's part, but they make nonsense of Theseus's claim to be a fair judge:

> And whan that Theseus hadde seyn this sighte,
> Unto the folk that foghten thus echon
> He cryde, 'Hoo! namoore, for it is doon!
> I wol be trewe juge, and no partie.
> Arcite of Thebes shal have Emelie,
> That by his fortune hath hire faire ywonne'.
> *The Knight's Tale*, 2654–9

[And when that Theseus had seen this sight, unto everyone of the folk that fought he cried: 'Hoo! no more, for it is done! I will be a true judge and take no sides. Arcite of Thebes shall have Emily, who by his fortune has won her fairly.']

It is no wonder that 'rancour and envye' subsequently break out among his warrior-guests and that Theseus has to take measures to stop it – even to the extent of being totally two-faced about the result:

> For which anon duc Theseus leet crye,
> To stynten alle rancour and envye,
> The gree as wel of o syde as of oother,
> And eyther syde ylik as ootheres brother;
> *The Knight's Tale*, 2731–4

[Because of this, Duke Theseus ordered announcements, to stop all rancour and envy, about the victory of one side as well as of the other, and either side alike, as if they were brothers.]

The break-up of such festivities must always have been a danger-ous time, with hundreds of warrior-knights wandering the streets, armed to the teeth, full of ale and wine and looking for a good time – it must have made modern football supporters on the rampage look like a pacifists' conference. In *Havelock the Dane*, for example, King Ubbe has to give Havelock and his wife protection for the night, after such feasting.[105] Things must have been even more hazardous if there were any cause for discontent – it is no wonder that Theseus loads the fractious barons with gifts and feasting and then – just for good measure – escorts them a day's journey out of town:

> And yaf hem yiftes after hir degree,
> And fully heeld a feeste dayes three,
> And conveyed the kynges worthily
> Out of his toun a journee largely.
> *The Knight's Tale*, 2735–8

[He gave them gifts according to their rank, and held a feast for a full three days, and escorted the kings a good day's journey out of his town.]

Once again, the Knight tries to pass off all this as courtly manners, but to escort visiting knights through one's own territory was far from an act of chivalry – it was a political expedient which could easily be taken as an insult. It was the sort of 'courtesy' a wise potentate would insist on paying to any of the Free Com-panies that wished to pass through his country, simply to prevent their doing too much destruction and pillage. If Theseus had been acting in a truly chivalrous context, he would not have escorted his visitors 'a good day's journey out of town' – he would have given them free passage and trusted on their honour as knights to behave themselves – as, indeed, happens in the *Teseida*: 'And so the kings departed, and each took the shortest route he could to return quickly to his own country.'[106] The Knight pretends to be depicting the manners of chivalry, but he is, in fact, doing no more than recording the military reality of his day. He attempts to create a world of romantic knighthood, but he ends up sounding more and more like the professional man of war. Even his attitude to the tournament itself is dubious:

> Ne ther was holden no disconfitynge
> But as a justes, or a tourneiynge:
> *The Knight's Tale*, 2719–20

[Nor was it considered that there had been any defeat except as in a joust or tournament.]

As Stuart Robertson has pointed out, tournaments and jousts were treated with just as much seriousness as real battles: 'It is to be observed throughout Froissart that there is very little difference indeed, from the standpoint of the knights, between a battle, supposedly fought to support a great and patriotic cause, and a tournament, nominally for exercise or to uphold the honor of one's lady.'[107] To be shamed in a tournament was just as serious a matter as to be shamed on the battlefield (see *Sir Launfal*, 574–9; *Sir Degaré*, 571–82). Once again the Knight's attitude, in dismissing the tournament as a thing of little consequence, is not courtly – it is, however, just the sort of thing one might expect of an old professional soldier, making light of the games of Court.

Allusions to mercenary life in the *Tale*

This glimpse of the narrator as a mercenary captain is by no means an isolated example. Similar allusions show through the romantic façade throughout *The Knight's Tale*.

At the start of the tournament, for example, the Knight records how a roll-call was held so that there should be no deception in the numbers of the two sides:

> Whan that hir names rad were everichon,
> That in hir nombre gyle were ther noon...
> *The Knight's Tale*, 2595–6

[... every one of their names was read out so that there should be no deception in their numbers.]

This suggestion that there might have been sharp practice in the ranks of knights simply does not belong in a chivalrous romance. It does recall, however, the sort of deception that was habitual among the hired armies of northern Italy, where an empty place answered for meant an extra wage packet to be shared out among the company. It was just the sort of thing their Italian employers tried vainly to prevent, as is clear from the following entry in the Military Code for mercenaries hired by the state of Pisa: the Constables of every troop were supposed to reveal

any fraud of which they know or are aware amongst the mercenaries of said Troop. That is to say: any empty place which has not been revealed, anyone answering to a name other than his own, any ordinary horseman answering for the head of his section. With the penalty for anyone of whatever position who goes against these orders of the forfeiture and loss of his arms and horses.[108]

The roll-call book or register played an important part in the lives of the mercenaries of the Free Companies, for it was by the register that they were accounted for, the quality of their horses and equipment checked and their wages subsequently paid. Every mercenary in the pay of the City of Florence, for example, was obliged to have all his details written down, and special registrars were employed to keep a constant check on them – to make sure he had not sold off a good horse and bought a cheaper one or pawned his armour etc. The whole business was taken very seriously: 'Each and every mercenary of the Commune of Florence ... must appear in person to make their review before these registrars, on penalty of being discharged and fined a hundred pounds of lesser florins....'[109] It is no wonder that the image of the roll-call and the register is important to Chaucer's Knight and recurs in his *Tale* when he dismisses speculation about Arcite's death with the contemptuous remark: 'Of soules fynde I nat in this registre' (*KT*, 2812).

As an itinerant mercenary, the Knight naturally also displays a wide knowledge of the world, and his speech is littered with allusions to the places he has visited – Turkish bows, Russian shields, Armenian cloth, Moroccan lions and Greek tigers.[110] He flaunts his travelling before the other pilgrims, with little concern for the strong feeling then prevalent that knights should stay in their own country during such troubled times.

I repeat Gower's lines in *Le Mirour de L'Omme*:

> O knight, you who go far off
> Into strange lands and seek only
> Praise in arms, know this:
> If your country and your neighbour
> Are at war themselves, all the honour
> Is in vain, when you flee from
> Your country and estrange yourself.
> For he who abandons his duties
> And does not wish to fulfil his obligations
> But rather fulfils his own desires
> Has no right to be honoured
> No matter how mighty he might be.[111]

With his homeland torn by internal revolt (1381) and threatened by invasion from abroad (1386), the Knight displays a flippancy towards the role of the knightly estate which would shock many of his listeners. He describes how the knights of ancient days flocked to Theseus's tournament and goes on to remark, with a sigh, that if such an event were to take place tomorrow, every 'lusty knight' would want to be there – *whether it were in England or elsewhere:*

> For if ther fille tomorwe swich a cas,
> Ye knowen wel that every lusty knyght
> That loveth paramours and hath his myght,
> Were it in Engelond or elleswhere,
> They wolde, hir thankes, wilnen to be there, –
> To fighte for a lady, *benedicitee!*
> It were a lusty sighte for to see.
>   *The Knight's Tale*, 2110–16

[For if there chanced, tomorrow, such a thing, you know quite well that every lusty knight who loves to make love and has the strength, whether it were in England or elsewhere, would, for their part, all want to be there – to fight for a lady, Lord bless us! That would be a fine sight to see.]

Such a statement would have been regarded by many of Chaucer's fellow-countrymen as the height of irresponsibility.

There are innumerable other images which sit ill in a chivalrous

romance but which recall the sort of life led by a mercenary
soldier, living by his wits among the lawless Free Companies. The
image of Palamon hiding in a bush

> ... that no man myghte hym se,
> For soore afered of his deeth was he.
>> *The Knight's Tale*, 1517–18

[... that no man might see him for he was sore afraid of his death]

has no place in Boccaccio's poem, where Palamon daringly
escapes from prison and fearlessly strides into the woods to seek
out Arcite (*T*, 5, 33–4). On another occasion, the Knight recalls
the sort of advice the leader of a gang of brigands might give
his men:

> But sooth is seyd, go sithen many yeres,
> That 'feeld hath eyen and the wode hath eres.'
> It is ful fair a man to bere hym evene,
> For al day meeteth men at unset stevene.
>> *The Knight's Tale*, 1521–4

[It's been truly said, many years long since, that 'the field has eyes
and the wood has ears.' It is wise for a man to keep a cool head, for
every day one comes across unexpected events.]

And when Theseus comes between Palamon and Arcite, gone is
the courtly concern of Boccaccio's Teseo: 'He said to them then,
"O knights, if Mars grants victory to him who desires it more,
let each of you draw to one side. If there is any courtesy in you,
tell me who you are and who urges you on to such cruel combat
in such a place, for you show by the way you strike that you
are killing one another." '[112] Instead, the Knight's Theseus sounds
more like a commander in the field breaking up a brawl in the
ranks:

> This duc his courser with his spores smoot,
> And at a stert he was bitwix hem two,
> And pulled out a swerd, and cride, 'Hoo!
> Namoore, up peyne of lesynge of youre heed!
> By myghty Mars, he shal anon be deed
> That smyteth any strook that I may seen.'
>> *The Knight's Tale*, 1704–9

[This duke stuck his spurs into his horse and with a bound he was
between them both, and pulled out his sword and cried: 'Hoo! No
more! On pain of losing your head! By mighty Mars he shall be dead
immediately who strikes any blow that I can see....']

But no passage tells us more about the Knight's scale of values in the military field than does his description of Mars's temple.

The temple of Mars

In both Boccaccio's *Teseida* and the *Thebaid* of Statius, Mars's temple is presided over by the allegorical figure of Valour (*Teseida*, 7, 34; *Thebaid*, 7, 51). In Chaucer's Knight's version, Valour has no place at all – he sees only Mischance (*KT*, 2009) and Conquest (*KT*, 2028). More significantly, Boccaccio specifies that the altars of Mars are stained *only* by blood shed in battle (*T*, 7, 35) – likewise Statius records: 'No blood but that of wars is on the altars' (*Thebaid*, 7, 51). Chaucer's Knight, however, includes in Mars's temple many a death that has not been in battle – but then since the advent of the mercenary armies and the Free Companies, was this not what had happened in real life? It was one of the greatest scandals of the age that the bloodshed of war was no longer confined to the knightly combatants on the battlefield but had spilled over onto the innocent inhabitants of town and country alike. The images of civil destruction which the Knight sees in the temple of Mars, and which are found in neither Boccaccio nor Statius, should be read alongside Jean de Venette's description of the destruction of the French countryside by the Free Companies in the 1360s or the wholesale massacre of the people of Cesena in northern Italy by Hawkwood's White Company in 1377:[113] the stable burning with black smoke (*KT*, 2000), people murdered in their beds (*KT*, 2001), the suicide (*KT*, 2005), the corpse in the bush with its throat slit (*KT*, 2013) the thousand slain and not dead of the plague (*KT*, 2014), the tyrant with his prey snatched by force (*KT*, 2015), the town destroyed so that there was nothing left (*KT*, 2016) and the ships burning on the water (*KT*, 2017). These are not the images of idealized chivalrous warfare. In the Knight's description of Mars's temple, war has become little distinguished from banditry – the images of the pick-purse (*KT*, 1998) and 'the smiler with the knife under his cloak' (*KT*, 1999) and more than just an attempt by Chaucer to be more 'urgent, visionary and … more down to earth than Boccaccio'.[114] War, as the Free Companies waged it in the name of tyrants such as Bernabò Visconti of Milan, had become merely an extension of banditry. Another of the Canterbury pilgrims puts this very succinctly: the tyrants who employ these mercenary armies, says the Manciple, are no different from thieves except that they commit crimes on a larger scale:

> Right so bitwixe a titlelees tiraunt
> And an outlawe, or a theef erraunt,
> The same I seye, ther is no difference.
> To Alisaundre was toold this sentence,
> That, for the tirant is of gretter myght,
> By force of meynee, for to sleen dounright,
> And brennen hous and hoom, and make al playn,
> Lo, therfore is he cleped a capitayn;
> And for the outlawe hath but smal meynee,
> And may nat doon so greet an harm as he,
> Ne brynge a contree to so greet mescheef,
> Men clepen hym an outlawe or a theef.
>
> *The Manciple's Tale*, 223–34

[In the same way between a usurping tyrant and an outlaw or a wandering thief, there is no difference, I say. This opinion was told to Alexander: that because the tyrant is stronger, by force of his men, to slay outright and burn house and home and lay all flat, Lo! for that he is called a captain! And because the outlaw has but a small company of men and cannot do such great harm, nor bring a country into such great mischief, men call him an outlaw or a thief.]

The Knight's own vision of war conjures up not the splendour of the battlefield but the sort of warfare waged by the mercenary armies, which had become the common experience, especially in northern Italy, during the last half of the fourteenth century.

And just in case the allusion to what was happening even then in Lombardy should have escaped his audience, Chaucer closes the Knight's description of Mars's temple with some specific references to the Italian city-states which would have made it clear. I was always rather puzzled by the fact that the statue of Mars is placed on a cart:

> The statue of Mars upon a carte stood
> Armed, and looked grym as he were wood;
>
> *The Knight's Tale*, 2041–2

[The statue of Mars stood upon a cart armed and looking as fierce as if he were mad.]

It seemed an odd sort of detail, until I discovered that the cart or *carroccio* was an important symbolic object which served the

Italian states as both standard and war-chariot. 'The *carroccio*', writes Geoffrey Trease, 'was both a mobile headquarters and a symbol of loyalty'.[115] The Knight thus places Mars firmly in the context of the Italian states whose wars at this period were fought almost entirely by the mercenaries of France, Germany and England. At the very end of his description of Mars's temple, he becomes even more specific, giving Mars an emblem almost

The *carroccio* of the Italian city-states, which the Knight depicts in Mars' temple

identical to that of Bernabò Visconti of Milan, in whose tyrannical quest for power Hawkwood was principally engaged and at whose Court Chaucer had met Hawkwood in 1378.[116]

> A wolf ther stood biforn hym at his feet
> With eyen rede, and of a man he eet;
> > *The Knight's Tale*, 2047–8

[A wolf stood there before him at his feet, with red eyes and eating of a man.]

The resemblance to the Visconti emblem is unmistakable. And the emblem itself must have been notorious in Chaucer's day. It adorned the books of the famous Visconti library, it was sculpted on the outside of buildings and it was emblazoned across Bernabo's chest on his tomb effigy by Benino Campione – one of the most famous pieces of sculpture of its day. More to the point, perhaps, the man-eating monster embellished the coinage of Milan, and in such a form it may well have found its way into the English Court, for in 1368 Bernabo paid no less than 2,000,000 gold florins for the privilege of marrying his niece into the English royal family. It must have seemed a peculiarly apt symbol for the man who more than any other of his time represented the inhumanity of ruthless tyranny – as Chaucer's Monk styles him 'God of delyt, and scourge of Lumbardye' (*Monk's Tale*, 2400).

Theseus as a typical Italian tyrant

If the Knight's vision of warfare is of the kind of warfare pursued by the tyrants of his day, it is also scarcely surprising that the ultimate hero of his *Tale*, Theseus, should himself turn out to be nothing more nor less than an archetypal tyrant – what is more, a tyrant in whose portrait are certain allusions that identify him with those 'tirauntz of Lumbardye' (*LGW*, 374).

I am by no means the first person to observe the tyrannical character of Theseus. Whereas, up to thirty years ago, he was seen as the omniscient, omnipotent executor of benign destiny, nowadays a number of cracks in his façade have become evident and have been charted by numerous commentators.

In 1947 H. J. Webb noted that Chaucer had deliberately made Theseus considerably harsher than his counterpart in the *Teseida* and that in *The Knight's Tale* Theseus bears some of the traits of a tyrant. 'One may well wonder', he concludes, 'if Palamon was not uttering the truth as Chaucer saw it, when he complained that his "lynage" was "so lowe ybroght by tirannye".'[117] More recently, in 1962, R. Neuse remarked that Theseus has 'many of the characteristics of the Renaissance machiavel', and Ian Robinson (1972) observed that in many of Theseus's actions, 'Chaucer is perhaps making the eternally true bourgeois comment on aristocratic statesmen: How magnificent they are – and how dangerous!'[118]

In the Middle Ages the nature of tyranny and the difference between kings and tyrants was the subject of continual energetic debate – and at no period more so than the fourteenth century, when the Italian tyrants emerged on the European horizon. The shock-waves from their bloody reigns were felt all over Europe, and their doings were a matter of concern to all. This was particularly so at the English Court, which had maintained close links

The allegorical figure of Milan, holding up the emblem of her tyrant-masters, the Visconti:

> A wolf ther stood biforn hym at his feet
> With eyen rede, and of a man he eet;
>
> *The Knight's Tale,* 2047–8

with the Visconti of Milan – links which became, of course, particularly close in Bernarbò Visconti's time with the marriage of his niece Violante to Edward III's son Lionel, Duke of Clarence in 1368.[119] Besides, a large proportion of the free armies employed by the Italian city-states consisted of Englishmen – the residue of Edward's armies in France. In fact one of the words for a mercenary in Italian was *inglese*. When Chaucer visited Milan in 1378 it was to meet both the tyrant Bernabò Visconti and the English *condottiere* John Hawkwood, so when he dealt with the subject of tyranny he was talking from first-hand observation.

The characteristics that turned a ruler into a tyrant for the thinkers of Chaucer's day have been summarized by Margaret Schlauch: 'Lordship, it was generally assumed, is primarily a duty; rulers were instituted for the sake of peoples, not peoples for rulers.... When a ruler abandons this objective and seeks rather his personal aggrandizement, employing violent or arbitrary courses and ignoring the common weal and the people's will, he becomes by his very actions a tyrant.'[120] Such opinions were being freely expressed in Italy when Chaucer visited Milan, and, as Margaret Schlauch suggests, it is reasonable to assume that 'Chaucer could very well have heard echoes of the Italian controversies on tyrannicide, even if he did not read any of the texts produced by it.'[121] But even if he had never visited Italy, Chaucer could have heard the same definition of tyranny being aired in London – by Thomas of Wimbledon in his sermon at St Paul's Cross in 1388: 'If you take on such an office more for your own worldly profit than for the benefit of the community, you are a tyrant, as the philosopher says.'[122] Whatever its origin, it is this definition of tyranny that Chaucer incorporated into his own writing, as Margaret Schlauch has convincingly demonstrated.[123] Equally there is no doubt that, by this yardstick, Theseus is a tyrant. His primary motivation is self-aggrandizement, his actions are arbitrary and oppressive, and his main concern is to assert his own authority and to satisfy his own will.

When he is confronted by the mourning women at the start of the *Tale*, his first concern is not for them but for his own triumphal entry:

> 'What folk been ye, that at myn homcomynge
> Perturben so my feste with criynge?'

> Quod Theseus. 'Have ye so greet envye
> Of myn honour, that thus compleyne and crye?'
>> *The Knight's Tale*, 905–8

['What folk are you who at my home-coming disturb my feast like this with your crying?' said Theseus. 'Have you such great envy of my glory that you thus complain and cry?']

He remembers his chivalry only as an afterthought (*KT*, 909–11), and even then he is still thinking of his own prestige:

> That al the peple of Grece sholde speke
> How Creon was of Theseus yserved...
>> *The Knight's Tale*, 962–3

[So that all the people of Greece would speak of how Creon was treated by Theseus.]

Even when Theseus orders Palamon and Emily to marry, he is not motivated by any noble concern for their happiness, nor by respect for the dead Arcite's last wishes, as in the *Teseida* (*T*, 12, 18): his motives are machiavellian, and he orders the marriage merely to bring Thebes under his total domination:

> Thanne semed me ther was a parlement
> At Atthenes, upon certein pointz and caas;
> Among the whiche pointz yspoken was,
> To have with certein contrees alliaunce,
> And have fully of Thebans obeisaunce.
> For which this noble Theseus anon
> Leet senden after gentil Palamon,
>> *The Knight's Tale*, 2970–6

[Then it seems that there was a parliament at Athens, to consider certain matters and affairs, amongst which matters it was discussed how they should make alliances with certain countries and how they should get the full submission of the Thebans. For which purpose, this noble Theseus at once sent for the noble Palamon....]

So much for his noble motives! The Knight reveals Theseus to be nothing more than a sordid political schemer, and yet he never wavers in his admiration for Theseus. This political motivation for the marriage plays, of course, no part in Boccaccio's story. It is a deliberate invention of Chaucer's which gives a hollow ring to all the expressions of joy and celebration with which *The Knight's Tale* closes.

Theseus's tyranny is also expressed in the arbitrariness of many of his actions. For example, when Palamon and Arcite are captured, Theseus allows no ransom, fails to reward those who found them and throws the Princes into perpetual prison without explanation. The ruthlessness of the tyrant, and his disregard for what are now called 'human rights', are highlighted by the Knight's own insensitivity to the situation which allows him, as story-teller, to hop from the abject distress of the young men to Theseus's self-glorification without any awareness of the incongruity involved:

> Out of the taas the pilours han hem torn,
> And han hem caried softe unto the tente
> Of Theseus; and he ful soone hem sente
> To Atthenes, to dwellen in prisoun
> Perpetuelly, – he nolde no raunsoun.
> And whan this worthy duc hath thus ydon,
> He took his hoost, and hoom he rit anon
> With laurer crowned as a conquerour;
> And ther he lyveth in joye and in honour
> Terme of his lyf; what nedeth wordes mo?
> And in a tour, in angwissh and in wo,
> This Palamon and his felawe Arcite
> For everemoore; ther may no gold hem quite.
>
> *The Knight's Tale*, 1020–32

[Out of the heap the pillagers have them torn and have them carried softly to the tent of Theseus; and he soon had them sent to Athens, to dwell in prison perpetually – he allowed no ransom. And when this worthy Duke had done all this he took his men and home he rode anon with laurel crowned as a conqueror. And there he lived in joy and in honour the rest of his life. What else is there to say? And in a tower, in anguish and in woe, lie Palamon and his friend Arcite for evermore – no gold can get them out.]

The treatment of Palamon and Arcite in the *Knight's Tale* is in vivid contrast to their treatment in the *Teseida*, where they are dealt with as humanely as possible and with respect for their high rank: 'The prisoners were all incarcerated and handed over to guards who knew how to do this well. And these two were set aside to put them more at their ease because they were born of royal blood. And he made them live in the palace and kept them in this way in a room where they were served at their pleasure.'[124] Similarly, when Boccaccio's Teseo comes across Palamon and Arcite fighting in the forest, he is impressed by their skill and

earnestness; in *The Knight's Tale* Theseus's first instinct is that
they are challenging his own authority:

> But telleth me what myster men ye been,
> That been so hardy for to fighten heere
> Withouten juge or oother officere,
> As it were in a lystes roially.
> *Knight's Tale*, 1710–13

[But tell me what sort of men you are, that are so daring as to fight
here without a judge or other officer, as if you were in a royal lists.]

When he learns their story and who they are, he immediately flies
into a violent fit of passion 'quaking and shaking' with rage (*KT*,
1762). At the same time he casually reveals that he is the sort
of pitiless tyrant who uses torture as a matter of course, except
that in this case their confession has saved him the trouble: 'It
nedeth noght to pyne yow with the corde' (*KT*, 1746) [There's
no need to torture you with the cord], and he can have them put
to death at once. Thereupon the women in his retinue plead with
him to be merciful. Theseus evidently enjoys this sort of supplica-
tion, for it is only when they offer to kiss his feet that '... at
the laste aslaked was his mood' (*KT*, 1760). Such 'moods' in a
ruler were themselves regarded as signs of despotism. The *Liber
Custumarum* (c. 1320) which was kept in the Guildhall in London, stated that the good ruler should be careful '... that he be
not too irritable, and that he continue not too long in his wrath
or in his indignation. For wrath that has its habitation in authority is like unto the thunder-bolt, in that it lets not the truth
be known or rightful judgement be given.'[125]

When Theseus does eventually pull himself together, it is clear,
as R. Neuse points out, 'that his pity is no instinctive matter of
the gentle heart'.[126] He carries out a sort of interior dialogue on
the pros and cons of showing mercy and decides that, in this case,
it will be in his own interests. He then abruptly switches his mood
from violent rage to a sort of coarse jokiness, which is far from
courtly. He turns to the women and, with amazing insensitivity,
holds up the still bleeding lovers to painful ridicule in front of
the whole Court and the girl they love:

> Who may been a fool, but if he love?
> Bihoold, for Goddes sake that sit above,
> Se how they blede! be they noght wel arrayed?
> Thus hath hir lord, the god of love, ypayed

> Hir wages and hir fees for hir servyse!
> And yet they wenen for to been ful wyse
> That serven love, for aught that may bifalle.
> But this is yet the beste game of alle,
> That she for whom they han this jolitee
> Kan hem therfore as muche thank as me.
> She woot namoore of al this hoote fare,
> By God, than woot a cokkow or an hare!
>
> *The Knight's Tale*, 1799–1810

[Is there a bigger fool than someone in love? Look! For God's sake that sits above, see how they bleed! Aren't they well decked out? Thus has their lord, the god of love, paid them their wages and their fees for their service! And yet the people who serve love think they're so wise – no matter what happens. But this is the best joke of all: that she for whom they've had all this fun can thank them for it as much as me, for she knows no more of all this hot affair than does a cuckoo or a hare!]

Even in his best humour, Theseus is insensitive and brutalized. And when he is finally moved to pity, the net result of his 'pity' is to multiply the suffering a hundredfold. Whereas Boccaccio's Teseo has in mind merely a 'palestral games' – i.e. non-mortal (*T*, 7, 4), the Knight's Theseus announces that Palamon and Arcite must find a hundred knights each and

> May with his hundred ...
> Sleen his contrarie, or out of lystes dryve...
>
> *The Knight's Tale*, 1858–9

[May with his hundred men slay his opponent or drive him out of the lists.]

Even though he is later to modify it, his first intention smacks of the gladiatorial games of the Roman emperors – to whom, indeed, men such as Bernabo Visconti have been compared.

The whole tenor of Theseus's manner is that of a tyrant. In the *Teseida*, Teseo is dignified and always respectful towards both Palamon and Arcite (*T*, 5, 94–8) and merely suggests his proposal as a way out of a difficult situation. The Knight's Theseus adopts the tone of an autocrat:

> My wyl is this, for plat conclusioun,
> Withouten any repplicacioun ...
> Ye shul noon oother ende with me maken ...
> This is youre ende and youre conclusioun.
>
> *The Knight's Tale*, 1845–6, 1865, 1869

[My will is this, for a flat conclusion to the matter, without any argument. ... You shall not make any other agreement with me ... This must be your aim and your destiny.]

Yet although his tone is so autocratic and he brooks no argument from Palamon and Arcite, nevertheless he still pays lip-service to getting their agreement:

> And if yow thynketh this is weel ysayd,
> Seyeth youre avys, and holdeth you apayd.
> *The Knight's Tale*, 1867–8

[And if you think that this is well said, say your opinion, and consider yourselves well treated.]

We are left in no doubt, however, that it is merely a rubber stamp that he requires – he is not interested if they do not agree with him. Such charades of justice are only too familiar in totalitarian societies even to this day.

It is, perhaps, a surprising fact that the consent of the people was a vital element in the right to rule of the medieval prince. Not all writers went as far as William of Ockham, who recognized the right of revolution in cases where a ruler had become tyrannical, but most political thinkers acknowledged the people's will as an ultimate source of authority.[127] As Dante wrote: 'Certainly the citizens do not exist for the counsellors, nor the people for the king, but on the contrary the counsellors exist for the citizens and the king for the people.'[128] Or, as Chaucer put it in the *Prologue* to *The Legend of Good Women* (379–80):

> He moste thinke yt is his lige man,
> And is his tresour, and his gold in cofre.

[He must believe that his loyal subjects are his treasure, and the gold in his coffer.]

It was therefore no less important for the medieval despot to maintain a façade of popular support than it is for the modern dictator. And this is exactly what we see portrayed in *The Knight's Tale*. The Knight never refers to the people of Athens bearing any love towards Theseus, their lord – he merely pictures them behaving like automata, applauding everything Theseus says, regardless of its good sense, wisdom or even justice.

When Theseus substitutes a battle to the death between two hundred knights for the deaths of Palamon and Arcite (*KT*, 1851–61), he is not acting mercifully or wisely, and yet his Court

responds with an exaggerated delight that strains our credulity to
the limit – everyone leaping for joy, falling down on their knees
and thanking Theseus with all their heart and might:

> Who looketh lightly now but Palamoun?
> Who spryngeth up for joye but Arcite?
> Who kouthe telle, or who kouthe it endite,
> The joye that is maked in the place
> Whan Theseus hath doon so fair a grace?
> But doun on knees wente every maner wight,
> And thonked him with al hir herte and myght ...
>
> *The Knight's Tale*, 1870–6

[Who now looks happier than Palamon? Who leaps up for joy more
than Arcite? Who could tell, or who could write, the joy that was
made in that place when Theseus has shown such a kindness? But
down on their knees went every single person and thanked him with
all their heart and might.]

In the *Teseida*, where Teseo's proposal is a genuinely wise com-
mutation of the original death sentence, there is no such exaggerated response (*T*, 5, 98–105): the Knight, without admitting
it, is depicting the sycophancy of a tyrant's Court.

A similar thing happens before the tournament, when Theseus
announces his intention to modify his first proposal. To
Chaucer's audience, familiar with the rules of tournament, his
modifications would have been quite ludicrous. It is absurd, for
instance, for Theseus to ban poll axes and yet allow maces (*KT*,
2544, 2559) since both were equally dangerous and designed for
the same purpose of breaking through armour; as Caxton has
it in *The Book of the Ordre of Chivalry* (p. 80): 'A mace or pollax,
is strong ageynst al armes and smyteth on al partes'. It is equally
absurd to ban short swords but allow long swords (*KT*, 2546,
2559). Similarly it is ridiculous to ban missiles and daggers (*KT*,
2544) and yet to allow lances (*KT*, 2549). Lances were, of course,
one of the most dangerous weapons, and in the *Teseida*, Teseo
bans them altogether: 'And to make sure that hate does not spring
up among you, leave your lances, which are more injurious,
aside....'[129] And yet in *The Knight's Tale* Theseus not only
allows lances but specifies that they are to have sharpened heads!
(*KT*, 2549). In the tournaments of Chaucer's day, such as the one
he himself helped to organize at Smithfield in 1390, lances were
usually blunted.[130] In fact, it was usual, by this time, for all

weapons of tournament to be blunted,[131] and swords, knives and maces were all equally banned, as one manuscript records: 'No one shall bear a sword, pointed knife, mace or other weapon, except for the sword for the tournament.'[132] In fact, by Chaucer's day, the general mêlée, in which large numbers of knights all fought at once, as Theseus is proposing, had long since been phased out precisely because it was considered too dangerous – and perhaps a little unedifying.[133] So the sort of tournament that Theseus is suggesting would have been regarded by Chaucer's contemporaries as little more than a licensed brawl, and his 'modifications' would have been seen as farcical. Yet, once again, the crowd in the *Tale* responds with well-orchestrated rapture:

> The voys of peple touchede the hevene,
> So loude cride they with murie stevene,
> 'God save swich a lord, that is so good,
> He wilneth no destruccion of blood!'
> *The Knight's Tale*, 2561–4

[The voice of the people touched the heaven, so loud they cried with a happy sound: 'God save such a lord, that is so good, he will allow no destruction of blood.']

And let us be quite clear what this means – 'destruction of blood' does not mean simply bloodshed. 'Blood' here means 'noble blood', and so what the crowd is shouting is 'God save such a lord that is so good he will allow no destruction of the aristocracy'! It is hard to imagine a medieval crowd getting worked up about what damage the aristocracy did to each other. One is inevitably led to the conclusion that, as Stuart Robertson suggested, 'the people feel compelled to applaud every decree of the King.'[134] It is the typical Pavlovian mob response demanded by tyrants all through history, from Rome to Nuremberg, and the Knight's simplistic vision of it is delightfully absurd, if a trifle sinister.

This absurdity reaches new heights at the end of the tournament. When Theseus announces his outrageous decision to award the prize to Arcite, regardless of the flagrant breaches of rules that have led to Palamon's capture, the crowd once again responds with ludicrous sycophancy. This time Chaucer emphasizes it with the characteristic stylistic device of splitting up the lines: 'Anon ther is a noyse of peple bigonne ...' (*KT*, 2660), he says, and his listeners would be expecting the 'noise' to be that

of a massive protest against Theseus's decision, but the next lines
are:

> For joye of this, so loude and heighe withalle,
> It semed that the lystes sholde falle.
> *The Knight's Tale*, 2661–2

It is easy to imagine that the other pilgrims, listening to *The
Knight's Tale*, would have had a lot to say about this travesty
of justice and about the Knight's blithe disregard for it. Indeed,
it probably sparked off a heated discussion among audiences
wherever *The Knight's Tale* was recited, and it is not surprising
to find, twelve lines further on, an injunction to the audience to
quieten down and pay attention: 'But herkneth me, *and stynteth
noyse a lite*' (KT, 2674). Whether this is the Knight talking to
the other pilgrims, or Chaucer talking to his audience, it was
probably a very necessary device in the oral performance of the
Tale.

Theseus's 'First Mover' speech

The ultimate expression of Theseus's tyranny and of the
Knight's own political creed is the long speech at the end of the
poem (*KT*, 2987–3089), which is generally referred to as the 'First
Mover' speech.

This speech has been regarded as the great philosophical climax of *The Knight's Tale*. It has been interpreted as Chaucer's
greatest and most complete exposition of the philosophy of
Boethius.[135] More recently, however, critics such as Elizabeth
Salter and Ian Robinson have begun to show up the inconsis-
tencies in the philosophical arguments. As Elizabeth Salter
writes: 'Only the confident flow of the poetry disguises the basic
illogicality of the appeals.'[136] R. Neuse goes further and
perceives that Theseus is 'a brilliant political opportunist',
observing how the supposedly philosophical argument 'does not
lead to a spiritual vision, but merely to the tyrant's plea "To
maken vertu of necessitee" '.[137]

Theseus certainly takes Boethian phrases and concepts, but he
produces an argument that is actually a travesty of Boethius's
De Consolatione. For Theseus, the 'First Mover' is Jupiter the
king, and he pictures Jupiter as a tyrant-prince against whom
rebellion is futile.[138] Basically the thread of the argument is this:

the 'First Mover' has created everything for his own purposes and has decreed that everything must eventually die (*KT*, 2994–9). Since we have only to look around us to see that everything does, indeed, die, we can see that the First Mover is stable and eternal (*KT* 3004–5) and that it is therefore useless to try to strive against him:

> What maketh this but Juppiter, the kyng,
> That is prince and cause of alle thyng ...
> And heer-agayns no creature on lyve,
> Of no degree, availleth for to stryve.
> Thanne is it wysdom, as it thynketh me,
> To maken vertu of necessitee,
> And take it weel that we may nat eschue,
> And namely that to us alle is due.
> And whoso grucceth ought, he dooth folye,
> And rebel is to hym that al may gye.
>
> *The Knight's Tale*, 3035–46

[Who causes this but Jupiter the king, who is the prince and cause of everything.... And no creature, no matter what his rank, can gain by striving against this. Then, it seems to me, that it is wise to make necessity one's strength, and to accept willingly what we cannot avoid, especially that which is due to all of us. And whoever complains in any way, is foolish and is a rebel against him that controls all.]

Now such a conclusion is a direct contradiction of Boethius's insistence that it is the duty of every man to strive to shape his own fortune: 'You are engaged in bitter mental strife with every kind of fortune.... For it is placed in your own hands, what kind of fortune you prefer to shape for yourselves; for all fortune that seems adverse, if it does not exercise or correct, punishes.'[139] Boethius certainly propounded stoic acceptance of adversity, but Theseus fails to carry Boethius's argument to its conclusion – that it is only in striving for the good that man can place himself beyond the vicissitudes of fortune. Theseus reduces Boethius's argument to a tyrant's demand for passive submission. He presents only the duties of the ruled to the ruler and nothing of the duties of the ruler to the ruled – which was the very thing which defined a tyrant to the Italian writers of Chaucer's day, such as Bartolus of Sassoferrato and Coluccio Salutati.[140]

As an exposition of Boethian thought, Theseus's speech is flawed from the start because he fails to make the distinction between Providence and Fate which is the nexus of Boethius's argument. For Boethius, Providence is: 'divine reason itself, the reason which disposes all things that exist'.[141] It is the good to which all things strive, and it is a unity with happiness, love and God. Fate, on the other hand, is merely the day-to-day happenings of chance, ' a disposition inherent in movable things, through which Providence binds all things together'.[142] We may not be able to make sense of the ups and downs of Fate, he continues, but we must keep our minds fixed on the single unmoving centre: *providentia*, which never changes and is always good. To illustrate the difference, he takes the example of regeneration: Fate is such that each of us is faced with death, but Providence has provided for the renewal of life through regeneration: 'That course moves the heaven and the stars, it mingles the elements with one another in proportion and transforms them by changing one with another; it renews all things that are born and die through the growth of their young and their seedlings in their likeness.'[143] Theseus takes this same argument and stands it on its head by claiming that Jupiter has organized species to endure 'by successiouns' merely to ensure that each individual will die:

> And therfore, of his wise purveiaunce,
> He hath so wel biset his ordinaunce,
> That speces of thynges and progressiouns
> Shullen enduren by successiouns,
> And nat eterne, withouten any lye.
> This maystow understonde and seen at ye.
> *The Knight's Tale*, 3011–16

[And therefore, through his wise foresight, he has so well arranged his commands that all species and things that reproduce shall endure by generations and not last for ever as individuals – and that's truth as you can see with your own eyes.]

Similarly, Theseus borrows from Boethius the images of the tree, the stone and the river, but he uses them merely to demonstrate that nothing lasts forever:

> Loo the ook, that hath so long a norisshynge
> From tyme that it first bigynneth to sprynge,
> And hath so long a lif, as we may see,
> Yet at the laste wasted is the tree.
> Considereth eek how that the harde stoon
> Under oure feet, on which we trede and goon,
> Yet wasteth it as it lyth by the weye.

The brode ryver somtyme wexeth dreye;
The grete tounes se we wane and wende.
Thanne may ye see that al this thyng hath ende.
The Knight's Tale, 3017–26

[Lo! The oak that takes so long to grow from the time that it first begins to spring up and has so long a life, as we can see, yet eventually the tree will waste away. Consider also how the hard stone under our feet, on which we tread and go about, still wears away, as it lies by the wayside. The broad river will eventually wax dry. We see the great towns wane and disappear. Then can you see that all things have an end.]

Boethius, on the other hand, used these same images as evidence of the harmony of the universe, by which the behaviour of even inanimate objects is consistent with their nature so as to *preserve* them:

You perceive first that plants and trees grow in places suitable to them, where, so far as their nature permits, they are able to avoid withering swiftly and perishing.
Whatever is suited to any thing preserves that thing, whatever it is; just as those things injurious to it destroy it.
Again, those things which are hard, like stones, cling most tenaciously to their parts and resist easy dissolution; but those things which are flowing, as air or water, yield easily it is true to forces dividing them, but the parts so divided swiftly flow together as one again.[144]

Nothing, however, could be more directly contrary to the whole spirit of Boethius's philosophy than the final conclusion which Theseus draws from all this philosophizing. The best thing that we can hope for in the 'foul prison of this life' (*KT*, 3061), he claims, is to die in our prime, because then we can be more certain of our good name enduring:

And certeinly a man hath moost honour
To dyen in his excellence and flour,
Whan he is siker of his goode name;
Thanne hath he doon his freend, ne hym, no shame.
And gladder oghte his freend been of his deeth,
Whan with honour up yolden is his breeth,
Than whan his name apalled is for age,
For al forgeten is his vassellage.
Thanne is it best, as for a worthy fame,
To dyen whan that he is best of name.
The Knight's Tale, 3047–56

[And certainly a man receives more honour when he dies in his excellence and flower, when he can be more certain of his good name; for then he does no shame to either himself or his friend, and his friend ought to be gladder for his death, when his breath is given up with honour than when his good name has been tarnished by old age, for then his prowess is all forgotten. Then is it best, for the sake of a high reputation, to die when one's good name is at its height.]

Theseus would have had to read no further than the Second Consolation to know that Boethius considered the long life of one's good name as nothing at all: 'But if you really consider the infinite space of eternity, have you any reason to rejoice in the long life of your own name? ... However long a time fame last, if it is thought of in the context of boundless eternity, it is clearly seen to be, not small, but nothing at all.'[145] And he considered 'the man who rushes after glory' as a fool:

> The man who rushes after glory
> And nothing else, thinking it highest of all,
> Let him compare the vastness of the heavens
> With the narrowness of earth:
> He'll blush for his proud name that cannot satisfy
> Even his brief ambition.
> Why do men in their pride – and yet in vain! –
> Long to shake from their necks the yoke
> Of their mortality?
> Though fame may spread abroad
> Loosing the tongues of many different peoples,
> And though a great house blaze with many a famous title,
> Death despises the heights of glory,
> Enfolds alike the humble and the proud,
> Making the lowest equal to the highest.
> Where now are the bones of good Fabricius?
> What is Brutus now, or stern old Cato?
> What little fame is left them – just their names
> In a few old stories!
> And if we read and learn their glorious names
> Do we then know the dead?
> And so you too will all be quite forgotten,
> Nor can fame make you known by any man.
> And if you think you may live longer yet
> At least as a name alive on the lips of men,
> When your last day takes even this from you,
> There's still to come
> That second death.[146]

Another work which had a profound influence on Chaucer was *The Dream of Scipio*, and there Cicero put the same idea – though perhaps more wittily: 'But in any case why do you regard it as so important to be talked about by people who have not yet been born? After all, you were never spoken of by all the multitudes who lived before you – and they were every bit as numerous, and were better men.'[147] Theseus does not rejoice because Arcite is one of those 'whose means to glory has been their virtue' (*'qui virtute gloriam petunt'*)[148] but because he has departed

> ... with duetee and honour
> Out of this foule prisoun of this lyf...
> *The Knight's Tale*, 3060–1

[... with duty and honour out of this foul prison of this life.]

The image of this life as a prison is also taken from Boethius, but again Theseus turns the argument on its head. He sees Arcite's triumph in the good name that he has left behind in this world, whereas Boethius says that the soul that is fully aware of its own nature (*bene sibi mens conscia*)[149] will despise *all* earthly things.

In short, Theseus's 'First Mover' speech certainly borrows from Boethius but gets it all wrong. It comes out not as Boethian philosophy but as the long-winded, sententious waffle of a conceited autocrat. And here it is worth remembering that the whole speech is motivated not by Theseus's love for Emily or concern for Palamon, but by his grubby political designs upon Thebes.

The key concept which is missing from Theseus's argument is love. He does, indeed, commence by referring to 'the faire cheyne of love', but even this very image has an ironic *double entendre*. At first one might take it to mean a chain in which all the elements are links and are thus bound inextricably together. But it soon becomes clear that Theseus is thinking of it in terms of a chain around the neck, which keeps everything in its appointed order. In the passage from Boethius, which Theseus's opening lines recall, Boethius pictures the world bound together by love itself – for him it is love which is the 'Prime Mover':

> What binds all things to order,
> Governing earth and sea and sky,
> Is love.
> If love's rein slackened
> All things now held by mutual love

> At once would fall to warring with each other
> Striving to wreck that engine of the world
> Which now they drive
> In mutual trust with motion beautiful.[150]

For Theseus, the 'First Mover' is Jupiter the king, who binds everything in its place by the chains of love. But what sort of love is it that so arranges everything merely so that everything must die?

Theseus's conclusion, that we should not struggle because we are impotent, betrays a dark, cynical pessimism, and his stern world of absolute power allows no room for real love. It is not only a travesty of Boethius, it is also a travesty of the political theories of Chaucer's day – again as the *Liber Custumarum* has it:

> Love ought to be in the one and in the other. For the sovereign ought to love his subjects with a great heart and with a clear faith, and to watch by day and by night for the common profit of the city and of all the people. So also ought the subjects to love their sovereign with a righteous heart and with true affection, and to give him counsel and aid for maintaining his office. For seeing that he is but one only among them, he could do or accomplish nothing without them.[151]

It is also a travesty of Chaucer's own insistence in *The Legend of Good Women* that the Prince is duty-bound to treat his subjects with compassion and mercy:

> Yit mot he doon bothe ryght, to poore and ryche,
> Al be that hire estaat be nat yliche,
> And han of poore folk compassyoun.
> For loo, the gentil kynde of the lyoun!
> For whan a flye offendeth him or biteth,
> He with his tayl awey the flye smyteth
> Al esely; for, of hys genterye,
> Hym deyneth not to wreke hym on a flye,
> As dooth a curre, or elles another best.
>   Prologue, *The Legend of Good Women*, 388–99

[Yet must he do right to both rich and poor, albeit their status is not the same, and he must have compassion for poor folk. For look at the noble nature of the lion: when a fly offends him or stings him he brushes it away with his tail all gently, for, through his nobility, he does not deign to avenge himself on a fly, as a cur does or some other beast.]

Even Theseus's language, in his final speech, is that of a tyrant. He introduces a subject which Boethius described as 'the matter greatest of all in the seeking, and such that almost no discourse, however exhaustive, is sufficient for it'[152] with the contemptuous 'Wel may men knowe, but it be a fool' (*KT*, 3005). With the consummate arrogance of a despot, he denies the need for any authorities to support his argument:

> Ther nedeth noght noon auctoritee t'allegge,
> For it is preeved by experience,
> But that me list declaren my sentence.
> *The Knight's Tale*, 3000–2

[One needs no authority to show this, for it is proved by experience, except that I wish to make my meaning clear.]

This summary dismissal of the need for higher authority goes deeper than mere phraseology or lack of book-learning, as I earlier characterized it. In everything he does, Theseus is the sole arbiter of right and wrong, good and bad. His will, and his will alone, determines his actions. He admits of no higher authority than his own – neither the will of the people nor the will of the gods. It is significant, for example, that Theseus in *The Knight's Tale* never prays to the gods, as does Boccaccio's Teseo (*T*, 7, 102), nor – even more significantly – does he throw away the symbols of his worldly power onto Arcite's funeral pyre as does Teseo in the *Teseida* (*T*, 11, 36). The Knight's Theseus is his own First Mover.

It is no accident that he often appears to be more like a god than a man. At times he takes it upon himself to hand out destiny like Providence itself:

> And forthy I yow putte in this degree,
> That ech of yow shal have his destynee
> As hym is shape, and herkneth in what wyse;
> *The Knight's Tale*, 1841–3

[Therefore I give you the following conditions, so that each of you shall have the destiny that has been shaped for him. Listen how it shall be.]

He appears to have a confidence in his own judgement that Boethius specifically warns against: 'Do men, then, really live with such soundness of understanding that those they have judged to be good or bad must necessarily also be as they think?'[153] He even compares himself with God, in a way which must have struck some of his listeners as almost blasphemous:

> The lystes shal I maken in this place,
> And God so wisly on my soule rewe,
> As I shal evene juge been and trewe.
> *The Knight's Tale*, 1862–4

[I shall make the lists in this place, and may God have mercy on my soul in the same way as I shall be a true and even judge.]

It is certainly no accident that the Knight sees Theseus as 'a god in throne':

> Duc Theseus was at a wyndow set,
> Arrayed right as he were a god in trone.
> The peple preesseth thiderward ful soone
> Hym for to seen, and doon heigh reverence...
> *The Knight's Tale*, 2528–31

[Duke Theseus was seated at a window, arrayed just as if he were a god on a throne. The people soon crowded round to see him and do reverence to him.]

This image brings us back to a consideration of the contemporary context in which the Knight is telling his *Tale*, for it is yet another specific allusion to one of the north Italian tyrants. This trick of sitting at a window, dressed in cloth of gold, so as to be seen by the crowd, was one of the unendearing habits of the usurper Giovanni dell' Agnello, Doge of Pisa. The Knight may say that the crowd pressed forward to do Theseus 'heigh reverence' as he sat at his window, but for dell' Agnello's contemporaries it was a habit which epitomized everything they disliked in him. The contemporary Italian chronicler Matteo Villani remarked caustically: 'Never was a ruler more odious or overbearing. When he rode forth he carried a golden staff in his hand and wore magnificent clothes. Back in the palace, he placed himself at the window where the people could see him, as if he were some sacred relic – seated in cloth of gold leaning on cloth of gold cushions.'[154] If we add this image of dell' Agnello to the already mentioned allusions to the Visconti and the *carroccio* of the Italian city-states, which occur in Mars's temple, one might be led to suspect that *The Knight's Tale* may carry a *leitmotif* of references to the Italian tyrants. Perhaps more allusions of this sort will come to light. It might be worth a brief diversion at this point to note that there also seems to be a *substratum* of Italian associations running through the portraits of the Knight, the Squire and the Yeoman, in the *General Prologue*.

The Knight's retinue

In the first place, the Knight and his little retinue together make up the perfect 'lance', which was the distinctive fighting unit of Hawkwood's White Company – consisting of a knight, a squire and an archer, as the contemporary Italian chroniclers Filippo Villani and Pietro Azario both record.[155] Chaucer cheerfully pretends that the heavily-armed Yeoman must be a forester, since he is wearing a green 'baldric' or belt. Green, however, was the distinctive dress of the lowest of all the ranks of mercenaries – the ubiquitous Welsh archers, who – like the Yeoman – were also noted for their daggers.[156] In fact the way the Yeoman is armed to the teeth makes him sound much more like a fighting man than a forester. The long-bow which he carries was of course a military weapon not a hunting one, and the 'peacock arrows' which he bears under his belt 'full thriftily' would have been particularly long ones and illegal for foresters who by law were supposed to use only short arrows or 'bolts'.[157] The Yeoman in fact fits Azario's description of the archers in Hawkwood's Company: 'The footsoldiers have big and powerful bows that reach from their heads to the ground, and being drawn, shoot great long arrows.'[158] There is even an Italian pun in the very suggestion that he might be a 'forester' at all, for in Italian *forestiere* meant at that time 'stranger' or more particularly 'foreign mercenary' – a meaning which follows very naturally from the allusion to St Christopher, the patron saint of travellers, around his neck.[159] It may not even be stretching things too far to infer that the Yeoman's 'broun visage' may have suggested Italian features (Hawkwood himself relied on an Italian bodyguard), but it certainly indicated a life spent in sunnier climes, and the Italian connotations of the foreign word 'armee' would have helped to locate at least a part of this little troop's career in Italy.[160]

There is even an ambiguity about the young Squire's addiction to 'floyting' all the day. The flute would certainly be found in the courtly entertainments of the day, but there is surprisingly little evidence that the actual *playing* of it was a courtly

accomplishment.[161] Moreover, although the end-blown type of
flute was found at court, the transverse or side-blown flutes
from Germany) had strong military connotations.[162] Indeed, we
find in the Code for Mercenaries in the pay of Florence in 1369,
the following injunction: 'that each and every constable, and any
other mercenary ... ought to keep a piper, drummer, bagpiper
or trumpeter ...'[163] and could be fined 'five pounds of lesser
florins' for failing to have one. So the Squire's fluting may have
simply been part of his professional duties.

The Knight's Tale as a hymn to tyranny

If there is, indeed, this *leitmotif* of Italian references running
through both the portrait of the mercenary Knight and his retinue
in the *Prologue* and the Knight's own eulogium of tyranny in his
Tale, it would be by no means surprising. In Chaucer's day, Italy
was the land of tyrants, as Bartolus of Sassoferrato observed:
'I say he is a tyrant because he rules "tyrannically", that is, his
actions are not directed toward the common good but to his own
advantage, and that means to rule unjustly – as is the case *de
facto* in Italy.'[164] And for Chaucer himself the 'tyrants of Lombardy' were almost proverbial:

> This shoolde a ryghtwis lord have in his thoght,
> And nat be lyk tirauntz of Lumbardye,
> That han no reward but at tyrannye.
> *Prologue, The Legend of Good Women*, 373–5

[This should a rightful lord bear in mind and not be like the tyrants
of Lombardy that have no regard but for tyranny.]

What is more, mercenaries, such as the Knight, were recognized
as the tools of the tyrants. The ruler who ruled by oppression
could not rely on the military services of the very people he was
oppressing, so he preferred to employ foreigners. As Egidio
Romano de Colonna noted, one of the trademarks of a tyrant
is that 'he fears to entrust himself to guards selected from his
fellow citizens' – an opinion seconded by Bartolus of Sassoferrato.[165] This was precisely why the rulers of Morocco, in Belmarye and Tramyssene, chose to employ Christian mercenaries
such as the Knight rather than Muslims.[166] In the second half of
the fourteenth century mercenary activity had become most
active in northern Italy. The freebooting Companies which

sprang up after the Treaty of Brétigny in 1360 served the purposes of the already powerful tyrants of Milan, Pisa and Florence: 'When tyrants, the inevitable result of faction, grew common in Italy,' wrote Sir Charles Oman, 'they habitually discouraged the native *levée en masse*, preferring to rely on mercenaries.'[167] In their turn, the very presence of these tyrants and their willingness to provide employment for the Free Companies ensured the survival of those notorious bands. Tyrants and mercenaries went together: the one nurtured and fostered the other.[168]

It is, therefore, only natural that Chaucer's Knight, as a mercenary, should tell a *Tale* that resounds with images of military despotism in northern Italy. Nor should it be surprising that he identifies the God of War with the Visconti of Milan and compares his hero Theseus with a despicable tyrant such as Giovanni dell' Agnello. The mercenary soldier did not question the right to rule of whatever dictator he happened to be supporting at the time: he could not afford to. The archetypal English *condottiere*, John Hawkwood, sold his services to the Visconti, to the Pope, to Cardinal Robert of Geneva or to dell' Agnello for money, he did not bother himself with metaphysical questions of morality or justice. Dell' Agnello, in fact, was his first employer, and no matter how odious that usurper may have been to his people, Hawkwood developed an intimate friendship with him – he was godfather to Agnello's son and even gave him his name 'Auto' or 'Aukud'.[169] Bernabo Visconti may have been 'the most ruthless tyrant in a ruthless age'[170] and the 'scourge of Lumbardye',[171] but Hawkwood put Bernabo's ruthlessness into action and in return was only too happy to marry one of his illegitimate daughters. Robert of Geneva (later Antipope Clement VII) may have been 'a man of ultimate barbarity'[172] and the 'butcher of Cesena',[173] but Hawkwood was quite prepared to serve him and, when ordered, even to organize the massacre of the inhabitants of Cesena.

Hawkwood was a plain soldier, and as such he had 'the professional soldier's common bias towards established authority, what he calls "law and order"'.[174] And this is exactly the character revealed by Chaucer's Knight throughout his *Tale*. Just like Hawkwood, he appears to believe implicitly in the right of might and to be totally unaware of the political arguments advanced by men such as Marsilius of Padua who claimed that the ruler drew his authority from the will of the people.[175]

I am not suggesting, by this, that Chaucer's Knight is a specific portrait of Sir John Hawkwood (in fact the Knight's wide-ranging career is at odds with Hawkwood's, which was concentrated mainly in northern Italy) but since Chaucer met and knew Hawk-

Sir John Hawkwood – the archetypal successful mercenary – whose monument still hangs alongside Dante's in the Duomo, Florence

wood, it is not unlikely that he should have based some of the elements of his characterization of a mercenary on that best-known of the English mercenary captains. Like Hawkwood, Chaucer's Knight reveals himself as a bluff man-of-action with little time for religion or metaphysics. He dismisses theological speculation with the cheerful contempt one might expect of an old professional soldier:

> His spirit chaunged hous and wente ther,
> As I cam nevere, I kan nat tellen wher.
> Therfore I stynte, I nam no divinistre;
> Of soules fynde I nat in this registre,
> Ne me ne list thilke opinions to telle
> Of hem, though that they writen wher they dwelle.
> Arcite is coold, ther Mars his soule gye!
>> *The Knight's Tale*, 2809–15

[His spirit changed house and went where I have never been, I cannot say where, therefore I say no more – I am no theologian; I find nothing about souls in this roll-book, nor do I care to talk about the opinions of theologians, even though they write about where souls dwell. Arcite is cold – may Mars guide his soul there!]

This is not the ascetic Christian idealist that scholars would have us believe the Knight to be. He even reduces Arcite's death to a cold technical description which has, as Ian Robinson noted, 'no more nobility than a death certificate'.[176] He shows the sort of clinical detachment appropriate to a man such as Hawkwood who has dealt out death on a vast scale and observed it at close quarters throughout his working life:

> Swelleth the brest of Arcite, and the soore
> Encreesseth at his herte moore and moore.
> The clothered blood, for any lechecraft,
> Corrupteth, and is in his bouk ylaft,
> That neither veyne-blood, ne ventusynge,
> Ne drynke of herbes may ben his helpynge.
> The vertu expulsif, or animal,
> Fro thilke vertu cleped natural
> Ne may the venym voyden ne expelle.
> The pipes of his longes gonne to swelle,
> And every lacerte in his brest adoun
> Is shent with venym and corrupcioun.
> Hym gayneth neither, for to gete his lif,
> Vomyt upward, ne dounward laxatif.
> Al is tobrosten thilke regioun;
> Nature hath now no dominacioun.
> And certeinly, ther Nature wol nat wirche,
> Fare wel phisik! go ber the man to chirche!
> This al and som, that Arcita moot dye;
>> *The Knight's Tale*, 2743–61

[The breast of Arcite swells up and the pain increases in his heart more and more. The clotted blood – despite all the skill of doctors – becomes corrupted and remains in his belly, so that neither bleeding nor cupping nor herbal potions can help him. The 'expulsive', or 'animal' power, which from its strength is called 'natural', can neither void nor expel the poison. The pipes of his lungs begin to swell, and every muscle down in his breast is destroyed by poison and gangrene. Neither upward vomit nor downward laxative can help him to save his life. All is shattered in that region; Nature now has no dominion, and certainly, where Nature will not work, fare well physic! Go, bear the man to church! The long and short is Arcite must die.]

This is not the stuff of romance; these are not the words of a courtier or of a devout Christian thinker – but of a man for whom death has become a business.

By putting a chivalric romance into the mouth of a new-style mercenary captain, Chaucer has created a cold, dark world of fear, oppression and death. He encapsulates what had happened to the military world of his day – how chivalry and knighthood, divorced from their underlying ideals, had become the tools of tyranny and destruction.

5 Why does the Knight interrupt the Monk?

By way of a conclusion, I would like to turn to the appearance of Chaucer's Knight later on in *The Canterbury Tales* – to the moment when he abruptly cuts the Monk off in the middle of his Tale.[1] Such an interruption seems an extraordinary breach of good manners on any level, and it is expressly contrary to the Knight's own undertaking:

> I wol nat letten eek noon of this route;
> Lat every felawe telle his tale aboute...
> *The Knight's Tale*, 889–90

[I will not hinder any of this crew; let every fellow tell his tale in turn.]

After all, they are still in competition to win the free supper, and by the agreed rules each pilgrim should be allowed his say – why then should the Knight want to prevent one of his companions from finishing his tale?

The explanation which is often put forward – that *The Monk's Tale* is genuinely dull and boring and that the Knight is echoing the feelings not only of the other pilgrims but also of Chaucer's own audience – seems to me so superficial as to be hardly worth considering.[2] Chaucer – that master of economy, whom Caxton eulogized for his concise, vigorous and dignified expressions 'exchewyng prolyxyte, castyng away the chaf of superfluyte'[3] – would not have written 776 lines of poetry (nearly as long as the *General Prologue* itself) merely to demonstrate that the Monk is a boring story-teller. There must be another reason for the Knight's outburst, and to find it one needs to read no further than the end of the Knight's own *Tale*.

When the Knight has finished what he himself admits is a 'long tale' (*KT*, 2966), the other pilgrims are all very polite and mumble about 'what a noble story it was' and 'how well worth remembering' (*Miller's Prologue*, 3110–12), but Harry Bailey, the Host, turns to the Monk and, rather surprisingly, asks him to 'quite with', that is to repay or balance, the Knight's tale:

> Now telleth ye, sir Monk, if that ye konne
> Somwhat to quite with the Knyghtes tale.
> *The Miller's Prologue*, 3118–19

[Now you tell, Sir Monk, if you can, something to answer the Knight's Tale.]

Whether Harry Bailey recognizes that the *Knight's Tale* has raised some highly contentious points on the subject of tyranny, or whether he is merely exercising his tact in asking the Knight's equal in 'degree' to complement the *Tale*, one thing is clear: Chaucer intended the *Monk's Tale* as some sort of reply to the *Knight's Tale*.

At this point, however, as if such a reply were too much of a political hot potato – or else, perhaps, just too obvious – Chaucer has the drunken Miller interrupt and insist on telling *his Tale*, which 'quits' *The Knight's Tale* on a more humorous level. Nevertheless, the fact remains that when the Monk eventually comes to tell his *Tale*, he is replying to the Knight, and he does so in unequivocally political terms.

The Knight told a *Tale* extolling the power and glory of a tyrant – a hymn to worldly success and the right of might. The Monk presents the other side of the coin:

> I wol biwaille, in manere of tragedie,
> The harm of hem that stoode in heigh degree,
> And fillen so that ther nas no remedie
> To brynge hem out of hir adversitee.
> *The Monk's Tale*, 1991–4

[I will bewail, in the style of tragedy, the fall of those that stood in high degree, and fell so that there was no remedy to bring them out of their adversity.]

I think it is very easy for us nowadays to miss the extremely provocative content of *The Monk's Tale* as it would have appeared to many of Chaucer's contemporaries. Here is the Monk telling a string of stories about the downfall of mighty and powerful rulers only a few years after the Peasants' Revolt, and at a time when the Court still lived in continual fear of further uprisings – and with good reason: there were disturbances in Norfolk in 1383 and an abortive rising in Kent in 1390, as well as attacks on property in London in 1412 and the Oldcastle revolt of 1415.[4] Look especially at the slant which the Monk gives to Nero's death. The downfall of Nero was a popular enough tale, with its gory details such as the opening-up of his mother's womb to see the place where he was conceived etc, but compare Chaucer's Monk's account with that of a rather more conservative churchman, John Mirk. In Mirk's version there is no mention of a popular uprising against the tyrant – instead Nero's death is glossed over by merely saying 'the Romans chased him out of the city'.[5] Of course, the simple listeners of the Middle Ages might not connect the glamorous and far-off 'Romans' with themselves; but in Chaucer's Monk's account it is very definitely 'the peple' who 'rombled up and down' – a frightening image for the well-to-do who had lived through those troubled times – and, what is most significant, the Monk clearly regards the revolt against Nero as a rightful act.

For John Gower, still quivering with fright in his study, the rebellious peasants of 1381 were no better than wild beasts with the Curse of God upon them. For him, the memory of the Revolt held nothing but horror and boded ill for the future: 'Although I may weep over it, I shall write of a tearful time, so that it may go down as an example for posterity.... As I write these things my pen grows wet with profuse weeping, and while I am carried forward by my zeal, my heart and hand tremble. ... One who looks further into this work and into the present time will find nothing consoling in the whole poem...."[6] And yet here is Chaucer, writing at the same time as Gower, calmly presenting a vivid instance from history of a revolt of the common people being totally justified. It is the ultimate answer to Theseus's tyrant's plea for unquestioning obedience

> To maken vertu of necessitee,
> And take it weel that we may nat eschue,
> And namely that to us alle is due.
> And whoso gruccheth ought, he dooth folye,
> And rebel is to hym that all may gye.
> *The Knight's Tale*, 3042–6

[To make necessity our strength, and take well, what we cannot avoid especially that which comes to us all. And whoever grumbles at all is foolish, and is a rebel against him who controls everything.]

In fact, in this 'tragedy' of Nero, the Monk is touching on that trickiest of subjects for medieval political thinkers: the question of how to get rid of a ruler who has become a tyrant. Many writers of the day, such as Bartolus of Sassoferrato and Marsilius of Padua, stop short of actually proposing the right of the ordinary people to revolt, but other writers, such as William of Ockham, claimed that revolution was justified, when the people were oppressed with tyranny and when there was no other remedy.[7] Even Wyclif, at times, suggested the duty of rebellion and even tyrannicide, but he usually laid emphasis on passive obedience for the sake of civil order, and probably with good reason.[8] After the shattering events of 1381, to be seen to support any form of revolution must have been very hazardous. In the troubled times of the late 1380s and 1390s any example of justified popular revolt – even if drawn from the far-off days of Nero's Rome – would have been considered highly inflammatory material. It is no wonder that the Monk dresses his tales up as 'tragedies', with a long diversionary preface on the metrical features of 'tragedy'. It is no wonder that he eases into his subject via safe examples of the downfall of individuals such as Lucifer, Adam, Hercules, Nebuchadnezzar. But, as he warms to his theme, he begins to home in on the question of tyranny and the disposal of tyrants. His targets move closer and closer to the Knight himself, until he is narrating the downfall of the Knight's own former war-lord Peter of Cyprus. In fact all the so-called 'modern instances' in *The Monk's Tale* (Pedro the Cruel, Peter of Cyprus, Bernabo Visconti of Milan and Ugolino of Pisa) must have cut the Knight to the quick. In the case of Pedro the Cruel of Castile, the Monk is being blatantly ironic when he calls him: 'O noble, O worthy Petro, glorie of Spayne' (*MT*, 2375), since all other contemporary writers – even the Spaniard Ayala – universally anathematized Don Pedro.[9] Pedro the Cruel was, in truth, a notorious tyrant, and his death was an unpleasant tale of treachery in which the King was slain by his own brother.[10] The whole episode was a considerable stain on the already tattered banner of chivalry, and the Monk brings it into the focus of the mercenary companies with which the Knight has been associated. He lays the blame for 'this cursednesse and al this synne' firmly at the door of Bertrand du Guesclin, then commander of the Free Companies in the service of Henry of Trastamara, and at the door of his nephew, Oliver Mauny – a Breton knight 'corrupt for mede'

(*MT*, 2389). Similarly with Peter of Cyprus, the Monk cheerfully recalls the winning of Alexandria – as if to remind his listeners of the Knight's connection with Peter – and then proceeds
to tell how Peter was killed in his bed by his 'owene liges' – among
whom, of course, we must count the Knight. The Monk blandly
remarks that Peter was killed 'for nothing but his chivalry', but
anyone familiar with Machaut's account of Peter's end (which
appears to have been the source of the Monk's account) would
have known that the Monk was being heavily ironic and that
Peter was murdered because he had become the very worst kind
of tyrant.[11] The Monk had really taken the gloves off now, and
the other pilgrims must have been holding their sides with sup-
pressed glee. With Bernabò Visconti, the Monk focuses on the
Italian tyrant as the typical employer of mercenaries, who meets
his death through the treachery of his own nephew, and with
the pitiable death of Ugolino – locked up in a tower to starve
to death with his three small children – the Monk presents the
ultimate image of the evil of tyranny. Ugolino was himself a tyrant, and he met the most inhuman death at the hands of another
– such is man's inhumanity to man.[12] The Monk has 'quitted'
The Knight's Tale in the most unequivocal terms by drawing on
at least one instance from the Knight's own military career and
including others which no doubt his audience would have recognized as the sort of tyrant-masters the Knight has been serving.
No wonder that under this onslaught – almost a personal attack
– the Knight suddenly bursts out: ' "Hoo!" quod the Knyght,
"good sire, namoore of this!" ' The whole thing is far too near
home for comfort, and he can obviously take no more.[13]

At this point I would like to put in a little plea for a reconsidera-
tion of the order of the stories in *The Monk's Tale*. At the
moment, the 'modern instances' are usually followed by the tales
of Nero, Holofernes, Alexander, Julius Caesar and Croesus, but
there is a large group of manuscripts including the two most auth-
oritative, Ellesmere and Hengwyrt, which concludes with the
modern instances.[14] This seems to me to make better sense of
the Knight's interruption. But even in the currently accepted
order, it is easy to see why the Knight gets so upset.

Far from finding *The Monk's Tale* boring, the other pilgrims
on that road to Canterbury must have been enjoying themselves
hugely at the Knight's expense. The Monk 'quits' the Knight's
eulogy of the proud conqueror Theseus by a compendious

exposition of the folly of those who, like the Knight, put their trust in Fortune and in worldly glory, for

> ...Fortune alwey wole assaille
> With unwar strook the regnes that been proude.
> *The Monk's Tale*, 2763–4

[Fortune will always bring low with an unexpected blow, the rulers that are proud.]

With *The Monk's Tale* and the Knight's irritable interruption, Chaucer completes a cycle within the overall structure of his great work. In the *Prologue* he describes a typical mercenary of his day, whose career has been one of bloodshed and oppression and yet who pretends to the dignity of the old-style feudal retainer. In *The Knight's Tale*, he presents a chivalric romance, seen through the eyes of a mercenary captain, which consequently turns into a hymn to tyranny – just as the mercenaries themselves had become the mainstay of the modern tyrant. In *The Monk's Tale*, he 'quits' the Knight's authoritarian and materialistic vision of the world by illustrating the debasement of modern chivalry and by asserting the right of the people to bring down tyrants. At the same time the Monk asserts the Boethian view of the folly of seeking human happiness in worldly power and glory.[15]

The whole cycle is vibrant with the political realities that Chaucer saw around him – the established tyrannies abroad and the nascent tyranny at home. It shows Chaucer as a concerned, committed writer, very much involved in and remarkably outspoken about the problems that most concerned the government and the ordinary people of his day.

Appendix: The meanings of 'chivalrie', 'trouthe', 'honour', 'fredom' and 'curteisie'

'Chivalrie'

In Chaucer's day, 'chivalrie' was still a word new to the English language, having been imported from the French only at the beginning of the century. (*The Middle English Dictionary* records no use in English prior to 1325.) Like so many new words, it started out with a specific technical meaning, which over the years has almost totally disappeared.

The word came from the Latin '*caballus*', and it originally specified an inferior kind of horse – a nag or pack-horse.[1] In the dialect of Latin spoken in northern France, the word became '*cheval*' and rose in the social scale – presumably because only people of importance were mounted. These mounted noblemen-warriors became known as '*chevaliers*', and, as a group, they were known as the '*chevalerie*'. This connotation of 'a host of armed, mounted warriors' was still the primary one in Chaucer's day.

Thus, when the Knight tells us in his *Tale* (KT, 865) that 'the regne of Femenye' was won by Theseus and by his 'chivalrye', he does not mean that it was won by Theseus and his 'noble conduct' but that it was won by Theseus and his cavalry.

The word could also be used to indicate 'the ethical code of chivalry', but it is important to realize that this was not the most common use of it. According to *The Middle English Dictionary*, 'chivalry' usually indicated 'a body of armed mounted warriors or knights, serving an overlord' or else it was simply applied to warfare in general or to feats of arms.[2]

A revealing illustration of what chivalry meant to Chaucer's contemporaries is contained in one of the first entries for the reign of Richard II in the *Rotuli Parliamentorum*. Here, in 1377 – a mere ten years before Chaucer started work on the *Tales* – we can see the word used in its clear technical meaning of 'mounted noblemen-soldiers' or 'cavalry' – while at the same time an attempt is made to define the ethical code which, it was felt, ought to go with it. This is a transcript of a complaint made by the Speaker of the House of Commons, Sir Peter de la Mare:

> He said, by way of complaint, that when the noble Chivalry of the Realm was well encouraged, cherished, honoured and rewarded for their great deeds, then the Chivalry urgently and ardently desired to make great expeditions and do great deeds of arms, each one vying with the other, and the Realm was greatly enriched and filled with good things, and its inhabitants feared by their enemies, of whom almost all nations spoke with honour and praise. And, what is more, the fame of their nobility spread across the whole earth. But today, because our Chivalry are put down, and held in disrespect, and, what is more, have their goods, which they won honourably from their enemies in War, taken away from them without just cause, and the use of Chivalry and all other virtue is neglected, and vice is prized, advanced and honoured and nowhere punished or chastised, then even the Chivalry themselves and the hearts of good and virtuous persons are greatly abashed, since there is no man who has the desire nowadays to do good, as experience would show. And so the Realm today newly suffers great damage and outrage from its said Enemies from diverse parts, and it is to be feared will suffer much more, unless God send a remedy to the Government of the Realm.[3]

For Chaucer's contemporaries, then, the word 'chivalry' had two broad meanings: the one carrying the overtones of idealism which we understand by the word today,[4] and the other being a precise technical term. In this latter sense, there was no automatic association with Christian spiritual idealism – on the contrary, the word might well be used in a wholly critical context. John Trevisa's translation of the *Dialogus inter Militem et Clericum*, for example, records the complaint that knights take the Church's wealth and spend it 'in chivalry and not for the benefit of Holy Church'.[5] Elsewhere, in an ironic poem of the period, an unknown poet brackets chivalry with 'riote and ribaudry' (*Song against the Friars*).[6] While Philippe de Mézières goes so far as to compare 'the two chivalries of France and England' with the twin perils of Scylla and Charybdis (*Letter to Richard II*).[7]

In short, the fact that the Knight loved *chivalrie* would not necessarily have meant the same to Chaucer's contemporaries as it does to us. It *could* have meant that he loved all the knightly virtues, but it could also have meant simply that he loved cavalry warfare and feats of arms – the sort of thing one might expect a knight to love, but without the automatic moral implications which we read into it.

'Trouthe'

When we turn to the next quality which the Knight admires, we find other questions raised. Modern translators normally render 'trouthe', in this particular context, as 'loyalty', but this was not the way in which Chaucer usually used the word. In an interesting study Gervase

Mathew distinguishes three different types of loyalty: fidelity to the pledged word; loyalty to an individual, owing to a transient relationship such as that of guest and host; and loyalty to an individual because of love or friendship. He continues: 'In the first case it was held to last until the pledge had been fulfilled; in the second until the mutual relationship which had given rise to it had ended. In the third it was ideally held to be irrevocable and of its nature incapable of change.'[8] 'Loyalty' in the Middle Ages was always a question of loyalty *to someone* – it was never loyalty to an abstract concept. Clearly it was this third kind of life-long allegiance which was one of the most cherished ideals of knighthood, and which we would expect the Knight of the *Prologue* to admire. It was this kind of loyalty that John of Gaunt tried to enshrine in his indentures of retinue, when he made knights swear their service to him 'in peace as in war for the duration of their lives'.[9] It was also this life-long loyalty which was most threatened by the change-over from feudal host to the mercenary armies of the fourteenth century, and it is precisely this kind of loyalty that is lacking from the Knight of the *Prologue*, with his record of fighting for a whole string of different masters all over the globe.

It is therefore significant that Chaucer chooses to tell us that his Knight admired 'trouthe'. In Anglo-Saxon, 'treoth' could mean 'truth, good faith, honour and fidelity', but it could also mean 'a pledge' or 'a covenant, an assurance of good faith'.[10] It is in this sense that Chaucer normally used the word, whereas he tended to express 'loyalty' by the word 'feythe'.[11]

'Feythe' came from the Latin '*fides*', 'faith, trust'. In Old French, it became '*fei*' or '*foi*', and also took on the specific meaning of 'fidelity towards one's sovereign'.[12] An itinerant mercenary would have no interest whatsoever in 'feythe' – he wanted to be free to contract out his services to whomsoever he pleased and wheresoever he pleased, exactly as the Knight of the *Prologue* has done. On the other hand, the mercenary was making war his business, and as a wise businessman he would do well to proclaim an interest in 'trouthe', in the sense of 'fulfilling his pledges'. All too often the mercenary captains of the Free Companies failed to fulfil their contracts, so they had to work hard to persuade any new prospective employer of their trustworthiness. Indeed it was precisely this quality which made Sir John Hawkwood the most famous English mercenary captain of his day. He might have changed sides, fighting for or against the Pope and for or against the Visconti, but it was his boast that, once he undertook a particular contract, he honoured it.[13] The Knight of the *Prologue* himself demonstrates this same sense of obligation to his pledged word when the 'cut' falls to him, and Chaucer here chooses his words carefully to emphasize the idea of contracts and agreements freely entered into and fulfilled:

And telle he moste his tale, as was resoun,
By foreward and by composicioun,
As ye han herd; what nedeth wordes mo?
And whan this goode man saugh that it was so,
As he that wys was and obedient
To kepe his foreward by his free assent,
He seyde, 'Syn I shall bigynne the game,
What, welcome be the cut, a Goddes name!'
General Prologue, 847–54

[And he must tell his tale, as was right
According to the agreement and the treaty,
As you have heard. What more need one say?
When this good man saw that it was so,
Then as a man who was prudent and scrupulous
In keeping his agreement, by his own free will
He said: 'Since I must begin the game,
What! Welcome be the cut in God's name!']

The distinction between a 'pledge entered into of one's own free will' and the kind of loyalty over which a man had no control (e.g. loyalty to one's sovereign or feudal lord) was a crucial one in Chaucer's day – it marked the transition from the old feudal world to the new. The Knight of the *Prologue* is to be commended for his love of 'trouthe', but I would suggest that this should be interpreted as 'honesty' or 'trustworthiness'. The concept of 'feythe' or 'loyalty' has played precious little part in his career.

'Honour'

The Knight's love of 'honour' is even more open to interpretation. To at least one other pilgrim, riding alongside the Knight on that road to Canterbury, the love of 'honour' was damnable – it condemned a man to the eternal fires of hell. For the modern reader, the primary sense of the word may be, as Dr Johnson defined it, 'nobleness of mind, scorn of meanness, magnanimity', but this was not what Chaucer's contemporaries necessarily or even usually understood by it. According to *The Middle English Dictionary*, by far the most usual connotations of the word 'honour' were: 'the action of honouring someone' or 'fame, repute, worldly glory'.[14] Such is the definition of 'honour' which the Knight himself offers –it provides, indeed, the philosophical climax to his long tale:

And certeinly a man hath moost honour
To dyen in his excellence and flour*,   [flower]
Whan he is siker* of his goode name;   [sure]
Thanne hath he doon his freend, ne hym*, no shame.   [nor himself]
And gladder oghte his freend been of his deeth,

Whan with honour up yolden* is his breeth,	[yielded up]
Than whan his name apalled is for age*,	[tarnished with old age]
For al forgeten is his vassellage*.	[prowess]
Thanne is it best, as for a worthy fame*,	[in order to leave behind a good name]
To dyen whan that he is best of name*.	[at the height of his fame]

Knight's Tale, 3047–56

Such a high opinion of wordly honour was not shared by the writers who influenced Chaucer's own thought and writing most profoundly.[15] Boethius, for example, in a book which Chaucer himself considered worth the pains of translating, wrote: 'If you really consider the infinite space of eternity, have you any reason to rejoice in the long life of your own name? ... However long a time fame last, if it is thought of in the context of boundless eternity, it is clearly seen to be, not small, but nothing at all.'[16] In another work which was a seminal influence on Chaucer, Cicero wrote to the same effect.[17]

Naturally a love of worldly glory remained a major characteristic of the knights of Chaucer's day, and it was one which was frequently condemned by the writers of his own acquaintance. Chaucer's close friend Sir John Clanvowe claimed that the kind of honour which knights all too often sought and the way in which they sought it was a cause for shame: 'For the world holds worshipful those that are great warriors and fighters and that destroy and win many lands.... But whatever the world thinks about such folk, let us learn that God, who is sovereign truth and a true judge, considers them shameful.'[18]

For the benefit of the other Canterbury pilgrims, the Poor Parson provides a definition of 'honour', and this is what he says:

... You know well that 'honour' is what men call the reverence that man does to man, but in Hell there is no 'honour' nor reverence. For certainly no more reverence will be done there to a king than to a knave.... 'Honour' is also what we call great lordship, but in Hell no man shall serve another but with harm and torment. 'Honour' is also what we call great dignity and highness, but in Hell they shall all be trodden under by devils.[19]

So much for the 'honour' which the Knight so admires.

'Fredom'

The next quality which the Knight loves is 'fredom'. Modern critics invariably interpret the word 'fredom' in this particular line as 'largess' or 'prodigal generosity' – but this was not the usual meaning of the word nor was it the way in which Chaucer himself normally used the word.[20] 'Largess' was perhaps the most crucial quality for a knight to possess – no other knightly quality is so widely illustrated in the popular literature of the day,[21] and even the Poor Parson regards moderate largess as the hall-mark of true 'gentility'.[22] The concept of largess found its origins in the liberality with which a war-leader rewarded his followers, thereby binding about himself a loyal band; it was thus a cornerstone of the feudal system and, consequently, of knighthood itself.[23] And yet the extraordinary fact remains that Chaucer never once associates the word 'largess' with the Knight of the *Prologue*, nor does the Knight himself ever use the word in his *Tale* of nearly three thousand lines supposedly dedicated to romantic chivalry. It is an unthinkable omission in a portrait that purports to represent the flower of knighthood. Therefore, it has been argued, since the only word that could possibly mean generosity is 'fredom', it must mean generosity here.[24]

There are, however, several objections to this argument. In the first place, Chaucer never seems to use 'fredom' to indicate the largess of a warlord to his followers. In fact, there are only three occasions when he unquestionably uses it to mean 'largess' at all, and these are all in a romantic context.[25] On the other occasions when Chaucer uses the word, it means either freedom of action (as when he translates the *'libertas'* of Boethius) or the concept which was known in Old French as *'fraunchise'* (as in his translation of the *Roman de la Rose*).[26] When Chaucer wished to indicate the concept of largess, he usually said 'largess' (as he does on some nineteen occasions).[27]

'Fraunchise' itself was also an important quality for a knight to possess. Gervase Mathew, in his study of chivalry in the late-fourteenth century, defined it as 'the mark of the wellbred ... a certain freedom and naturalness in manner and form of approach'.[28] The Black Prince displayed it, for instance, when he made his triumphal entry into Bordeaux on foot and holding the hands of his wife and son. It was that independence which comes from non-servile status – the easy naturalness of the privileged.[29]

Thus, since Chaucer normally used 'fredom' to mean liberty of action or *'fraunchise'*, and since *'fraunchise'* was an important knightly quality, there seems little reason for not concluding that that is what it means here. Indeed, it is quite apparent from the Knight's treatment of the other pilgrims and from the manner in telling his *Tale* that he possesses both liberty of action and *'fraunchise'*.[30] He never displays, however, the slightest trace of 'largess'.

'Curteisie'

'Curteisie' was another quality which it was only natural for a 'gentil knyght' to admire – indeed it would have been unthinkable for an exponent of chivalry to be without it. Like *'fraunchise'* it was one of the five virtues symbolized by the points of the pentangle which that doyen of chivalry Sir Gawain carried on his shield.[31]

The Latin word for an enclosed area, a yard or courtyard was 'cohors'. In the Latin of the Middle Ages this became 'curtis' and in Old French: 'cort'.[32] Since a house large enough to have a courtyard inevitably belonged to the rich and noble families, the cort began to refer to the gatherings of people who assembled round these grand folk. The behaviour which was expected from people attending a nobleman's cort became known in Old French as 'corteisie' and in Middle English as 'curteisie'. By Chaucer's day, the meaning of 'curteisie' was wide and flexible. It could refer to the whole complex of courtly ideals, to a benevolent or humane disposition, or even to the grace or mercy of God.[33] But it could also mean no more than 'refined manners'. According to Gervase Mathew, this was, by the late-fourteenth century, the dominant meaning of the word, even though it frequently retained some of the earlier moral implications. Mathew writes: 'The sense of "courtoisie" had been slowly narrowing. At this time it primarily means good manners, whether in action, as in the 'cortaysie" books, or in conversation – the "teccheles termes of talkyng noble" as in Gawain and in the careful courtliness of Degrevant.'[34]

Chaucer himself frequently uses 'curteisie' to mean simply 'refined manners', and, when he does, he sees it not as a moral strength but more often as a cloak for evil-doing. In his beautiful poem Complaint Unto Pity he describes how 'Crueltee' hides 'hir tirannye' under the guise of 'Beaute ... Bounte, Gentilesse and Curtesye' (l. 68). Without that crucial quality of Pity, fine manners are just the tool of evil:

> Eke what availeth Maner and Gentilesse
> Withoute yow, benygne creature?
> Shal Cruelte be your governeresse?
> *Complaint Unto Pity*, 78–80

In *The Canterbury Tales*, 'curteisie' is not necessarily a profound moral virtue; it is a quality found in villains as much as in heroes and heroines. Those confidence tricksters the Canon and his Yeoman are 'ful of curteisye'; so is the swindling Monk in the *Shipman's Tale*, and so is the scheming, lecherous Friar.[35] The greatest exponent of 'curteisie' on the whole pilgrimage is, of course, the Prioress. 'In curteisie was set ful muchel hir lest' (*General Prologue*, 132) and there is no question but that Chaucer is using the word ironically here. The Prioress's concept of 'curteisie' is simply to imitate the fine manners of the Court:

> And peyned hire to countrefete cheere
> Of court, and to be estatlich of manere,
> And to ben holden digne of reverence.
> *General Prologue*, 139–41

> [She strove to imitate the appearances
> Of Court and have a stately manner
> And be considered worthy of reverence.]

Her human charity and pity, on the other hand, do not extend beyond dead mice and little dogs, and in her *Tale* her sentimental pity for the little choirboy is overshadowed by her bloodthirsty and pitiless treatment of the Jews.[36]

In short, the Knight's love of 'curteisie' is open to interpretation. It may indeed be an admirable trait, but equally it could be no more than a love of fine manners. We shall have to hold our judgement over which it is.

To summarize: 'Chivalrie', 'Trouthe', 'Honour', 'Fredom' and 'Curtesie' are all concepts which we might expect a knight to admire, but they are not necessarily the idealized moral virtues that they seem. They could equally well be interpreted as: 'deeds of arms, trustworthiness, worldly glory, freedom of action and fine manners'.

It is also worth noting what qualities are missing from this list. Chaucer is ominously silent about such qualities as: magnanimity, physical beauty and, above all, pity – that knightly quality which, for the Gawain poet, surpassed all others and without which, according to Chaucer himself, fine manners and high birth all too easily become a cloak for cruelty.[37]

Notes to the illustrations

191 From *De re militari* by Roberto Valturius (1472) in the British Museum. Reproduced in G. Trease, *The Condottieri*, p. 121.

193 From *De natura deorum et de divinatione* by Cicero. Italian fourteenth century. Now in Bibliothèque Nationale, Paris. MS Latin 6340. Also reproduced in G. Trease, *The Condottieri*, p. 81.

214 Paolo Uccello, *Sir John Hawkwood*. From the monument to Hawkwood which still hangs in the Duomo, Florence.

Notes

Abbreviations used in the Notes and Bibliography

ANTS	Anglo-Norman Text Society
Arch	Archaeologia
ChauR	Chaucer Review
CJH	Canadian Journal of History
CMH	Cambridge Medieval History
EconHR	Economic History Review
EETS	Early English Text Society
EHD	English Historical Documents
EHR	English Historical Review
ELH	English Literary History
EPS	English Philological Studies
JEGP	Journal of English and German Philology
LTR	London Topographical Review
MED	Middle English Dictionary
MLN	Modern Language Notes
MLQ	Modern Language Quarterly
MLR	Modern Language Review
MP	Modern Philology
N&Q	Notes and Queries
PLPLS	Proceedings of the Leeds Philosophical and Literary Society
PMLA	Proceedings of the Modern Language Association
P&P	Past and Present
PQ	Philological Quarterly
RES	Review of English Studies
STS	Scottish Text Society
TAPA	Transactions of the American Philological Association
TCAAS	Transactions of the Connecticut Academy of Arts and Sciences
TRHS	Transactions of the Royal Historical Society
UTQ	University of Toronto Quarterly

Notes

Preface

1. Steven Runciman, *A History of the Crusades*, III, pp. 444–5.
2. Charles Mitchell, 'The Worthiness of Chaucer's Knight', *MLQ*, XXV, 1964, pp. 66–75.
3. See Comte de Mas Latrie, *Relations et commerce de l'Afrique septentrionale ou Magreb avec les nations Chrétiennes au Moyen Age*; also Norman Daniel, *The Arabs and Medieval Europe*, p. 309; also A.A. Dent, 'Chaucer and the Horse' in *PLPLS*, IX, 1959–62, pp. 1–12.
4. The argument of the guide-book, by W. Douglas Simpson, is reproduced in his article 'Bastard Feudalism and the Later Castles' in *Antiquaries Journal*, XXVI, 1946, pp. 145–71.
5. Chaucer, *The Miller's Prologue*, 3118–19.
6. In P.M. Holt (ed.) *The Eastern Mediterranean Lands in the Period of the Crusades*, Warminster, 1977 pp. 90–105.
7. *Journal of Medieval History*, VI, 1980.
8. Holt, *op. cit.* p. 99.
9. For the translation of *envie* as 'harms or ills' see *MED*.

Traditional interpretation of Chaucer's Knight

1. J.M. Manly, 'A Knight Ther Was', *TAPA*, XXXVIII, 1907, p. 107.
2. *The Complete Works of Geoffrey Chaucer*, F.N. Robinson, p. 652n.
3. Muriel Bowden, *A Commentary on the General Prologue to the Canterbury Tales*, p. 45.
4. *Chaucer's Poetry*, ed. E. T. Donaldson, p. 881.
5. *Ibid*, p. 882.
6. Jill Mann, *Chaucer and Medieval Estates Satire*, p. 113.
7. David M. Zesmer, *Guide to English Literature*, 1961, p. 213.
8. In addition to the works already quoted cf: Emile Legouis, *Geoffrey Chaucer*, trans. L. Lailavoix, p. 148; A.S. Cook, 'The historical background of Chaucer's Knight', *TCAAS*, XX, 1916, p. 237; Charles Muscatine, 'Form, texture and meaning in Chaucer's Knight's Tale', *PMLA*, LXV, 1950, pp. 911–29; Nevill Coghill, *The Poet Chaucer*, pp. 44–5; R.M. Lumiansky, *Of Sondry Folk: the Dramatic Principle in the Canterbury Tales*, pp. 29–49; William Frost, 'An interpretation of Chaucer's Knight's Tale', *RES*, XXV, 1949, pp. 290–304, even the admirable H.A. Patch, *On Rereading Chaucer*, p. 155. The only dissenting voice in all this is that of Charles Mitchell who speculated, without any concrete evidence, on whether the Knight's motives were really self-serving. See Charles Mitchell, 'The Worthiness of Chaucer's Knight', pp. 66–75. Otherwise it is only historians, primarily concerned with other topics, who see the Knight clearly as a mercenary: cf Norman Daniel, *The Arabs and Medieval Europe*, p. 309; A.A. Dent, 'Chaucer and the Horse', IX, pp. 1–12.
9. Bernard F. Huppé, *A Reading of the Canterbury Tales*, p. 31.

What was a 'knight' in the fourteenth century?

1. *Middle English Dictionary*, ed H. Kurath and Kuhn.
2. Sally Harvey, 'The Knight and the Knight's Fee in England', *P&P*, II, 1970, p. 27 and p. 15; see also *Domesday Book 11 Middlesex* (trans. J. Morris), Appendix.
3. Harvey, 'The Knight's Fee', p. 42.
4. See P.D.A. Harvey, 'The English Inflation of 1180–1220' in *Peasants, Knights and Heretics: studies in Medieval English Social History*, ed. R.H. Hilton, pp. 57–84.
5. See Harvey, 'The Knight's Fee', pp. 39–40.
6. *Ibid*, p. 40.
7. For prices of plough horses see D.L. Farmer, 'Some Livestock Price Movements in Thirteenth-Century England' in *EconHR*, XXII, 1969, pp. 1–16. For the price of knights' horses see J.E. Morris, who quotes direct from Exchequer Accounts in *Welsh Wars of Edward I*, p. 49. For Chaucer's house see *Chaucer Life-Records*, Martin M. Crow and Clair C. Olson, p. 537.
8. See M.R. Powicke, *Military Obligation in Medieval England*, p. 103.
9. *Ibid*, p. 109.
10. *Ibid*, pp. 176–7.
11. Cf. H.S. Bennett, *The Pastons and their England*, p. 13; also *The Paston Letters and Papers of the Fifteenth Century*, ed. N. Davies, p. lxvii.
12. Powicke, *Military Obligation*, p. 175; Richard Barber, *The Knight and Chivalry*, p. 18.
13. F.J. Child (ed.), *The English and Scottish Popular Ballads*, III, p. 58, 'A geste of Robyn Hode' st. 45 – my modernization.
14. Harvey, 'The Knight's Fee', p. 42: 'By the early-thirteenth century men of noble birth were proud to style themselves knight [*miles*] in their formal documents. When only the wealthy could be accoutred as a knight, knighthood appeared socially desirable, and the burden of the knightly role acceptable to some.' See also Powicke, *Military Obligation*, p. 103. Powicke states that at the end of Henry III's reign (1216–72) the obligation to bear arms as a knight had degenerated into 'a mere question of status easily escaped by the payment of a relatively light fine'. See also: J. Riley-Smith, *The Feudal Nobility and the Kingdom of Jerusalem, 1174–1277*, p. 11.
15. See Caxton's translation of Ramon Lull (1233–1316) in the *Book of The Ordre of Chyualrye*, pp. 58–9, quoted below in 'Is the Knight "gentil"?' note 3 (p. 269).
16. Child, *loc. cit.*, note 13 above, st. 47 – my modernization.
17. See Harvey, 'The Knight's Fee', p. 31.
18. See A.E. Prince, 'The Indenture System under Edward III' in *Historical Essays in Honour of James Tait*, p. 287. As a measure of how unpopular such service abroad was, even in the twelfth century, it is recorded how in 1159 Henry II employed mercenaries in order to spare his 'country knights' the burden of military service in Toulouse. See Harvey, 'The Knight's Fee', p. 35.
19. See Powicke, *Military Obligation*, p. 172.
20. *Ibid*, also *Rolls of Parliament*, III, p. 66.
21. Powicke, *Military Obligation*, p. 103:

> The gap between knightly arms and those of ordinary men-at-arms was now steadily increasing. Heavier and more complicated armour, and therefore heavier horses, and the ever-developing practices and rites of chivalry, such as the assumption of coats of arms, raised a barrier between the knight and the ordinary man-at-arms.

22. See Powicke, *Military Obligation*, p. 102.
23. *Ibid*, p. 102.
24. See H.J. Hewitt, 'The Organization of War' in *The Hundred Years' War*, ed. Kenneth Fowler, p. 80. For example, in 1341 the Earl of Warwick undertook to raise two bannerets, twenty-six knights, seventy-one men-at-arms, forty armed men and one hundred archers.
25. For good definitions of the phrase 'feudal system' see: J.M.W. Bean, *The Decline of English Feudalism, 1215–1540*, p. 6, also p. 3 and pp. 306–7; S.H. Steinberg and I.H. Evans, *Steinberg's Dictionary of British History*, p. 135; Marc Bloch, *Feudal Society*, trans. L. A. Manyon, p. 444. I use 'feudal' as applied to that system instituted by William I, in which all lands belonged to the king and were granted to tenants-in-chief in return for specific services – generally military though not exclusively so. These tenants-in-chief would pass off some of the lands which the king had granted them, forming a pyramidical society with the king at its apex.
26. See Barber, *The Knight and Chivalry*, p. 13; also Harvey, 'The Knight's Fee', p. 7.
27. Honoré Bonet, *The Tree of Battles*, trans. G.W. Coopland, p. 146.
28. My translation of the French in *Camden Misc.*, XXII (4th ser. vol. 1), 1964, pp. 93–4.
29. *Ibid*, p. 98.
30. Harvey, 'The Knight's Fee', p. 28 writes:

> Contemporaries as well as historians ran into likely misinterpretations by the use of the single word for all military men from the magnate who went on campaigns downwards, and so in prose they often use distinguishing adjectives to make themselves plain. William of Poitiers's account of the preparations for the Norman Conquest depicts Duke William giving instructions first to his compeers, then to 'middling noble knights' (*milites mediae nobilitatis*), then to the 'common knights' (*milites gregarios*).

31. Barber, *The Knight and Chivalry*, p. 21; Harvey, 'The Knight's Fee', pp. 40–1; Steinberg, *Dic. Brit. Hist.*, p. 198.
32. *General Prologue*, 356. See *Chaucer Life-Records*, ed. Crow and Olson, p. 364.
33. Thomas Wimbledon's Sermon, ed. Nancy M. Owen, *Medieval Studies*, XXVIII, 1966, p. 178.

> Right so in the chirche beeth nedeful thes thre offices: presthod, knyghthod, [and] laboreris. [To] prestes [it fallith to] k[utt]e awey the voide braunchis of synn[i]s with the swerd of here tonges. To knyghtis it fallith to lette wrongis and thefitis to be do and to mayntene Goddis Lawe and hem that ben techeris therof, and also to kepe the lond fro enemyes of other londes. And to laboreris it falleth to trauayle bodily and with here sore swet geten out of the erth [b]odily liflode for hem and for other parties. And these statis beth also nedeful to the chirche that non may wel ben withouten other.

Gower emphasizes the knight's role as the strong arm of the law:

> Each estate, whichever it may be
> Is ordained after its own kind
> To do a particular job in the world;
> Therefore in order to guard the common right
> Knights must do battle,
> Because it behoves their honour.
> Gower, *Mirour de l'Omme*, 23617–22 (my trans.)

The same use of the word 'knight' to mean 'the lay power' is found all through official records – e.g. *Rolls of Parliament*, v, p. 504; see also Lydgate, *Fall of Princes*, i, xii.

34. Thomas Hoccleve, *The Regement of Princes*, 442–5 (my trans.); *Thomas Wimbledon's Sermon of 1388*, ed. Nancy H. Owen, *Medieval Studies*, XXVIII, 1900, p. 182. 'It is to wondry trewly how the lif of prestis is chaunged they beth clothed as knyghtes....'

35. John Myrc, the prior of Lilleshall in Shropshire, complained that nowadays one could not tell priests from knights – in an unpublished homily (*Lib.* i, *cap. xiii*, MS York Minster Libr., xvi o. 11, fols. 396–400) translated by Owst, *Literature and Pulpit*, p. 277:

> A knight is addressed as 'Sir'; a priest is also called 'Sir'. A knight makes use of gold; and so does that priest. A knight is dressed according to the form and fashion of the world. But neither here is there any differences between the two. Thus he (the priest) conforms to the world in such a way that in nothing does he differ from the people, save possibly in the tonsure which is reserved for him.

36. See also Myrc, *Instructions for Parish Priests*, ed. E. Peacock, pp. 1–3. In the thirteenth and early-fourteenth centuries Edward I tried hard to enforce a royal monopoly but was not all that successful. In the fourteenth century there are many records of such knighting (particularly after Crécy and Calais). For example, in 1333 an Exchequer return records that one William Morant of Kent had taken up knighthood on the Feast of Holy Trinity from Richard de Grey of Thodenore.

37. See *Dictionary of National Biography* and J. Temple-Leader and G. Marcotti, *Sir John Hawkwood*, p. 9. For an account of Hawkwood knighting his own men, see Geoffrey Trease, *The Condottieri*, p. 70.

38. Barber, *The Knight and Chivalry*, p. 24.

39. See K.B. McFarlane, *Lancastrian Kings and Lollard Knights*, pp. 148–85. And in particular, Sir Richard Sturry was a most prominent counsellor of both Edward III and Richard II, earning for himself the name of '*regi familiarissimus*' (*Chron. Angl.*, ed. E.M. Thompson, p. 87). See J.F. Baldwin, *The King's Council in England during the Middle Ages*, pp. 89–90, especially the journal kept by John Prophet, clerk of the Council, from 1392–5, Baldwin, pp. 489–507.

40. For an account of the breakdown of the old patriarchal structure in later centuries see Peter Laslett, *The World We Have Lost*, p. 1 ff, especially p. 17.

41. Bloch, *Feudal Society*, pp. 443, 444–5, notes the complexity of the feudal relationship. He stresses the quasi-family character of the relationship and the 'necessary personal contact':

> But much as feudal society differed from societies based on kinship as well as from those dominated by the power of the State, it was their successor and bore their imprint.
>
> From this necessary personal contact the relationship derived the best part of its moral value.

42. See Jean de Meung, *Roman de la Rose*, ed. Sutherland, ll. 5091–100. The Chaucerian translation amplifies the medical side:

> Physiciens and aduocates
> Gone right by the same yates;
> They sell her science for wynnyng,
> And haunte her crafte for great gettyng.

> Her wynnyng is of suche swetnesse,
> That if a man fall in sicknesse,
> They are ful glad, for her encrese;
> For by her wyll, without lese,
> Eueryche man shulde be seke,
> And though they dye, they set not a leke
> After, whan they the golde haue take,
> Ful lytel care for hem they make.
> They wolde that fourty were sicke at ones,
> Ye, two hundred, in flesshe and bones.
> And yet two thousande, as I gesse,
> For to encresen her rychesse,
> They wol not worchen, in no wyse
> But for lucre and couetyse;
> For physicke gynneth first by phy,
> The phisycien also sothely;
> And sythen it gothe from (phy) to (sy);
> To truste on hem, it is folye;
> For they nyl, in no maner gre,
> Do right nought for charyte.
> *Romaunt of the Rose*, ed. Sutherland, 5721–44

The father-in-law of Chaucer's patron, John of Gaunt, Henry Duke of Lancaster, wrote that if medicine is expensive and a man poor, then the doctor should give him medicine free out of the goodness of his heart:

si l'omme est poure et la medicine chiere, c'est trop fort si lui meistres ne soit [si] curtois q'il le voille garrir sanz plus prendre de soen forsqe soulement grant mercy, mes qe ceo soit de bon coer.

Henry, Duke of Lancaster, *Le Livre Seynt Medicines*, ed. E.J. Arnold, p. 7. See also Wyclif, *English Works of Wyclif*, and Langland, *Piers Plowman*, C1, 158–68; Gower, *Vox Clamantis*, IV, 1–4. Against this background I think it is possible to see the sharpness of Chaucer's barb against the Doctor of Physic:

> And yet he was but esy of dispence;
> He kepte that he wan in pestilence.
> For gold in phisik is a cordial,
> Therfore he lovede gold in special.
> *General Prologue*, 441–4

Chaucer is talking about the Black Death – the helplessness of people confronted by that terrible plague was still vivid in their minds as was the well-known inadequacy of the medical profession to deal with it (see Ziegler, *The Black Death*, pp. 71–2). The callousness with which the Doctor of Physic has nevertheless simply lined his own pockets must have been even more disgusting to Chaucer's contemporaries for the way it is underplayed.

43. Printed in Sir P. Horton-Smith Hartley and H.R. Aldridge, *Johannes de Mirfield of St Bartholomew's Smithfield*, p. 133, quoted in W.O. Hassall, *How they Lived*, p. 223.
44. See Corrado Pallenberg, *Vatican Finances*, Chapter 1, for a good account of how usury became respectable.
45. That there are alternatives to a medical culture dependent on paid professionals see: Ivan Illich, *Medical Nemesis*, London, 1975, pp. 87–93.

The rise and rise of the mercenaries

1. H.G. Richardson and G.O. Sayles, *The Governance of Medieval England*, pp. 463–5. See also: J.M.W. Bean, *The Decline of English Feudalism, 1215–1540*, pp. 306–9; T.F. Tout, *Chapters in the Administrative History of Medieval England*, pp. 134–5.
2. Harvey, 'The Knight's Fee', pp. 29–30.
3. *Ibid*, p. 35.
4. *Ibid*, p. 6.
5. C. Stephenson and F.G. Marcham, *Sources of English Constitutional History*, p. 123, 51: 'And immediately after the restoration of peace we will remove from the kingdom all alien knights, crossbowmen, serjeants and mercenaries, who have come with horses and arms to the injury of the kingdom.'
6. C.T. Allmand, *Society at War: the experience of England and France during the Hundred Years' War*, pp. 5–6: 'The need for bigger armies, ready to serve outside England and for longer than the forty days specified in the feudal agreement, meant that an army whose existence and cohesion depended largely upon financial reward was coming into being by the time the Hundred Years' War began. It is the ever-increasing emphasis upon financial and material reward which characterizes the period.'
7. Charles Oman writes in *CMH*, VIII, pp. 655–6: 'When tyrants, the inevitable result of faction, grew common in Italy, they habitually discouraged the native levee *en masse*, preferring to rely on mercenaries. But the cities which never fell into the hands of a tyrant, such as Venice, were no less given to the employment of foreign bands than were the lords of Milan, Verona, or Padua.' For the early history of the *condottieri* see G. Trease, *The Condottieri*, pp. 11–40.
8. J.J.N. Palmer, *England, France and Christendom, 1377–99*, p. 12, and M. Mallett, *Mercenaries and their Masters*, p. 36.
9. Froissart notes in his *Chronicles*, trans. Johnes, I, p. 298: 'There were at that time in France, besides these Companies [French] many other pillagers, English, Gascons and Germans, who were desirous of living there and who maintained many garrisons in fortresses. Although the commissaries from the king of England had ordered them to evacuate these castles, and to leave the country, they had not obeyed, which was very displeasing to the king of France, as well as to his council.'
10. Henry Knighton, *Chronicon*, II, pp. 114–15: '*Eodem tempore crevit quaedam societas virorum fortium vocata Societas fortunae, et per quosdam vocata est La grant companye. Et adunati sunt de diversis partibus non habentes unde vivere nisi de suo labore post initam pacem inter regna. Isti erant viri fortes et bellicosi, elegantes et strenui et vivebant de suo perquisito per guerram, in pace nil habentes.*'
11. Jean de Venette, *Chronicle*, trans. Birdshall, p. 106.
12. See Froissart. *Chronicles*, trans. Johnes, I, p. 297. Also *CMH*, VII, p. 358.
13. Jean de Venette, *Chronicle*, pp. 106–7.
14. Froissart, *Chronicles*, trans. Johnes, I, p. 295–9.
15. Walsingham, *Historia Anglicana*, ed. H.T. Riley, I, pp. 295–6, and Murimath. *Chronica*, ed. T. Hog, pp. 194–5.
16. Froissart, *Cronycle*, trans. Berners, III, p. 70 (my modernization).
17. H. Trease, *The Condottieri*, p. 73.
18. London, *Calendar of Select Pleas and Memoranda of the City of London, 1381–1412*, ed. A.H. Thomas, p. 257.
19. Temple-Leader and Marcotti, *Sir J. Hawkwood*, p. 14; p. 27.
20. Pietro Azario, '*Liber gestorum in Lombardia*' in L.A. Muratori, *Rerum Italicarum Scriptores – Storici Italiani*, XVI, IV, p. 128: '*Carcerabant homines*

singuli suos in scrineis et ipsos intus clavabant de nocte quando equitant et de die tenent ipsos inclusos et custoditos; quam terram studentes evacuare....'

21. Matteo Villani's chronicle is actually a continuation of his father Giovanni's: Villani, *Cronica*, V, pp. 259–60: '*Costoro tutti giovani, e per la maggoir parte nati e accresciuti nelle lunghe guerre tra' Franceschi e Inghilesi, caldi e vogliosi, usi agli omicidii e alle rapine, erano correnti al ferro, poco avendo loro persone in calere.*'

22. G. Trease, *The Condottieri*, p. 73.

23. For a description of the appalling massacre at Cesena, see Temple-Leader and Marcotti, *Sir J. Hawkwood*, pp. 118–23.

24. G. Trease, *op. cit.*, p. 38.

25. Froissart, *Chronicles*, trans. Johnes, I, p. 295; see also J.W. Sherborne, 'Indentured Retinues and English Expeditions to France, 1369–1380', *EHR*, LXXIX, 1964, p. 735.

26. See R.J. Barnet and R.E. Muller, *Global Reach – The Power of the Multinational Corporations*, pp. 15–25. The annual sales of General Motors, for example, are greater than the Gross National Product of Switzerland, Pakistan and South Africa, while Goodyear Tyre has a turn-over higher than the GNP of Saudi Arabia.

Fourteenth-century attitudes to mercenaries

1. See G. Trease, *The Condottieri*, p. 34.

2. See Temple-Leader and Marcotti, *Sir John Hawkwood*, pp. 7–8.

3. C.T. Allmand, *Society at War*, pp. 5–6, 188. See also K. McRobbie, 'The Concept of Advancement in the Fourteenth Century', *CJH*, VI, 1971, pp. 1–19.

4. Froissart, *Cronycle*, trans. Berners, II, p. 183.

5. Alain Chartier, *Quadriloque Invectif*, ed. M.S. Blayney, p. 230 – my modernization.

6. 'Ac sith bondemenne barnes han be mad bisshopes, And barnes bastardes han ben archidekenes, And sopers and here sones for siluer han be knyghts, And lordene sones here laborers and leid here rentes to wedde.' Langland, *Piers Plowman* C-Text, VI, 70–3.

7. Gower, *The Major Latin Works of John Gower*, ed. and trans. E.W. Stockton: 'Vox Clamantis', VII, IV, p. 260: 'Arms are more of a business now than a mark of nobility; as a result, the tailor's boy now goes about in a helmet. The gilded spur is all too common now, and for this reason there is not the honor in feats of arms that there used to be.'

8. *Ibid*, p. 260.

9. For Roger di Flor and Andronicus II see: Geoffrey Trease, *The Condottieri*, p. 32. For an example of trouble with the English companies in Italy, see *Calendar of Papal Register relating to Great Britain and Ireland 1342–1404*, ed. Bliss, Johnson and Twemlow, IV, pp. 121, 154, 265–6.

10. Ramon Lull, *The Book of the Ordre of Chyualry*, trans. William Caxton, ed. A.T.P. Byles, pp. 62–3: 'Chyualry may not be mayntened withoute harnoys which apperteyneth to a knyght/nor without thonourable costes and dispences whiche apperteyne to chyualrye/By cause a squyer beyng withoute harneys/And that hath no rychesse for to make his dispences/yf he be made knyght/hym shold peraduenture happe for nede to be a robbour/a theef/traitre lyar or begylour/or haue some other vyces whiche ben contrary to Chyualry.'

11. Barber, *The Knight and Chivalry*, pp. 16–17.

12. See Charles Oman in *CMH*, VIII, p. 655.

13. Machiavelli, *The Prince*, ed. 1640, pp. 92–3.
14. Jean de Bel, *Chronique*, ed. Viard and Deprez, II, pp. 294–6. Edward III did, of course, use foreign troops but always within the retinue of some indentured knight. See Sherborne, 'Indentured Retinues', p. 723.
15. Froissart, *Chronicles*, trans. Johnes, I, p. 355.
16. The Cypriot chronicler Makhairas records that Peter sent envoys to recruit from the Free Companies in Lombardy. In all of this, of course, he was being encouraged by the Pope, who was only too anxious to get the Free Companies out of Italy. Cf Makhairas, *Recital concerning the Sweet Land of Cyprus entitled 'Chronicle'*, ed. and trans. R.M. Dawkins, I, p. 97; G. Canestrini, *Documenti della Milizia Italiana*, p. 85; Froissart, *Cronycle*, trans. Berners II, p. 93, and Jean de Venette, *Chronicle*, trans. Birdshall, p. 132.
17. Guillaume de Machaut, *La Prise d'Alexandrie*, ed. Mas Latrie, I, 3583.
18. Christine de Pisan, *The Book of Fayttes of Armes and of Chyualrye*, trans. William Caxton, ed. A.T.P. Byles, p. 26:

more profytable is to a kyng or prynce to see his men vsed & wel taught in the said art and fait of armes how fewe or lytyl quantite of peple he hath/than to take and reteyne vnder hym grete foison of strange souldeours that he knoweth not

19. W. Douglas Simpson, *Doune Castle*, guidebook, 1973.
20. See W. Douglas Simpson, 'Bastard Feudalism and the Later Castles', *Antiquaries Journal*, XXVI, 1946, pp. 145–71.
21. For example, Bonet, *Tree of Battles*, p. 153; also J. Barnie, *War in Medieval Society*, pp. 67–8.
22. Gower, 'Mirour de l'Omme' in *Complete Works* I, *The French Works*, ed. G.C. Macaulay, ll. 24037–49:

> Selonc l'entente que tu as,
> Du bien et mal resceiveras,
> Car dieus reguarde ton corage:
> En juste cause tu porras
> Tort faire, car si tu t'en vas
> Plus pour le gaign de ton pilage
> Qe pour le droit, lors vassellage
> Par ton maltolt se desparage,
> Qe nul honour deserviras:
> Mais si pour droit fais ton voiage.
> Lors pris, honour et avantage
> Trestout ensemble avoir porras.

23. Lull, *Book of the Ordre of Chyualry*, pp. 45–6.
24. Hawkwood's entry in *DNB*.
25. Wyclif, *Tractatus De Officio Regis*, ed. A.W. Pollard and C. Sayle, pp. 271–2.
26. Machiavelli, *The Prince*, p. 93 (my modernization).
27. Gower, *Mirour de l'Omme*, XI, 24049–24060:

> Mais certes ore je ne say
> De ces gens d'armes quoy dirray.
> Q'ensi disant les ay oïz:
> 'Es guerres je travailleray.
> Je serray riche ou je morray,
> Ainz que revoie mon paiis
> Ne mes parens ne mes amys.'

> *Mais riens parlont, ce m'est avis,*
> '*Je pour le droit combateray,*'
> *Ainz sont de covoitise espris;*
> *Mais cil n'est digne d'avoir pris.*
> *Qui d'armes fait ensi l'essay.*

28. See Sir John Clanvowe, *The Two Ways*, ed. V.J. Scattergood, in *EPS*, x, 1967, pp. 33–56; *Eustache Deschamps, Le Lay des Douze Estats du Monde*, Rheims, 1870, pp. 10–15, and 'Le Lay de Vaillance' in *Œuvres Complètes*, XI, 55–71, and Petrarch, *Lettere senili*, v, 2nd ed. G. Fracassetti, 5, 2. Clanvowe was almost certainly a close friend of Chaucer's. He stood as a witness for him, for example, in the notorious rape case (see M.M. Crow and C.C. Olson, *Chaucer Life-Records*, p. 347). Deschamps, of course, sent Chaucer a poem via Clifford, which is still preserved (see J.A. Burrow, *Geoffrey Chaucer: a critical anthology*, p. 26). Petrarch was certainly someone Chaucer was acquainted with in the literary field and possibly someone he actually met (see E. Hutton, 'Did Chaucer meet Petrarch and Boccaccio?' *Anglo-Italian Review*, I, 1918, pp. 121–35). But perhaps Sir John Clanvowe's comment is the most appropriate to the Knight of the *Prologue*:

> For the world holds them worshipful that are great warriors and fighters and that destroy and win many lands ... and also the world worships greatly those who would be proudly revenged and without pity for every wrong that is said or done to them. And of such folk, men make books and songs and read and sing of them in order to keep their deeds in mind the longer here upon this earth. For that is a thing that worldly men desire greatly – that their name might last long after them here upon this earth.
> Clanvowe, *The Two Ways*, pp. 47–8.

The poor knight

1. C.T. Allmand makes the point that it was the commercialization of war that made the ideals of chivalry so important to men of the fourteenth century (*Society at War*, pp. 186–7).
2. The generally accepted explanation for the Knight's shabby appearance has been, of course, that he avoids showy dress as a sign of his piety. See Bowden, *Commentary*, p. 50. For the argument against this and details of the Knight's dress see my commentary on lines 77–8.
3. Barber, *The Knight and Chivalry*, p. 18: 'The poor knight was a common figure throughout the Middle Ages, ranging from the younger son making his fortune in tournament and the old knight fallen on harsh days who could not find a dowry for his daughter, to the mercenaries and men of the "great companies" fighting and plundering for a living or the robber knights turned to evil ways. Knighthood and wealth were by no means synonymous.'
4. Cf Child, *Ballads*, III, 'Geste of Robyn Hode', p. 59:

> 'In what maner,' than sayde Robyn,
> 'Hast thou lorne thy rychesse?'
> 'For my greate foly,' he sayde,
> 'And for my kynd(e)nesse.
> I hade a sone, forsoth, Robyn,
> That shulde hau(e) ben myn ayre,
> Whanne he was twenty wynter olde.
> In felde wolde iust full fayre.

> He slewe a knyght of Lancaster,
> And a squyer bolde;
> For to saue hym in his ryght
> My godes both sette and solde.'

5. Venette, *Chronicle*, pp. 135–6.
6. E. Ricotti, 'Military code for mercenaries in the pay of the Pisan Republic 1327–31', Article 22 in *Storia delle Compagnie di Ventura in Italia*, II, p. 302:

> *Item quod nullus stipendiarius dicte masnade possit vel debeat vendere aut barac-tare aliquem equum curserium vel ronzinum scriptum ad soldum predictum aut eius arma piqnorare alicui persone vel loco sine licentia dictorum Anthianorum ad penam soldorum centum denariorum et plus arbitrio suprastantis dicte masnade, et nullus possit vel debeat ab ipsis stipendariis recipere in pignus eorum equos vel arma. Et si contrafecerit aliquis amictat creditum et restituat equos et arma que habuerit in pignus eis quorum essent. Et insuper condempnetur arbitrio suprastan-tum.*

7. See Temple-Leader and Marcotti, *Sir J. Hawkwood*, p. 42.
8. See *Calendar of Papal Registers*, IV, p. 8.
9. Jean le Bel, *Chronique*, ed. J. Viard and E. Deprez, II, pp. 295–6:

> *Celle response ne pleut pas a ces seigneurs estrangiers qui avoient ainsy durement traveillié et souffert grande famine et poureté, ainsy que vous avez ouy; et toutesfoys on bailla a chascon certaine somme d'argent en prest pour retourner en son pays, mais ce fut moult petit. Si s'en retournerent les ungs mal montez, les aultres a pye, les ungs vendoient leur harnas ou leurs costes, et laissoient a leurs hostes en gaage les aultres leurs houseaulx; c'estoit toute poureté que de leur fait.*

10. *Rotuli Parliamentorum*, II, p. 332: '*Et quant as autres qi se sont par lour dit Gentils, & Hommes d'armes, ou Archers, & sont devenuz a meschief par les guerres, & autrement, s'ils furent gentz de mestier, & ne soient en nully service, soient artez de servir, ou de repairer a lours mesiters quielles ils userent devant.*'
11. Wyclif, *Sermones* ed. I. Loserth, II, p. 341; see also H.B. Workman, *John Wyclif*, II, p. 303.
12. See commentary on lines 75–8.

The Ellesmere illustration of the Knight

1. For this suggestion see J.M. Manly and Edith Rickert, *The Text of The Canterbury Tales*, I, 159.
2. According to the sixteenth-century historian John Stow, the habit of riding side-saddle was first introduced into this country by Richard II's queen, Anne of Bohemia; cf John Stow, *The Survey of London*, ed. H.B. Wheatley, p. 77.
3. Cf A.A. Dent, 'Chaucer and the Horse', *PLPLS*, IX, 1959–62, pp. 10–11.
4. *Ibid.*, pp. 9–10.
5. Printed in G. Canestrini, *Documenti per Servire Alla Storia Della Milizia Italiana*, Florence, 1851, XV, p. 542.

> *Item, che tutti et singuli cavalli, palafreni et ronzini et muli consignare si debbiano per pelo et per sengno, et marcare col ferro caldo con segno apparente; et che li decti cavalli debbiano essere extimati per quelli mariscalchi li quali fieno electi per li officiali della conducta che seranno per li tempi.*

The Knight's ideals

1. See commentary to lines 68–9 for a discussion of 'worthy' and 'worthiness'.
2. For the meaning of 'chivalrie' see Appendix.
3. Nor does it mean, as some modern commentators assume, 'since boyhood'. See, for example, T. J. Hatton, 'Chaucer's Crusading Knight, a Slanted Ideal', *ChauR* III, 1968, p. 84.
4. This is what Gower refers to when he speaks of knights who make 'many hasty rodes'. Gower, *Confessio Amantis*, 1629–30.
5. My modernization of:
   No man make roode withoute licence.
   Also that no man make no ridyng by day ne by night but by licence and knowleche of the chevestens of the battaille, so that the chevesten may know what way they draw theime, and that they may have socour and helpe, if nede be, upon peyn of them that offendeth of their bodyes and good to the kyng wille.
   Also that the capiten of no warde graunte no roode withoute licence of the kyng.
   No man breke no array ne goo of the ooste withoute licence.
   Black Book of the Admiralty, ed. Travers Twiss, I, p. 294.

   There is some dispute about the date of these particular ordinances, but the manuscript bears a side-note saying that they were of the time of Richard II (see *ibid*, p. 282). There is a similar ordinance in the time of Henry V, 1419 (*ibid*, p. 471).
6. See the discussion of 'trouthe', 'honour', 'fredom' and 'curteisie' in the Appendix.
7. Cf G. Trease, *The Condottieri*, p. 73, also discussion of 'trouthe' in the Appendix.
8. See discussion of 'fredom' in the Appendix.
9. See *The Parson's Tale*, 185–190, quoted in the Appendix. For Chaucer's own attitude to 'honour' see his translation of Boethius, *De Consolatione Philosophiae* and *Tractates, De Consolatione etc*, trans. Stewart, Rand and Tester, II, 7. Also quoted in Appendix.
10. For a discussion of 'loyalty', 'largess' and 'pity' see the Appendix.

Crusading into Christendom

1. My translation of William Caxton's Proem to his Second Edition of the Canterbury Tales (1484): 'Short, quyck and hye sentences, eschewyng prolyxyte, castyng away the chaf of superfluyte, and shewyng the pyked grayn of sentence ...', in J. A. Burrow, *Geoffrey Chaucer: a Critical Anthology*, p. 45.
2. Cf E. T. Donaldson, *Chaucer's Poetry*, p. 882; Stillwell and Webb, 'Chaucer's Knight', pp. 45–7; Hatton, 'Chaucer's Crusading Knight', pp. 80–7.
3. Bowden, *Commentary*, p. 45.
4. Hatton, 'Chaucer's Crusading Knight', p. 80.
5. Stillwell and Webb, 'Chaucer's Knight', pp. 45–7.
6. Quoted in F.M. Powick, *Christian Life in the Middle Ages*, pp. 41–2. See Roger Bacon, *Opus Majus*, translated in Richard McKeon, *Selections from Medieval Philosophers*, II, p. 106. See also F.H. Russell, *The Just War in the Middle Ages*, p. 225.
7. John Gower, '*Confessio Amantis*' in *The English Works of John Gower*, ed. G.C. Macaulay, IV, 1659–81.
8. Roger Bacon, for example, singled out the activities of the Teutonic Knights in Germany and Poland. See note 17 below.

9. Bonet, *Tree of Battles* (trans. Coopland) p. 127.
10. My modernization of the original Middle English text found in the manu-
    script of Roger Dymok edited by H.S. Cronin, *EHR*, XXII, 1907, pp. 292–
    304:

    > It is an holy robbing of the pore puple qwanne lordis purchase indulgencis *a pena
    > et a culpa* to hem that helpith to his oste, and gaderith to slen the Cristene men
    > in fer londis for god temporel, as we have seen. And knythtis, that rennen to heth-
    > nesse to geten hem a name in sleinge of men, geten miche maugre of the king of
    > pes; for be mekenesse and suffraunce oure beleue was multiplied, and fythteres and
    > mansleeris Ihesu Cryst hatith and manasit. *Qui gladio percutit, gladio peribit.*

11. Bonet, *Tree of Battles*, p. 126.
12. See Jusserand, *English Wayfaring Life*, p. 237; Manly, 'A Knight Ther Was',
    p. 91; A.S. Atiya, *Crusade, Commerce and Culture*, pp. 205–50.
13. See A.C. Crombie, *Augustine to Galileo: science in the Middle Ages*, 1, pp.
    51–79. This includes a very useful chart showing the principal sources of an-
    cient science in western Christendom between AD 500 and 1300 (pp. 56–63).
    See also Daniel, *Arabs and Medieval Europe*, pp. 263–98.
14. See Chaucer, *The Book of the Duchess*, ll. 435–42; *Canterbury Tales*, Gen.
    Prol., ll. 429–34.
15. Chaucer, *Treatise on the Astrolabe*, Prologue, 21–4.
16. Froissart, *Cronycle*, trans. Berners, V, p. 433.
17. Roger Bacon, *Opus Majus*, translated in McKeon, *Selections from Medieval
    Philosophers*, II, p. 106.
18. Walsingham, *Historia Anglicana*, II, p. 198.
19. For the English conviction that the Pope favoured the French, see *Anoni-
    malle Chronicle*, ed. V.H. Galbraith, 1970, p. 39; Henry Knighton, *Chroni-
    con*, ed. J.R. Lumby, II, p. 28; Adam Murimath, *Continuatio Chronicarum*,
    ed. Thompson, p. 162, and Barnie, *War in Medieval Society*, pp. 52, 87–8.
20. Gower, 'Confessio Amantis', IV, l. 1625 et seq.
21. See Machaut, 'Dit dou Lion', 1412–55 in *Œuvres*, ed. E. Hoepffner, II, pp.
    208–10, and 'Le Confort d'Ami', 2924–9 (*Œuvres*, III, p. 102).
22. Froissart, *Cronycle*, trans. Berners, II, p. 183. For distant adventures as a
    means of making money see: Geoffroi de Charny, 'Le Livre de Chevalerie'
    in *Œuvres de Froissart* (ed. K. de Lettenhove), I, 3, p. 468, and M. McKisack,
    The Fourteenth Century, p. 248, note 5.

23.
> Ne sende men into Walakye,
> To Pruyse and into Tartarye,
> To Alisaundre, ne into Turkye,
> And bidde him faste, anoon that he
> Go hoodles to the drye see,
> And come hoom by the Carrenare;
> And seye, "Sir, be now right ware
> That I may of yow here seyn
> Worship, or that ye come ageyn!"
> She ne used no suche knakkes smale.
>   *The Book of the Duchess*, 1024–33

24. The use of lists of remote places as part of the stock-in-trade of the *chanson
    de geste* has been amply illustrated by Mann, *Chaucer and Med. Estates
    Satire*, pp. 111–13.
25. See Runciman, *History of Crusades*, III, pp. 427, 471, and Powicke, *Christian
    Life in the Middle Ages*, pp. 41–7.

26. See P.A. Throop, 'Criticisms of Papal Crusade policy in Old French and Provençal', *Speculum*, XIII, 1938, pp. 379–412.

27. '*Lo principe de' novi Farisei,/avendo guerra presso a Laterano,/e non con Saracin ne con Giudei,/che ciascun suo nimico era Cristiano.*' Dante, *Inferno*, 27, 85–8.

28. See Temple-Leader and Marcotti, *Sir J. Hawkwood*, pp. 118–22, for an account of Cesena.

29. For example, in 1383 the Bishop of Norwich's disastrous attempt to drive the French out of Flanders was dignified as a crusade by Pope Urban, because he hoped it would damage Pope Clement. Similarly, John of Gaunt's attempt to win the throne of Castile in that same year obtained from Urban 'the privileges and indulgences granted for the Holy Land crusade' merely because his adversary, Juan I, had declared for Pope Clement (*Calendar of Papal Registers*, IV, p. 265). See also Runciman, *History of Crusades*, III, pp. 471–2.

30. In 1397 the Pope wrote to the Archbishops of Canterbury and York and to Master James Dardani, clerk of the *camera* and collector in England:

> Whereas the insolence of the schismatic adherents of Robert, cardinal priest of the Twelve Apostles, of damned memory, and the son of perdition, Peter de Luna, sometime cardinal deacon of St Mary's in Cosmedin [i.e. anti-popes Clement VII and Benedict XII] ... and of other enemies of the Pope and the Roman Church, has grown strong and daily grows stronger in Italy, and especially in the patrimony of St Peter; the Pope commends the laudable purpose of John Holland, Earl of Huntingdon, and grants the usual Holy Land indulgence and remission of sins to penitents who join his crusade to Italy, or contribute to the expenses.
> *Calendar of Papal Registers* IV, pp. 294–5.

31.
> Helas! mais c'est des cristiens
> Dont est destruite sainte eglise,
> Et la justice en sa franchise
> Ne prent mais garde de les gens.
> Gower, *Mirour de l'Omme*, 24111–13

32. My modernization of Wyclif, *Select English Works*, ed. T. Arnold, I, pp. 229–30:

> For bodili turment is now ful greet, whanne oo pope sendith bishopis and many men to sle many men, wymen, and children, and for the tother pope comen many agens hem; and cause of his fightinge is a fendis cause, for no men of erthe woot whether of thes popis be a fend to be dampnyd in helle, or ellis thei bothe.... For if the pope shal be dampned, as God woot whether thei both shal, thanne men figten for falshede in cause of a fend; and sich a cause was never herd so opynli agens treuthe.

33. See Henry Knighton, *Chronicon*, II, pp. 151–2. There is a fuller translation in W.O. Hassall, *They Saw it Happen*, I, pp. 188–9.

34. My modernization of Langland, *Piers the Plowman*, ed. W. Skeat, C-Text, XVIII, 233–8:

> For were preest-hod more parfyt that is, the pope formest,
> That with moneye menteyneth men . to werren vp-on cristine,
> A-gens the lore of oure lorde . as seynt Luk wytnesseth,
> *Michi uindictam, et ego retribuam, dicit dominus* & c.,
> Hus prayers with hus pacience to pees sholde brynge
> Alle londes to loue . and that in a lytel tyme;
> The pope with alle preestes . *pax-uobis* sholde make.

35.

> *Si tost come le Pape voet avoir Monoie pur meintenir ses Guerres de Lumbardie,*
> *ou aillours, pur despendre, ou pur raunson' ascuns de ses amys prisoners Franceys*
> *pryses par Engleys, il voet avoir Subside de Clergie d'Engleterre. Et tantost ce luy*
> *est grantez par les Prelatz, a cause que les Evesqes n'osent luy contrestere. Et est*
> *leve del Clergie sanz lour assent ent avoir devant. Et le Seculers Seigneurs n'y*
> *preignent garde, ne ne font force coment le Clergie est destruit, & la Monoye de*
> *Roialme malement emporte.*
> *Rotuli Parliamentorum*, II, p. 339.

36. Murimath, *Continuatio Chronicarum*, p. 175.
37. For Chaucer's commission to negotiate with Hawkwood see Crow and Olson, *Chaucer Life-Records*, pp. 58–9; see also Temple-Leader and Marcotti, *Sir J. Hawkwood*, pp. 118–22, and Gower's disparaging reference to Hawkwood quoted above, p. 19.
38. For the meaning of 'worthynesse' see commentary on line 43.

The Knight and Peter of Cyprus at Alexandria

1. J. M. Manly, for example, claimed that the siege of Alexandria 'made upon the minds of the men of the time an impression not altogether unlike that made in our own day by the Russo-Japanese naval battle of Tshushima' ('A Knight Ther Was', p. 99). See also Bowden, *Commentary*, pp. 58–63 (quoted below).
2. See Runciman, *History of Crusades*, III, pp. 44–5. See also G. Hill, *History of Cyprus*, II, pp. 331–4.
3. Atiya, *Crusade, Commerce and Culture*, pp. 134–5.
4. Paraphrase in A.S. Atiya, *The Crusades in the Later Middle Ages*, p. 367, note 4, of Al-Nuwairi, Al-Ilman. For details of the Arabic work see his p. 349, note 1.
5. Runciman, *History of Crusades*, III, p. 448.
6. H.W. Hazard, *A History of the Crusades*, III, p. 17.
7. Walsingham, *Historia Anglicana*, I, pp. 301–2.
8. See Bowden, *Commentary*, pp. 58–63; Hazard, *History of Crusades*, III, p. 18.
9. See *Calendar of Papal Registers (1362–1404)*, IV, p. 25. It had long been recognized that the most difficult thing was not the winning of places from the Saracen but the keeping of them. See, for example, Pierre du Bois, 'De recuperatione Terre Sancte', translated in *The Portable Medieval Reader*, ed. Ross and McLaughlin, pp. 291–2.
10. For Chaucer's knowledge of Machaut's account of the siege of Alexandria see H. Braddy, 'The Two Petros in The Monk's Tale', *PMLA*, L, 1935, pp. 78–80.
11. Guillaume de Machaut, *La Prise d'Alexandrie*, ed. M.L. de Mas Latrie, 3274–85.
12. Machaut, *Prise d'Alexandrie*, 3298–306.
13. *Ibid*, 3308.
14. *Ibid*, 3307–13.
15. *Ibid*, 3378–85.
16. *Ibid*, 3498–503:

> *Jamais n'aray parfaite joie*
> *Pour vostre honnour et pour la meie,*
> *Que je tieng pour toute perdue*
> *Se courages ne vous remue.*
> *Si vous pri que chascuns demeure,*
> *Qu'autrement il se deshonneure.*

17. *Ibid*, 3504–7:

> *Quant il et finé sa parole,*
> *Les estranges, dont je parole,*
> *Respondirent qu'il s'en iroient,*
> *Et que tenir ne le porroient.*

18. *Ibid*, 3520–34:

> *'Aussi vous estes ci venu*
> *Disans que vous estes tenu*
> *Pour faire son très dous service,*
> *Dont le partir yert trop grant vice,*
> *Et s'arez perdu et deffait*
> *Tout le bien que vous avez fait;*
> *Car bien et deshonneur ansamble*
> *Ne puelent estre, ce me samble.*
> *Aussi dit-on que cils qui sert,*
> *S'il ne parsert, son louier pert.'*
> *Bien leur moustra la sainte page;*
> *Mais il perdi tout son langage,*
> *Qu'il respondirent brief et court:*
> *'Nous en yrons; la vie y court.*
> *Nous ne volóns mie morir.'*

19. *Ibid*, 3583–5:

> *'Honneur, or yes tu morte!*
> *Certes dou tout perdu t'avons*
> *Sans recouvrier, bien le savons.'*

20. It was on battles like Poitiers and Crécy that the laurels of English chivalry rested. See J. Barnie, *War in Medieval Society*, p. 25. Froissart puts the following complaint in the mouths of the English populace (1387):

> Where be nowe these grete entrepryses and these valyaunt men of Englande that were in the dayes of kynge Edwarde the Thyrd, and with the Prynce his sone. We were wonte to go into Fraunce, and put backe our enemyes in suche maner that none durst make batayle with us; yf they dydde, they were soone dyscomfyted. O what a dede was that when the noble kynge Edwarde aryved in Normandy and in Constantyne, and passed thrugh the royalme of Fraunce, and what goodly entrepryse he acheved in his ways; and after at Cressy he dyscomfyted kynge Phylyp and all the puyssaunce of Fraunce, and or he retourned he wan the towne of Calays. But as nowe the knyghtes and men of warre in Englande doo none suche feates. Also the prynce of Wales, sone to this noble kynge, dyd he not take the Frensshe kynge John, and dyscomfyted his puyssaunce at Poyeters with a smal nombre of people agaynste the people that kynge John hadde. In those dayes Englande was fered and doubted, and we were spoken of thrughe al the worlde for the floure of chyvalry; but as nowe no man speketh of us, for nowe there is noo warre made but at poore mennes purses.

Froissart, *Cronycle*, trans. Berners, IV, p. 437.

21. 'Letter from Peter Thomas to the Pope, 1365' in Philippe de Mézières, '*Vita Sancti Petri Thomasii*' in the *Acta Sanctorum bollandiana* (ed. Jean Carnadet), 29 *januarii*, III, pp. 611–38. On p. 632 we read:

> *Heu dolor intolerabilis! Numquam auditus similis. Quos Deos conjunxerat, ut caperetur civitas, divisit iniquitas . . . Et recesserunt Anglici, qui videbantur fortiores,*

facta conjuratione cum Principe, cujus ex parentela et dolosa sequela nomen taccere debeo. Quia cum voluisset caput, Rex, resumere vires, velut probus miles, noluerunt hi resistere: sed cum suis Anglicis, qui nolentes in civitate in crastinum pernoctare devicta....

22. Chaucer may even have met Philippe de Mézières in 1395, when the Frenchman appeared at the English Court to present his *Letter to King Richard II.*

23. Petrarch, in fact, saw the current spate of mail robberies as the result of the paranoia of the 'tyrants of Lombardy' who subjected everything that went into or out of their territory to careful scrutiny. In a letter to Boccaccio dated 4 June 1374 (*Lettere Senili*, 17, 4) he complained that the border guards:

> ... not only glance over the letters that they open, but they read them with the utmost curiosity. They may, perhaps, have for an excuse the orders of their masters, who, conscious of being subject to every reproach in their restless careers of insolence, imagine that everyone must be writing about and against them; hence their anxiety to know everything. But it is certainly inexcusable, when they find something in the letters that tickles their asinine ears, that instead of detaining the messengers while they take time to copy the contents, as they used to do, they should now, with ever increasing audacity, spare their fingers the fatigue, and order the messengers off without their letters ...

The translation is taken from *Petrarch*, an anthology, ed. David Thompson, pp. 239–40.

24. When composing *The Clerk's Tale*, Chaucer appears to have had in front of him both Petrarch's Latin letter and an anonymous French translation of it. Cf. J. Burke Severs in Bryan and Dempster, *Sources and Analogues*, p. 289.

25. Cf E. Hutton, 'Did Chaucer Meet Petrarch and Boccaccio?' *Anglo-Italian Review*, I, 1918, pp. 121–35. See also R. A. Pratt, 'Chaucer and the Visconti Libraries', *ELH*, VI, 1939, pp. 189–99.

26. Petrarch, *Lettere Senili*, I, 8, Letter 8, p. 495:

> *Pietro re di Cipro s'impadroni di Alessandria nell' Egitto: grande e memoranda impresa, e ad amplificare l'impero di nostra religione immensamente utile, se quanto fu il valore nel prendere la citta, tanto fosse stato nel conservarla. Ne in lui, secondo che narra la fama, quel valor venne meno. Ma le sue schiere, quasi tutte composte di genti raccogliticcie d'oltr'Alpe, migliori sempre ad imprendere che a consumare le imprese, lo lasciarono in sul piu bello, e mosse come erano a seguirlo non da pieta, ma da cupidigia, fatte bottino, se la dettero a gambe poco curando che il pietoso voto del Re rimanesse deluso, quando gli avari loro voti ebbero soddisfatti.*

27. See Runciman, *History of Crusades*, III, p. 443. See also: Hazard, *History of Crusades*, III, p. 355.

28. Froissart, *Chronicles*, trans. Johnes, I, p. 306.

29. *Calendar of Papal Registers*, IV, p. 8.

30. This statement is contained in a letter from the Pope to the Signoria of Florence of 8 June 1365. See Canestrini, *Documenti della Milizia Italiana*, p. 85.

31. Froissart, *Chronicles*, trans. Johnes, I, p. 303.

32. Jean de Venette, *Chronicle*, p. 132.

33. Makhairas (who flourished in the first half of the fifteenth century) describes in his *Chronicle*, I, p. 97, how two Cypriot envoys were returning from Rome

in 1360: 'And when they were returning to Cyprus, they fell in with John of Verona, whom the king had sent to recruit men at arms at a monthly wage. And at once they landed in Lombardy and recruited many men at arms, and came back together to Cyprus in company with the said John of Verona.'

The Knight and the Teutonic Order

1. See Bowden, *Commentary*, p. 63; Mann, *Chaucer and Med. Estates Satire*, pp. 113–14; Manly, 'A Knight Ther Was', p. 101.
2. See A. Tuck, *Richard II and the English Nobility*, p. 153, for a useful summary of the Order of Teutonic Knights, and Barber, *The Knight and Chivalry*, pp. 263–82. See also Henry, Earl of Derby, *Expeditions to Prussia and the Holy Land*, ed. L.T. Smith, pp. xi–xix.
3. See McKeon, *Selections from Medieval Philosophers*, II, p. 106.
4. J. Huizinga, *The Waning of the Middle Ages*, p. 83.
5. See *CMH*, VII, p. 260.
6. N. Canter, *Medieval History*, p. 411.
7. In 1197, for example, we learn of Frankish barons warning the Sultan that the Germans were not wont to spare lives. See Runciman, *History of Crusades*, III, p. 97.
8. *Scriptores Rerum Prussicarum*, III, 164–7, translated in A.S. Cook, 'Historical background of Chaucer's Knight', *TCAAS*, XX, 1916, p. 200.
9. *CMH*, VII, pp. 259, 260.
10. Both the horse and foot soldiers who followed Henry of Lancaster to Prussia in 1352 did so at their own expense. See *Calendar of Papal Registers*, III, p. 459: 'To Henry, duke of Lancaster. Indult that he and his company of horse and foot who are going, mainly at their own expense, against the Prussians, enemies of the Christian faith in Prussia, may choose confessors, who shall give them plenary remission at the hour of death.'
11. Froissart, *Cronycle*, trans. Berners, II, p. 183.
12. Gower, *Mirour de l'Omme*, 23893–988:

> O chivaler, je t'en dirray,
> Tu qui travailles a l'essay
> Devers Espruce et Tartarie.
> Le cause dont tu vas ne say,
> Trois causes t'en diviseray,
> Les deux ne valont une alie;
> La primere est, si j'ensi die
> De ma prouesce enorguillie,
> 'Pour loos avoir je passeray;'
> Ou autrement, 'C'est pour m'amye,
> Dont puiss avoir sa druerie,
> Et pour ce je travailleray ...'
> La tierce cause n'est ensi,
> Pour quelle ly prodhons travaille;
> Ainz est par cause de celluy
> Par qui tous bons sont remery ...
> Mais d'autre part sanz contredit
> Pour luy servir en chascun plit
> Le siecle ad large retenue;
> Car d'orguil ou du foldelit
> Au jour present sicomme l'en dist
> Chivalerie est maintenue.

13. Gower, *Confessio Amantis*, IV, 1625–40, quoted above, pp. 37–8.
14. *The Book of the Duchess*, ll. 1024–33.
15. Text in *Scriptores Rerum Prussicarum*, III, 619, note 3, translated in A.S. Cook, 'Beginning the Board in Prussia', *JEGP*, XIV, 1915, p. 377.
16. *Ibid.*
17. Gower, *Confessio Amantis*, IV, ll. 1612–17.
18. Cook, 'Beginning the Board', pp. 376 ff.
19. Tuck, *Richard II*, p. 153.
20. Cook, 'Beginning the Board', p. 383.
21. For example, here is an indulgence which Pope Clement VI granted in 1349: 'Relaxation of a year and forty days of enjoined penance to those who lend helping hands to the building, by certain English knights and other persons, of a castle in the territory of the king of Lithuania [*Regis deletwinorum*], on the borders of Prussia [*Spurcie*], which is to serve as a refuge for the Christians against the pagans of those parts, and to contain a chapel to be served by five chaplains. The relaxation holds good for ten years.' *Calendar of Papal Registers*, III, p. 331. See also Runciman, *History of Crusades*, III, pp. 471, 479. In 1365 Urban V commended the Earl of Warwick for 'his discretion and devotion in taking the cross whether he goes to the Holy Land or against the pagans in Prussia', *Calendar of Papal Registers*, IV, p. 19.
22. One chronicle records, for example, how in 1376 the Teutonic Knights organized an expedition *pedestres more latrunculorum* ('on foot, in the manner of thieves or free-booters'). See *CMH*, VII, p. 258.
23. See Cook, 'Beginning the Board', p. 377.
24. See Philippe de Mézières, *Letter to King Richard II*, trans. G. W. Coopland, p. xviii.
25. See for example the account of the high spending and eventual ruin of the mercenaries in Lombardy in Temple-Leader and Marcotti, *Sir J. Hawkwood*, p. 42; see also Jean de Venette, *Chronicle*, pp. 135–6 (quoted in commentary to lines 75–6).
26. Cook, 'Beginning the Board', p. 377.
27. See Barber, *The Knight and Chivalry*, p. 18, and also 'The Shabby Knight', above, pp. 125–35.

What was the Knight doing in 'Ruce'?

1. For the identification of 'Ruce' with Russia see F.P. Magoun, *A Chaucer Gazetteer*, p. 136. In the fourteenth century it consisted of the principalities of Vladimir, Tver, Smolensk, Riazan and the Republic of Novgorod.
2. Cf indexes to Froissart, *Œuvres*, ed. Lettenhove, Gower, '*Vox Clamantis*', '*Mirour de l'Omme*' and '*Confessio Amantis*', and Tatlock, *Concordance*. It is true that Machaut mentions 'Russe' as a place where the King of Behaigne won fame and honour, but this is in a list including other Christian countries such as France and Germany. See Machaut, '*Le Confort d'Ami*', l. 2928 in *Œuvres*, III, p. 103.
3. Russia accepted Christianity from the Greeks under St Vladimir in 988. See *CMH*, VII, p. 599, and *Chronicle of Novgorod*, trans. R. Mitchell and N. Forbes, p. v.
4. *Chronicle of Novgorod*, p. xi.
5. See B. Dmytryshyn, *Medieval Russia*, pp. 159–60.
6. There had even been moves for a reconciliation between the two Churches under the rule of John V who was Emperor of the Eastern Roman Empire from 1332 to 1391. See Denys Hay, *Europe in the Fourteenth and Fifteenth Centuries*, pp. 242–8. An early traveller to Russia, John de Carpini, records the communication between the Russian Church and Rome. See *The Travels*

of Sir John Mandeville with three narrations in illustration of it, ed. A.W. Pollard, p. 232, and *Chronicle of Novgorod*, p. xi.

7. See W. Urban, 'The Organization of Defense of the Livonian Frontier in the Thirteenth Century', in *Speculum*, 48, 1973, p. 525, note 2: 'The Battle on the Ice' in 1242, known to most from Eisenstein's film *Alexander Nevski*, and a great battle in 1268 are the only important conflicts after the Teutonic Knights came to Livonia. There were, however, constant complaints from German merchants about robberies on the overland route to Novgorod.' For a useful summary of relations between Russia and the Knights of the Teutonic Order see *Chronicle of Novgorod*, pp. xxvii–xxix.

8. *Chronicle of Novgorod*, p. 151. For the origin of the word *Nemtsy* see *ibid*, p. xxvii.

9. See Urban, 'Defense of Livonian Frontier', p. 525.

10. See *Europe*, p. 262; see also G. Vernadsky, *A History of Russia*, III: The Mongols and Russia.

11. Translated in Dmytryshyn, *Medieval Russia*, p. 152.

12. The *Polnoe Sobranie Russkikh Letopisei* ('Complete Collection of Russian Chronicles'), XI, pp. 95–101, translated in Dmytryshyn, *Medieval Russia*, p. 160. The area actually being described in this extract is Riazan (see map).

13. See Atiya, *Crusade in Later Middle Ages*, p. 141.

14. Translation in Dmytryshyn, *Medieval Russia*, p. 165, of *Polnoe Sobranie Russkikh Letopisei*, XXIII, pp. 124–7.

15. See *Squire's Tale*, ll. 12–27, for the Squire's description of 'This noble kyng, this Tartre Cambyuskan'. He does not claim to have been there himself but to have heard stories from older knights 'as tellen knyghtes olde' (l. 69) – perhaps he is alluding to his father.

What was the Knight doing at Algezir?

1. See Magoun, *Gazetteer*, p. 79.

2. *Ibid*, p. 17.

3. For example, Manly, 'A Knight Ther Was', p. 92; Bowden, *Commentary*, p. 53, and Robinson, *Works*, p. 652.

4. See for example: Allmand, *Society at War*, pp. 40–3; Russell, *The Just War*, p. 292, and Barnie, *War in Medieval Society*, pp. 12–13.

5. *CMH*, p. 571.

6. See J.M. Abun-Nasr, *History of the Maghrib*, pp. 125–6. For example, in 1281 Alfonso X, King of Castile, found his second son, Don Sancho, in open rebellion against himself. He therefore allied himself with the Banū-Marīn, while Don Sancho allied himself with the Moors of Granada. Similarly, Froissart tells us how, in 1365, during the dynastic feud between Pedro the Cruel and his brother Henry Trastamara, Pedro was reputed to be in league with 'the kings of Gernade, Belmarye and Tramissene' (Froissart, *Cronycle*, trans. Berners, II, p. 152).

7. Hazard, *History of Crusades*, III, pp. 11–12.

8. See J.N. Hillgarth, *The Spanish Kingdoms*, I, p. 342.

9. *Crónica de Alfonso XI*, pp. 319, 322, 325–9 (quoted in Hillgarth, *Spanish Kingdoms*, I, p. 342).

10. Jean le Bel, *Chronique*, I, p. 213: '*Je ne vueil mye mettre en oubli la grande aventure et la tres heureuse fortune qui avint au roy d'Espaigne, a Castelet, en ce prens* [sic] *contre les Sarrasins dont toute crestienté doibt à tousjours mais regracier Nostre Seigneur de la grande vertu qu'il monstra adoncques.*'

11. See Rymer, *Fœdera*, V, pp. 257, 415.

12. See Walsingham, *Historia Anglicana*, I, p. 262, and Hillgarth, *Spanish Kingdoms*, I, pp. 343–4.

13. See Ibn-Khaldun, *Histoire des Berbers*, trans. Slane, IV, p. 381, quoted in Cook, 'Historical Background', pp. 219–21.
14. See, for example, Walsingham's account, *Historia Anglicana*, I, p. 262:

> At this time the city of Algezir was captured by the King of Spain, who had been besieging it for three years by land and sea, with innumerable pains to the Christian people.

15. Jean le Bel, *Chronique*, I, p. 219: '*et y furrent veues moult d'abilitez d'armes, entre les estranges pelerins et les Sarrasins, par devant la ville, en une place qui la estoit. Les crestiens perdoient plus souvent que les Sarrasins aux paletis et aultres armes, car ilz s'abondonnoient trop à la folie pour avancer leur honneur envers les grands seigneurs et les barons qui là estoient venus de tous pays comme pelerins l'ung pour l'autre.*'
16. *Crónica del Rey Alfonso el Onzeno*, ed. F. Cerdá y Rico, I, p. 551:

> *Et un dia, que fue en el comienzo del mes de Agosto, entraron compañas de pie de los que y eran de fuera del regno dentro de la barrera que tenian fecha los Christianos, et comenzaron á pelear con los Moros de la ciubdat entre amas las villas. Et el Rey desque lo vió, entendió, que si aquellos omes non fuesen acorridos, que eran en peligro de muerte, ca los Moros eran muchos, et salian de la ciubdat mas. Et por esto mandó á algunos de los suyos que se armasen et entrasen sacar fuera á aquellos omes: et aquellos á quien lo el Rey mandó, fueron aliá, et non pudieron tirarlos luego á fuera, ca los Moros comenzaron luego la pelea con estos tambien como con los otros. Et estando en esto los Condes de Arbi et de Solusber, et otras gentes de Ingleses et de Alemanes, armaronse, et entraron mucho apriesa á la pelea: et los Moros de la ciubdat salieron todos asi los de caballo como los de pie, et esperaronlos en el campo, et fué las pelea muy fuerte entre ellos. Et los Christianos que andaban en la pelea, non estaban bien firmes con los Condes, et dexaronlos como omes que avian entrado arrebatadamente á la pelea. Et el Rey veyendo esto, mando luego que todos los que posaban enderredor de la barrera, que se armasen luego, et entrasen á acorrer á los Christianos: et ellos ficieronlo asi.*

For translations of other extracts from the *Crónica* see Cook, *Historical Background*, p. 225.
17. In his letter of congratulation to Alfonso in 1340, Edward wrote: 'The re-establishment of peace between ourselves and our enemy of France was most pleasing to you, both because of the affection for us that you feel, and also because of the aid and support that we could provide, along with other Princes against the said enemies of the faith.' There is no such observation in his letter of 1344 at the conclusion of the siege of Algezir; in fact Edward seems to be more concerned at receiving replies to his secret envoys which, he notes rather ruefully, had been sent to Alfonso 'a long time ago'. (See Rymer, *Fœdera*, V, p. 257; 415–16.)
18. See McKisack, *The Fourteenth Century*, p. 130.
19. See Knighton, *Chronicon*, II, pp. 8–9, also H. J. Hewitt, *The Organization of War Under Edward III*, pp. 4–5. The second Portsmouth raid is mentioned in *Annals of England: an Epitome of English History*, Oxford and London, 1876, p. 192.
20. See McKisack, *The Fourteenth Century*, pp. 131–2.
21. *Rotuli Parliamentorum*, II, p. 140.
22.

> *Et outre ce, le dit Adversaire ... est il en ferme purpos, a ce que nostre Seign' le Roi & son Conseil ont entenduz en certeyn, a destruire la Lange Engleys, & occuper*

> *la terre d'Engleterre, que Dieu defend, si remeide ne soit mys contre sa malice par force.*
> Rotuli Parliamentorium, II, p. 147.

23. Cf *City of London Letter-Book F*, p. 94.
24. See Cook, 'Historical Background', p. 219.

What was the Knight doing in Belmarye?

1. See Magoun, *Gazetteer*, p. 92; Abun-Nasr, *History of Maghrib*, p. 127; Hillgarth, *Spanish Kingdoms*, I, p. 37.
2. See, for example, Manly, 'A Knyght Ther Was', p. 93; Bowden, *Commentary*, p. 53. Manly quotes only Edward's letter to Alfonso of 12 June 1341, but this of course refers to Alfonso's victory over the King of Belmarye on the River Salado which is in Granada and not in Belmarye itself. Bowden gives a string of references: Froissart, *Œuvres*, VII, pp. 93, 116, 267; IX, p. 429; XIV, p. 278; XVII, p. 425; however, none of these contains a reference to any expedition into Belmarye itself.
3. Hillgarth, *Spanish Kingdoms*, I, p. 267.
4. See Cook, 'Historical Background', p. 234; Froissart, *Œuvres*, VII, p. 93.
5. See Abun-Nasr, *History of Maghrib*, p. 133.
6. Daniel, *Arabs and Medieval Europe*, p. 219.
7. Abun-Nasr, *History of Maghrib*, pp. 135, 153–4.
8. Hillgarth, *Spanish Kingdoms*, I, pp. 158–9.
9. Ibn-Khaldun, *The Muqaddimah*, trans. F. Rosenthal, II, p. 80.
10. Le Comte de Mas Latrie, *Relations et Commerce de l'Afrique septentrionale ou Magreb avec les Nations chrétiennes au Moyen Age*, p. 274.
11. Hillgarth, *Spanish Kingdoms*, I, p. 158.
12. Abun-Nasr, *History of Maghrib*, p. 154.
13. *Ibid*.
14. Hillgarth, *Spanish Kingdoms*, p. 160.
15. Froissart, for example, makes a clear distinction between the realms of 'Aufryke, Thunes, Bogy, Marroke, Melmaryn, Tremessyans and Granade'. See *Cronycle*, trans. Berners, V, p. 433.
16. Hillgarth, *Spanish Kingdoms*, I, p. 157.
17. Mas Latrie, *Relations et Commerce*, p. 270.
18. Daniel, *Arabs and Medieval Europe*, p. 309.

Further adventures with Peter of Cyprus

1. See Magoun, *Gazetteer*, pp. 139–40; for Lyeys see p. 103.
2. Bowden, *Commentary*, p. 55. See also Mitchell, 'The Worthiness of Chaucer's Knight', pp. 66–75.
3. The *Chronicle* of Makhairas, for example, makes no mention of a bloodbath, but then nor does Makhairas mention the massacre that took place at Alexandria. Atiya, however, states that the townsfolk of Adalia surrendered quickly to avoid bloodshed. His authorities are presumably Strambaldi and Amadi. Cf Makhairas, *Chronicle*, I, pp. 107, 151–5, and Atiya, *Crusades in the Later Middle Ages*, pp. 326–7.
4.

> *Il s'en ala, lui et sa gent,*
> *Parmi la haute mer nagent,*
> *Tant qu'il vint devant Satalie,*
> *Une cité qu'est en Turquie,*
> *Grande & puissaunt, & ferme, et forte;*
> *Mais il n'i ot ne mur, ne porte,*

> *Ne gens qui la peust deffendre*
> *Que li bons rois ne l'alast prendre,*
> *Et destruire, et mettre a l'espee;*
> *Et si l'a toute arse et bruslée.*
> *Là veist on maint drap de soie,*
> *Et de fin or qui reflamboie*
> *Ardoir, et mainte dame belle,*
> *Maint Sarrazin, mainte pucelle,*
> *Maint Turc et maint enfant perir,*
> *Par feu, ou par glaive morir.*
> Machaut, *La Prise d'Alexandrie*, ll. 643–58

5.

> *Alayas est un chastiaus*
> *Qui est fors et puissans et biaus.*
> *Ville y a et siet seur la mer*...
> *Quant il y vint, il assailly*
> *Le chastel, mais il y failly,*
> *Car sa gent estoient lassé,*
> *Grevé, travillié et soulé*
> *Dou grant chaut et de la bataille,*
> *Et s'avoient po de vitaille;*
> *Et li Sarracin qui estoient*
> *Eu chastel, bien se deffendoient.*
> *Mais la ville arse et si destruite*
> *Fu, qu'elle ne vaut une truite.*
> Machaut, *La Prise d'Alexandrie*, 6964–6, 7096–7105

Makhairas confirms the accuracy of Machaut's account, although, as an apologist for Peter of Cyprus, he naturally puts it in a better light, and concludes that 'they departed with honour' (Makhairas, *Chronicle*, pp. 193–5).

6. See Froissart, *Cronycle*, trans. Berners, IV, p. 228.
7. See, for example, Hatton, 'Chaucer's Crusading Knight', p. 86.
8. Machaut, *La Prise d'Alexandrie*, XI, 6972–7011:

> *Alayas est un chastiaus*
> *Qui est fors et puissans et biaus.*
> *Ville y a et siet seur la mer,*
> *Et si vous vueil bien affermer*
> *Qu'aus Ermins a fait maint ahan.*
> *C'est l'heritage dou soudan*
> *Et si est assis en la marche*
> *D'Ermenie, et aus Ermins marche.*
> *Li nobles roys au fier corage*
> *Estoit outre mer davantage*
> *Et au pays des Sarrazins,*
> *Si vuet conforter les Ermins.*
> *Li roys de Triple se parti*
> *Et s'en ala, a cuer parti*
> *De joie et de merencolie,*
> *Car moult souvent merencolie*
> *A ses annemis damagier*
> *Et au roy d'Ermenie aidier;*
> *Et s'a joie de son emprise*
> *Quant la cite de Triple est prise,*

> *Seur la mer de Triple chevauche,*
> *Mais il n'i a maison de bauche,*
> *De terre, ne d'autre marrien*
> *Qu'il n'arde, et n'i espargne rien.*
> *Souvent s'espée en sanc a taint,*
> *Chascuns tue quanqu'il ataint.*
> *Einsi s'en va tout combatant*
> *Et les Sarrazins ociant,*
> *A Alayas droite voie,*
> *Boutant les feus; que vous diroie?*
> *Trois bonnes villes y a pris*
> *Et destruites li roys de pris,*
> *Dont vesci les noms, sans doubtance:*
> *C'est Tourtouze, Liche et Valence,*
> *Et maintes grandes et petites,*
> *Qui de peler les aus sont quittes,*
> *Car c'est tout mors et mis en cendre,*
> *Sans espargnier homme ne prendre.*
> *Et quant la nuit venir veoit,*
> *En navige se retraioit.*
> *Et y faisoit sa gent retraire.*
> *Mais de jours aloient meffaire*
> *Sus Sarrazins, et destruisoient*
> *Et tuoient quanqu'il trouvoient.*
> *Li nobles roys, frans et gentis*
> *A son fait est si ententis*
> *Qu'avoir ne puet autre penser*
> *N'il ne saroit ailleurs penser.*

9. For evidence that Chaucer had read Machaut's account of Peter of Cyprus' death see Braddy, 'The Two Petros', pp. 69–80.
10. See Machaut, *La Prise d'Alexandrie*, ll. 8196–359.
11. See Makhairas, *Chronicle*, pp. 239–69.
12. *Ibid*, p. 249.
13. *Ibid*, p. 269.
14. See 'Why does the Knight interrupt the Monk?' above, p. 217.

Why does Chaucer use the word 'armee'?

1. There has in the past been some discussion as to whether the 'Grete See' means the Mediterranean or the Black Sea, but nowadays it is generally agreed that it must mean the Mediterranean. Gower, for example, uses it unequivocally in this sense:

> Mi fader, understonde it is,
> That ye have said; bot over this
> I prei you tell me nay or yee,
> To passe over the grete See
> To werre and sle the Sarazin,
> Is that the lawe?
> Gower, *Confessio Amantis*, iii, ll. 2485–90

(You would not sail over the Black Sea to slay Saracens.) For discussion, cf: Bowden, *Commentary*, p. 71, note 69; Robinson, *Works*, p. 652, note 60; Skeat, *Works*, v, p. 8, note 59. For the suggestion that it means Black Sea, cf: *The Buke of John Maundevill*, ed. G. F. Warner, p. 211, and *The Book of Ser Marco Polo*, ed. Yule, i, p. 3.

2. See Skeat, *Works*, v, p. 8, note 60; Robinson, *Works*, p. 652, note 60, and Donaldson, *Chaucer's Poetry*, p. 7. For a full discussion of the problem see Manly-Rickert, III, p. 421, and also M. Gorlach, 'The Knight's Army', *N&Q*, xx, 1973, pp. 363–5. Although to my mind, Gorlach turns the argument on its head by concluding (p. 365) that 'the growing popularity of the word [army] in the fifteenth century may well have led the scribes of Chaucer to substitute the modern "army" for the difficult "arive"'.

3. '*Armee*' does not appear in an undisputed usage until 1472–3, cf: *Rotuli Parliamentorum*, VI, p. 42.

4. *Promptorium Parvulorum*, ed. A.L.Mayhew, p. 15.

5. Dante, *Paradiso*, VI, l. 25 – S. Battaglia, *Grande Dizionario della Lingua Italiana*, I, p. 661.

6. '*Armee*' was first used in France by Machaut c. 1360; see *Œuvres*, 'Histoire de Chypre', I, 239; also *La Grande Larousse* and *Trésor de la Langue Française*, ed. P. Imbs, III, p. 505; E. Littré, *Dictionnaire de la Langue Française*, I.

7. Gorlach, 'The Knight's Army', p. 365.

8. For the word's appearance in English see *Middle English Dictionary*.

9. *Piu presto noceranno al bene publico l'armi forestiere, che le proprie, perche sono le piu facili a corrompersi*, quoted in S. Battaglia, *Grande Dizionario*, I, p. 661.

10. See Froissart, *Chronicles*, ed. Kervyn, IV, p. 64.

11. See G. Gougenheim, 'Notes sur le Vocabulaire de Rabelais' in *Word*, v, p. 148.

12. '...the Duyk of Gloucestre, whiche by that tyme was redy at London with his power and armee to come to the rescows of Caleis ...', *The Brut*, ed. F.W.O. Brie, *EETS*, os 136, II, p. 584. For date of composition cf *MED*, A4 p. 382.

13. See above, p. 8.

14. See for example David Wright's translation of *The Canterbury Tales*, pp. 13–14, also Robinson, *Works*, p. 652, note 60.

15. J.J.N. Palmer, *England, France and Christendom*, pp. 12–13.

16. Temple-Leader and Marcotti, *Sir J. Hawkwood*, pp. 27, 14.

The Knight as an efficient killer (1)

1. See *MED* for 'mortel bataille', cf: F. Godefroy, *Dictionnaire de l'ancienne Langue Française*, suppl. 2, p. 177; also Langland, *Piers Plowman*, C-Text, ll. 288–93; Chaucer, *The Knight's Tale*, l. 1632.

The Knight's tournaments in Tramyssene

1. See Magoun, *Gazetteer*, pp. 158–9.

2. See Bowden, *Commentary*, p. 53; Mann, *Chaucer and Med. Estates Satire*, p. 113.

3. See Abun-Nasr, *History of Maghrib*, pp. 135, 153–4; Cook, 'Historical Background', p. 233.

4. See Abun-Nasr, *History of Maghrib*, pp. 128–32, 156–7. Here is a synopsis of Tramyssene's troubled history during the fourteenth century:

1236–1337	Under Zayanid control. Commercial and military ties with Spain. Christian mercenaries in militia.
1337–1349	Occupied by Abul-Hasan of the Marinids.
1349–1352	Reverts to Zayanid control. Abul-Hasan fails to recapture it.
1353–1359	Recaptured by Abul-Hasan's son. Marinid control.

1359–1383	Recaptured for Zayanids by Abu Hamuw II.
1383–1388	Recaptured by the Marinids.
1388	Abu Hamuw II of the Zayanids regains it. His son rebels and recaptures Tlemcen under Marinid suzerainty.

5. See commentary to line 57, p. 64 ff.
6. Daniel, *Arabs and Medieval Europe*, p. 222.
7. In 1344 and in 1358, for example, Edward III offered safe-conducts to 'all foreigners from whatever parts of the world' who wished to take part in his tournament. *See Eulogium Historiarum*, III, p. 227; Rymer, *Fœdera*, 1818, III, i, p. 5, and Knighton, *Chronicon*, II, pp. 98–9.
8. Honoré Bonet, *Tree of Battles*, p. 207.
9. Jean de Bueil, *Le Jouvencel*, ed. C. Favre and L. Lecestre, II, p. 100.
10. See Froissart, *Chronicles*, ed. S. Luce, IV, p. 115: '*Si fu en pluiseurs lieus ceste avenue comptée et recordée. Li aucun le tenoient a proece, et li aucun a outrage et grant outrecuidance.*'
11. Huizinga, *Waning of Middle Ages*, p. 96.
12. See Froissart, *Chronicles*, ed. Kervyn, XIV, pp. 50–1.
13. Quoted in: Owst, *Literature and Pulpit*, p. 334; 'What praise is it that such are glorious and seek praise in prohibited deeds of arms, as in tournaments and the like, while in deeds of virtue, such as in just wars and in defence of their own country, they are timorous, cowardly and fugitive, allowing the enemy to devastate the land, to plunder and to pillage, to burn the towns, destroy the castles, and carry off captives?'
14. See Philippe de Mézières, *Le Songe du Vieil Pèlerin*, ed. and trans. G. W. Coopland, III, 337 recto; also Atiya, *Crusades in Later Middle Ages*, p. 146.
15. See F.H. Cripps-Day, *The History of the Tournament in England and in France*, Appendix 1, pp. vi–vii.
16. For the softening of the Church's attitude in the fourteenth century see Barnie, *War in Medieval Society*, pp. 83–4.
17. *Calendar of Papal Registers*, 1362–1404, IV, p. 27.
18. See Crow and Olson, *Chaucer Life-Records*, pp. 472–6.
19. My modernization of:

> We saie that for to aske a thynge ayenst nature or aboue nature is presumpcyon & it displeaseth god/& for to trowe that the feble shalle ouercome the stronge/ & and the olde the yonge or the sike the hole/by strengthe of goode right/to haue/ as haue had & haue confidence they that therto putte hemself/suche a thing is but atemptyng of god & I saye for certeyn that yf it happe them to wynne/it is but an aduenture/& not for the gode ryght that they therto haue.
> Christine de Pisan, *Fayttes of Armes*, trans. Caxton, p. 259.

20. See Froissart, *Cronycle*, trans. Berners, V, pp. 414–15.
21. *Monty Python's Flying Circus* (BBC TV, 1969), project no. 1149/0451.
22. *The Knight's Tale*, l. 1706 ff.

The Knight as an efficient killer (2)

1. Froissart, *Chronicles*, trans. Johnes, II, pp. 440–1.
2. See Froissart, *Cronycle*, trans. Berners, V, p. 423. When an accident does occur, Froissart seems almost to apologize for it, as when the Frenchman Raynolde du Roy wounds an English knight in the St Inglebert tournament: 'Of that course sir Raynolde du Roy was greatly praised, for all the hurtyng of the knight, for suche is the adventure of armes: to some good, to some yvell' (*ibid*, p. 349).
3. See Barnie, *War in Medieval Society*, p. 184; for deaths in the thirteenth

century see Cripps-Day, *History of Tournament*, Appendix I, p. vi and pp. 44–5.

4. *Idem*, Appendix I, p. vi.

5. Higden, *Polychronicon*, IX, pp. 219–20, translated in Rickert, *Chaucer's World*, p. 216; see also *Sir Launfal*, ll. 601–6:

> Alle the lordes of Atalie
> To Sir Launfal hadde greet envie
> That Valentine was y-slawe
> And swore that he shold die
> Er he wente out of Lumbardie
> And be hongede and todrawe.

6. Rymer, *Fœdera*, 1818, II, i, p. 358; see also Cripps-Day, *History of Tournament*, p. 43.

7. *A Geste of Robyn Hode*, ll. 51–5:

> 'In what maner,' than sayde Robyn,
> 'Hast thou lorne thy rychesse?'
> 'For my greate foly,' he sayde,
> 'And for my kynd(e)nesse.
> 'I hade a sone, forsoth, Robyn,
> That shulde hau(e) ben myn ayre,
> Whanne he was twenty wynter olde,
> In felde wolde iust full fayre.
> He slewe a knyght of Lancaster,
> And a squyer bolde;
> For to saue hym in his ryght
> My godes both sette and solde.
> My londes both sette to wedde, Robyn,
> Vntyll a certayn day,
> To a ryche abbot here besyde
> Of Seynt Mari Abbey.'
> 'What is the som?' sayde Robyn;
> 'Trought than tell thou me.'
> 'Sir,' he sayde, 'foure hundred pounde;
> The abbot told it to me.'

8. See the Duke of Gloucester's *Ordenaunce & Fourme of Fightyng within the Listes* which he presented to Richard II. It is reprinted with the French original alongside the translation made for John Paston in *The Black Book of the Admiralty*, I, p. 325:

> And yif the saide batell be of treason, he that is convicte and discomfite, shalbe disarmed in the listes by the commandement of the conestable, and a corner of the liste brokyn in the reprove of hym, by the which shalbe drawen oute with hors fro the same place, there he is so disarmede, thorugh the listes unto the place of justice, where he shalbe hedid or hanged aftir the usage of the countrey ...

9. Daniel, *Arabs and Medieval Europe*, p. 227.

10. My modernization of:

> Lord, what honour falles to a knyght, for he killes mony men? Wil I wot that honge-men killen mony moo, and by more just titel, and so by vertue, and so schulden thei be preysid more then soche knyghtis. And bochere of bestis dos oft tyme his offis by right and by charite, and so he dos hit wil; bot bocher of his brether

by not so gret evydense slees men in charite, and so not so justly. Why schulde not this bocher, for his better dede, be preysid more then this knyght that the world hyees? sith more virtuous dede is more for to pryse. And so hit were better to mon to be bocher of bestis then to be bocher of his brether, for that is more unkyndely. The passioun of Crist is myche for to preyse, bot sleeyng of his tormentoures is odiouse to God.
Wyclif, *Select English Works*, III, p. 139.

Cf also: *ibid*, p. 138.
11. Gower, 'Vox Clamantis', pp. 207–8.
12. Brief of Pope Urban V, 17 February 1364, quoted in Temple-Leader and Marcotti, *Sir J. Hawkwood*, p. 51.
13. 'Riden' was often used in Middle English to mean: 'to go on a pillaging foray or raid on horseback', see *OED* and, for example, 'Statutes & Ordinaunces to be Keped in Time of Werre' in *Black Book of the Admiralty*, I, p. 294. See also my commentary to lines 43–6.
14. Mathew, *The Court of Richard II*, p. 122.
15. There is a comparison of the tournament in Chaucer and in Boccaccio, see p. 178 ff.

The Knight in the service of a heathen
1. H.H. Gibbons, *The Foundation of the Ottoman Empire (1300–1403)*, pp. 277, 295.
2. See S. Runciman, *History of Crusades*, III, pp. 473–4.
3. See H.A.R. Gibb ed., *Encyclopaedia of Islam*, I, pp. 987–8.
4. Gibbons, *Foundation*, p. 295.
5. See Cook, 'Historical Background', p. 235. That the Lord of Palatye was indeed a heathen is clear from the contemporary chronicles. See Makhairas, *Chronicle*, II, p. 114; Strambaldi, *Chroniques d'Amadi et de Strambaldi*, ed. Mas Latrie, II, p. 166. See also Robinson, *Works*, p. 652. Muriel Bowden, however, suggests the possibility that the Lord of Palatye might have been a Christian paying homage to a Turkish overlord (*Commentary*, p. 58), but I have been unable to find anything to support this idea. According to Gibbons, there were only two independent Christian states in Asia Minor during the fourteenth century: Little Armenia and Trebizond (Gibbons, *Foundation*, pp. 298–9). Muriel Bowden's authority is Froissart (Berners, IV, p. 231; Johnes, II, pp. 140–1), who is, in turn, reporting a remark of the King of Armenia. But the King of Armenia does not in fact say that the Lord of Palatye is a Christian. He merely says that he wishes Armenia had been conquered by Murad (Amarat) the Turk instead of by the Tartars, because Murad leaves his tributaries alone to follow their own customs and religion, as he does with the Lords of Satalye, Palatye and Haut-Loge (Altologo). Savvage even suggests there might be a mistake in these names. See *L'Histoire et Chronique de Froissart*, ed. D. Savvage, 1560, III, p. 79.
6. See Bowden, *Commentary*, p. 58; Robinson, *Works*, p. 652; also Mann, *Chaucer and Med. Estates Satire*, p. 113; D. Zesmer, *Guide to English Literature*, p. 213, and Donaldson, *Chaucer's Poetry*, p. 882.
7. Strambaldi, *Chroniques*, II, p. 70.
8. Mézières, 'Vita St Petri Thomasii', p. 629.
9. 'And the Grand Master and all the Brethren besought the king to maintain peace with Ephesus and with Miletus, because they were afraid of them ...'
Makhairas, *Chronicle*, I, p. 149.

Was the Knight too successful?

1. See N. Coghill, *The Canterbury Tales*, p. 21; D. Wright, *The Canterbury Tales*, p. 14. 'Prys' could also mean 'praise' or 'renown', see Skeat, *Works*, v, p. 8; E.T. Donaldson, *Chaucer's Poetry*, p. 7. F. King and B. Steele, *The Prologue etc*, p. 5. F.N. Robinson gives all three readings: price, praise and prize (see Robinson, *Works*, p. 971).

2. *General Prologue*, 815. Other occasions on which Chaucer uses 'prys' in the sense of price are: 'the whiche man thow woldest byen redyly with the pris of thyn owene lif' (*Boethius*, 2, pr. 4 29); 'And many other folk han bought honourable renoun of this world by the prys of a glorious deth' (*Boethius*, 4, pr. 6 276); 'But by the pris of ryghtwisnesse and of verray mekenesse we disserven the gerdon of the devyne grace ...' (*Boethius*, 5, pr. 3 193).

3. *General Prologue*, 237. See also when Chaucer says of Hercules: 'he disservide eftsones the hevene to ben the pris of his laste travaile' (*Boethius*, 4, m. 7 60). See also 'Thei that rennen in a furlong, alle forsoth rennen, but oon takith the preys', *Wyclif Bible*, 1 *Corinthians* 9, 24.

4. See *OED* under 'prize'.

5. See *Parson's Tale*, 355. Gower writes in *Confessio Amantis*, II, 2592–5:

> Such was the knyht in his degre:
> Wher he was armed in the feld,
> There dorste non abide his scheld;
> Gret pris upon the werre he hadde.

See also *Hymns to the Virgin and Christ* (c. 1430, EETS, 1867), 53:

> 'I haue brought hidir manye a greet price
> Hidir into helle of al kinde of man.'

6. See *Elegy on the Death of Edward I*, l. 28, i, Robbins, *Hist. Songs of the XIV & XV Centuries*, p. 22. *Guy of Warwick*, Abbotsford Club, 1840, 168; see also *The gest hystoriale of the destruction of Troy*, EETS, 1869–74, 1693: 'Mykell pepull of prise & proude men of Armys'.

7. Of the fifty-seven times that Chaucer uses the word 'prys' (listed in Tatlock's *Concordance*), he only twice uses the word with the indefinite article, and only eleven times with the definite article. On each other occasion it has no article at all. Of these eleven, four times 'prys' is being used in the sense of 'price or cost' – *General Prologue*, 815, *Boethius*, 2, pr. 4 29; *ibid*, 4, pr. 6 276; *ibid*, 5, pr. 3 193. Twice it is used in the sense of 'worth, esteem': *The Clerk's Tale*, 1026; *Romaunt of the Rose*, 286. On only three occasions is 'prys' used with the definite article to mean 'praise or honour': 'I ne trowe nat that the pris and the grace of the peple nys worthi to ben remembered', *Boethius*, 3, pr. 6 28; 'The same pris of Troilus I seye', *Troilus & Criseyde*, 2, 181; 'thilke pris echid or encresed to the', *Boethius*, 3, pr. 6 14. Thus one can say that when Chaucer used the word 'prys' to mean 'esteem, honour, value', he overwhelmingly used it without either the indefinite or the definite article – thirty-seven times out of forty.

8. 'Wurthy of prys', Chaucer, *Boethius*, 1, pr. 5 44; 'holden in prys', *Franklin's Tale*, 934; 'alle prys hath he', *Troilus & Criseyde*, 2, 188; 'Gret loos hath Largess and gret prys', *Romaunt of the Rose*, 1161; 'a lady bright/Of high prys and of grete degre', *Romaunt of the Rose*, 1005.

9. On 3 May 1375 the Pope wrote to the English mercenary captain John Thornbury, urging him to remain faithful, 'as he has lately learned that the men-at-arms under his command, especially the English, are grumbling

because they are not paid, and seem to be withdrawing their services ...'
Calendar of Papal Registers, IV, 154. See also *Calendar of Papal Registers*,
IV, 122, 121, 136, 206.

10. See *Calendar of Papal Registers*, IV, 263. In 1382 Pope Urban VI was having
to pay Hawkwood considerable sums in order to draw him into his service
(*ibid*, IV, 263). In 1377 Gregory XI owed John Thornbury 15,625 gold florins
for keeping the castle of Castricari. That same year he also owed Thornbury
and his men 11,700 gold florins for 'the restitution by them of the city of
Cesena and the spoils obtained there ...' (*ibid*, IV, 158–9).

11. See Allmard, *Society at War*, p. 77.

12. D. Hay, 'The Division of the Spoils of War in fourteenth-century England',
TRHS, 5th series, London, 1954, IV, p. 91.

13. My modernization of: 'For that whiche they doo is doon as of the kynges
owne werk men that he sette awerke for hym and in his name/therfore ought
not the proye to be theyrs wyth theyre wages/but onely thys that the prynce/
wyl gyue them of a specyall grace' (Christine de Pisan, *Book of Fayttes of
Armes*, trans. Caxton).

14. See Hay, 'Division of Spoils', p. 100; also A.E. Prince, 'The Indenture System
under Edward III' in *Historical Essays in Honour of James Tait*, ed.
Edwards, Galbraith and Jacob, p. 295, note 4.

15. See *Black Prince's Register*, III, pp. 251–2; 'Indentures of Retinue John of
Gaunt', *Camden Miscellany*, XXII, 1964, p. 88; P.W. Topping, *Feudal Institutions as Revealed in the Assizes of Romania*, p. 163.

16. See J.L. La Monte, *Feudal Monarchy in the Latin Kingdom of Jerusalem,
1100–1291*, p. 163.

17. Hay, 'Division of Spoils', pp. 103–6.

18. 'Ordinances of War at Durham 1385' in *The Black Book of the Admiralty*,
pp. 456–7. The same conditions are more or less repeated in Henry V's Ordinances of War 1419, *ibid*, pp. 463–4.

19. Cf Bonet, *Tree of Battles*, p. 147; Machaut, *Prise d'Alexandrie*, ll. 3370–
3507, 3518–39; Petrarch, *Lettere Senili*, I, 5, note 4.

20. Bonet, *Tree of Battles*, p. 153; 'Let him ask reasonable and knightly ransom,
such as is possible for the prisoner to pay and according to the usage of
arms and of his country, and not such as to disinherit his wife, children,
relations and friends; for justice demands that they should have the wherewithal to live after the ransom has been paid. If he do otherwise he is not
a gentleman but a tyrant, and no knight.'

21. Froissart, *Chronicles*, trans. Johnes, I, pp. 223–4.

22. Bonet, *Tree of Battles*, p. 153.

23. Geoffroi de Charny's '*Livre de Chevalerie*' in Froissart, *Œuvres*, ed. Kervyn,
I, iii, p. 472:

> Si peut avenir encores de tels gens qui grant volenté ont de gaigner, que, quant
> ce avient que l'en a à faire sur les champs, pluseurs sont qui regardent à prendre
> prisons et autre gaing, et quant il les ont pris et autres biens, ils ont plus grant
> volenté et desir de sauver leurs prisons ou leur gaing que de secourir et aidier de
> mettre la journée à bonne fin. Et bien puet avenir que par tele manière peut-l'en
> perdre la journée. Et l'en doit bien doubter le gaing qui fait perdre honneur, corps
> et avoir.

24. For a fuller discussion of Largess see: Mathew, 'Ideals of Knighthood', p.
360; also Barnie, *War in Medieval Society*, p. 60.

25. '*Liber custumarum*' in *Liber Albus*, ed. H.T. Riley, II, ii, pp. 519–20.

26. In fact the Knight uses neither 'largess', 'bounty' nor even the word 'liberal',
despite the fact that they are words which Chaucer himself is constantly

using, and despite the fact that the Knight is telling a tale which purports to be about chivalry. See Appendix.

Where had the Knight not fought?

1. In 1360, for example, a writ was issued compelling all citizens of London to elect four of their number to attend a council 'touching a threatened invasion by the enemy' – cf *City of London Letter-Book G*, pp. 113–14. Similarly, in 1370 'certain livery companies' were entrusted with the 'defence of the City, the enemy's fleet being reported to be lying off le Foreland de Tenet', *Letter-Book G*, p. 264.

2. Knighton, *Chronicon*, II, pp. 8–9; Murimath, *Continuatio Chronicarum*, p. 87.

3. See *The Brut*, ed. F.W.D. Brie, II, pp. 299, 303–4, 317; Walsingham, *Historia Anglicana*, I, pp. 380, 274, 287; Barnie, *War in Medieval Society*, p. 15.

4. *Rotuli Parliamentorum*, II, p. 147.

5. See Hewitt, *Organization of War*, pp. 4–5.

6. See *City of London Letter-Book G*, p. 295.

7. See *Rotuli Parliamentorum*, II, p. 303; also Powicke, *Military Obligation*, p. 242.

8. *Brut*, II, p. 335.

9. Rymer, *Fœdera*, VII, p. 185.

10. *Rotuli Parliamentorum*, III, pp. 63, 69, 70.

11. Froissart, *Cronycle*, trans. Berners, IV, pp. 306–8.

12. Walsingham, *Historia Anglicana*, II, p. 127.

13. Froissart, *Cronycle*, trans. Berners, IV, p. 312.

14. For population estimates, see H.C. Darby, *An Historical Geography of England*, p. 231; for call-up figures, see Froissart, *Cronycle*, trans. Berners, IV, pp. 314–15.

15. Froissart, *Cronycle*, trans. Berners, IV, pp. 314–15.

16. Walsingham, *Historia Anglicana*, II, p. 145.

17. My translation of Gower: *Mirour de l'Omme*, 24061–72:

> O chivaler qui vas longtein
> En terre estrange et quiers soulein
> Loenge d'armes, ce sachietz,
> Si ton paiis et ton prochein
> Ait guerre en soy, tout est en vein
> L'onour, qant tu t'es eslongez
> De ton paiis et estrangez:
> Car cil qui laist ses ductés,
> Et ne voet faire son certein,
> Ainz fait ses propres volentés,
> N'est resoun qu'il soit honourés,
> Combien qu'il soit du forte mein.

18. See Barnie, *War in Medieval Society*, pp. 24–8. The shortage of knights brought about the need for compulsory service, see Hewitt, *Organization of War*, p. 36. This shortage was the result partly of the depredations of the Black Death, partly of losses suffered in the Hundred Years' War and particularly of the increasing unpopularity of having to fulfil one's feudal obligations abroad. See Harvey, 'The Knight's Fee', pp. 31–5. For the need to increase wages as military service became less popular, see Prince, 'Indenture System', p. 292.

19. See Walsingham, *Historia Anglicana*, II, p. 202:

At this time, the Duke of Gloucester, Thomas of Woodstock, amidst many lamentations, took his way towards Prussia. Neither the pleadings of the Londoners, nor the grief of the common people could stop him, for he wholly wished to set out. Without doubt the ordinary sort of people, both in the city and in the country, feared that in his absence some new evil would follow. While he was present they feared nothing, since the hope and solace of the whole nation was seen to be placed in him.

20. Froissart, *Cronycle*, trans. Berners, v, p. 360.
21. Walsingham, *Historia Anglicana*, I, p. 371. For the fuller account of Philpot's exploit see *ibid*, pp. 370–1, also Barnie, *War in Medieval Society*, pp. 108 ff.
22. My modernization of Froissart, *Cronycle*, trans. Berners, IV, p. 437.
23. Barnie, *War in Medieval Society*, p. 45.
24. See Robinson, *Works*, p. 652; *The Canterbury Tales*, trans. Coghill, p. 20; *The Canterbury Tales*, trans. Wright, p. 13.
25. John Barnie writes: 'Edward III was not backward in proposing a crusade when it suited his purpose, but neither he nor the Black Prince ever seriously projected an expedition. It was always an instrument of policy directly related to his continental ambitions' (*War in Medieval Society*, p. 87). The Pope was always urging Edward to take up the crusade but without success – see *Calendar of Papal Registers*, IV, pp. 15, 140–2. As for Richard II, Philippe de Mézières wrote a long letter to him urging him to take up the crusade but to no effect. See Philippe de Mézières, *Letter to King Richard II*, also Hazard, *History of Crusades*, III, p. 21, and Runciman, *History of Crusades*, III, pp. 427, 456. The most Richard seems to have done is to contribute a very small amount to the fund for Constantinople. See 'Anglo-Norman Letters and Petitions', ed. M.D. Legge, *ANTS*, III, 1941, p. 103.
26. See Knighton, *Chronicon*, II, pp. 65–6:

> In the year of grace 1349, the general absolution of Rome was declared and many set out to travel to Rome; but the King prohibited their passage on account of the war with France. For which reason the pope sent messengers to the king of England concerning the principle of pilgrimage. In the first place the king clearly should not obstruct the sacred pilgrimage to the holy places of the saints.... And to the first article the reply was: that the king was occupied in a war and therefore stood in need of support, so that as yet it was necessary to take care that the treasure of his kingdom should not be spent outside his kingdom, to the harm of himself and his people, while the war lasted. And in addition, the King had it proclaimed that all Englishmen who were in Rome as well as in other places beyond the sea, should make haste to return as quickly as possible under pain of forfeiting their body and all goods....

27. See *City of London Letter-Book F*, p. 94;

> Writ to the Sheriffs for proclamation to be made forbidding any earl, baron, knight, esquire, or any other person bearing arms, religious or pilgrim, to leave the kingdom for foreign parts without special licence, on pain of arrest. Witness the King at Westminster, 9 Feb., 18 Edward III [AD 1343–4]. Proclamation made accordingly on Thursday before the Feast of St Valentine [14 Feb.].

City of London Letter-Book G, p. 7:

> Writ to the Sheriffs to make proclamation forbidding any Earl, Baron, Knight, or any one else to join in tournaments and jousts, seek adventures, or exercise other feats of arms without special command, under pain of forfeiture of horse, arms, &c., and imprisonment. Witness the King at Westminster, 20 May, 27 Edward III [AD 1353].

Ibid, p. 40:

> Writ to the Sheriffs to make proclamation forbidding any one leaving the Port of

London for foreign parts without special licence. Witness the King at Westminster, 12 June, 29 Edward III [AD 1355].

Ibid, p. 105:
Writ to the Sheriffs to make proclamation against men-at-arms, hobelers, and archers quitting the realm without especial leave. Witness the King at Westminster, 1 Feb, 33 Edward III [AD 1358–9]. Proclamation made accordingly Sunday after the Purification [2 Feb.].

28. See Froissart, *Cronycle*, trans. Berners, v, p. 360.
29. See for example Skeat, *Works*, v, p. 5; Robinson, *Works*, p. 652.
30. See N. Coghill, *Chaucer's Idea of what is Noble*, p. 9; Bowden, *Commentary*, p. 67; Manly, 'A Knyght Ther Was', pp. 104–7; Mann, *Chaucer and Med. Estates Satire*, pp. 110–11.
31. See *Scrope and Grosvenor Roll*, ed. H. Nicolas, II, pp. 106–8; *Brut*, II, pp. 303–4. For other members of the Scrope family see: *Scrope and Grosvenor Roll*, II, pp. 120, 130.
32. For Chaucer's acquaintance with Clanvowe, Neville, Montagu, Clifford and Sturry see G.L. Kittredge, 'Chaucer and some of his Friends', *MP*, I, 1903, pp. 1–5, also F.R.H. de Boulay in D. Brewer (ed.), *Geoffrey Chaucer*, pp. 44–7. For Chaucer and Clanvowe see Crow and Olson, *Chaucer Life-Records*, 347, 343; for Neville: *ibid*, 343–7; for Sturry: *ibid*, 492 n. 2, 101–2, 24–5; for Clifford: *ibid*, 104, 307, 545 n. 1. See also McFarlane, *Lancastrian Kings and Lollard Knights*, pp. 148–85.

The wisdom of being meek

1. See Robinson, *Works*, p. 652, note 68; Bowden, *Commentary*, p. 49.
2. Among them *Song of Roland*; *Erec and Enide*; *Erexsaga*. For this statement I am indebted to Malcolm Andrew of the University of East Anglia.
3. Muriel Bowden tells us that 'Even without the word "wys", Chaucer sometimes uses "worthy" to mean "brave", as in *Boece*, where "worthynesse" translates the Latin "*valentiam*" which is equivalent to the Latin "*virtus*" or "bravery".' Now '*virtus*' certainly does mean 'bravery', but '*valentia*' does not: it means 'bodily strength' and by the Middle Ages had come to mean 'power' in a more general, political sense. The most recent translation of Boethius's *De Consolatione* consequently renders *valentiam* as 'influence': '*Robur enim magnitudoque videtur praestare valentiam, pulchritudo atque velocitas celebritatem, salubritas voluptatem*' is translated as: 'Physical strength and size seem to provide influence; beauty and swiftness, fame; and health, pleasure' (Boethius, '*De Consolatione*', III, pr. 2).
   To grasp the significance of this, it is important to understand the context. Boethius is saying that purely physical characteristics (such as strength, size, beauty, speed, health) can bring only material benefits (such as fame, pleasure, and worldly power) – things which cannot, in themselves, bring true happiness. To read '*valentiam*' as 'bravery' – an inward, moral characteristic – would be nonsense. Chaucer himself translates '*valentiam*' as 'power and worthynesse'. The fact that he uses 'worthynesse' as a reinforcing word for 'power' once again confirms that for him it signified social rank or worldly influence.
4. Other examples of 'worthy' and 'wise' being used together in Chaucer's work are: 'Ye wise, proude, and worthy folkes alle,' *T&C*, I, 233; 'The wise worthy Ector the seconde', *T&C*, II, 158; 'This knoweth many a wis and worthy wight,' *T&C*, II, 180; 'The goode, wise, worthy, fresshe & fre', *T&C*, II, 317; 'Wyse and werthy for to nevene', *HofF*, III, 348; 'Worthy, wyse and gode also', *HofF*, III, 666.

5. See *OED*: 'The seyd meir … made com afore hym thes wurthymen foloweng …', *Coventry Leet Book*, 1907, III; see also *Rotuli Parliamentorum*, VI, p. 338. In Chaucer's own day, 'worthiness' was quite clearly equated with what was also called 'estate in the town'. In 1384, for example, Thomas Usk complained that a proclamation against usurers had been used as an excuse to bring about the downfall of the well-to-do citizens: '& in thys wise, be fals compassement & ymaginacion to-forn cast, many of the worthiest of the town sholde haue [be] ther-by enpesched, & be execucion ydo so vpon hem, that they sholde noght haue bore nomore estat in the town', 'Appeal of Thomas Usk against John of Northampton', in Chambers and Daunt, *A Book of London English*, p. 26.

Similarly, an anonymous vernacular homilist at the end of Richard II's reign regarded 'worthinesse' as a question of 'gret estaat' and how many horses and yeomen a man possessed: 'There also, as sum tyme a worthi bacheler of gret estaat hilde him apaied to ride with 5 or 6 hors, now a pore squyer wole ride with 9 or 10 yemen, alle of sute of as gret araie as sumtyme weren ful worthi squyers' – cited in Owst, *Literature and Pulpit*, p. 337.

6. In W. F. Bryan and G. Dempster, *Sources and Analogues of Chaucer's Canterbury Tales*, p. 600.

7. *General Prologue*, 217.

8. See Chaucer, *The Wife of Bath's Prologue*, 6–8:

> Housbondes at chirche dore I have had fyve,
> If I so ofte myghte have ywedded bee,
> And alle were worthy men in hir degree.

In this particular case, it is clear that 'worthy' also has connotations of wealth, because of the allusion to the 'church door' – legal jargon relating to the claims of a widow to her dead husband's estate. The thirteenth-century jurist Henry Bracton tells us: '… that a woman cannot claim dower unless she was endowed at the door of the church … if a woman has omitted these words: "and of which so-and-so my husband endowed me at the church door", she will lose her dower without any recovery' (Henrici de Bracton, *De Legibus et Consuetudinibus Anglie*, IV, 509, 510). So, by mentioning the 'church door', the Wife of Bath is merely emphasizing her legal claim on her five dead husbands' properties – a precaution which would only be worthwhile, of course, if they were 'worthy' men – i.e. men of substance.

9. Chaucer's application of the word 'worthy' to the Pilgrims:

Knight	5 times
Friar	4 ,,
Merchant	2 ,,
Clerk	2 ,,
Franklin	1 ,,
Wife of Bath	1 ,,
Monk	1 ,,
Canon	1 ,,

10. Chaucer, *Romaunt of the Rose*, 1197–9:

> Largesse, that worthy was and wyse,
> Helde by the honde a knyght of prise,
> Was sybbe to Arthour of Breteigne.

The French reads:

> *Largeice la uaillant, la sage,*
> *Tint .i. cheualier dou lignage*
> *Le bon roi Artu de Bretaigne.*
> *Le Roman de la Rose*, 1173–5

11. *Havelock the Dane*, 1632–6.
12. Andrew of Wyntoun, *Original Chronicle*, VI, B8.
13. The original French reads:

> Mout est fox hauz hom qui est [chiches],
> Hauz hom ne puet auoir nul uice
> Qui tant le griet come auarice;
> Car auers hom ne puet conquerre
> Ne seignorie ne grant terre.
> Car il n'a pas d'amis planté
> Dont il face sa uolenté.
> Mes qui amis uoudra auoir,
> Si n'ait mie chier son auoir.
>
> *Roman de la Rose*, 1148–57

14. See H.J. Hewitt, *The Organization of War under Edward III*, p. 31; see also: Walsingham, *Historia Anglicana*, I, p. 327.
15. Henry of Grosmont, *Le Livre de Seyntz Medicines*, p. 28: 'Car de humblesce venent toutes les autres vertues.'
16. See my sections on 'The Knight and the Teutonic Order' and 'The Knight's tournaments in Tramyssene', pp. 49 ff. and 77 ff. See also Cook, 'Beginning the Board'. On the vainglory of fighting in the lists see: J. Huizinga, *Waning of the Middle Ages*, trans. F. Hopmen, p. 96.
17. It would be a mistake to imagine that Chaucer was using the phrase 'of port' lightly – whatever may have been the habit of other poets of his age. Elsewhere he describes people's 'port' in such terms as 'plesaunt and amyable', 'noble', 'hauteyn', 'heighe' and 'faire' but never as 'meek'. See *General Prologue*, 138; *The Book of the Duchess*, 834; *The Parliament of Fowls*, 262; *Troilus & Criseyde*, I, 1084; *Romaunt of the Rose*, 1307. In *RR*, 3403, the narrator describes himself as kneeling before 'Daunger' 'ful meke of port' but this is generally not reckoned to be by Chaucer.
18. *The Merchant's Tale*, 1745 and 1851.
19. *The House of Fame*, III, 1402.
20. H.E. Watts, *Spain*, p. 201.

The Knight's lack of bad language

1. See *OED*; for 'villein', see Steinberg, *Dic. Brit. Hist.*, p. 392.
2. 'Ordinances of War made by Henry V at Mantes, 1419' in *Black Book of the Admiralty*, I, pp. 469–70:

> For theim that gyve men reproche.
> Also, that nomaner man gyve no reproche to none other, bicause of the cuntrey that he is of, that is to say be he Frenshe, Englissh, Walsh, or Irissh, or of any other cuntrey, whens that ever he be, that noman say no vilony to none other, thorough the whiche vilony saying may falle sodeyn manslaughter or reysyng of people; alle suche barratourz shal stond at the Kynges will, what deth thay shall have for their noys makyng.

3. '*Halmota Prioratus Dunelmensis*', pp. 126–32, translated in Stephenson and Marcham, *Sources*, pp. 247–8.
4. 'Oaths of Heralds' in *Black Book of the Admiralty*, I, pp. 298–9: 'Item ye shal promise to your power to forsake all vices, and take you to all virtues, and to be no commyn goerse to tavernes, the which might cause unvirtuousness and uncleane langage, and that ye be not dyse player, nother has-harder, and that ye flee places of debate and unhoneste places, and the companye of women unhoneste....'

5. Hewitt, *Organization of War*, p. 30.
6. 'The Simonie' – a poem on the evil times of Edward II, ll. 259–64 in *Political Songs*, ed. T. Wright, p. 335:

> Thus is the ordre of kniht turned up-so-doun,
> Also wel can a kniht chide as any skolde of a toun.
> Hii sholde ben also hende as any levedi in londe,
> And for to speke alle vilanie nel nu no kniht wonde
> for shame;
> And thus knihtshipe (is) acloied and waxen al fot lame.

7. Chaucer, *Romaunt of the Rose*, ll. 4233–6.

> Thanne Wikked-Tunge, ful of envye,
> With soudiours of Normandye,
> As he that causeth all the bate,
> Was keper of the fourthe gate.

8. See Canestrini, *Documenti della Milizia Italiana*, p. 58:

> Item, that the trial and judgement of each and every complaint or controversy, and in what fair way it may be settled among those concerned, provided they are of the said company, is the responsibility and duty of the captains or marshals of the said company ...
> *1364. 28 Iuglio. Patti Stabiliti Con La Compagnia Inglese Dello Sterz, detta la Compagnia Bianca.*

9. 'Richard II's Ordinances of War at Durham 1385' in *Black Book of the Admiralty*, I, p. 454:

> *Item, pur nul debat darmes, prisons, loiges, ne de nulle autre chose quelcconqe, qe nul face riote, contek, ne debat en lost ... sur peine de perdre lour chivalx et hernoys, et lour corps en areste a la voluntee de Roy, et, sil soit garceon ou page, il perdera son senestre oraille....*
> *Item, qe nul soit si hardiz de faire contek ou debat en lost, par hayne du temps passe, ne du temps avenir, dont si aucun soit mort par tiel contek ou debat, cely ou ceux qe sont encheson ou concer dycelx, serront penduz ...*

10. C.T. Allmand writes:

> Certain military leaders, but by no means all, might rule their men by force of character or sheer ability. But even great leaders sometimes found this difficult; Henry v himself could not guarantee that all his men obeyed orders. The problem, as many contemporaries realised, lay in the existence of war's material gains which were there for the taking. An army which went unpaid would seek its rewards from other sources, often from those least able to afford them or to protect themselves. The lure of material gain, or the enticements of war, presented not only war leaders, but society at large, with one of its greatest problems: how could might be prevented from always imposing itself? It was in order to achieve some measure of control that the laws of war were frequently reiterated to the soldiers.
> *Society at War*, p. 4.

11. Makhairas, *Chronicle*, I, pp. 97–9.
12. See W.H. Schofield, *Chivalry in English Literature*, pp. 30–8; Bowden, *Commentary*, p. 46; Mann, *Chaucer & Med. Estates Satire*, p. 107.
13. Watriquet, 'Li dit du Connestable de France' in *Dits de Watriquet de Couvin*, ed. A. Scheler, ll. 42–5:

> *Tant fust plains de courouz ne d'ire*
> *Onques n'issi hors de sa bouche*

> Vilains mos; maniere avoit douche,
> Plus que dame ne damoisele.

14. For example, Henry of Grosmont condemned evil speech because it was the result of anger (*corouce*) which had already entered the body, and Christine de Pisan described how, in the old days, youths were trained to fight as knights without 'noo rancour ne anger'. Cf *Livre de Seyntz Medicines*, p. 42, and Christine de Pisan, *Fayttes of Armes*, p. 30.
15. *The Parson's Tale*, ll. 534–6: 'This synne of Ire, after the discryvyng of Seint Augustyn, is wikked wil to been avenged by word or by dede./Ire, after the philosophre, is the fervent blood of man yquyked in his herte, thurgh which he wole harm to hym that he hateth.'
16. *Ibid*, ll. 561–2: 'Of Ire comen thise stynkynge engendrures: First, hate, that is oold wratthe; discord, thurgh which a man forsaketh his olde freend that he hath loved ful longe;/and thanne cometh werre, and every manere of wrong that man dooth to his neighebor, in body or in catel.'
17. See Tatlock, *Concordance*, pp. 1004–5. As an example of the usual sense in which Chaucer uses 'vileynye' – i.e., as a deed or action – *Tale of Melibeus*, ll. 1460–1: 'Melibee answerde, "If I ne venge me nat of the vileynye that men han doon to me,/I sompne or warne hem that han doon to me that vileyne, and alle othere, to do me another vileynye,"'
18. Cf Lull, *Book of the Ordre of Chyualry*, trans. Caxton.
19. My modernization of *ibid*, p. 113: 'To a knyght apperteyneth to speke nobly and curtoisly/and to haue fayr harneys and to be wel cladde/and to holde a good houshold/and an honest hows/For alle these thynges ben to honoure Chyualrye necessarye.'
20. See *Sir Gawain and the Green Knight*, ed. J.R.R. Tolkien and E.V. Gordon, l. 917.

Is the Knight 'gentil'?

1. For definitions, see Lewis and Short, *A Latin Dictionary* and *MED*.

2.   *Il me semble qe qi qe deveroit a droit jugger la gentilesce d'une persone, il lui covendroit a savoir trois choses, avant q'omme lui tenisoit a droit gentil: La primere est de savour si son pier estoit gentil; la seconde, si sa miere estoit genti famme ausi; et la tierce est a savoir s'il se contient en ditz, en faitz, com gentil et ayme la compaignye de gentils – et grant honte fait a sa miere qi en bien ne contrefait son pier. Et s'il soit ensi par pier et par miere gentil et de lui meismes, come j'ai dite devant, bien le doit homme appeller et tenir gentil.*
     Henry of Grosmont, *Le Livre de Seyntz Medicines*, p. 27.

3. My modernization of Caxton's translation:

   Parage and chyualrye accorden to gyder/... yf thou make a knyght that is not of parage/thou makest chyualrye to be contrary to parage/and by this same reason/he whom thou makest knyght is contrary to parage & to chyualry
   Ramon Lull, *Book of the Ordre of Chyualry*, trans. Caxton, p. 58

4. For a full discussion of these influences on Chaucer's ideas of 'gentillesse' see B.L. Jefferson, *Chaucer and the 'Consolation of Philosophy' of Boethius*, pp. 94–104.
5. Jean de Meung, *Romance of the Rose*, trans. Robbins, ll. 18607–29, p. 395.
6. Boethius, '*De Consolatione*', trans. Stewart *et al*. III, vi. p. 255.

7. See Dante, *The Convivio*, IV, pp. 224–7:

> So inured is such false thought amongst us, that folk call that man a gentleman, who can aver: 'I was grandson or son of such an one of worth,' though he himself be nought ... Gentlehood is wherever there is virtue, but not virtue where she is; even as the heaven is wherever is the star, but not conversely.

See also Jefferson, *Chaucer and the 'Consolation'*, p. 96, also J.L. Lowes, 'Chaucer and Dante's *Convivio*' in *MP*, XIII, 1915, pp. 19–27.

8. Dante, *The Convivio*, IV, 15, pp. 303–4.
9. See *The Legend of Good Women*, Prologue, F. 374.
10. Dante, *The Convivio*, IV, 20, p. 326.
11. See M. Schlauch, 'Chaucer's Doctrine of Kings and Tyrants', *Speculum*, XX, 1945, pp. 145–6:

> In Italy, contemporary political theory and practice had now to deal with local 'tyrants' who concentrated in their persons the new power which had been playing pope against emperor for its own ends in an earlier generation. It was the ruling families of Milan, Florence and other cities, usurpers in many cases of republican or at least oligarchic administrations, which now challenged the attention of writers ... It is impossible to say how much of the discussion may have reached Chaucer's attention, directly or indirectly, but it may at least be pointed out that the subject was much to the fore among Italian thinkers in the cities he visited.

12. Walsingham, *Historia Anglicana*, II, pp. 32–3.
13. See Coghill, *Chaucer's Idea of what is Noble*, p. 15.
14. Cf *Prologue*, 567, 669; *Cook's Prol.*, 4353; *Prologue*, 718. The irony of calling the Tabard 'this gentil hostelrye' revolves around the next line in which he draws attention to the Tabard's proximity to the Bell, which was a notorious brothel. Cf Stow, *Survey of London*, p. 361.
15. Cf *Gentilesse*, ll. 9–11: Jefferson, *Chaucer and the 'Consolation'*, pp. 101–2, note 18.
16. See Dante, *The Convivio*, IV, 17. Jefferson, *Chaucer and the 'Consolation'*, p. 102, note 18.
17. For example,

> But pite renneth soone in gentil herte;
> That maistow seen, she kytheth what she ys.
> > Chaucer, *The Legend of Good Women*, ll. 503–4

> And thus for pite and for gentillesse
> > *Legend of Dido*, l. 1080

> Have mercy on oure wo and oure distresse!
> Som drope of pitee, thurgh thy gentillesse.
> > *The Knight's Tale*, ll. 919–20

> This Alla kyng hath swich compassioun,
> As gentil herte is fulfild of pitee,
> That from his eyen ran the water doun.
> > *The Man of Law's Tale*, ll. 659–61

> Lo, pitee renneth soone in gentile hert!
> > *The Merchant's Tale*, l. 1986

18. See Temple-Leader and Marcotti, *Sir J. Hawkwood*, pp. 118–22.
19. Even when Theseus appears to take pity on the weeping women at the very start of *The Knight's Tale* (952–6), his motives are far from unquestionable. See Ian Robinson, *Chaucer and the English Tradition*, p. 120.
20. See Harvey, 'The Knight's Fee', pp. 1–7; Bloch, *Feudal Society*, p. 444; Bean,

Decline of English Feudalism, pp. 306–7. The fact that more and more land-holders sought to avoid their military obligations as the Knight of the *Prologue* must have done was a constant source of complaint. See, for example: Owst, *Literature and Pulpit*, p. 73; Froissart, *Cronycle*, trans. Berners, IV, p. 437; *Political Poems and Songs relating to English History*, ed. Wright, I, p. 216; *Rotuli Parliamentorum*, III, p. 5; *Petrarch, an Anthology*, p. 211.

A gay horse?

1. There has in fact been some debate as to whether or not 'His hors were gode' *is* plural – see G. Ethel, 'Horse or Horses?', *MLN*, LXXV, 1960, pp. 97–101, who thinks it is not, and W.H. French, 'Horse or Horses?' *MLN*, LXXVI, 1961, pp. 293–5, who thinks it is. But it is generally accepted now to be plural.

   The construction in detail is as follows: 'Hors' could be singular or plural; 'were' is plural Pret. Ind. (see F. Mossé, *A Handbook of Middle English*, p. 84); 'were' is also subj. sing. and plural, but would not be subjunctive here; 'gode' is plural – although there was also a weak form of the singular; (*ibid*, p. 64); 'he' could be sing. or plural (*ibid*, p. 55); but 'was' is singular.
2. Printed in E. Ricotti, *Storia Delle Compagnie di Ventura*, II, 302.
3. See Skeat, *Works*, V, p. 8.
4. Bowden, *Commentary*, p. 50.
5. *Sir Amadace*, Camden Society, 1842, lvi (cf. *OED*).
6. As in *Sir Gawain and the Green Knight*, ll. 970, 2035.
7. John Lydgate, *The Minor Poems* (ed. H. N. MacCracken), II, p. 417.
8. See *The Romaunt of the Rose*, ll. 7243–5. False Semblant, dressed as 'an Holy heremyte' (l. 6481) confesses to Love: 'Sothe is, but I am but an ypo-cryte' (l. 6482). He then goes on to deliver a typical friar's sermon to demon-strate how friars criticize the gaiety of others in order to escape criticism themselves: 'That we may folke repreue echone,/And we nyll haue reprefe of none' (ll. 7237–8). As part of this sermon, False Semblant declares that friars say such things as: 'And where is more woode folye/Than to enhaunce chiualrye,/and loue noble men and gay,/That ioly clothes weren alway?' (ll. 7243–5).
9. See Godefroy, *Dictionnaire de l'Ancienne langue française*.
10. See *An Alphabet of Tales* (ed. M.M. Banks), p. 168, 6.
11. See J.E. Mansion, *Harrap's New Standard French–English Dictionary*.
12. The '*Ortus Vocabulorum*' (1530) quoted in the *Catholicon Anglicum* of 1483, ed. S.J. Herrtage, pp. 146–8, note 5. See also a dictionary of 1468, the '*Medulla Grammatica*' Manuscript in St John's College, Cambridge.
13. *Catholicon Anglicum*, p. 147; see also Lewis and Short, *A Latin Dictionary*, p. 1107, also *MED* under 'gay'.
14. *Catholicon Anglicum*, pp. 147–8, note 5, quotes the '*Medulla Grammatica*': '*Manducus*, in Plaut. A disguised or ugly picture, such as was used in May games and shows, seeming terrible, by reason of his broad mouth and great crashing teeth, and made to cause the people to give room.'

The shabby Knight

1. On the importance of flamboyant trappings see: Barnie, *War in Medieval Society*, p. 73. For example, see the description of Sir William Marmion 'all resplendent with gold and silver, marvellously arrayed'. Thomas Gray, *Scalacronica*, ed. J. Stevenson, p. 145, translated in G.G. Coulton, *Life in the Middle Ages*, II, pp. 89–90.

For a good popular account of how a 'gentyll knyght' should be dressed, see 'A Geste of Robyn Hode', stanzas 70–8; Child, *Ballads*, III, pp. 59–60.

2. Chaucer, *The Knight's Tale*, ll. 2128–84, 2529.

3. See C. Blair, *European Armour circa 1066–1700*, p. 46.

4. 'Expenses of the Great Wardrobe of Edward III from 21 Dec. 1345 to 31 Jan. 1349', ed. N.H. Nicolas, in *Arch*, XXXI, 1846, pp. 34, 35, 49.

5. Blair, *Armour*, pp. 75–6; C.H. Ashdown, *British and Foreign Arms and Armour*, pp. 167–8.

6. For 'fustian', see Elisha Coles, *An English Dictionary*, 1676, and also MED. Henry VI, for example, had a fustian and a sheet under his feather bed, and then over the bed another sheet and then 'the over fustian above', see *The Babees Book*, ed. F.J. Furnivall, p. 179, note 1.

7. See Jacques de Hemricourt, *'Le Traité des Guerres d'Awans et de Waroux'* in *Œuvres*, ed. Borman, Bayot and Poncelet, III, para. 41, quoted below, note 32. Presumably fustian was too coarse a material for fine embroidery and the like. Certainly Hemricourt takes it for granted that fustian gypons would be plain.

8. In his accounts (1462–71) John Howard, Duke of Norfolk, records that he had a 'doublet of defence' made out of fustian and linen: 'I took to the doublet maker in the Holte, to make me a doublet of defence ... eighteen-fold thick of white fustian, and four-fold of linen cloth', in T.H. Turner (ed.), *Manners and Household Expenses of England in the thirteenth and fifteenth centuries*, p. 239, also 'Fusten ffor my lord to make doblettys off ffence' *ibid*, p. 158. While there is nothing infra-dig about fustian itself, as is clear from the above extracts, it is worth noting that in 1464 an Act of Parliament established the minimum income for wearing fustian at forty shillings, and prescribed it for '... the meniall servauntes of Yomens degree, of Lordes, Knyghts, Squiers and other Gentilmen.' See *Rotuli Parliamentorum*, V, p. 504.

9. See H.A. Dillon, 'A manuscript collection of Ordinances of Chivalry of the fifteenth century' in *Arch*, LVII, i, pp. 43–4.

10. Others bearing elaborate gypons are Count de la Roche (otherwise known as 'the Bastard of Burgundy'), who wore a gypon of arras, when he arrived in Gravesend in 1467: '... accompanyde with many noble lordes ... his gabon also hangid with arasse within and withoute richely beseen ...', *Excerpta Historica*, ed. S. Bentley, p. 197; and Sir Ferumbras (the Saracen champion) who had a gypon of 'riche entaylle', 'Sir Ferumbras', l. 745 in *English Charlemagne Romances*, i, ed. S.J. Herrtage.

11. Muriel Bowden thinks we are meant to visualize the Knight actually riding in his chain-mail on the pilgrimage (Bowden, *Commentary*, p. 50). Skeat thinks not (Skeat, *Works*, V, p. 9). For what it is worth, I agree with Skeat. It was a common cry that the armour of the day was too heavy:

> *D'une autre chose vous dy tant*
> *Que vous vous armez trop pesant,*
> *Tant que quant estez tout armez,*
> *En pou d'eure estes foulez ...*
> Bonet, *L'Apparicion Maistre Jehan de Meun*,
> ed. I. Arnold, ll. 517–20

And although this must refer to the use of plate-armour in addition to chain-mail, the chain-mail itself must have been very heavy. When we made the film *Monty Python and the Holy Grail*, most of us wore imitation chain-mail made out of knitted wool, which was uncomfortable enough, but Graham Chapman, as King Arthur, wore a genuine metal chain-mail coif and found the weight of it unbearable for more than short periods. See also Eric Rohmer's remarks about the weight of real chain-mail during the making of his film *Perceval* in *Sight and Sound*, XLVII, 4, 1978, p. 231. See also: R.C. Clephan, *The Defensive Armour and Weapons of Medieval Times and of the Renaissance*, p. 51.

12. '*Knyghthode & Bataile*' a XVth Century verse paraphrase of Flavius Vegetius Renatus' Treatise *De Re Militari*, eds R. Dyboski & Z. M. Arend, p. 36:

> And vse wel a dart, a shaft, a spere,
> And teche chiualers vndir his cure,
> Right as himself to torne hem in her gere
> The brigandyn, helmet, and al procure,
> It oftyn wipe clene, – and knowe sure,
> With herneysing and myghti poort affrayed
> Is ofte a foo, and forto fight dismayed.

The verse continues as follows:

> Is it to sey: 'he is a werrely knyght,'
> Whos herneys is horribil & beduste,
> Not onys vsed in a fourte nyght,
> And al that iron is or steel, beruste;
> Vnkept his hors, how may he fight or juste?
> The knyghtis and her horsys in his tourme
> This Capitayn shal procure & refourme.

13. See Ashdown, *British and Foreign Arms*, p. 168; Blair, *Armour*, p. 53.
14. *Ibid*, p. 40.
15. See *London: Calendar of Select Pleas and Memoranda, 1381–1412*, p. 62. See also the inventory of Richard Tokey's goods, *ibid*, p. 213.
16. *Ibid*, p. 128.
17. 'The Assize of Arms 1181', translated in Stephenson and Marcham, *Sources*, pp. 85–7.
18. Translated in *EHD*, III, pp. 461–2.
19. Powicke, *Military Obligation*, p. 145.
20. *Ibid*, pp. 147–8.
21. *Ibid*, p. 192.
22. See the 'Tariff of Fines for the City of Florence, 1368', printed in E. Ricotti, *Storia della Compagnie di Ventura in Italia*, II, p. 342:

PENALTIES		
Captain of a lance:	L.	s.
lacking helmet	5	
——— cuirass or panciera	5	
having panciera without a coat of mail or breastplate		20
lacking a lance	2	
——— arm-pieces		20
——— gloves	2	
——— sword	3	
——— knife or dagger		20
——— thigh armour		20
——— leg armour		40
Foot-soldiers:		
lacking panciera	3	
——— armour for the head or a lance	2	

	L.	s.
—— gloves		20
—— sword	2	
—— knife or dagger		10
—— bow or balista	3	
—— arrows	2	
Archers:		
lacking panciera	3	
—— small helmet or bacinet		20
—— sword	2	
—— bow	6	
—— arrows	3	
And for each of the above-named, lacking spurs	2	

23. Compare sections II and VII in the 'Codice degli stipendiarii della repubblica di Firenze 1369' in E. Ricotti, Storia delle Compagnie, II, pp. 315–16.

24. For definition of panciera see Gay, Glossaire Archéologique. See also Jean le Bel, Chronique, I, pp. 126–7, and Jacques de Hemricourt, 'Traité des Guerres d'Awans et de Waroux', para. 41, quoted below in notes 32 and 33.

25. M. Villani, Cronica, V, p. 260:

Loro armadura quasi de tutti erano panzeroni, e davanti al petto un'anima d'ac- ciaio, bracciali di ferro, cosciali e gamberuoli, daghe e spade sode, tutti con lance da posta, le quali scesi a piè volentieri usavano, e ciascuno di loro avea uno o due paggetti, è tali piu secondo ch'era possente, e come s'aveano cavate l'armi di dosso i detti paggetti di presente intendeano a tenerle pulite, sicche quando com- pariano a zuffe loro armi pareano specchi, e per tanto erano più spaventevoli.

26. Pietro Azario, 'Liber Gestorum in Lombardia' in L. A. Muratori, Rerum Italicarum Scriptores – Storici Italiani, XVI, iv, p. 128: 'Nam mos ipsorum est cum necessario habeant in aperto debellare, descendentes ab equis, sola diploide armati, ut plurimum, vel placa una ferrea supra pectus et capite ut plurimum decoperto vel cum solo cupo barbute et lanceis grandibus.'

27. See 'Codice degli stipendiarii etc 1369' in Ricotti, Storia della Compagnie di Ventura, I, iv, pp. 313–27.

28. For origin of 'brigante' see A. J. Greimas, Dictionnaire de l'Ancien Français p. 83; also OED and the continuation of Chronique de Richard Lescot, ed. J. Lemoine: 'Five hundred crossbowmen with one hundred servants lightly armoured with armour who then were called "brigantes"', quoted in Jean de Venette, Chronicle, trans. Birdshall, p. 217, note 35. John Gower also uses the word in connection with the dominance of the Free Companies in Lombardy, when he rebukes the Church for employing companies such as the White Company of John Hawkwood. He says they have stooped to 'brygantaille':

The cherche keye in aventure
Of armes and of brygantaille
Stod nothing thanne upon bataille;
To fyhte or for to make cheste
It thoght hem thanne noght honeste;
Gower, 'Confessio Amantis' Prol., ll. 213–17

29. John Trevisa, in his translation of Higden's Polychronicon (c. 1387), notes that no one dared to take the road to Rome for fear of the 'robbours and

for brigantes that was ther armed' (*Polychronicon*, VII, p. 151). For *coterel* see Greimas, *Dictionnaire*, p. 146.

30. Jean le Bel, *Chronique*, I, pp. 126–7:

> *A ce temps ne faisoient les grands seigneurs compte de gens d'armes s'ilz n'avoient les heaumes couronnez, et à ce temps de maintenant fait on compt de gens à glaives, à panchiéres, à haubergons et à chapeaulx de fer. Sy me semble le tempts estre bien changé de mon souvenant, car les chevaulx couvers, les heaumes couronnés, dont on se souloit parer, les plates, les tourniqués d'armes de congnoissance sont alez à neant, et les haubergons, que on appelle maintenant panchieres, les juppes de wanbisons et les chapeaulx de fer sont venuz en avant. Aussy bien et aussy noblement est maintenant armé ung povre garchon, qu'est ung noble chevaliers.*

* wanbison = gambeson: a military tunic, worn especially in the fourteenth century made of leather or thick cloth, sometimes padded, originally worn under the habergeoun to prevent chafing or bruises, but sometimes used as a defence without other body armour.

31. J. de Hemricourt, '*Traité des Guerres*', para. 41.

32. *Ibid*:

> *Mais, à present, cascons est armeis d'unne cotte de fer appelée panchire, sor petis chevaz; et ont vestut on joupon de festaine alle deseur, sy que nus n'est conus encontre son compangnon. Et, en liu de wardecors d'armes, ith portent on eskuchet de leur blazon, atagiet a leur barbire. Neisly prinches n'ont atres habit, excepteit que leurs desoirtrains warnimens est overeis d'alconne envozure, sains atre connissance, si qu'il ne semblent nint saingnors ne gens d'armes, mais garchons. Et ensy est perie tout honeur et tout gentilhece, car à poynes seit on, al jour d'uy, queis armes ne queilz blazons ly nobles et gens de linage doiient porteir, ne queis timbres sor leur heame.*

33. *Ibid: Si que c'estoit ly plus gran plaisanche, ly plus riches habis et ly plus grans solas que on powist avoir, de nobles gens d'armes à veioir en teil estat. Car nus n'ozoit estre coars, par tant que on conissoit les bons et les mavais à leurs blazons. Et duroit plus longement une batailhe adont que maintenant trois.*

34. Froissart, *Chronicles*, trans. Johnes, I, pp. 293–300.

35. For an account of Hemricourt's life see: J. de Hemricourt, *Œuvres*, eds C. de Borman, A. Bayot, E. Poncelet, III, pp. xii–xxix.

Is the Knight's shabbiness a sign of piety?

1. See, for example, Chaucer's explanation of the Canon's obvious haste in getting out of town and his consequent lack of luggage: 'Al light for somer rood this worthy man', *The Canon's Yeoman's Prol.*, l. 568.

2. For example, E. T. Donaldson, *Chaucer's Poetry*, p. 882: 'Of all the pilgrims the Knight (with the Parson) seems most aware of the real purpose of the pilgrimage. Having just returned from his latest campaign, he proceeds at once in his travel-stained clothing.'

3. Bowden, *Commentary*, pp. 49–50.

4. Cf *Epilogue of the Man of Law's Tale*, 1170–83:

> The Parson hem answerde, 'Benedicite!
> What eyleth the man, so synfully to swere?'
> Oure Host answerde, 'O Jankin, be ye there?
> I smelle a Lollere in the wynd,' quod he.
> 'Now! goode men,' quod oure Hoste, 'herkeneth me;
> Abydeth, for Goddes digne passioun,
> For we shal han a predicacioun;

> This Lollere heer wil prechen us somwhat.'
> 'Nay, by my fader soule, that schal he nat!'
> Seyde the Shipman; 'heer schal he nat preche;
> He schal no gospel glosen here ne teche.
> We leven alle in the grete God,' quod he;
> 'He wolde sowen som difficulte,
> Or springen cokkel in our clene corn.'

For a discussion of the possible Lollardy of the Parson see: Loomis in *Essays in Honour of Carelton Brown*, pp. 141–4; Robinson, *Works*, p. 765; Manly, *The Canterbury Tales*, p. 528.

5. Chaucer, *The Parson's Tale*, l. 419: 'Forthwith the superfluitee in lengthe of the forseide gownes, trailynge in the dong and in the mire, on horse and eek on foote, as wel of man as of womman, that al thilke trailyng is verraily as in effect wasted, consumed, thredbare, and roten with donge, rather than it is yeven to the povre, to greet damage of the forseyde povre folk.'

6. A homily c. 1380–1440, quoted in Owst, *Literature and Pulpit*, p. 369:

   Now a wrecchid cnave, that goth to the plough and to carte, that hath no more good but serveth fro yer to yer for his liflode, there-as sumtyme a white curtel and a russet gowne wolde have served suchon ful wel, now he muste have a fresch doublet of fyve schillynges or more the price; and above, a costli gowne with bagges hangynge to his kne, and iridelid undir his girdil as a newe ryven roket, and an hood on his heved, with a thousand ragges on his tipet; and gaili hosid an schood as though it were a squyer of cuntre.

7. The cause of this social upheaval can be traced back partly to the Black Death and the subsequent labour shortage and demand for higher wages, as writers of the fourteenth century were aware. Robert Rypon of Durham whose sermon is quoted here, for example 'tells how, according to the account of elderly persons, at the beginning of the Pestilence and for a long while before, men were simple and clad in homely fashion. But, after the Pestilence, when the war with France began, then began also the pride of the French to infect the English, and now the present age is surfeited with it.' Quoted in Owst, p. 406.

   The sight of these churls, who formerly went about in rags, now being able to buy better clothes, was evidently more than the conservative preacher could stand (*ibid*, p. 360): 'This pride schulle ther maistirs a-buye, whanne that thei schul paie hir wages. For, there-as thei weren wont to serve for x or xii schillingis in a yer, now thei musten have xx oor thritti and his lyverei also therto; not for he wol do more werk, but for to meynten with that pride.'

8. MS Harley 4894, fol. 27b, translated in *ibid*, pp. 369–70.

9. See Jusserand, *English Wayfaring Life*, p. 204:

   If the distances were great between class and class at this period, familiarity was still greater. The distance has indeed diminished at the present day, and familiarity also, as though in compensation. The noble felt himself sufficiently raised above the common people not to be afraid of using a kind of jovial intimacy with them on occasion; at the present time, when superiority of rank is of less importance, many are more attentive and take care not to overstep a limit which is not now so patent as before.

10. According to the sixteenth-century antiquary John Stow, coaches were a comparatively recent importation in his day, and in the fourteenth century even great lords rode either on horseback or – at most – in a 'chariot' or

'whirlicote'. Even then, Richard II's Queen Anne introduced the side-saddle, and hence, in Chaucer's time, everyone went about either on foot or on horseback. Stow complains:

> Of old time coaches were not known in this island, but chariots or whirlicotes, then so called, and they only used of princes or great estates, such as had their footmen about them; and for example to note, I read that Richard II, being threatened by the rebels of Kent, rode from the Tower of London to the Myles end, and with him his mother, because she was sick and weak, in a whirlicote, the Earls of Buckingham, Kent, Warwicke, and Oxford, Sir Thomas Percie, Sir Robert Knowles, The Mayor of London, Sir Aubery de Vere, that bare the king's sword, with other knights and esquires attending on horseback. But in the next year, the said King Richard took to wife Anne, daughter to the King of Bohemia, that first brought hither the riding upon side-saddles; and so was the riding in wherlicoates and chariots forsaken, except at coronations and such like spectacles; but now of late years the use of coaches, brought out of Germany, is taken up, and made so common, as there is neither distinction of time nor difference of persons observed; for the world runs on wheels with many whose parents were glad to go on foot.
> John Stow, *The Survey of London*, ed. H.B. Wheatley, p. 77.

11. The origin of the word 'almoner' lies in the official whose duty it was to look after the alms-dish and place it on the table or 'on the copborde yf no rome be vppon the borde'. He saw to it that the dish was filled with meat from the first cut of the joint:

> And when all the lordes messe is sewid, then shall another esquyre next the hande sewe the other messes at the borde or in his presence. And anone forthewyth the amener shall bryng in the almesse dyshe with a loofe there inne and set it bynethe the lordes salt or elles vppon the copborde yf no rome be vppon the borde; and a litill afore the seconde cours the amener shall take of euery standarde or grete mete that comys byfore the lorde at the first cours a sertayne, wyth the helpe of the kerver, and put it in the almes dysshe and send the voyde dysshes to the kechyn. *A Fifteenth-Century Courtesy Book*, ed. R.W. Chambers and W.W. Seton, p. 12.

When Abbot Samson of Bury St Edmunds (d. 1212) forswore meat after the fall of Jerusalem, he still had meat set before him on the table so 'that the alms might be increased'. See Jocelin of Brakelond, *Chronicle*, trans. L.C. Jane, p. 63.

12. On the increasing privileges of the modern 'executive class' see Ivan Illich, *Tools for Conviviality*, pp. 70–1:

> Never before have tools approached present power. Never before have they been so integrated at the service of a small elite. Kings could not claim divine right with as little challenge as executives claim services for the sake of greater production. The Russians justify supersonic transport by saying it will economize the time of their scientists. High-speed transportation, broad band-width communication, special health maintenance, and unlimited bureaucratic assistance are all explained as requirements to get the most out of the most highly capitalized people. A society with very large tools must rely on multiple devices to keep the majority from claiming the most expensive packages of privilege.

13. Hoccleve, *Regement of Princes*, 442–5:

> Som tyme, afer men myghten lordes knowe
> By there array, from other folke; but now
> A man schal stody and musen a long throwe
> Whiche is whiche....

14. *Ibid*, 445–8.
15. Hawkwood was generally reckoned to have started out in life as a tailor's apprentice, presumably before he was swept into the service of the Hundred Years' War. See the account in the *DNB*, also Temple-Leader and Marcotti, *Sir J. Hawkwood*, pp. 1 ff.
    For another possible reference to him in this context see Gower, *Vox Clamantis*, VII, 263.
16. Alain Chartier, *Quadrilogue Invectif*, pp. 200–2: 'Take me a taylours man and woman of powr degre and loke whethir thei be nat bolde to wer suche arraye as dothe a wourshipfull knyght or a noble lady, wherfor euery man hath suche wise lernyd this conseite that it is an harde thing to knowe the states of persones by their array or to knowe a wourshipfull man from a craftis man.'
17. *Rotuli Parliamentorum*, II, p. 278:

    25. ITEM Monstrent les Communes, que come diverses Vitailles dedeinz le Roialme sont grandement encherrez, par cause que diverses gentz de diverses Condicions usent diverse Apparaill nient appertenant a lour Estat; c'est assaver, Garceons usent Apparaill des gentz de Mestire, & gentz de Mestire Apparaile des Valletz, & Valletz Apparaile des Esquiers, & Esquiers Apparaill de Chivalers; l'un & l'autre Pellure que seulment de reson appertienent as Seigneurs & Chivalers; Femmes povres & autres Apparaile des Dames, povres Clercs Pellure come le Roi & autres Seigneurs. Issint sont les Marchandises susdites a plus grant pris que ne soleient estre, & le Tresor de la terre destruit, a grant damage des Seigneurs & Communes. Dont ils priont remede, si ce soit avys as Seigneurs du Conseil.

18. 'The Simonie', 253–4, printed in *Political Songs of England*, ed. T. Wright, p. 335.
19. The Dominican Friar John Bromyard represents the typical establishment support of the 'crusades': see Owst, *Literature and Pulpit*, pp. 412, 335. In fact the Papacy was continually assigning money for the dissemination of crusade propaganda in England. See, for example, *Calendar of Papal Registers*, IV, p. 267.

The Knight's Tale

1. A.E. Housman, *The Name and Nature of Poetry*, 1933, quoted in J.A. Burrow, *Geoffrey Chaucer – a critical anthology*, p. 136.
2. Robinson, *Chaucer and Tradition*, p. 109.
3. See Donaldson, *Chaucer's Poetry*, p. 901; John Speirs, *Chaucer the Maker*, p. 121.
4. Stuart Robertson, 'Elements of Realism in the Knight's Tale', *JEGP*, XIV, 1915, pp. 226–55.
5. Patch, *On Rereading Chaucer*, p. 211.
6. Paull F. Baum, *Chaucer, A Critical Introduction*, pp. 90, 95, 96, 101 – quoted by R. Neuse, 'The Knight: the First Mover in Chaucer's Human Comedy', *UTQ*, XXXI, 1962, p. 314.
7. Charles Muscatine, 'Form, texture and meaning in Chaucer's Knight's Tale', *PMLA*, LXV, 1950, pp. 917–18.
8. *Ibid*, pp. 919, 920, for this and preceding quotation.
9. See Stephen Knight, *Rymyng Craftily – Meaning in Chaucer's Poetry*, p. 98. See also W.H. French, 'The Lovers in the *Knight's Tale*', *JEGP*, XLVIII, 1949, pp. 320–8; William Frost, 'An Interpretation of Chaucer's *Knight's Tale*', *RES*, XXV, 1949, pp. 289–304.
10. Muscatine, 'Form and meaning', p. 919.
11. Knight, *Rymyng Craftily*, p. 98.

12. Frost, 'An Interpretation', p. 302. William Frost's essay is reprinted in *Chaucer Criticism*, eds R. Schoeck and J. Taylor, I, pp. 98–116, and see p. 113.
13. Dale Underwood, 'The First of the Canterbury Tales', *ELH*, XXVI, 1959, p. 455.
14. *Ibid*, p. 466.
15. Neuse, 'Knight: First Mover', p. 300.
16. Elizabeth Salter, *The Knight's Tale and The Clerk's Tale*, p. 34.
17. Salter, *The Knight's Tale*, pp. 32–3.
18. Robinson, *Chaucer and Tradition*, pp. 120, 127.
19. *Ibid*, p. 144.
20. See Bowden, *Commentary*, p. 69; 'There is every indication in many of his works that the poet frequently saw only the excitement, the adventure, and the pageantry of war. We cannot find in Chaucer the openly avowed pacifist we find in his friend Gower, who boldly condemns "dedly werre" as a "foule horrible vice", forbidden by both God and nature.' See also Barnie, *War in Medieval Society*, p. 134.
21. See *Chronique de la Traison et Mort de Richard II*, ed. B. Williams, pp. 118–21:

> It is to be observed that King Richard held a feast at Westminster, when he declared his intention of going to Bristol. And straightway at this feast arrived the said soldiers who had held Brest for the King, who were received at dinner in the King's Hall. When the dinner was over and the King had taken wine and comfits, the Duke of Gloucester said to the King, 'My lord, have you not remarked at dinner our companions which are here?' The King replied, 'Good uncle, what companions do you mean?' 'My lord,' said the Duke, 'they are your people who have come from Brest, who have faithfully served you, but have been badly paid, and know not what to take to.' And the King said that they should be paid in full; and, in fact, commanded that four good villages near London should be given up to them, that they might there live at his expense until they received their due. Then replied the Duke of Gloucester very proudly, 'Sire, you ought first to hazard your life in capturing a city from your enemies, by feat of arms or by force, before you think of giving up or selling any city which your ancestors, the Kings of England, have gained or conquered.' To which the King answered very scornfully, 'What is that you say?' The Duke, his uncle, then repeated what he had before said. Upon which the King was very wroth, and said to the Duke, 'Do you think that I am a merchant or a traitor, that I wish to sell my land? By St John the Baptist, no, no; but it is a fact that our cousin of Britanny has restored, and well and truly paid us the sum which our ancestors had lent him on the city of Brest; and since he has honestly paid us, it is only just he should have his pledge back again.' Thus began the quarrel between the King and the Duke of Gloucester. It is true that they parted politely and with civil words, as they were bound to do; but their distrust was by no means the less because they separated with civil words before the people; and the mistrust continued between the King and the Duke of Gloucester without any more disputes until a short time afterwards; and they continued to give each other a civil reception, but with a bad will, as is too much the case with the Duke and many others of the kingdom of England.

22. See Díez de Games Gutierre, *El Victorial, Crónica de Don Pero Niño*, ed. J. de Mata Carriazo, Madrid, 1940, p. 182 ff; also Philippe de Mézières, *Songe du Vieil Pelérin*, III, pp. 373 ff – both cited in Barnie, *War in Medieval Society*, p. 126 and note 28, p. 178.
23. See Anthony Tuck, *Richard II and the English Nobility*, p. 158; also Froissart, *Cronycle*, trans. Berners, VI, pp. 38–9.

24. Chaucer, *Tale of Melibeus*, ll. 2226–31, 2860. See also 2477–83.
25. See M.H. Keen's important article 'Chivalry, Nobility and the Man-at-Arms' in *War, Literature and Politics in the Late Middle Ages*, ed. C.T. Allmand, pp. 32, 44.
26. Boccaccio, *The Book of Theseus (Teseida delle Nozze d'Emilia)*, trans. Bernadette Marie McCoy. The book can be purchased from the publishers Teesdale Publishing Associates Inc., Box 1375, 299 Sea Cliff Avenue, Sea Cliff, New York 11579, USA.
27. *Sir Gawain and the Green Knight*, l. 917.
28. See Eustache Deschamps, *Art de Dictier Ballade*, edited with translation and commentary by T.A. Jenkins in *MLN*, XXXIII, 1918, pp. 268–78; also translation in J.A. Burrow, *Geoffrey Chaucer*, pp. 26–8. See also Gower, *Confessio Amantis*, VIII, 2942.
29. See J. Lempriere, *Classical Dictionary of Proper Names*, new ed. by F.A. Wright, p. 274. Lemprière is a good source for all the stories cited by Chaucer here.
30. Neuse, 'Knight: First Mover', p. 308.
31. Boccaccio, *Teseida*, trans. McCoy, III, 13.
32. *Ibid*, III, 15, 17.
33. Jean de Meung identified 'Wikked-Tunge' with 'soudiours of Normandye' (*Romaunt of the Rose*, 4234). For full argument see my commentary to l. 70 of the *General Prologue*, pp. 110 ff.
34. Boccaccio, *Teseida*, trans. McCoy, VII, 7–8.
35. In *Sir Degaré* the emphasis is on the romantic success of the young hero in the tournament – the hatred of his enemy, the violence of the jousting are designed merely to set off his strength, courage and beauty. See *Sir Degare*, 481–582. In *Sir Launfal* the emphasis is again on the beauty of the hero and his loneliness 'with litel companie' in a foreign land (*Sir Launfal*, 553–606). Froissart always stresses the courage of the contestants and their courtesy to one another – he plays down the violence of the tournament and often the worst that happens is that some of the contestants get 'knocked off their horses' – see Froissart, *Cronycle*, trans. Berners, V, pp. 419–424. See also Froissart's account of a 'goodly feat of arms' in 1381 – Froissart, trans. Berners, III, pp. 182–3. Also in translation in Edith Rickert, *Chaucer's World*, pp. 214–15.
36. Boccaccio, *Teseida*, trans. McCoy, XII, 25.
37. My translation of 'The Boke of Curtesye', (Sloane MS, 1986), printed in *The Babees Book*, ed. F.J. Furnivall, pp. 306–7, ll. 259–63:

> Speke neuer vnhonestly of woman kynde
> Ne let hit neuer renne in thy mynde:
> The boke hym calles a chorle of chere,
> That vylany spekes be wemen sere;
> For alle we ben of wymmen born.

38. For a good summary of courtesy and *druerie* see: Gervase Mathew, *The Court of Richard II*, pp. 123–4, which contains all the points he made in 'Ideals of Knighthood', pp. 354–62.
39. See Mathew, 'The Court of Richard II', p. 124.
40. My translation of Hoccleve's 'Letter of Cupid', ll. 134–54 in *Hoccleve's Works, The Minor Poems*, ed. F.J. Furnivall and I. Gollancz, p. 78:

> To sclaunder women thus, what may profyte?
> too gentils namely that hem armen sholde,
> and in defence of women hem delyte,
> as that the ordre of gentilesse wolde ...

> Al-be hyt that man fynde o woman nyce,
> in-constant, recheles or varriable,
> Deynouse, or proude fulfilled of malice,
> Wythouten feyth or love and deceyvable,
> sly, queynt, and fals in al vnthrift coupable,
> Wikked, and feers and ful of cruelte,
> yt foloweth nat that swich, al wommen be.

41. Boccaccio, *Teseida*, trans. McCoy, x, 60.
42. For a further discussion of this see my commentary to line 46 of the *General Prologue*, pp. 33–4.
43. Mathew, 'The Court of Richard II', pp. 122–3.
44. See Boethius, '*De Consolatione*', III, pr. 3, p. 241.
45. Chaucer was, of course, translating the French *Le Livre de Mellibee et Prudence*: '*Et le couvoiteux ne puet riens juger fors que en la fin sa couvoitise soit acomplie, qui acomplir ne se puet, car tant com plus a li couvoiteux, plus desirre.*' The original is published *in toto* in *Sources and Analogues of Chaucer's Canterbury Tales*, ed. W.F. Bryan and Germaine Dempster, pp. 560–614.
46. With reference to this association of gold with death, however, one must not forget that gold was supposed to have special medical properties – see *General Prologue*, 443.
47. Clifford's Will is given in Sir W. Dugdale, *The Baronage of England*, I, pp. 341–2. In full it reads:

> *In Nomine Patris & Filii & Spiritus Sancti, Amen.* The sevententhe day of September, the yere of our Lord Jesu Christ, a thousand foure hundred and foure, I Lowys Clyfforth fals and Traytor to my Lord God, and to all the blessed company of heuene, and unworthi to be clepyd a Cristen man, make and ardeyne my Testament, and my last Will, in this manere. At the begynning I most unworthi and Goddis Traytor, recommaunde my wrechid and synfule Soule hooly to the Grace and to the grete mercy of the blessed Trynytie, and my wrechid Careyne to be beryed in the ferthest corner of the Chirchyard, in which Pariche my wrechid Soule departeth fro my Body. And I prey and charge my Survivors and myne Executors, as they wollen answere tofore God, and as all myne hoole trust in this matere is in hem; that on my stinking Careyne be neyther leyd Clothe of Gold, ne of Silk, but a black Clothe, and a Taper at myne hed, and another at my fete, ne Stone, ne other thinge, whereby any man may witt where my stinkyng Careyne liggeth. And to that Chirch do myne Executors all thingis, which owen duly in such caas to be don, without eny more cost saaf to pore men. And also I prey my Survivors and myne Executors, that eny dette that eny man kan axe me, by true title, that hit be payd. And yf eny man kan trewly sey, that I have do hym eny harme, in body or in good, that ye make largely his gree, whyles the goodys wole strecche. And I wole also that non of myne Executors meddle, or mynystre eny thingw of my goodys withouten avyse and consent of my Survivors, or sum of hem.
>
> Now first I bequethe to Sire Phylype la Vache, Knight, my Masse-booke, and my Porhoos; and my Book of Tribulacion to my Daughter hys Wyf....

The rest follows in Latin. It is dated 5 December 1404.

48. Latimer's Will is given in *The Ancestor*, 10 July 1904, 19–20: 'That ther be non maner of cost don aboute my biryngge neyther in mete nether in dryngg non in no other thynge by yt be to any swych on that nedyth it after the lawe of God save twey tapers of wex and anon as i be ded thud me in the erthe.' Sir John Cheyne's Will is in K. B. McFarlane, *Lancastrian Kings*, p. 211.

49. See McFarlane, *Lancastrian Kings*, p. 211. See also *Chaucer Life-Records*, pp. 343–7.
50. Died 1422. See *Fifty Earliest English Wills* ed. F.J. Furnivall, p. 49.
51. See McFarlane, *Lancastrian Kings*, pp. 210–13.
52. See *Medieval Studies*, XXVIII, 1966, p. 187.
53. *The Knight's Tale*, 2919–66.
54. Stephen Knight, *Rymyng Craftily*, p. 143.
55. William Frost, 'An Interpretation of Chaucer's Knight's Tale', *RES*, XXV, 1949, p. 304.
56. See also Boccaccio's own explanation for his choice of trees in his glossary, trans. McCoy, pp. 307–8.
57. Frost, 'An Interpretation', p. 304.
58. The importance of Largess may be assessed from the fact that in the pseudo-Aristotelian *Secretum Secretorum*, one of the most influential books of its day on the governances of kings and princes, Largess is the first subject to be dealt with at length. See *Secretum Secretorum*, ed. M.A. Manzalaoui, I, pp. 232–3.
59. See Tatlock, *Concordance*, pp. 99, 504.
60. Boccaccio, *Teseida*, trans. McCoy, II, 84.
61. See Hay, 'Division of Spoils', pp. 100–1.
62. For Largess as a political necessity see *Romaunt of the Rose*, 1149–86.
63. For useful definitions of all the medieval figures of style, see Knight, pp. 236–42. This quotation is from p. 240; see also pp. 136–7.
64. *Ibid*, p. 136.
65. *The Knight's Tale*, 985; 1000; 2052; 2965–6.
66. My modernization of Gower, '*Confessio Amantis*', Prologue, 81–6:

> Bot for my wittes ben to smale
> To tellen every man his tale,
> This bok, upon amendment
> To stonde at his commandement,
> With whom myn herte is of accord,
> I sende unto myn oghne lord.

67. My modernization of *Mum and the Sothsegger*, Prologue 57–60:

> And if ye ffynde ffables . or ffoly ther-amonge,
> Or ony ffantasie yffeyned . that no ffrute is in,
> Lete youre conceill corette it and clerkis to-gedyr,
> And amende that ys amysse . and make it more better.

68. See *Knight's Tale*, 889–91, also *MED* under *felau* meanings 5 and 7:

5. (a) Used in friendly address to a social inferior.
   (b) Used in condescending or contemptuous address to an inferior or to one so treated.
   (c) A person of low social position; servant, slave; also a contemptible person ...
7. An associate in crime, accomplice, accessory ...

69. Charles Muscatine, '*The Canterbury Tales* – style of the man and style of the work' in *Chaucer and Chaucerians: critical studies in Middle English Literature*, ed. Derek S. Brewer, p. 92.
70. Frost, 'An Interpretation', p. 304; Salter, *The Knight's Tale*, p. 23.
71. Neville Coghill, *Chaucer's Idea of what is Noble*, English Association, Presidential Address, 1971, p. 15.

72. Robinson, *Chaucer and Tradition*, p. 118.
73. See Geoffrey Trease, *The Condottieri*, p. 73.
74. See, for example, the opening lines of the *General Prologue*, 1–12; also the Prologue to *The Legend of Good Women*, 115–66 (F).
75. *General Prologue*, 450; 370; 743–6.
76. Gervase Mathew, *The Court of Richard II*, p. 125.
77. My modernization of Caxton, *The Book of the Ordre of Chyualry*, ed. A.T. Byles, pp. 30–1: 'Knyghtes shold be lerned/so that by scyence they were suffysaunt to be juges/none office shoulde be so couenable to be a juge as chyualry.'
78. See Mathew, *Court of Richard II*, p. 125, n. 73, where he quotes the *Livre des faicts de Jean Bouciquaut*, IV, cap. 7.
79. See *The Wife of Bath's Tale*, 1126; 1165; 1166; 1168. *The Miller's Tale*, 3227; 3208; 3483; 3582.
80. See Introduction to *The Man of Law's Tale*, 25.
81. In fact Chaucer seems to have thought that Statius came from Toulouse, perhaps following Dante; see *The House of Fame*, III, 1460; see also Magoun, *Gazetteer*, p. 154.
82. See *The Nun's Priest's Tale*, 2970–3156.
83. See Commentary on the *General Prologue*, l. 75, pp. 125 ff.
84. See Commentary on *General Prologue*, l. 51, pp. 42 ff.
85. Boccaccio, *Teseida*, trans. McCoy, II, 84.
86. Walsingham, *Historia Anglicana*, I, 328, translated in John Barnie, *War in Medieval Society*, p. 141.
87. See *Sir Gawain and the Green Knight*, 1273: 'bewte and debonerte and blith semblaunt'. On the importance of physical beauty to chivalry see Mathew, *Court of Richard II*, pp. 124–5.
88. Patch, *On Rereading Chaucer*, p. 203.
89. J. Melterman, 'The Dehumanizing Metamorphoses of the Knight's Tale', *ELH*, XXXVIII, 1971, pp. 493–511.
90. Cripps-Day, *History of Tournament*, appendix 1, p. vi.
91. Boccaccio, *Teseida*, trans. McCoy, VII, 7–8.
92. Referred to by Cripps-Day, *ibid*, and Henry Knighton, *Chronicon*, ed. Lumby, I, pp. 265–6. See also Matthew Paris's account of the death of Gilbert Marshal at a tournament in Hertford in 1241 in *Chronica Majora*, IV, p. 135.
93. See Léon Gautier, *Chivalry*, p. 60; also Barnie, *War in Medieval Society*, p. 66.
94. Froissart, *Cronycle*, trans. Berners, III, pp. 182–3. See also *Sir Degare*, 501–81, and *Sir Launfal*, 553–606.
95. Malcolm Andrew's observation is contained in a lecture delivered to the University of East Anglia, the notes of which he kindly allowed me to read.
96. John Tiptofte's *Ordinances of Tournament*, 1464, reprinted in Cripps-Day, *History of Tournament*, appendix 4, p. xxviii.
97. Robertson, 'Elements of Realism', p. 240.
98. See for example, Froissart, *Cronycle*, trans. Berners, III, pp. 183–4.
99. *King Alexander*, 3906.
100. My modernization of *King Alexander*, 3974–83:

> 'Thow,' he saide, 'traytour,
> Yursturday thow come in aunture,
> Yarmed so on of myne;
> Me byhynde at my chyne

Smotest me with thy spere;
No hadde myn hawberk beo the strengore,
Thou hadest me vyly yslawe.
Thou schalt beo honged and todrawe,
And beo tobrent al to nought,
For thou soche traytory wroughtest.

101. *Havelock the Dane*, 1837–40.
102. J.F.C. Fuller, *Decisive Battles of the Western World*, I, p. 300.
103. Venette, *Chronicle*, p. 92. For other references see Barnie, *War in Medieval Society*, pp. 167, 72.
104. See Dillon 'Ordinances of Chivalry', p. 65; also Thomas, Earl of Gloucester, 'Ordenaunce and Fourme of Fightyng Within the Listes' in *The Black Book of the Admiralty*, pp. 300–29.
105. See *Havelock the Dane*, 1736–55.
106. Boccaccio, *Teseida*, trans. McCoy, XII, 83.
107. Robertson, 'Elements of Realism', p. 237.
108. 'Codice Militare per le Masnade stipendiarie di Pisa' in E. Ricotti, *Storia delle Compagnie di Ventura in Italia*, II, p. 297.
109. 'Codice degli Stipendiarii della Repubblica di Firenze', *ibid*, II, p. 327.
110. *The Knight's Tale*, 2895, 2122, 2160, 2630, 2626.
111. Gower, *Mirour de l'Omme*, 24061–72; for the French text see 'Where had the Knight not fought?' Note 17 above, p. 263.
112. Boccaccio, *Teseida*, trans. McCoy, V, 83.
113. Venette, *Chronicle*, pp. 75–6, 105–7, 110–13 etc. For an account of Cesena see Temple-Leader and Marcotti, *Sir J. Hawkwood*, pp. 118–23.
114. Robinson, *Chaucer and Tradition*, p. 111.
115. Trease, *The Condottieri*, pp. 120–1.
116. For Chaucer's visit to Italy in 1378 see Crow and Olson, *Chaucer Life-Records*, pp. 53–61; also H. Braddy, 'New documentary evidence concerning Chaucer's mission to Lombardy' in *MLN*, XLVIII, 1933, pp. 507–11; J.M. Manly, 'Chaucer's mission to Lombardy' in *MLN*, XLIX, 1934, pp. 209–16, and R.A. Pratt, 'Chaucer and the Visconti Libraries' in *ELH*, VI, 1939, pp. 189–99.
117. H.J. Webb, 'A Re-interpretation of Chaucer's Theseus' in *RES*, III, 1947, pp. 289–96.
118. See Neuse, 'Knight: First Mover', p. 307, and Robinson, *Chaucer and Tradition*, p. 121.
119. McKisack, *Fourteenth Century*, p. 267.
120. Margaret Schlauch, 'Chaucer's doctrine of Kings and Tyrants', *Speculum*, XX, 1945, p. 134.
121. *Ibid*, p. 134.
122. 'Thomas of Wimbledon's Sermon', ed. N.H. Owen, *Medieval Studies*, XXVIII, 1966, p. 183.
123. For a full analysis of tyranny as it appears in Chaucer's works see Schlauch, 'Chaucer's Doctrine of Kings', pp. 150–5.
124. Boccaccio, *Teseida*, trans. McCoy, II, 99.
125. 'Twelve requisites of a Good Ruler' in *Liber Albus, Liber Custumarum et Liber Horn*, ed. H.T. Riley, II, ii, p. 520.
126. Neuse, 'Knight; First Mover', p. 251.
127. William of Ockham, 'Octo Quaestiones de Poteste Papae' in *Opera Politica*, ed. J.G. Sikes *et al.*, I, q. viii, cap. 5, pp. 201 ff. quoted by Schlauch, 'Chaucer's doctrine of Kings', p. 143.
128. Dante, *De Monarchia*, I, 12.

129. Boccaccio, *Teseida*, trans. McCoy, VII, 12.
130. Froissart, *Cronycle*, trans. Berners, V, p. 419. The word Berners uses is 'rokette', which means a blunt tournament lance.
131. Léon Gautier, *Chivalry*, p. 276.
132. MS Harl. 69 is quoted in Skeat, *Works*, V, p. 89.
133. Robertson, 'Elements of Realism', p. 237.
134. *Ibid.*
135. Robinson, *Works*, p. 682; E.T. Donaldson, *Chaucer's Poetry*, p. 901; Muscatine, 'Form and Meaning', p. 922; Bernard F. Huppé, *A Reading of the Canterbury Tales*, p. 73. There is also a very interesting exposition of the speech in P.M. Kean, *The Art of Narrative*, pp. 41–8.
136. Salter, *The Knight's Tale*, p. 35.
137. Neuse, 'Knight: First Mover', p. 305.
138. The incongruity of this image of rebellion within the context of the speech has been noted by Kean, *Art of Narrative*, p. 47.
139. Boethius, '*De Consolatione*', IV, pr. 7, p. 379.
140. Ephraim Emerton, *Humanism and Tyranny*, pp. 74–8; 140.
141. Boethius, '*De Consolatione*', IV, pr. 6, p. 359.
142. *Ibid.*
143. *Ibid*, p. 363.
144. Boethius, '*De Consolatione*', III, pr. 10, p. 293.
145. *Ibid*, II, pr. 7, pp. 219–21.
146. *Ibid*, p. 223.
147. Cicero, 'The Dream of Scipio', p. 351.
148. Boethius, '*De Consolatione*', II, pr. 7, p. 220.
149. *Ibid.*
150. *Ibid*, II, pr. 8, p. 227.
151. 'The Twelve Requisites of a good Ruler' in *Liber Albus* etc, II, ii, pp. 517–18.
152. Boethius, '*De Consolatione*', IV, pr. 6, p. 357.
153. *Ibid*, pp. 363–5.
154. Translation in Trease, *The Condottieri*, p. 73.
155. F. Villani, *Cronica*, XI, p. 81; P. Azario, *Gestorum in Lombardia*, p. 128.
156. McKisack, *Fourteenth Century*, p. 241.
157. The 'Ordinance for the Preservation of the Peace' of 1242 stated: 'Furthermore, all who, outside the forest, can have bows and arrows are to have them; but those in the forest are to have bows and bolts [*pilettos*]', translation in Stephenson and Marcham, *Sources*, pp. 139–40. For the use of peacock arrows with long bows see Skeat, *Works*, V, p. 11, where he quotes Ascham's *Toxophilus*.
158. Azario, '*Liber Gestorum in Lombardia*', p. 128: '*pedestres tam magnos et acutos arcus, quod ipsos fingunt a testa inferiori in terra et, trahendo, magnas et longas sagitas emitunt.*'
159. S. Battaglia, *Grande Dizionario della Lingua Italiana*, who quotes Machiavelli using '*forestiere*' in this way. As regards the St Christopher round the Yeoman's neck, most modern critics seem to follow F.N. Robinson's assertion that St Christopher was the patron saint of foresters (Robinson, *Works*, p. 653). But Robinson offers no evidence for his assertion, and I have been unable to find any connection between St Christopher and foresters. The patron saint of woodmen and woodcutters was St Gummarus or Gomer (see Helen Roeder, *Saints and their Attributes*, p. 45), while the patron saint of hunters was St Hubert (see *Catholic Encyclopedia*, ed. C.G. Herbermann, XI, p. 566, and Charles Muscatine, 'The Naming of Chaucer's Friar', *MLN*, LXX, 1955, pp. 169–72; also *Webster's Bio-*

graphical Dictionary, p. 739). St Christopher, of course, was the patron saint of travellers. According to the *Catholic Encyclopedia*, ed. C.G. Herbermann, XI, p. 566, he was also the patron saint of bookbinders, gardeners and sailors – but there is absolutely nothing in his legend or in his associations to connect him with foresters. Interestingly enough, he was also reputed, in Chaucer's day, to have been a Saracen. See *The South English Legendary*, ed. C. D'Evelyn & A.J. Mill, I, p. 340.

160. For a discussion of *armee* see my Commentary to l. 60, pp. 73 ff.

161. The playing of some instruments, such as guitars and harps, appears to have been regarded as a courtly accomplishment, but other instruments, such as the rebec and the fiddle, were definitely the province of professional minstrels (see *The Book of the Knight of La Tour-Landry*, ed. T. Wright, p. 159). In the *Romance of the Rose* 'flowtours' are equated with other professional entertainers:

> There myghtist thou see these flowtours,
> Mynstrales, and eke jogelours,
> That wel to synge dide her peyne.
> *Romance of the Rose*, 763–5

In fact 'Fluter' was a not uncommon surname amongst the (presumably) artisan class – e.g. Richer le Fleuiter, John le Floyter, Will the Floutere, Rob. Flouter, Rog. Floyter (see *M.E.D.* under 'flouter').

The only reference I can find to *playing* the flute as a courtly skill comes in Guillame de Lorris' section of the *Roman de la Rose* (2207–10), when the God of Love tells the dreamer: 'it is a great advantage for a young man to know how to play the viol, to flute and to dance. By these means he can further himself greatly.' This, however, would have been written sometime before 1228, and when Chaucer's contemporary came to translate it, some 170 years later, it is noticeable that he omitted the reference to fluting. Could it be that the social role of fluting had changed? Eustache Deschamps, however, also refers to fluting as a way of advancement for a young man – although whether ironically or not I don't know (see 'Du metier profitable' in *Oeuvres complètes*, vol. 6, p. 128).

162. Edmund Bowles writes: 'Transverse, or side-blown flutes, on the other hand, were most favoured in Germany (hence, *flauste d'Allemand*), and became widely used in a military connection. From the Crusades on the fife and drum were the principal instruments of the infantry.'

Edmund A. Bowles, 'Haut and Bas: The Grouping of Musical Instruments in the Middle Ages', *Musica Disciplina*, VIII, 1954, p. 127.

163. '*Codice degli Stipendiarii della Repubblica di Firenze*' in E. Ricotti, *Storia delle Compagnie di Ventura in Italia*, II, p. 318:

> *XVII. Item pro omnibus et singulis conestabilibus et aliis quibuscumque stipendiariis conductis a kalendis mensis decembris proxime venturi in antea ad stipendia seu ad provisiones comunis Florentiae, quod retinere debeant pifferum naccherinum vel cornamusam vel trombectam et eum non teneatur,* [sic] *retineatur et retineri debeat de suis stipendiis et provisionibus quolibet mense et ad rationem mensis floren. quinque auri.*

164. Bartolus of Sassoferrato, '*Tractatus de Tyrannia*', VIII, 27, translated in E. Emerton, *Humanism and Tyranny*, p. 140.

165. See Schlauch, 'Chaucer's Doctrine of Kings', p. 140; Emerton, *Humanism and Tyranny*, p. 143.
166. Abun—Nasr, *History of the Maghrib*, pp. 128–32, 156–7.
167. *CMH*, VIII, pp. 655–6.
168. See also M.H. Keen, 'Chivalry, nobility and the man-at-arms' in *War Literature and Politics in the Late Middle Ages*, ed. C.T. Allmand, p. 43, where he quotes Philippe de Mézières" introduction to the statutes of his crusading Order of the Passion: 'The second and third born sons, and others, who by the custom of the land have little or no portion in the inheritance of their fathers, and who by poverty are often constrained to follow wars that are unjust and tyrannical so as to sustain their estate of nobleness, since they know no other calling but arms; and therein they commit so much ill that it would be frightening to tell of all the pillaging and crimes with which they oppress the poor people' (Bodleian Library, Oxford, MS Ashmole 865 fol. 423).
169. Temple-Leader and Marcotti, *Sir J. Hawkwood*, p. 35.
170. Trease, *The Condottieri*, p. 76.
171. Chaucer, *Monk's Tale*, 2400.
172. *CMH*, VII, p. 299.
173. Trease, *The Condottieri*, p. 92.
174. *Ibid*, p. 73.
175. Marsilius of Padua, *Defensor Pacis*, ed. Previté-Orton, I, 12, par. 3, p. 49, quoted in Schlauch, 'Chaucer's Doctrine of Kings', p. 142.
176. Robinson, *Chaucer and Tradition*, p. 135.

Why does the Knight interrupt the Monk?

1. *Prologue to The Nun's Priest's Tale*, 2767.
2. See Emile Legouis, *Geoffrey Chaucer*, trans. Lailavoix, p. 186; R.D. French, *A Chaucer Handbook*, p. 248; Trevor Whittock, *A Reading of The Canterbury Tales*, p. 221; R.M. Lumiansky, *Of Sondry Folk*, p. 103, and Joyce E. Peterson, *ChauR*, V, 1970, p. 65.
3. Caxton, *Proem* to second edition of *The Canterbury Tales*, 1484, reprinted in J.A. Burrow, *Geoffrey Chaucer*, p. 45.
4. R.B. Dobson, *The Peasant's Revolt of 1381*, p. viii.
5. John Mirk, *Festial*, I, p. 194.
6. John Gower, *Vox Clamantis*, I, ch. 2, trans. Stockton, pp. 50, 54.
7. Margaret Schlauch, 'Chaucer's doctrine of Kings', pp. 142, 147.
8. *Ibid*, p. 149.
9. Braddy, 'The Two Petros', pp. 69–80.
10. See Froissart's account of Pedro's death in *Chronicles*, trans. Johnes, I, pp. 388–9.
11. For the relation of the Monk's account to Machaut's see Braddy, 'The Two Petros', pp. 69–80. See also above, p. 72.
12. For a discussion of Dante's treatment of Ugolino's death, in which Ugolino is seen as tyrant as much as victim, see C. Salvadori Lonergan in *Dante Commentaries*, ed. David Nolan, pp. 74–84.
13. The uncomfortable relevance of the Monk's remarks to the Knight's own career has already been remarked by several critics. See William C. Strange, 'The Monk's Tale: a generous View', *ChauR*, I, 1967, pp. 167–80; also Trevor Whittock, *A Reading of The Canterbury Tales*, p. 221.
14. Manly-Rickert, *The Text of The Canterbury Tales*, II, pp. 406–9.
15. Since writing this I have received Douglas L. Lepley's interesting article 'The Monk's Boethian Tale' which convincingly substantiates this view of the philosophical nature of the Tale. See *ChauR*, XII, 3, 1978, pp. 162–70.

Notes to Appendix

1. See Lewis and Short, *A Latin Dictionary*, p. 257.
2. The frequency for each meaning up to 1400 listed by the *Middle English Dictionary*, ed. H. Kurath and S.M. Kuhn, fasc. C 2, pp. 233–5 is as follows:

A body of armed mounted warriors or knights serving an overlord	15 times
Warfare; a feat of arms	12 ,,
The nobility as a social class	2 ,,
Knighthood as a ceremonially conferred rank	2 ,,
The ethical code of chivalry, comprising allegiance, valour, generosity, courtly manner	2 ,,

3. My translation of *Rotuli Parliamentorum*, III, p. 516:

Y dist, en compleignant que tant come le noble Chivalrie del Roialme estoit bien nurriz, encherriz, honores, & noblement guerdonez, pur lours grantz bienfaitz, si estoit celle Chivalrie molt urgerouse, & ardantment desirouse a faire grantz emprises & grantz faitz d'armes, chescun devant autre, puis ont le Roialme fust grantement enrichez & pleintinouse de toute bien, & les habitanz en ycelle doutez de lours enemys, dont toutes nations a poy en parlerent d'onour & de nobleye; & que pluis est, lour fame de nobleye estoit espandue parmy le monde. Mais ore, depuis que celle Chivalrie ad este rebuquiz & tenuz en viletee, & que pluis est, lours biens noblement gaignez de lours Enemys de Guerre lour tolluz sanz jouste cause, & auxint celle Chivalrie & toute autre vertu mys a derire, & vice preisee, avancee, & honouree, & nullement puniz ou chasticee, si est mesme la Chivalrie & les coers des bones & vertuouses persones grantement abeissez, puis ont nul homme ad talent al jour de huy, a ce que semble par experience de fait, de bien faire: de qoy le Roialme ad ore novellement suffert grantz damages & outrage de lours ditz Enemys des plujours partz, & est a douter que pluis soeffrera, si Dieu n'y remede au gouvernaille d'ycell.

4. See, for example, E.T. Donaldson, *Chaucer's Poetry*, p. 881: 'The medieval chivalric ideal combined, perhaps more explicitly than any other to which men might aspire, the spiritual with the secular aspects of human life.'
5. John Trevisa's translation of the *Disputatio inter Clericum et Militem* was probably written between 1296 and 1302. It includes the following passage: 'Clericus: This kyng toke nought the godes & catel to his owne use, but he spende it al in holy chirche use. Ye [i.e. you knights] takith oure catel and spendith hit in chivalrie and nought in use of holy chirche' (Trevisa, *Dialogus inter Militem et Clericum*, ed. A.J. Perry, p. 23). See also: T.J. Renna, 'Kingship in the *Disputatio inter Clericum et Militem*', *Speculum*, XLVIII, 1973, p. 675.
6. *Political Poems and 'Song against the Friars'* in *Songs relating to English History*, ed. T. Wright, I, p. 263:

> Preste, ne monke, ne yit chanoun,
> Ne no man of religioun,
> Gyfen hem so to devocioun,
> As done thes holy frers.
> For summe gyven ham to chyvalry,
> Somme to riote and ribaudery;
> Bot ffrers gyven ham to grete study,
> And to grete prayers,
> Who so kepes thair reule al,
> Bothe in worde and dede;

> I am ful siker that he shal
> Have heven blis to mede.

7. Philippe de Mézières, *Letter to King Richard II*, trans. G.W. Coopland, pp. 61–2.
8. Gervase Mathew, 'Ideals of Knighthood in late fourteenth-century England', in R.W. Hunt *et al.*, *Studies in Medieval History presented to F.M. Powicke*, pp. 358–9.
9. 'Indentures of Retinue of John of Gaunt', *Camden Miscellany*, IV, ser. 1, 1964, 22, pp. 77–112.
10. Bosworth-Toller, *An Anglo-Saxon Dictionary*, p. 1014.
11. The following table has been compiled from my own analysis of Chaucer's use of the words throughout his works. I do not pretend that such a table is definitive, since the meaning of words in any particular context is clearly open to interpretation, but I have followed through every citation of the words given in J.S.P. Tatlock and A.G. Kennedy's *Concordance to the complete Works of Geoffrey Chaucer* and tried to evaluate them in their full context.

Chaucer's use of the word 'Trouthe'

A pledge	57	times
As an oath	50	,,
Honesty	31	,,
Constancy in love	25	,,
A truth	15	,,
Religious truth	12	,,
Correctness	7	,,
Loyalty (other than romantic)	3	,,
Total (approximate)	200	

Chaucer's use of the word 'Feythe'

As an oath	36	times
Religious belief	16	,,
Trust	15	,,
A pledge	8	,,
Loyalty	8	,,
Constancy in love	6	,,
Total (approximate)	89	

Possibly the distinction I have made between 'constancy in love' and 'loyalty other than romantic' may be objected to as arbitrary, since the constancy of lovers could be called 'loyalty'. The three undoubted instances where 'trouthe' means 'loyalty other than romantic' all occur in the *Romaunt of the Rose*, ll. 266, 5216, 5562. Hence, even of these, only one need be considered as by Chaucer himself. There are also occasions in the *Romaunt of the Rose* when Jean de Meung's expression '*loialment*' is translated as 'in trouthe' or 'ful of trouthe' (*RR*, 6722, 2060). Once again these are in the section of the poem not normally considered to be by Chaucer. In any case, in the first instance '*loialment*' does not mean 'loyally' but 'legally', and in the second case the sense is 'honesty'.

12. A.J. Greimas, *Dictionnaire de l'Ancien Français*, p. 281.
13. G. Trease, *The Condottieri*, p. 73.
14. The frequency of meanings for the word 'honour' given in the *Middle English Dictionary* is as follows:

The action of honouring someone	78 times
Fame, repute, worldly glory	40 ,,
A gift, reward, mark of distinction	25 ,,
A state inspiring respect, dignified manner	22 ,,
Domain of a feudal lord	19 ,,
Position, rank	17 ,,
Nobleness of character	14 ,,

15. For the influence of Boethius on Chaucer see Bernard L. Jefferson, *Chaucer and the Consolation of Philosophy of Boethius*. As for the other work alluded to, Cicero's *Somnium Scipionis*, Chaucer alludes to it in *The Nun's Priest's Tale*, 3124; *The Book of the Duchess*, 284; *The House of Fame*, 514.

16. Boethius, '*De Consolatione Philosophiae*' in *Tractates, De Consolatione etc*, trans. Stewart, Rand and Tester, II, 7.

17. Cicero, 'The Dream of Scipio' in *Cicero: On the Good Life*, trans. M. Grant, p. 351.

18. Sir John Clanvowe, *The Two Ways*, 450–75. Printed in *EPS*, X, 1967, pp. 47–8.

19. My modernization of:

> For wel ye woot that men clepen honour the reverence that man doth to man; but in helle is noon honour ne reverence. For certes, namoore reverence shal be doon there to a kyng than to a knave.... Honour is eek cleped greet lordshipe; ther shal no wight serven other, but of harm and torment. Honour is eek cleped greet dignytee and heighnesse, but in helle shul they been al fortroden of develes.
> *The Parson's Tale*, 187–9.

20. Here is my analysis of Chaucer's use of the word 'fredom' based on Tatlock's *Concordance*:

Liberty of action	15 times
Franchise (liberty of manner)	7 ,,
A lady's 'generosity' to her lover	3 ,,
Ambivalent uses	6 ,,

21. Mathew, 'Ideals of Knighthood', p. 360. Mathew goes on: 'For an epic hero largesse is essentially an act of justice; he shares his spoils freely with his war band, as his recognition of their due. It has been suggested that for the hero of a *roman courtois* largesse is a social accomplishment used to ensure esteem. For the fourteenth-century knight it is a sign that he sits lightly to all possessions. Its antithesis is "covetesse".' 'Covetesse' or greed was held to cloud a man's judgement: '... "covetousness is the root of all harms." And trust well that a covetous man cannot judge nor think, except to fulfil the end of his own covetousness; and certainly that can never be accomplished – for ever the more riches he has, the more he desires' (*The Tale of Melibeus*, 1130). The leaders of chivalry of the day – men such as Edward III and Henry of Grosmont – were praised for their largess. Walsingham says of Edward III: 'He was without doubt beyond all men living always lavish and prompt in conferring favours.... He was liberal with gifts and good cheer; prodigal in expenses' (Walsingham, *Historia Anglicana*, I, p. 328). Andrew of Wyntoun praises Henry of Grosmont:

.... ay worthi, wycht and wysse,
And mast ranownyt of bownte,
Of gentrice and of honeste,
That in til Inglande liffande was.

Andrew of Wyntoun, *The Original Chronicle*,
ed. F.J. Amours, 688, l. 5134.

22. 'Now been ther general signes of gentilesse: as eschewing vyce ... usinge
vertu ... and to be liberal, that is to seyn, large by mesure ...' (*The Parson's Tale*, 464–5).

23. Jean de Meung outlined the theory of largess as a political necessity in his *Roman de la Rose*:

Gret loos hath Largesse and gret pris;
For bothe wys folk and unwys
Were hooly to hir baundon brought,
So wel with yiftes hath she wrought
And if she hadde an enemy
I trowe that she coude craftely
Make hym full soone hir freend to be,
So large of yift and free was she.
Therfore she stod in love and grace
Of riche and pover in every place.
A full gret fool is he, ywys,
That bothe riche and nygard is.
A lord may have no maner vice
That greveth more than avarice.
For nygart never with strengthe of hond
May wynne him gret lordship or lond;
For freendis all to fewe hath he
To doon his will perfourmed be.
And whoso wole have freendis heere,
He may not holde his tresour deere.

Romaunt of the Rose, 1161–80

24. Bowden, *Commentary*, pp. 48–9, presents the following rather circular argument: 'The objection may be raised, however, that Chaucer sometimes uses the word *fredom* in other senses. But here Chaucer is describing a knight, and one of the virtues which are emphasized as necessary in nearly every medieval book of instruction for knights is material generosity.... Surely Chaucer would not have omitted such an important chivalric virtue from the description of the Knight, and we must therefore be correct in saying that Chaucer's "fredom" is one with Watriquet's "largesce".'

25. See Chaucer, *Anelida and Arcite*, 106, *The Legend of Good Women*, 1126–7, *The Man of Law's Tale*, 162–8.

26. Boethius, '*De Consolatione*' II, pr. 6, l. 10. See also *Romaunt of the Rose and Le Roman de la Rose*, ed. Sutherland.

And leseth fredom and fraunchyse,   Qui ne set garder la franchise
That Nature in him had sette.   Que Nature auoit en li mise.
   ll. 4906–7
Fredom of kynde so loste hath he   La franchise qu'il a perdue
That never may recured be.   Qui ne li peut estre rendue.
   ll. 4919–20.

27. See Tatlock, *Concordance*, p. 99. Otherwise he would use the older English word 'bounty'; cf *MED* and *Concordance*.

28. Mathew, 'Ideals of Knighthood', p. 360.

29. There is a good summary of this easy but superior familiarity by the late-nineteenth-century historian J.J. Jusserand, *English Wayfaring Life in the Middle Ages*, p. 204. It is quoted above in 'Is the Knight's shabbiness a sign of piety', note 9, p. 276.

30. For example, the Knight displays 'fredom' or 'franchise' in his character when he takes it upon himself to cut the Monk off in the middle of his *Tale*, in the authority with which he gets the Host and the Pardoner to kiss and make up their quarrel, and the ease with which he accepts the honour of telling the first tale. See *Prol. Nun's Priest's Tale*, 2767 (B3957); *The Pardoner's Tale*, 960–8; *Prologue*, 845–55. He does not, on the other hand, display any concept of largess when he comes to tell his tale. In the first place he sets himself up in competition with the others with the avowed intent of winning the free supper, instead of assuming that the winning of something meant nothing, as true largess would demand he do. When he tells his *Tale*, even when he touches on the subject of gift-giving – the very stuff of largess – he does not associate it with largess. For him it is merely a symbol of worldly wealth, or else, on occasion, merely a political device to settle fractious knights. Thus the only two times he mentions gift-giving are once to demonstrate Theseus's power and wealth and his ability to 'do things properly' (*KT*, 2190–2208) and once in order to quieten the disputes that have arisen after Theseus's extraordinary decision to give the prize to Arcite – despite the most flagrant breaches of all the rules of tournament, 'To stinten alle rancour and envye' (*KT*, 2731–40).

31. *Sir Gawain and the Green Knight*, 652–3.

32. R.E. Latham, *Revised Medieval Latin Word-List from British and Irish Sources*, p. 127. Greimas, *Dictionnaire*, p. 144.

33. See *Middle English Dictionary*.

34. See Gervase Mathew, *The Court of Richard II*, p. 123.

35. *Canon's Yeoman's Prol.*, 587. The 'eke' implies that the epithet also applies to the Canon himself, who has just spoken with a display of courtesy: *Shipman's Tale*, 69; *General Prologue*, 250.

36. Indeed, when the Prioress goes on to tell her *Tale*, it is one singularly lacking in 'pity'. It is a piece of popular racist anti-Semitism, wallowing in sentimentality over a little choirboy killed by the Jews, but never showing one ounce of true humanity. For a contrary view to mine see A.B. Friedman, 'The Prioress's Tale and Chaucer's Anti-Semitism', in *Chaucer*, IX, 1974, pp. 118–27.

37. See *Complaint Unto Pity*, 78–80. John Gower and Ramon Lull both include 'pity' in their lists of knightly qualities. Gower, for example, includes: prouesce, honour, valour, bonte [mercy], largesce, and loyalte (Gower, *Mirour de l'Omme*, 24085–91). Ramon Lull, in Caxton's translation, lists: 'Pryualte and acqueyntaunce of good folke/loyalte and trouthe/hardynesse/largesse/honeste/Humylyte/pyte/and other thynges semblable to these apperteyne to Chyualry' (Caxton, *The Book of the Order of Chyualry*, p. 113).

Bibliography

Chaucer editions

All quotations and line references are to Robinson's second edition.

Donaldson, E.T., *Chaucer's Poetry*, New York, 1958
King, F. and Steele, B., *The Prologue and three Tales*, London, 1969
Manly, John M. and Rickert, Edith (eds), *The text of the Canterbury Tales studied on the basis of all known manuscripts*, 8 vols, Chicago and London, 1940
Robinson, F.N. (ed.), *The complete works of Geoffrey Chaucer*, 2nd ed. London, 1957
Skeat, Walter W. *The complete works of Geoffrey Chaucer*, 7 vols, Oxford, 1894–7; repr. 1972

Primary sources (including modern collections)

An Alphabet of Tales, ed. M.M. Banks, *EETS*, 126, 127, London, 1904–5
Amis and Amiloun, ed. M. Leach, *EETS*, 203, London, 1937
Anonimalle Chronicle 1331–81 from a manuscript written at St Mary's Abbey, York, ed. V.H. Galbraith, 1st ed. 1927; Manchester, 1970
Azario, Pietro, 'Liber gestorum in Lombardia (*c 1368*)', L.A. Muratori, *Rerum Italicarum scriptores – storici Italiani*, 16, iv, Bologna, 1939
Babees Book, The, ed. F.J. Furnivall, *EETS*, os 32, London, 1868; repr. Greenwood, New York, 1969
Black Book of the Admiralty, The, ed. Travers Twiss, 1, London, 1871
Boccaccio, Giovanni, *The Filostrato of Giovanni Boccaccio a translation with parallel text*, N.E. Griffin and A.B. Myrick, Philadelphia and London, 1929
—— *The Nymph of Fiesole*, trans. D.J. Donno, New York, 1960
—— *The Book of Theseus (Teseida delle Nozze d'Emilia)*, trans. Bernadette Marie McCoy, New York, 1974
—— '*Teseida delle Nozze d'Emilia*' in *Tutte le Opere*, 2, ed. Vittore Branca, Verona, 1964
Boethius '*De Consolatione Philosophiae*' in *Tractates, De Consolatione etc*, trans. H.F. Stewart, E.K. Rand, and S.J. Tester, Loeb Classical Library, Cambridge, Mass., 1973

Bonet, Hororé, *The Tree of Battles*, trans. G. W. Coopland, Liverpool, 1949
—— *L'apparicion Maistre Jehan de Meun*, ed. Ivor Arnold, Strasbourg, 1926
Book of the Knight of La Tour-Landry, ed. Thomas Wright, *EETS*, 33, London, 1868
Bracton, Henricus, *De legibus et consuetudinibus Angliae*, ed. Travers Twiss, 4, London, 1881
Brinton, Thomas, *The Sermons of Thomas Brinton, Bishop of Rochester (1373–1389)*, ed. Sister Mary Aquinas Devlin, 2 vols, Camden Society, 3rd ser., 85, 86, London, 1954
Brut, The or The Chronicles of England, ed. Friedrich W.D. Brie, 2 vols, *EETS*, os 136, London, 1908
Bryan, W.F. and Dempster, Germaine (eds), *Sources and Analogues of Chaucer's Canterbury Tales*, New York, 1941
Bueil, Jean de, *Le Jouvencel*, ed. C. Favre and L. Lecestre, 2 vols, Paris, 1887–9
Calendar of Papal Registers relating to Great Britain and Ireland: Papal Letters 1342–1404, ed. W.H. Bliss and C. Johnston, London, 1897; ed. J.A. Twemlow, London, 1902
Canestrini, Giuseppe (ed.), *Documenti ... della milizia italiana dal xiii secolo al xvi*, Florence, 1851
Carpini, 'The Voyage of Johannes de Plano Carpini' in *The Travels of Sir John Mandeville*, ed. A.W. Pollard, New York, 1964, pp. 213–60
Catholicon Anglicum, an English-Latin wordbook dated 1483, ed. S.J.H. Herrtage, *EETS*, os 75, London, 1881; Camden Society, NS 30, London, 1882
Chambers, R.W. and Daunt, M. *A book of London English 1384–1425*, Oxford, 1931; repr. Oxford, 1967
Chartier, Alain, *Fifteenth-century English translations of 'Le Traité de l'Espérance' and 'Le Quadrilogue Invectif'*, ed. Margaret S. Blayney, *EETS*, 270, London, 1974
Child, F.J. (ed.), *The English and Scottish popular ballads*, 5 vols, New York, 1965
Chrimes, S.B. and Brown, A.L., *Select documents of English constitutional history 1307–1485*, London, 1961
Christine de Pisan, *The Book of Fayttes of Armes and of Chyvalrye*, trans. Caxton, *EETS*, os 189, London, 1932; repr. 1971
The Chronicle of Novgorod 1016–1471, trans. R. Mitchell and N. Forbes, Camden Society, 3rd ser. 25, London, 1914
Chronique de le traison et mort de Richard II, ed. B. Williams, London, 1846
Chronique des règnes de Jean II et de Charles V, I, 1350–64, ed. R. Delachenal, Paris, 1910
Cicero, 'The Dream of Scipio' in *Cicero: On the Good Life*, trans. M. Grant, Harmondsworth, 1971
Clanvowe, John, *The Two Ways*, ed. V.J. Scattergood, *EPS*, 10, 1967
Coles, Elisha, *An English Dictionary*, London, 1676; repr. Scolar Press, London, 1971
Coulton, G.G., *Life in the Middle Ages*, 4 vols, Cambridge, 1910, repr. as 1 vol. 1954
'Crónica del Rey Alfonso el Onzeno' in *Colección de las crónicas ... de Castilla*, 7, ed. F. Cerdá y Rico, Madrid, 1787

Crow, Martin M. and Olson, Clair C., *Chaucer Life-Records*, Oxford, 1966

Cuvelier, *Chronique de Bertrand du Guesclin*, ed. P.E. Charnière, 11 vols, Paris, 1839

Dante, *The Convivio*, trans. P.H. Wicksteed, London, 1903

—— *The selected works*, trans. Paolo Milano, London, 1972

—— *The Divine Comedy: Italian text with translation and commentary*, John D. Sinclair, 3 vols, Oxford, 1971

Déguileville, Guillaume de, *The Pilgrimage of the Life of Man, Englished by John Lydgate AD 1426*, ed. F.J. Furnivall, Roxburghe Club, London, 1905

Deschamps, Eustache, *Le Lay des douze Estats du Monde*, Reims, 1870

—— *Œuvres complètes*, ed. Le Marquis de Queux de Saint-Hilaire and Gaston Raynaud, 11 vols, Paris, 1878–1903

—— *Poésies morales et historiques*, ed. G.A. Craplet, Paris, 1832

—— 'L'Art de Dictier', ed. and trans. T.A. Jenkins, *MLN*, 33, 1918, pp. 268–78

Dmytryshyn, B., *Medieval Russia, a sourcebook 900–1700*, 2nd ed., Hinsdale, Ill., 1973

Dobson, R.B., *The Peasants' Revolt of 1381*, London, 1970

Domesday Book, 11: Middlesex, text and trans. John Morris, Chichester, 1975

English historical documents, III, 1189–1327, ed. Harry Rothwell, London, 1975. IV, 1327–1485, ed. A.R. Myers, London, 1969

Excerpta historica, ed. S. Bentley, London, 1833

'Expenses and accounts of Sir John Howard' in *Manners and household expenses of England in the 13th and 15th centuries*, ed. T.H. Turner, Roxburghe Club, London, 1841

'Expenses of the Great Wardrobe of Edward III', ed. N.H. Nicholas, *Arch*, 31, 1846, pp. 1–103

Fasciculi Zizaniorum Magistri Johannis Wyclif cum Tritico, ed. W.W. Shirley, Rolls Series, London, 1858

Fifteenth-Century Courtesy Book, ed. R.W. Chambers and W.W. Seton, *EETS*, os 148, London, 1914; repr. 1962

Fifty Earliest English Wills, ed. F.J. Furnivall, *EETS*, os 78, London, 1882; repr. 1964

French, W.H. and Hale, C.B., *Middle English metrical romances*, 2 vols, New York, 1930; repr. 1964 (includes 'Havelock the Dane' and 'Sir Launfal')

Froissart, *The Cronycle of Sir John Froissart*, trans. Sir John Bourchier, Lord Berners, 6 vols, London, 1903

—— *Chronicles of England, France, Spain by Sir John Froissart*, trans. T. Johnes, 2 vols, London, 1852

—— *Chroniques*, ed. S. Luce and G. Raynaud, Paris, 1869

—— *Œuvres*, ed. Kervyn de Lettenhove, 25 vols, Brussels, 1867–77

—— *L'histoire et chronique de Froissart*, ed. Denis Savvage, Lyons, 1560

Geoffroi de Charny, 'Le Livre de Chevalrie', ed. Kervyn de Lettenhove in *Œuvres de Froissart*, I, iii, Brussels, 1873, pp. 462–533

'Geste of Robyn Hode' in *English and Scottish Popular Ballads*, ed. F.J. Child, 3, New York, 1885; new ed. 1965

Gloucester, Thomas, Earl of, 'Ordenaunce and fourme of fightyng within the listes presented to Richard II', Travers Twiss (ed.), *The Black Book of the Admiralty*, I, London, 1871

Gower, John, *Complete works*, ed. G.C. Macaulay, 4 vols, Oxford, 1899–1902 (includes '*Confessio amantis*' and '*Mirour de l'Omme*')

—— *Major Latin works of John Gower*, ed. and trans. E.W. Stockton, Seattle, 1962 (includes '*Vox Clamantis*')

Gray, Sir Thomas, *The Scalacronica of Sir Thomas Gray of Heaton*, ed. J. Stevenson, Edinburgh, 1836

Halmota Prioratus Dunelmensis, Surtees Society, 82 Durham, 1889

Hassal, W.O., *They saw it happen: 55 BC to AD 1485*, 1, Oxford, 1957; repr. 1973

—— *How they lived*, Oxford, 1962

'Havelock the Dane' in French and Hale, *Middle English metrical romances*, New York, 1930

Hemricourt, Jacques de, *Œuvres*, ed. C. de Borman, A. Bayot and E. Poncelet, 3 vols, Commission royale d'Histoire de Belgique, Brussels, 1910–31 (includes '*Le Traité des Guerres d'Awans et de Waroux*')

Henry, Earl of Derby, *Expeditions to Prussia and the Holy Land made by Henry, Earl of Derby, 1390–91, 1392–3, being the account kept by his treasurer*, ed. L. Toulmin Smith, Camden Society, NS 52, 1894

Henry of Grosmont, *Le Livre de Seyntz Medicines*, ed. E.J. Arnould, ANTS, 2, Oxford, 1940

Higden, Ranulph, *Polychronicon Randulphi Higden Monachi Cestrensis*, ed. C. Babington and J.R. Lumby, 9 vols, Rolls Series, London, 1865–86

Hoccleve, Thomas, *The Regement of Princes*, ed. F.J. Furnivall, EETS, os 72, London, 1897; repr. 1973

—— *The Minor Poems*, ed. F.J. Furnivall and I. Gollancz; revised by J. Mitchell and A.I. Dovle, EETS, os 61, 73, London, 1892, 1925; repr. in 1 vol, 1970

Ibn-Khaldun, *The Muqaddimah*, trans. F. Rosenthal, 3 vols, London, 1958

'Indentures of the Retinue of John of Gaunt enrolled in Chancery 1367–99', *Camden Miscellany*, 22, 4th ser., London, 1964, pp. 77–112

Jack Upland, Friar Daw's reply and Upland's Rejoinder, ed. P.L. Heyworth, Oxford, 1968

Jean le Bel, *Chronique de Jean le Bel*, ed. J. Viard and E. Deprez, 2 vols, Paris, 1904

Jocelin of Brakelond, *The Chronicle of Jocelin of Brakelond*, trans. L.C. Jane, London, 1907

John Prophete's Journal: 'A Journal of the Clerk of the Council during the fifteenth and sixteenth years of Richard II', in J.F. Baldwin, *The King's Council in England during the Middle Ages*, Oxford, 1913, pp. 489–507

Knighton, Henry, *Chronicon Henrici Knighton, Monachi Leycestrensis*, ed. J.R. Lumby, 2 vols, Rolls Series, London, 1889–95

'Knyghthode and Bataile' a xvth-century verse paraphrase of Flavius Vegetius Renatus' treatise 'De Re Militari', ed. R. Dyboski and Z.M. Arend, EETS, os 201, London, 1935

Kritzeck, J., *Anthology of Islamic literature*, Harmondsworth, 1964

Lanterne of Ligt, The, ed. Lilian M. Swinburn, EETS, os 151, London, 1917; repr. 1971

Legge, M. Dominica, *Anglo-Norman letters and petitions*, ANTS, 3, Oxford, 1941

Lescot, Richard, *Chronique de Richard Lescot*, Paris, 1896

Liber Albus, Liber Custumarum et Liber Horn, ed. H.T. Riley, 2, ii: *Liber Custumarum*, Rolls Series, London, 1860

London – *Calendar of early mayor's court rolls*, 1298–1307, ed. A.H. Thomas, Cambridge, 1924

—— *Calendar of letter books preserved among the archives of the Corporation of the City of London. Letter Book F: 1337–52; Letter Book G: 1352–74; Letter Book H: 1375–99; Letter Book I: 1400–22*, ed. R.R. Sharpe, London, 1904–9

—— *Calendar of Pleas and Memoranda Rolls of the City of London, 1324–1381*, ed. A.H. Thomas, 2 vols, Cambridge, 1926–9

—— *Calendar of Select Pleas and Memoranda of the City of London, 1381–1412*, ed. A.H. Thomas, Cambridge, 1932

Loomis, R.S. and Willard, R., *Medieval English verse and prose in modernized versions*, New York, 1948

Lorris, Guillaume and Clopinel, J., *Romance of the Rose*, trans. F.S. Ellis, 3 vols, London, 1900

Lorris, Guillaume and Meung, Jean de, *Romance of the Rose*, trans. Harry W. Robbins, New York, 1962

Lorris, Guillaume and Chaucer, *Romaunt of the Rose and le Roman de la Rose a parallel-text edition of the original French and Chaucer's translation*, ed. Ronald Sutherland, Oxford, 1968

Lull, Ramon, *The Book of the Ordre of Chyualry*, trans. W. Caxton, ed. A.T.P. Byles, EETS, os 168, London, 1926; repr. 1971

Lydgate, John, *The Minor Poems*, ed. H.N. MacCracken, 2 vols, EETS, os 107; os 192, London, 1911, repr. 1961; 1934, repr. 1961

Machaut, Guillaume, *La Prise d'Alexandrie*, ed. M.L. de Mas Latrie, Geneva, 1877

—— *Œuvres*, ed. E. Hoepffner, 3 vols, Paris, 1908–21

Machiavelli, Niccolo, *The Prince*, English translation, London, 1640; Scolar Press facsimile, London, 1969

Makhairas, Leontios, *Recital Concerning the sweet land of Cyprus entitled 'Chronicle'*, ed. and trans. R.M. Dawkins, 2 vols, Oxford, 1932

Mandeville, *The Travels of Sir John Mandeville with three narrations in illustration of it*, ed. A.W. Pollard, New York, 1964

—— *The Buke of John Maundevill*, ed. G.F. Warner, Roxburghe Club, 119, London, 1889

Marco Polo, *The Book of Ser Marco Polo*, ed. and trans. Henry Yule, London, 1903

McKeon, Richard, *Selections from medieval philosophers*, 2 vols, New York, 1930; repr. 1958

'"Metrical history of the Deposition of Richard II"', attributed to Jean Creton', ed. J. Webb, *Arch*, 20, 1814

Mézières, Philippe de, *Le Songe du Vieil Pélerin*, ed. and trans. G.W. Coopland, 2 vols, Cambridge, 1969

—— '*Vita Sancti Petri Thomasii*', *Acta Sanctorum Bollandiana*, ed. Jean Carnadet, 3, 29 Januarii, Brussels, 1863, pp. 611–38

—— *Letter to King Richard II*, trans. G.W. Coopland, Liverpool, 1975

Murimath, Adam, *Chronica*, ed. Thomas Hog, London, 1846

—— *Continuatio Chronicarum*, ed. E.M. Thompson, London, 1889

Myrc, John, *Festial: a collection of homilies*, ed. T. Erbe, *EETS*, os 96, London, 1905

—— *Instructions for parish priests*, ed. E. Peacock, *EETS*, os 31, London, 1902

Ockham, William, *Opera politica*, ed. J.G. Sikes *et al*, 3 vols, Manchester, 1940–56

O'Faolain, Julia and Martines, Lauro, *Not in God's image: documents showing women in history*, London, 1974

Paston letters and papers of the fifteenth century, ed. N. Davis, Oxford, 1971

Pauphilet, Albert, *Poetes et romanciers du Moyen Âge*, Bruges and Paris, 1973

Petrarch, Francesco, *Lettere senili di Francesco Petrarca*, ed. Giuseppe Francassetti, 1, Florence, 1869

Petrarch: an anthology, ed. and trans. David Thompson, New York, 1971

Piers the Plowman in three parallel texts by William Langland, ed. W.W. Skeat, 2 vols, Oxford, 1886; repr. with bibliography, 1969

Powell, E. and Trevelyan, G.M., 'The Peasants' Rising and the Lollards', unpublished documents forming an appendix to *England in the Age of Wycliffe*, London, 1899

Promptorium parvulorum, ed. A.L. Mayhew, *EETS*, ES 102, Oxford, 1908

Prynne, W. *An exact abridgement of the records in the Tower of London*, London, 1689

Reading, John of, *Chronica Johannis de Reading et anonymi Cantuarensis*, ed. J. Tait, Manchester, 1914

Relation of the Island of England, trans. C.A. Sneyd, Camden Society, London, 1847

Rickert, Edith, *Chaucer's world*, ed. C.C. Olson and M.M. Crow, New York and London, 1948

Ricotti, Ercole, *Storia delle Compagnie di Ventura in Italia*, 1, 2, Turin, 1844

Riley, H.T., *Memorials of London and London life in the xiiith, xivth and xvth centuries*, London, 1868

Ross, Woodburn O. (ed.), *Middle English sermons*, *EETS*, os 209, London, 1940

Ross, J.B. and M.M. McLaughlin, *The Portable Medieval Reader*, New York, 1949; repr. 1975

Rotuli parliamentorum et petitiones et placita in parliamento, 6 vols, Record Commission, London, 1783

Rymer, *Fœdera Conventiones Litterae etc*, ed. G. Holmes, 20 vols, 2nd ed., London, 1704–35

Salutati, Coluccio, 'De Tyranno', trans. in E. Emerton, *Humanism and Tyranny*, Cambridge, Mass., 1925, pp. 24–116

Sands, D.B., *Middle English verse romances*, New York, 1966 (includes 'Sir Launfal')

Scrope, *The Dicts and sayings of the philosophers*, ed. C.F. Buhler, *EETS*, 211, London, 1941

Scrope and Grosvenor Roll, *De controversia in curia militari inter Ricardum le Scrope et Robertum Grosvenor milites: rege Ricardo Secundo 1385–90*, ed. H. Nicolas, 2 vols, London, 1832

Secretum secretorum in nine English versions, ed. M.A. Manzalaoui, 1, *EETS*, 276, London, 1977

' "The Simonie" also known as "Poem on the evil times of Edward ii" ', *Political songs of England*, ed. T. Wright, Camden Society, 6, London, 1839, pp. 323–45

'Sir Ferumbras' in *English Charlemagne romances*, 1, ed. S.J. Herrtage, *EETS*, ES 34, London, 1879; repr. 1903

Sir Gawain and the Green Knight, ed. J.R.R. Tolkien and E.V. Gordon, Oxford, 1925; repr. 1960

'Sir Gawain and the Green Knight' in *The Complete works of the Gawain poet in a modern English version*, trans. J. Gardner, Chicago, 1975

'Sir Launfal' in W.H. French and C.B. Hale, *Middle English metrical romances*, 1, pp. 345–80, and D.B. Sands, *Middle English verse romances*, pp. 201–32

South English legendary, ed. Charlotte D'Evelyn and Anna J. Mill, 3 vols, *EETS*, 235; 236; 244, London, 1956–9

Statutes at large from the Magna Carta to the end of the last Parliament, 1761, ed. Owen Ruffhead, 8 vols, London, 1769

Stephenson, C. and Marcham, F.G., *Sources of English constitutional history*, New York and London, 1937

Stow, John, *The survey of London (1598)*, ed. H.B. Wheatley, London, 1912; rev. ed. 1970

Strambaldi, *Chronique d'Amadi et de Strambaldi*, 2, ed. M.R. de Mas Latrie, Paris, 1893

Tale of Beryn, ed. F.J. Furnivall and W.G. Stone, 2 vols, Chaucer Society, London, 1876–7

Trevisa, John, *Dialogus inter militem et clericum*, ed. A.J. Perry, *EETS*, os 167, London, 1925

Trokelowe, *Johannis de Trokelowe et Henrici de Blaneforde chronica et annales*, ed. H.T. Riley, Rolls Series, London, 1866

Turner, T.H., *Manners and household expenses of England in the thirteenth and fifteenth centuries*, Roxburghe Club, London, 1841

'Twelve conclusions of the Lollards affixed to St Paul's and Westminster Abbey: English and Latin translation in Ms of Roger Dymok', ed. H.S. Cronin, *EHR*, 22, 1907, pp. 292–304

Usk, Adam, *Chronicon Adamae de Usk 1377–1421*, ed. and trans. E.M. Thompson, London, 1904

Venette, Jean de, *Chronicle*, ed. and trans. J. Birdshall and R.A. Newhall, New York, 1953

Villani, Filippo, *Cronica di Filippo Villani*, vol. 5 in *Cronica di Matteo Villani*, 8 vols, Florence, 1825–6

Walsingham, *Thomas Walsingham Historia Anglicana*, ed. H.T. Riley, 2 vols, Rolls Series, London, 1863–4

Watriquet, *Dits de Watriquet de Couvin*, ed. A. Scheler, Brussels, 1868

Wimbledon, Thomas, 'Thomas Wimbledon's Sermon *Redde Racionem Villicacionis Tue* (1388)', ed. Nancy H. Owen, Medieval Studies, 28, 1966, pp. 176–97

Wright, R., *Political poems and songs relating to English history composed during the period from the accession of Edward III to that of Richard III*, 2 vols, Rolls Series, London, 1859; 1861

—— *Political songs of England from the reign of John to that of Edward II*, Camden Society, 6, London, 1839

Wyclif, *De Civili Dominio*, ed. I. Loserth, 3 vols, Wyclif Society, London, 1903
—— *The English works of Wyclif hitherto unprinted*, ed. F.D. Matthew, *EETS*, os 74, London, 1880
—— *Polemical works in Latin*, ed. Rudolf Buddensieg, 2 vols, Wyclif Society, London, 1883
—— *Select English works*, ed. Thomas Arnold, 3 vols, Oxford, 1869–71
—— *Sermones*, ed. I. Loserth, 4 vols, Wyclif Society, London, 1889
—— *Tractatus De Officio Regis*, ed. Alfred W. Pollard and Charles Sayle, Wyclif Society, London, 1887
Wyntoun, Andrew of, *The Original Chronicle*, ed. F.J. Amours, 6 vols, *STS*, Edinburgh, 1903–14

Secondary works

Abun-Nasr, J.M., *History of the Maghrib*, Cambridge, 1971
Allmand, C.T., *Society at War: the experience of England and France during the Hundred Years' War*, Edinburgh, 1973
—— *War, Literature and Politics in the Late Middle Ages*, Liverpool, 1976 (includes an important article by M.H. Keen: 'Chivalry, nobility and the man-at-arms', pp. 33–45)
Ashdown, C.H., *British and foreign Arms and Armour*, London, 1909
Aston, Margaret, 'Lollardy and sedition, 1381–1431' in R.H. Hilton (ed.), *Peasants, knights and heretics: Studies in Medieval English Social History*, pp. 273–318
Atiya, A.S., *Crusade in the Later Middle Ages*, London, 1938
—— *Crusade, Commerce and Culture*, London, 1962
Baldwin, J.F., *The King's Council in England during the Middle Ages*, Oxford, 1913
Barber, Richard, *The Knight and Chivalry*, London, 1970
Barnes, A.S., 'The Teutonic Knights and the Kingdom of Prussia' in *Dublin Review*, 157, 1915, pp. 272–83
Barnie, John, *War in medieval society: social values and the Hundred Years' War 1337–99*, London, 1974
Battaglia, S., *Grande Dizionario della Lingua italiana*, Turin, 1961
Baum, Paull F., *Chaucer, a Critical Introduction*, Durham, North Carolina, 1958
Bean, J.M.W., *The decline of English feudalism, 1215–1540*, Manchester, 1968
Bennett, H.S., *The Pastons and their England*, repr. Cambridge, 1968
Bennett, J.A.W., *Chaucer at Oxford and at Cambridge*, Oxford, 1974
Blair, Claude, *European armour circa 1066–1700*, London, 1958
Bloch, Marc, *Feudal society*, trans. L.A. Manyon, London, 1962
Bowden, Muriel, *A commentary on the General Prologue to the Canterbury Tales*, 2nd ed. London, 1969
Boyd, Beverly, *Chaucer and the Medieval Book*, Huntingdon, 1973
Braddy, H., 'The two Petros in The Monk's Tale', *PMLA*, 50, 1935, pp. 69–80
—— *Geoffrey Chaucer: literary and historical studies*, New York and London, 1971
Brent, John, *Canterbury in the olden times*, London, 1879
Brewer, Derek S. (ed.), *Chaucer and Chaucerians: critical studies in Middle English literature*, London, 1966

—— *Geoffrey Chaucer*. Writers and their background, London, 1974

Brunner, K., *An outline of Middle English grammar*, trans. G.K.W. Johnston, Oxford, 1963; repr. 1967

Burrow, J.A., *Geoffrey Chaucer: a critical anthology*, Harmondsworth, 1969

Canestrini, *Documenti per servire alla Storia della Milizia italiana*. Archivo Storico Italiano, 15, Florence, 1851

Canter, N., *Medieval history*, New York, 1969

Carelton Brown, *Essays in honor of Carelton Brown*, New York, 1940

Chrimes, S.B., *An introduction to the administrative history of Medieval England*, Oxford, 1959; repr. 1966

Clephan, R.C., *The defensive armour and weapons of war of medieval times and of the Renaissance*, London, 1900

Coghill, Nevill (trans.), *The Canterbury Tales*, London, 1951

—— *The poet Chaucer*, London, 1967

—— *Chaucer's Idea of What is Noble*, English Association presidential address, London, 1971

Cohn, Norman, *The pursuit of the Millennium*, London, 1957

Cook, A.S., 'The historical background of Chaucer's Knight', *TCAAS*, 20, 1916, pp. 161–240

—— 'Beginning the board in Prussia', *JEGP*, 14, 1915, pp. 375–84

Cottle, Basil, *The triumph of English 1350–1400*, London, 1969

Coulton, G.G., *Chaucer and his England*, London, 1909

Cowgill, B.K., '*The Knight's Tale* and the Hundred Years' War', *PQ*, 54, 1975, pp. 670–7

Cripps-Day, F.H., *The History of the tournament in England and in France*, London, 1918

Crombie, A.C., *Augustine to Galileo: science in the Middle Ages*, Harmondsworth, 1969

Daniel, Norman, *The Arabs and medieval Europe*, London, 1975

Darby, H.C., *An historical geography of England before AD 1800*, Cambridge, 1936; revised 1963

Deansley, Margaret, *The Lollard Bible*, Cambridge, 1920

Dent, A.A., 'Chaucer and the horse', *PLPLS*, 9, 1959–62, pp. 1–12

Dillon, H.A., 'A manuscript collection of Ordinances of Chivalry of the fifteenth century', *Arch*, 57, 1, 1900, pp. 29–70

Douglas Simpson, W., 'Bastard Feudalism and the Later Castles', *Antiquaries Journal*, 26, 1946, pp. 145–71

Dugdale, W., *The Baronage of England*, 1, London, 1675–6

Edwards, J.G., Galbraith and Jacob (eds), *Historical essays in honour of James Tait*, Manchester, 1933

Emerton, Ephraim, *Humanism and Tyranny*, Cambridge, Mass., 1925 (contains very useful introductions and translations of treatises on tyranny by the Italian political theorists Coluccio Salutati and Bartolus of Sassoferrato etc)

Encyclopaedia of Islam, ed. H.A.R. Gibb *et al.*, Leiden and London, 1960–

Ethel, G., 'Horse or horses', *MLN*, 75, 1960, pp. 97–101

Fowler, Kenneth (ed.), *The Hundred Years' War*, London, 1971

French, R.D., *A Chaucer Handbook*, New York, 1927; rept. 1955

French, W.H., 'The lovers in *The Knight's Tale*', *JEGP*, 48, 1949, pp. 320–8

French, W.H., 'Horse or horses', *MLN*, 76, 1961, pp. 293–5

Friedman, A.B., '*The Prioress's Tale* and Chaucer's Anti-Semitism', *ChauR*, 9, 1974, pp. 118–27

Frost, William, 'An interpretation of Chaucer's Knight's Tale', *RES*, 25, 1949, pp. 289–304

Fuller, J.F.C., *The decisive battles of the Western World, 480 BC–1757*, ed. John Terraine, 2 vols, London, 1954; abridged 1972

Gautier, Léon, *Chivalry*, London, 1891

Gay, Victor, *Glossaire archéologique*, 2 vols, Paris, 1882–1928

Gibbons, H.H., *The foundation of the Ottoman Empire, 1300–1403*, Oxford, 1916

Godefroy, F., *Dictionnaire de l'ancienne langue française du ixe au xve siècle*, 10 vols, Paris, 1881–1902

Gorlach, M., 'The Knight's army', in *N&Q*, 20, 1973, pp. 363–5

Gougenheim, G., 'Notes sur le Vocabulaire de Rabelais' in *Word*, 5, 1949, p. 148

Greimas, A.-J., *Dictionnaire de l'ancien français*, Paris, 1968

Harvey, Sally, 'The Knight and the Knight's Fee in England', *P&P*, 49, 1970, pp. 1–43

Hatton, Thomas, J., 'Chaucer's Crusading Knight – a slanted ideal' in *ChauR*, 3, 1968

Hay, Denys, 'The division of the spoils of war in fourteenth-century England', *TRHS*, 4, 1954, pp. 91–109

—— *Europe in the fourteenth and fifteenth centuries*, London, 1966; 2nd ed. 1973

Hazard, H.W., *A history of the Crusades*, 3, Wisconsin, 1975

Helterman, Jeffrey, 'The dehumanizing metamorphoses of the Knight's Tale', *ELH*, 38, 1971, pp. 493–511

Hewitt, H.J., *The organization of war under Edward III 1338–62*, Manchester and New York, 1966

Hill, G., *History of Cyprus*, 2, 3, Cambridge, 1948

Hillgarth, J.N., *The Spanish kingdoms, 1250–1516*, 1, Oxford, 1976

Hilton, Rodney, *Bond men made free: medieval peasant movements and the English Rising of 1381*, London, 1973

Hilton, R.H., *Peasants, knights and heretics: studies in medieval English social history*, Cambridge, 1976

Hilton, R.H. and Fagan, H., *The English Rising of 1381*, London, 1950

Honeybourne, M.B., 'The reconstructed map of London under Richard II', *LTR*, 22, 1965, pp. 29–76

Hudson, Anne, 'A Lollard sermon cycle', *Medium Ævum*, 40, 1971

Huizinga, J., *The waning of the Middle Ages*, Harmondsworth, 1972

Hunt, R.W., Pantin, W.A. & Southern, R.W. (eds), *Studies in medieval history presented to F.M. Powicke*, Oxford, 1948; repr. 1969

Huppé, Bernard F., *A reading of The Canterbury Tales*, New York, 1964

Hutton, E., 'Did Chaucer meet Petrarch and Boccaccio?' *Anglo-Italian Review*, 1, 1918, pp. 121–35

Imbs, P. (ed.), *Trésor de la langue française*, 1– , Paris, 1974–

Jefferson, B.L., *Chaucer and the 'Consolation of Philosophy' of Boethius*, New York, 1917; repr. 1968

Jones, Richard H., *The royal policy of Richard II*, Oxford, 1968

Jorga, N., *Philippe de Mézières*, Paris, 1896

Jusserand, J.J., *English wayfaring life in the Middle Ages*, London, 1889; new ed., 1961

Kean, P.M., *The art of narrative: Chaucer and the making of English poetry*, 2 vols, London, 1972

Keeney, B.C., 'Military Service and the Development of Nationalism in England, 1212–1327' in *Speculum*, 22, 1947, pp. 534–49

Kilgour, R.L., *The Decline of Chivalry*, Harvard Studies in Romance Languages, 12, Harvard, 1937

Kingsford, C.L., 'Historical notes on medieval London houses', *LTR*, 10–12

Kittredge, G.L., 'Chaucer and some of his friends', *MP*, 1, 1903–4, pp. 1–18

Knight, S., *Rymyng Craftily: meaning in Chaucer's poetry*, London, 1973

Kuhl, Ernest P., 'Some friends of Chaucer' in *PMLA*, 29, 1914, pp. 270–6

—— 'Why was Chaucer sent to Milan in 1378' in *MLN*, 62, 1947, pp. 42–4

La Monte, J.L., *Feudal Monarchy in the Latin Kingdom of Jerusalem 1100 to 1291*, Cambridge, Mass., 1932

Latham, R.E., *Revised Medieval Latin word-list from British and Irish sources*, London, 1965

Legouis, Emile, *Geoffrey Chaucer*, trans. Lailavoix, London, 1913

Lemprière, J., *Classical dictionary of proper names*, New ed. ed. F.A. Wright, London, 1949; repr. 1972

Lewis, C.T. and Short, C., *A Latin dictionary*, Oxford, 1879; repr. 1969

Littré, E. *Dictionnaire de la langue française*, Paris, 1956

Lowes, J.L., 'Chaucer and Dante's "Convivio"', in *MP*, 13, 1915, pp. 19–27

Lumiansky, R.M., *Of Sondry Folk: the dramatic principle in the Canterbury Tales*, Austin, Texas, 1955

Magoun, F.P., *A Chaucer gazetteer*, Chicago and London, 1961

Mallett, M., *Mercenaries and their masters*, London, 1974

Manly, J.M., 'A Knight ther was', *TAPA*, 38, 1907, pp. 89–107

Mann, Jill, *Chaucer and Medieval Estates Satire*, Cambridge, 1973

Mansion, J.E., *Harrap's new standard French and English dictionary*, rev. and ed. R.P.L. and M. Ledéserk, 2 vols, London, 1934; rev. 1972

Manual of the Writings in Middle English based upon the Manual by J.E. Wells, vols I and II, ed. J. Burke Severs, New Haven, 1967 and 1970; vols III and IV, ed. Albert E. Hartung, New Haven, 1972 and 1973

Mas Latrie, le Comte de, *Relations et commerce de l'Afrique septentrionale ou Magreb avec les nations chrétiennes au Moyen Age*, Paris, 1886

Mathew, Gervase, 'Ideals of Knighthood in late fourteenth century England' in R.W. Hunt, W.A. Pantin and R.W. Southern (eds), *Studies in Medieval History presented to F.M. Powicke*, pp. 354–62

—— *The Court of Richard II*, London, 1968

McEvedy, C., *The Penguin Atlas of Medieval History*, Harmondsworth, 1961

McFarlane, K.B., 'England and the Hundred Years' War', *P&P*, 22, 1962

—— *Lancastrian Kings and Lollard Knights*, Oxford, 1972

McKisack, May, *The Fourteenth Century 1307–1399*, Oxford, 1959; repr. 1971

McRobbie, K., 'The Concept of advancement in the fourteenth century', *CJH*, 6, 1971, pp. 1–19

Mersand, J., *Chaucer's Romance Vocabulary*, Washington, New York, 1939

Metlitzki, Dorothee, *The Matter of Araby in medieval England*, New Haven and London, 1977

Middle English Dictionary, ed. H. Kurath and S.M. Kuhn, Ann Arbor, 1956–

Mitchell, Charles, 'The Worthiness of Chaucer's Knight', *MLQ*, 25, 1964, pp. 66–75

Morris, J.E., *Welsh Wars of Edward I*, Oxford, 1901

Mossé, F., *A handbook of Middle English*, trans. J.A. Walker, Baltimore, 1952

Muscatine, Charles, 'Form, texture and meaning in Chaucer's Knight's Tale', *PMLA*, 65, 1950, pp. 911–29

Neuse, R., 'The Knight – the first mover in Chaucer's Human Comedy', in *UTQ*, 31, 1962, pp. 299–315

Nolan, David, *Dante Commentaries*, Dublin, 1977

Oman, Charles, *A History of the art of war in the Middle Ages*, vol. II, 1278–1418, London, 1924

Owst, G.R., *Literature and pulpit in medieval England*, Oxford, 1933; new ed. 1961

Pallenberg, Corrado, *Vatican Finances*, London, 1971; new ed., 1973

Palmer, J.J.N., *England, France and Christendom 1377–99*, London, 1972

Patch, H.A., *On Rereading Chaucer*, Cambridge, Mass., 1967

Petit-Dutaillis, C., *Studies and notes supplementary to Stubbs's 'Constitutional History'*, II, Manchester, 1914

Postan, M.M., 'Some Social Consequences of the Hundred Years' War', *EconHR*, 12, 1942, pp. 2–12

Powicke, F.M., *The Christian life in the Middle Ages and other essays*, Oxford, 1935

—— *Handbook of British chronology*, London, 1939

Powicke, M.R., *Military Obligation in Medieval England*, Oxford, 1962

Pratt, R.A., 'Geoffrey Chaucer Esq., and Sir John Hawkwood', *ELH*, 16, 1949, pp. 188–93

—— 'Chaucer and the Visconti Libraries', *ELH*, 6, 1939, pp. 191–9

Prince, A.E., 'The Indenture System under Edward III' in *Historical Essays in honour of James Tait*, ed. J.G. Edwards, Galbraith and Jacob, pp. 283–97

—— 'The Payment of Army Wages in Edward III's Reign', *Speculum*, 19, 1944, pp. 137–60

Renna, T.J., 'Kingship in the Disputatio inter Clericum et Militem', *Speculum*, 48, 1973, pp. 675–93

Rickard, Peter, *Britain in medieval French literature 1100–1500*, Cambridge, 1956

Rickert, Edith, 'Thou Vache', in *MP*, 11, 1913, pp. 209–26

Riley-Smith, J., *The Feudal nobility and the kingdom of Jerusalem 1174–1277*, London, 1973

Robertson, Stuart, 'Elements of realism in *The Knight's Tale*', *JEGP*, 14, 1915, pp. 226–55

Robinson, Ian, *Chaucer and the English tradition*, Cambridge, 1972

Roeder, Helen, *Saints and their Attributes*, London, 1955

Runciman, Steven, *A History of the Crusades*, 3 vols, Cambridge, 1951; repr. Harmondsworth, 1965

Russell, F.H., *The Just War in the Middle Ages*, Cambridge, 1975

Salter, Elizabeth, *The Knight's Tale and the Clerk's Tale*, Studies in English Literature, v, London, 1962

Schlauch, Margaret, 'Chaucer's Doctrine of Kings and Tyrants', *Speculum*, 20, 1945, pp. 133–56

Schoeck, R. & Taylor, J., *Chaucer Criticism*, 2 vols, Notre Dame, 1960

Schramm, W.L., 'The cost of books in Chaucer's time', *MLN*, 48, 1933

Sherbourne, J.W., 'Indentured retinues and English expeditions to France 1369–1380', *EHR*, 79, 1964, pp. 718–46

—— 'The English Navy, Shipping and Manpower, 1369–1389', *P&P*, 37, 1967, pp. 163–75

Speirs, John, *Chaucer the Maker*, London, 1951

Steinberg, S.H. and Evans, I.H., *Steinberg's Dictionary of British History*, London, 1970

Stillwell, G. and Webb, H.J., 'Chaucer's Knight and the Hundred Years' War', *MLN*, 59, 1944, pp. 45–7

Storey, R.L., *Chronology of the Medieval World 800–1491*, London, 1973

Strange, William C., 'The Monk's Tale: a generous view', *ChauR*, 1, 1966–7, pp. 167–80

Stubbs, W., *Seventeen lectures on medieval and modern history*, Oxford, 1886

Sullivan, Sheila, *Critics on Chaucer*, London, 1970

Tatlock, J.S.P., *The Development and chronology of Chaucer's Works*, Chaucer Society, 1907

—— and Kennedy, A.G., *A concordance to the Complete Works of Geoffrey Chaucer*, Washington, 1927

Temple-Leader, J. and Marcotti, G., *Sir John Hawkwood*, Trans. Leader-Scott, London, 1889

Throop, P.A., 'Criticism of Papal Crusade policy in Old French and Provençal', *Speculum*, 13, 1938, pp. 379–412

Topping, P.W. (ed. and trans.), *Feudal Institutions as revealed in the assizes of Romania: the Law Code of Frankish Greece*, Philadelphia and London, 1949

Trease, Geoffrey, *The Condottieri*, London, 1970

Trevelyan, G.M., *England in the age of Wycliffe*, London, 1899; repr. with an introduction by J.A. Tuck, London, 1972

Tuck, Anthony, *Richard II and the English nobility*, London, 1973

Underwood, Dale, 'The First of the Canterbury Tales', *ELH*, 26, 1959, pp. 455 ff

Urban, W., 'The Organization of defense of the Livonian frontier in the thirteenth century', *Speculum*, 48, 1973

Vernadsky, G., *A History of Russia*, III: *The Mongols and Russia*, New Haven and London, 1953

Vinogradoff, Paul, *Villainage in England*, Oxford, 1892; repr. 1968

Watts, H.E., *Spain, being a summary of Spanish history from the Moorish Conquest to the Fall of Granada 711–1492*, London, 1893

Webb, Henry J., 'A Re-interpretation of Chaucer's Theseus', *RES*, 23, 1947, pp. 289–96

Whittock, Trevor, *A reading of the Canterbury Tales*, Cambridge, 1970

Workman, Herbert B., *John Wyclif*, 2 vols, Oxford, 1926

Wright, David, *The Canterbury Tales: a prose translation*, London, 1965

Index